Jeremiah
and
Lamentations

TEACH THE TEXT COMMENTARY

John H. Walton
Old Testament General Editor

Mark L. Strauss
New Testament General Editor

Volumes now available:

Old Testament Volumes

New Testament Volumes

Visit the series website at www.teachthetextseries.com.

TEACH the TEXT
COMMENTARY SERIES

Jeremiah
and
Lamentations

J. Daniel Hays

Mark L. Strauss and John H. Walton
GENERAL EDITORS

ILLUSTRATING THE TEXT

Kevin and Sherry Harney
ASSOCIATE EDITORS

Dann Stouten
CONTRIBUTING WRITER

BakerBooks
a division of Baker Publishing Group
Grand Rapids, Michigan

© 2016 by J. Daniel Hays
Illustrating the Text sections © 2016 by Baker Publishing Group

Published by Baker Books
a division of Baker Publishing Group
P.O. Box 6287, Grand Rapids, MI 49516-6287
www.bakerbooks.com

Printed and bound by CPI Group (UK) Ltd, Croydon, CR0 4YY

Library of Congress Cataloging-in-Publication Data
Names: Hays, J. Daniel, 1953– author.
Title: Jeremiah and Lamentations / J. Daniel Hays; Mark L. Strauss and John H. Walton, general
    editors; Kevin and Sherry Harney, associate editors; Dann Stouten, contributing writer.
Description: Grand Rapids, MI : Baker Books, 2016. | Series: Teach the text commentary series |
    Includes bibliographical references and index.
Identifiers: LCCN 2015041516 (print) | LCCN 2015042412 (ebook) | ISBN 9780801092121 (cloth) |
    ISBN 9781493403073 (ebook)
Subjects: LCSH: Bible. Jeremiah—Commentaries. | Bible. Lamentations—Commentaries.
Classification: LCC BS1525.53 .H39 2016 (print) | LCC BS1525.53 (ebook) | DDC 224/.207—dc23
LC record available at http://lccn.loc.gov/2015041516

16   17   18   19   20   21   22   7   6   5   4   3   2   1

To my dad, Jim Hays (1925–2013),
who passed down to me his love for the Prophets

Contents

Welcome to the Teach the Text Commentary Series

Why another commentary series? That was the question the general editors posed when Baker Books asked us to produce this series. Is there something that we can offer to pastors and teachers that is not currently being offered by other commentary series, or that can be offered in a more helpful way? After carefully researching the needs of pastors who teach the text on a weekly basis, we concluded that yes, more can be done; the Teach the Text Commentary Series (TTCS) is carefully designed to fill an important gap.

The technicality of modern commentaries often overwhelms readers with details that are tangential to the main purpose of the text. Discussions of source and redaction criticism, as well as detailed surveys of secondary literature, seem far removed from preaching and teaching the Word. Rather than wade through technical discussions, pastors often turn to devotional commentaries, which may contain exegetical weaknesses, misuse the Greek and Hebrew languages, and lack hermeneutical sophistication. There is a need for a commentary that utilizes the best of biblical scholarship but also presents the material in a clear, concise, attractive, and user-friendly format.

This commentary is designed for that purpose—to provide a ready reference for the exposition of the biblical text, giving easy access to information that a pastor needs to communicate the text effectively. To that end, the commentary is divided into carefully selected preaching units (with carefully regulated word counts both in the passage as a whole and in each subsection). Pastors and teachers engaged in weekly preparation thus know that they will be reading approximately the same amount of material on a week-by-week basis.

Each passage begins with a concise summary of the central message, or "Big Idea," of the passage and a list of its main themes. This is followed by a more detailed interpretation of the text, including the literary context of the passage, historical background material, and interpretive insights. While drawing on the best of biblical scholarship, this material is clear, concise, and to the point. Technical material is kept to a minimum, with endnotes pointing the reader to more detailed discussion and additional resources.

A second major focus of this commentary is on the preaching and teaching process itself. Few commentaries today help the pastor/teacher move from the meaning of the text to its effective communication. Our goal is to bridge this gap. In addition to interpreting the text in the "Understanding the Text" section, each unit contains a "Teaching the Text" section and an "Illustrating the Text" section. The teaching section points to the key theological themes of the passage and ways to communicate these themes to today's audiences. The illustration section provides ideas and examples for retaining the interest of hearers and connecting the message to daily life.

The creative format of this commentary arises from our belief that the Bible is not just a record of God's dealings in the past but is the living Word of God, "alive and active" and "sharper than any double-edged sword" (Heb. 4:12). Our prayer is that this commentary will help to unleash that transforming power for the glory of God.

The General Editors

Introduction to the Teach the Text Commentary Series

This series is designed to provide a ready reference for teaching the biblical text, giving easy access to information that is needed to communicate a passage effectively. To that end, the commentary is carefully divided into units that are faithful to the biblical authors' ideas and of an appropriate length for teaching or preaching.

The following standard sections are offered in each unit.

1. *Big Idea*. For each unit the commentary identifies the primary theme, or "Big Idea," that drives both the passage and the commentary.
2. *Key Themes*. Together with the Big Idea, the commentary addresses in bullet-point fashion the key ideas presented in the passage.
3. *Understanding the Text*. This section focuses on the exegesis of the text and includes several sections.
   a. The Text in Context. Here the author gives a brief explanation of how the unit fits into the flow of the text around it, including reference to the rhetorical strategy of the book and the unit's contribution to the purpose of the book.
   b. Outline/Structure. For some literary genres (e.g., epistles), a brief exegetical outline may be provided to guide the reader through the structure and flow of the passage.
   c. Historical and Cultural Background. This section addresses historical and cultural background information that may illuminate a verse or passage.

d. Interpretive Insights. This section provides information needed for a clear understanding of the passage. The intention of the author is to be highly selective and concise rather than exhaustive and expansive.

e. Theological Insights. In this very brief section the commentary identifies a few carefully selected theological insights about the passage.

4. *Teaching the Text*. Under this second main heading the commentary offers guidance for teaching the text. In this section the author lays out the main themes and applications of the passage. These are linked carefully to the Big Idea and are represented in the Key Themes.

5. *Illustrating the Text*. At this point in the commentary the writers partner with a team of pastor/teachers to provide suggestions for relevant and contemporary illustrations from current culture, entertainment, history, the Bible, news, literature, ethics, biography, daily life, medicine, and over forty other categories. They are designed to spark creative thinking for preachers and teachers and to help them design illustrations that bring alive the passage's key themes and message.

Abbreviations

Old Testament

Gen.	Genesis	2 Chron.	2 Chronicles	Dan.	Daniel
Exod.	Exodus	Ezra	Ezra	Hosea	Hosea
Lev.	Leviticus	Neh.	Nehemiah	Joel	Joel
Num.	Numbers	Esther	Esther	Amos	Amos
Deut.	Deuteronomy	Job	Job	Obad.	Obadiah
Josh.	Joshua	Ps(s).	Psalm(s)	Jon.	Jonah
Judg.	Judges	Prov.	Proverbs	Mic.	Micah
Ruth	Ruth	Eccles.	Ecclesiastes	Nah.	Nahum
1 Sam.	1 Samuel	Song	Song of Songs	Hab.	Habakkuk
2 Sam.	2 Samuel	Isa.	Isaiah	Zeph.	Zephaniah
1 Kings	1 Kings	Jer.	Jeremiah	Hag.	Haggai
2 Kings	2 Kings	Lam.	Lamentations	Zech.	Zechariah
1 Chron.	1 Chronicles	Ezek.	Ezekiel	Mal.	Malachi

New Testament

Matt.	Matthew	Eph.	Ephesians	Heb.	Hebrews
Mark	Mark	Phil.	Philippians	James	James
Luke	Luke	Col.	Colossians	1 Pet.	1 Peter
John	John	1 Thess.	1 Thessalonians	2 Pet.	2 Peter
Acts	Acts	2 Thess.	2 Thessalonians	1 John	1 John
Rom.	Romans	1 Tim.	1 Timothy	2 John	2 John
1 Cor.	1 Corinthians	2 Tim.	2 Timothy	3 John	3 John
2 Cor.	2 Corinthians	Titus	Titus	Jude	Jude
Gal.	Galatians	Philem.	Philemon	Rev.	Revelation

General

//	parallel text(s)	etc.	*et cetera*, and the rest
ca.	*circa*, around, approximately	ibid.	*ibidem*, in the same place
cf.	*confer*, compare	i.e.	*id est*, that is
e.g.	*exempli gratia*, for example	lit.	literally
esp.	especially		

Ancient Versions

LXX   Septuagint (ancient Greek version of the Old Testament)

MT   Masoretic Text (majority Hebrew text tradition)

Modern Versions

ESV   English Standard Version
HCSB   Holman Christian Standard Bible
KJV   King James Version
NASB   New American Standard Bible
NIV   New International Version
NLT   New Living Translation
NRSV   New Revised Standard Version

Secondary Sources

ANET   James B. Pritchard, ed. *Ancient Near Eastern Texts Relating to the Old Testament*. 3rd ed. Princeton, NJ: Princeton University Press, 1969.

BIBD   Tremper Longman III, Peter Enns, and Mark Strauss, eds. *The Baker Illustrated Bible Dictionary*. Grand Rapids: Baker Books, 2013.

DBI   Leland Ryken, James C. Wilhoit, and Tremper Longman III, eds. *Dictionary of Biblical Imagery*. Downers Grove, IL: InterVarsity, 1998.

GBPET   J. Daniel Hays, J. Scott Duvall, and C. Marvin Pate. *An A-to-Z Guide to Biblical Prophecy and the End Times*. Grand Rapids: Zondervan, 2007.

NIDOTTE   Willem A. VanGemeren, ed. *New International Dictionary of Old Testament Theology and Exegesis*. 5 vols. Grand Rapids: Zondervan, 1997.

ZIBBCOT   John H. Walton, ed. *Zondervan Illustrated Bible Backgrounds Commentary: Old Testament*. 5 vols. Grand Rapids: Zondervan, 2009.

Introduction to Jeremiah

Author

The prophet Jeremiah is from a priestly family that resides in the town of Anathoth, not far from Jerusalem (1:1). God appoints Jeremiah to be a prophet while in his youth, and Jeremiah serves in this capacity for over forty years, most of which were very difficult. Snippets and representative events portraying the serious challenges that Jeremiah faces in his prophetic ministry are woven into the book, providing us with more insight into Jeremiah as a person than for any other prophet. In fact, Jeremiah expresses many of his fears and struggles in a series of passages often referred to as his "laments" or "confessions." Because these "laments" are associated with weeping, Jeremiah has frequently been labeled as "the weeping prophet." This title, however, misses the point of the personal information about Jeremiah presented in this book. The "laments" of Jeremiah are provided to underscore the emotional and physical burden that he carries as a persecuted prophet. The hostility from the powers in Jerusalem (the king, nobles, priests, etc.) toward Jeremiah and his message is a central theme throughout much of the book. Within the Old Testament Jeremiah serves as the paradigmatic persecuted prophet whose story illustrates how thoroughly Judah and Jerusalem reject the message of God and his messenger.[1] So the title "the persecuted prophet" is more accurate.[2]

Also, although Jeremiah is the one who received the visions and oracles from God and is the one who delivered the word of God orally to the leaders and people of Jerusalem, it is his friend and scribe Baruch who actually converts much of Jeremiah's message and narrative into written text, at least that portion that took place before 605 BC, the date connected with Baruch's composition in Jeremiah 36 (see esp. 36:1–4, 28, 32; 45:1). Although the book of Jeremiah is clear and frequent in identifying the message as being the word of God mediated through the prophet Jeremiah, and although Baruch is identified as the one who wrote down large portions of it, the text is silent about who finalized it into the form we have now. Note that Jeremiah 51 ends with "The words of Jeremiah end here" (51:64), indicating that Jeremiah 52 was added by someone else, perhaps a scribe who took the work of Baruch and finalized it into the form we have today.

Historical Setting

Jeremiah's prophetic ministry began in 627 BC, during the reign of Josiah, the last "good" king of Judah, and continued through Josiah's reign (640–609 BC) and across the reigns of the four kings who followed: Jehoahaz (609 BC), Jehoiakim (609–598 BC), Jehoiachin (598–597 BC), and Zedekiah (597–586 BC).

Several important historical events during this time had huge impacts on Jeremiah and his audience in Jerusalem. In 612 BC the Babylonians captured Nineveh, the capital of Assyria, thus challenging the Assyrians as the major power in the region. The Egyptians, who had aligned themselves with the Assyrians, marched north through Judah in 609 BC to help fight the Babylonians. King Josiah apparently tried to stop the Egyptians and was killed. Judah then fell under Egyptian control, and the Egyptians appointed Jehoahaz as the new king. Within a year they changed their minds and replaced him with Jehoiakim. At the Battle of Carchemish (605 BC), however, the Babylonians soundly defeated the Assyrian-Egyptian alliance, ending the era of Assyrian domination and sending the remains of the Egyptian army retreating back into Egypt. The Babylonians then controlled the region, and King Jehoiakim in Judah quickly submitted to them as a vassal. Yet before long the foolish Jehoiakim formed an alliance with neighboring countries and rebelled against the Babylonians. In 598 BC the Babylonian king Nebuchadnezzar marched his army to Judah to punish Jehoiakim and the Judahites. As the Babylonian army approached, Jehoiakim died (he was probably murdered), and the eighteen-year-old Jehoiachin became king. Wisely, he quickly surrendered to Nebuchadnezzar and was taken into exile, along with many of the leading citizens and artisans of Jerusalem. The Babylonians replaced him with a new puppet king, Zedekiah, the brother of Jehoiakim. Before long, however, Zedekiah also rebelled against the Babylonians, resulting in another, and more devastating, invasion by the Babylonians. This time the Babylonians plundered and destroyed Jerusalem, executing many of the inhabitants and taking many others into exile. They then replaced Zedekiah with the governor Gedaliah.

Jeremiah lived and preached throughout this tumultuous time. Indeed, most of the misfortune that fell on Judah and Jerusalem was a result of their rejection of his message. Most of the book of Jeremiah is focused during the reigns of Jehoiakim and Zedekiah, the two kings with whom the prophet and his message most frequently collide. Likewise, two major events dominate the story. The surrender of Jerusalem leading to the exile of many of its inhabitants in 597 BC and the fall and destruction of Jerusalem leading to the execution of many of its leaders and the exile of others in 586 BC are the two central events that form the major historical background for the book of Jeremiah.

Central Message and Purpose

The book of Jeremiah is also tied into the central story of the Old Testament. After God saves the Israelites from Egypt, as recounted in the book of Exodus, he leads them into the promised land. He gives them the book of Deuteronomy to define the covenant terms by which they can live in the promised land with God in their midst and be wonderfully blessed by him. But Deuteronomy also delineates the terrible consequences that they would face if they chose to reject God and serve pagan idols instead. The sad story of Joshua through 2 Kings narrates how the kingdom of Israel (falling to the Assyrians in 722 BC) and the kingdom of Judah (falling to the Babylonians in 586 BC) chose to ignore Deuteronomy and worship idols instead of the true God of Israel.

Jeremiah proclaims God's message in this context. King Josiah had valiantly tried to reverse the slide into idolatry that had taken place in Judah and Jerusalem, but once he dies, the nation embraces the pagan worship of its neighbors. Therefore, acting like God's prosecuting attorney, and with Deuteronomy in one hand, Jeremiah confronts the leaders and people of Jerusalem, calling on them to repent and warning them of the terrible consequences of continuing on their present disobedient path. The central themes of Jeremiah's message can be condensed into three main points:

1. *You (people of Judah) have broken the covenant by your repeated sin; you must repent immediately!* Throughout much of the book, and especially in the first twenty-nine chapters, Jeremiah focuses on three major sins that indicate how seriously the people have broken their covenant relationship with God: idolatry, social injustice, and reliance on hypocritical religious ritualism.

2. *No repentance? Then terrible judgment will fall upon you.* The lack of repentance in Jerusalem and among its leaders is not just a passive indifference; it is a hostile and direct rejection of both God's word and God's messenger, played out through the persecution of Jeremiah and the attempt to replace God's word with the deceitful message of the false prophets. Jeremiah proclaims that because of this failure to repent, along with the persecution

of God's messenger, a horrific judgment will fall on Jerusalem. He proclaims that such judgment will also fall on the surrounding pagan nations.

3. *Yet beyond the judgment, there is hope for a glorious future restoration both for Israel/Judah and for the nations.* At the heart of this future restoration is the promise of a "new covenant" that will replace the old covenant (as defined in Deuteronomy).[3]

Also keep in mind that during the story within the book of Jeremiah, the prophet is speaking most of the time to the leaders and inhabitants of Judah and Jerusalem. They are his target audience, and he is calling on them to repent and turn back to God. The written book of Jeremiah, however, probably reaches its final form as the written word of God sometime shortly after the events of the book, early in the exile. Thus the initial target audience for the written book of Jeremiah is probably primarily those who were in exile in Babylon, and perhaps also those Judahites who remained behind in the land. At that point the message is reflecting back on what has already happened, reminding those in exile that this terrible event occurred because they and their forebears had rejected God and sinned against him. The primary purpose is to vindicate the message of Jeremiah and to encourage those in exile to trust in God and to look forward to the future restoration.

Literary Features

The book of Jeremiah is a mixture of narrative stories, oracles (prophecies and proclamations) from God, and "conversations" between Jeremiah and God. Most of the oracles and conversations are in verse, characterized by terse lines of poetry, colorful figures of speech, numerous wordplays, and other poetic features.

Also, even though the book refers frequently to kings and historical events, only Jeremiah 37–44 is in chronological order. The rest of the book moves back and forth throughout the various reigns of the kings whom Jeremiah confronts. While the overall message of Jeremiah is redundantly clear, and while large central themes emerge that connect multiple chapters, tight organizational strategies fitting the smaller sections together are not always easily discernible. In many cases the smaller sections are connected thematically or through word repetition using "catchwords."

The broad major themes that provide continuity across multiple chapter units are the following:

Jeremiah 1–29	The broken covenant and the consequent judgment
1:1–19	The call of Jeremiah
2:1–37	The formal lawsuit against Judah

3:1–4:4	The call to repentance
4:5–6:30	The coming Babylonian invasion
7:1–10:25	False religion and its punishment
11:1–29:32	The prophet in conflict
Jeremiah 30–33	**The Book of Restoration**
Jeremiah 34–35	**Covenant faithfulness**
Jeremiah 36–45	**The fall of Jerusalem and the aftermath**
Jeremiah 46–51	**Judgment on the Nations**
Jeremiah 52	**Recapping the fall of Jerusalem**

Another interesting literary feature of the book of Jeremiah is the stark difference in the text between its two major textual traditions. Most English Bibles are primarily translations of the Hebrew manuscript tradition known as the Masoretic Text (MT). Since Jeremiah was written in Hebrew, this makes good sense. Yet, although Jeremiah was written in the sixth century BC, the earliest complete Hebrew manuscript of Jeremiah that we have extant today dates to around AD 900. On the other hand, around 200–150 BC the Hebrew Old Testament, including Jeremiah, was translated into Greek. This Greek translation is known as the Septuagint (LXX). We have copies of Jeremiah from the Septuagint that date to the fourth century AD. Among the Dead Sea Scrolls (DSS) discovered at Qumran there are six Hebrew scrolls of Jeremiah. The date of these scrolls ranges from 200 BC to about 50 BC. Unfortunately, all of these six scrolls have suffered extensive damage and are only fragmentary. In fact, due to this damage there are over twenty-one chapters of Jeremiah (including 1:1–4:4) that are not present at all in any of the six DSS manuscripts. In Jeremiah, the Masoretic Text (Hebrew text tradition) and the Septuagint (the Greek text tradition) vary in several significant ways. First of all, the Greek text (LXX) is one-eighth shorter than the Hebrew text (MT). There are numerous words, verses, and even some paragraphs in the Masoretic Text that are not in the Septuagint (e.g., 33:14–26; 39:4–13; 51:44b–49a; 52:27b–30). Also, the placement of Jeremiah 46–51 (Judgment on the Nations) is different; in the Septuagint these chapters follow Jeremiah 25:13 and precede Jeremiah 26. Complicating the situation is the fact that two of the Dead Sea Scrolls Hebrew manuscripts of Jeremiah discovered at Qumran seem to follow the shorter Septuagint reading while the other Jeremiah manuscripts seem to follow the longer Masoretic Text reading (although the fragmentary nature of all six of these manuscripts raises some doubt about this identification).

Scholars disagree over what to make of these differences. Does the shorter Septuagint version reflect a Greek translation of an ancient Hebrew text that was indeed shorter than the Masoretic Text but expanded over time to develop into the Masoretic Text as it is today? If so, which text tradition should be viewed as the "original" one? Or should both text traditions be treated as equally valid and authoritative? Since the Reformation, most Protestant traditions have favored the Masoretic Text, using it as the primary source for Bible translation. The early church, on the other hand, favored the Greek Septuagint for the first several centuries. Because of the extremely complicated nature of this problem, and because most English translations being used in churches today reflect the Masoretic Text, this commentary follows the Hebrew tradition of the Masoretic Text in its discussion of Jeremiah.[4]

The Call of Jeremiah

Big Idea

God appoints his servants to difficult tasks but empowers them with his presence.

Key Themes

- The word of God plays a critical role in Jeremiah's call.
- God selected Jeremiah to be his prophet even before he was born.
- God reassures Jeremiah by promising the power of his presence.
- The word of God that Jeremiah is to proclaim will bring both destruction and restoration.
- God's presence will deliver Jeremiah from those who will oppose him and his message.

Understanding the Text

The Text in Context

The opening verses in Jeremiah summarize the entire book. While many of the sections within the book of Jeremiah are not in chronological order, the opening and closing of the book follow the format laid out in 1:1–3. That is, the book starts with the word of God coming to the young Jeremiah (1:4–19) and ends with the fall and exile of Jerusalem (52:1–34). From the beginning, there is no mystery about how this story will end: the exile of the people of Jerusalem.

Ominously, this introductory passage notes that the "fifth month of the eleventh year of Zedekiah" was the time when "the people of Jerusalem went into exile," thus removing all mystery or question in the reader's mind about whether the people of Jerusalem might respond to Jeremiah's message. The fact of the exile is stated unequivocally here at the beginning of the book, thus providing a clear point of reference. Jeremiah delivers his spoken prophecies in the present tense, warning and rebuking the inhabitants of Jerusalem and Judah and calling on them to repent. The written prophetic collection that is the book of Jeremiah, however, reflects a theological explanation of the fall of Jerusalem and the exile, events that vindicate the word of God as proclaimed by Jeremiah.

The rest of Jeremiah 1 recounts how God calls him to be a prophet and then gives him a specific commission, describing what he is called to do. The chapter's structure follows a chiastic arrangement (A B B' A') as follows:[1]

A The articulation of the call (1:4–10)
B The vision illustrating the call (1:11–12)
B' The vision illustrating the commission (1:13–14)
A' The articulation of the commission (1:15–19)

Jeremiah 1 is a mix of prose (narrative) and poetry. The story moves along in prose with God's divine words appearing in poetry interspersed in several locations.[2]

Historical and Cultural Background

The opening verses in Jeremiah place the events of the book and the prophet's proclamation into a very specific historical setting. The word of God first comes to him in "the thirteenth year of the reign of Josiah" (627 BC) and continues through the reign of Jehoiakim and down to the "fifth month of the eleventh year of Zedekiah" (587 BC). Thus the work of Jeremiah as a prophet covers a period of forty years (627–587 BC).

Jeremiah's call came at a momentous time in history. In 628 BC Josiah, the last good king of Judah, began his valiant but futile attempt to reform Judah's religious practice and belief (cf. 2 Chron. 34:3–7). In the very year in which Jeremiah was called (627 BC), Ashurbanipal died. He was the last of several powerful Assyrian kings, and his death facilitated the rapid decline of the Assyrian Empire. Indeed, in the following year (626 BC) an independent Babylonian state was established.[3] The rise of the Babylonian Empire had a profound impact on the life and times of Jeremiah.

Interpretive Insights

1:1 *The words of Jeremiah . . . one of the priests at Anathoth.* Jeremiah is a priest, but surprisingly he is not from Jerusalem. He is from Anathoth, a small town near Jerusalem. Years earlier Solomon had banished the priest Abiathar to Anathoth (1 Kings 2:26), and it is probable that Abiathar's descendants still lived in the town. Anathoth plays an important role in Jeremiah and will show up again several times (11:21, 23; 29:27; 32:7–9). It is precisely from those in his hometown of Anathoth that Jeremiah will receive some of his harshest persecution (11:18–23).

1:4 *The word of the LORD came to me.* The noun translated as "word" (*dᵉbar*) in "word of the LORD" occurs seven times in this passage (1:1, 2, 4,

9, 11, 12, 13), while the verb form of this word occurs three more times as well (1:6, 16, 17). The "word of the LORD" is central to Jeremiah's call and his work as a prophet. It is not the plans or ideas of Jeremiah that drive his tumultuous ministry, but rather the plans of God—indeed, the very words of God. As God's prophet, Jeremiah will serve as God's spokesman, speaking the very words of God to the nation.

1:5 *Before I formed you in the womb I knew you, before you were born I set you apart.* In this construction and context the verb "knew" (*yada‘*) implies an intimate, personal knowledge. "Set apart" (*qadash*) implies the concept of "consecration" or "setting apart for a special use by God." It is the same Hebrew term often translated as "holy."

I appointed you as a prophet to the nations. Most of Jeremiah's prophetic ministry focuses on Judah. A significant portion of his prophecies, however, are directed at foreign nations (chaps. 46–51), and in 27:1–7 he proclaims the word of God directly to the foreign emissaries who have gathered in Jerusalem. God is sovereign over all the nations, and the word of God that Jeremiah proclaims will impact all the nations throughout the entire region.

1:6 *I do not know how to speak; I am too young.* The Hebrew behind "I am too young" is *na‘ar* ("child, youth"), which can be used of boys of any age up until marriage. Jeremiah probably is a young man at this time, perhaps even a teenager. In Exodus 4:10 Moses too objects to God's calling, but whereas Moses claims an inability to speak eloquently, Jeremiah simply pleads that he is too young to be able to speak well enough to be a prophet.

1:7 *You must go to everyone I send you to and say whatever I command you.* As in the case of Moses in Exodus 3–4, God waves aside Jeremiah's objection and focuses on the task. This verse has two parallel clauses and literally reads, "To everyone I send you to, you will go; and everything I command you, you will say." This echoes the description of the true prophet in Deuteronomy 18:18: "He will tell them everything I command him."

1:8 *Do not be afraid of them, for I am with you and will rescue you.* This verse is repeated and expanded at the end of this passage (1:17–19). Thus, like bookends, this promise frames the basic description of the task that God gives Jeremiah (1:9–16). From the very beginning of his call Jeremiah is told to "fear not," strongly implying that if he obeys God and answers his call, there will be something quite tangible to fear. The strong, hostile opposition to Jeremiah's words by the king and other powerful officials in Jerusalem is a major theme throughout the book. As with Moses (Exod. 3:12), so God declares to Jeremiah what is probably the most important element of his calling: God's presence will be with him. Translated literally, this phrase reads, "I will be with you to deliver you." Not only does God protect Jeremiah from the persecution that he experiences throughout the book, but also, toward the end of the story, as Jerusalem falls and all of Jeremiah's opponents are executed or exiled by the Babylonians, Jeremiah is safely delivered (39:1–40:6), just as God promises here at the beginning.

1:9 *I have put my words in your mouth.* As with 1:7, this phrase alludes to the true prophet of Deuteronomy 18:18 ("I will put my words in his mouth"), thus identifying Jeremiah as a true prophet of God and a legitimate successor to Moses.

1:10 *I appoint you over nations and kingdoms to uproot and tear down, to destroy and overthrow, to build and to plant.* This describes the twofold nature of Jeremiah's prophetic message. He proclaims the coming judgment (chaps. 2–29) and then the restoration after the judgment (chaps. 30–33). Note the reverse parallel structure (called "chiasm") of the opposite verbs that God uses:

A "uproot"
  B "tear down"
    C "destroy and overthrow"
  B′ "build"
A′ "plant"

These terms will continue to appear throughout the book. It is also perhaps helpful to note what is not included in Jeremiah's job description. He is not appointed specifically just to predict the future. Such a notion is a modern misunderstanding and does not describe the biblical role of God's prophets.

1:11 *almond tree.* God gives Jeremiah a visual image that communicates through a clever wordplay. The word for "almond tree" (*shaqed*) sounds very much like the word for "watching" (*shoqed*) in 1:12. Furthermore, almond trees were also the first to blossom in the spring, and as such they served as signs or signals of the changing season.[4]

1:13 *a pot that is boiling.* God explains that the invaders who will bring his judgment will come the north, like boiling water spilled out on the ground. At this point the reference to the enemy coming from the north is ambiguous, for with the sea to the west and the desert to the east, Judah could be approached only from the north and the south. That is, any invading nation other than Egypt (to the south) would have to attack Judah from the north. We learn later in the book, however, that the reference is to the Babylonians.

1:15 *set up their thrones in the entrance of the gates.* In the ancient world, kings and rulers "sat at the city gates" to hold court and pass judgment. To "sit at the gates" is to rule the city. Jeremiah 39:3 describes the fulfillment of this prophecy as the Babylonian lords come and take their seats at the gates of Jerusalem.

1:16 *because of their wickedness in forsaking me.* Jeremiah will speak a lot about the various sins of the people in Judah, but their most serious sin was the "forsaking" or "abandonment" of God, usually in conjunction with turning to idolatry. The concept of forsaking also has emotional connotations, and God will often express his pain and sorrow over the fact that his people have abandoned their relationship with him in favor of something or someone else.

Theological Insights

This opening chapter indicates that Jeremiah's ministry will be a proclamation of the word of God that will destroy the disobedient in judgment and yet will also afterward build up and restore. Throughout the Bible we often see both of these aspects of God revealed simultaneously, as if two sides of the same coin. God's holiness, righteousness, and justice demand that he judge sin and disobedience. Thus we frequently see passages describing how the wrath of God will be poured out on rebellious and unrepentant sinners. On the other hand, God is regularly portrayed throughout the Bible, including the Old Testament, as one whose very essence is characterized by love and grace. It is his great desire that people turn to him in trust, repenting and turning away from sin so that he can deliver and restore them rather than judge them. Thus in the midst of proclaiming judgment on Judah, a judgment that is certainly well earned, God also reveals a spectacular future plan to deliver and restore his people, a plan characterized by his love and his grace.

Teaching the Text

As in the life of Jeremiah, it is certainly still true for us that the word of God should define who we are, what we are to do, and how we are to do it. It is the word of God that gives us the direction for engaging the world around us and the strength to endure the difficulties that we might encounter as we obey that word.

There is no "health and wealth gospel" in Jeremiah, and the implications for us are important to note. Being in the will of God and doing the work that he has called us to do not automatically equate to a comfortable life or a "successful" ministry, as far as numbers go. In fact, as with Jeremiah, it is quite possible that the opposite will be true. We may undergo severe difficulty, even persecution, precisely because we are following God in obedience. The call to follow Christ is never a call to an easy life with promises of health and wealth; rather, it is a call to "take up your cross" and follow him.

We all have our objections when God calls us to a certain task: "I am not trained well enough," "I am too busy with other critical activities," "I do not have adequate resources," or "I do not have the talent or skill." As he did with Jeremiah, God sweeps our lame excuses away and reminds us that he gives us the power and skill needed to accomplish the tasks that he calls us to through his powerful presence manifested in us through the Holy Spirit. It is the powerful presence of God that dispels our fear and anxiety and enables us to do the work of God, no matter how difficult it is and no matter how insurmountable the opposition may seem.

Like Jeremiah, we live in a world where people have blatantly rejected God and embraced a life of sin and rebellion. Thus, while it is essential to stress the "good news" of the salvation offered through faith in Jesus Christ, both aspects of God's word, his salvation and his judgment, must be proclaimed.

Illustrating the Text

When God calls us, he will empower us.

Film: *The Matrix.* In this 1999 movie the hero, Neo, has a gradual awakening that he has been called to be the leader of a revolution that would result in the destruction of the Matrix and the freedom of the human race from its bondage. His coming has been prophesied for some time, and those in the know have been anticipating his arrival. They even have a special name for this coming messiah. They refer to him as "The One." Morpheus and The Oracle help Neo to discover that he is in fact The One and that he is capable of much more than he could ever imagine. The problem is that he must choose to accept the role for which he was born.

This same thing is true for Jeremiah and for all of us. God has a plan and a purpose for our lives, but we must be willing to accept the mission that he has for us and believe that he will equip us to accomplish the task. As with Jeremiah, there is often a momentum to God's call on our lives. It gradually builds and grows inside us until one day we realize that God's call on our lives defines who we are and how we interact with the world around us. At times, particularly early in the call process, this feels daunting, but we can take our inspiration from those who have gone before us. For example, at the first Russian Prayer Breakfast in Moscow in 1992, when he was asked about the qualities of leadership needed in our world today, Billy Graham said, "I often think of Dr. Martin Luther King, who was my friend. He said many times that one plus God is a majority."

God knows us better than we know ourselves.

Television: In the television show *The Newlywed Game*, which premiered in 1966 and ran for over thirty years, husbands were asked three questions about their wives. The wives were asked the same questions offstage, and then their answers were revealed. This game often revealed how little married couples knew about each other. God, however, knew before Jeremiah was even born that he would be a prophetic voice in this troubled world.

Technology: Speech recognition software is designed to turn your talk into text. With many of these programs, the more you use it, the more accurate it becomes because it learns to recognize your speech patterns and inflections. In essence, the software gets to know you. God has no need to learn about us; he knows us before we utter our first sound.

The Unfaithful Bride

Big Idea

Abandoning God and turning to idols is like abandoning a faithful spouse for a life of prostitution.

Key Themes

- Judah's forsaking of God is without cause or reason.
- When his people forsake him, God takes it personally and is hurt emotionally.
- Forsaking God is stupid, with devastating consequences.

Understanding the Text

The Text in Context

One of the foundational points of Jeremiah's message is that the people of Judah have broken the Mosaic covenant, as defined in Deuteronomy. Jeremiah 2 presents a formal, legal lawsuit against the Judahites for breaking this covenant. The three main indictments against the Judahites proclaimed throughout the book of Jeremiah are idolatry, social injustice, and religious ritualism. In Jeremiah 2, at the beginning of the book, it is idolatry that is stressed as the primary indictment. Also, although the lawsuit is formal, the injury is personal, and God uses the imagery of a husband and his unfaithful wife to convey the betrayal and pain that he feels because of Judah's idolatry. This will be a major image throughout the book of Jeremiah.

Running throughout Jeremiah 2 are numerous connections and allusions to Deuteronomy (esp. Deut. 32).

Historical and Cultural Background

Baal (2:8, 23) was one of the primary gods of the Canaanites and others in the region. Baal was a storm-god, closely connected with rain, fertility, and agricultural production. The worship of Baal was officially incorporated into the worship of Israel by Ahab (1 Kings 16:31–33) and into the worship of Judah by Manasseh (2 Kings 10:18–27).[1] The name "Baal" means "lord" or "master." It can also mean "master of the house" (i.e., "husband"), so later in Jeremiah Baal will be used in wordplays involving idolatry as well as in the analogy of marital unfaithfulness.

Interpretive Insights

2:2 *proclaim in the hearing of Jerusalem.* This could be translated more literally as "cry out in the ears of Jerusalem." In the ancient world oral proclamation was the primary means of public communication. In the New Testament Jesus probably is alluding to prophetic statements like this when he says, "Whoever has ears to hear, let them hear" (e.g., Mark 9:4).

I remember . . . how as a bride you loved me. The analogy of the husband and wife runs throughout this chapter. Here at the beginning (2:2–3), God reflects back on the exodus, which he compares to the "honeymoon" period of the relationship. All the "you" and "your" pronouns in this section are feminine singular in Hebrew.

2:5 *What fault did your fathers find in me, that they strayed so far from me?* Like an unjustly jilted husband, God asks what he could possibly have done wrong to warrant this abandonment.

2:6 *They did not ask, "Where is the* Lord, *who brought us up out of Egypt?"* Ironically, even though God had delivered them from Egypt and given them a wonderful and fruitful land, they had no interest in seeking him to continue the relationship (2:6–8).

2:8 *The priests . . . Those who deal with the law . . . the leaders . . . The prophets.* Throughout the book of Jeremiah, God will find the leaders of Judah and Jerusalem particularly culpable of leading the people away from him and into sin. These were the ones who had the responsibility of passing the faith on to each generation. These were the ones responsible for keeping the memory of the great salvation events in the exodus alive and for teaching the people to obey the book of Deuteronomy. The word translated as "leaders" is the word for "shepherds." The analogy of leaders (i.e., the king, his nobles, etc.) to shepherds is frequent in Jeremiah. Note also that later in this unit (2:26) groups of leaders will be mentioned again (kings, officials, priests, prophets).

2:9 *I bring charges against you.* The word used here refers to bringing a "covenant lawsuit" against someone. Using legal terminology, God declares that he is bringing a case against Judah and Jerusalem. In the book of Deuteronomy, the Israelites had agreed to keep the law and be faithful to God, worshiping him alone. But they broke this agreement, and now God is formally charging them with this "breach of contract." In essence, Jeremiah will function as God's prosecuting attorney, pressing his case continuously throughout Jeremiah 2–29.

2:12 *Be appalled at this, you heavens.* Addressing the heavens as if they were a person is a fairly common figure of speech (anthropomorphism) in the

Old Testament. The usage here is probably a direct reference back to Deuteronomy, where "the heavens" serve as "witnesses" to the covenant agreement between Israel and God (see esp. Deut. 30:19; 31:28). Isaiah does the same thing (Isa. 1:2).

2:13 *two sins: They have forsaken me, the spring of living water, and have dug . . . broken cisterns.* God uses a water analogy to continue his accusation against the people of Jerusalem. The twofold nature of their sin is stressed once again: they have forsaken God, and they have turned to other gods. The accusation of forsaking God was introduced back in 1:16. It is stressed in this unit as well, occurring three times (2:13, 17, 19). The water analogy conveys that the relationship with God is like having a fresh spring bubbling up with good, clean water (the phrase "living water" implies a spring, where water bubbles up by itself). Following idols, on the other hand, is like hewing a cistern out of the stone to try to catch rainfall runoff. This is hard work, the water is not as fresh and clean, and in this case the cistern is cracked and therefore leaks, not holding any water at all. When Jesus alludes to himself as the "spring of living water" (John 4:10–14), he is most likely alluding to this passage.

2:20 *on every high hill . . . you lay down as a prostitute.* In Canaanite religion hilltops, especially if there were large trees present, were often the sites of fertility cult practices. Thus there is a double analogy in this verse. To abandon God and to go after Canaanite gods (which often were worshiped on hilltops) is compared to being a prostitute on these hills. But also it is likely that on these hilltops there was literal cultic prostitution taking place as well, in which Israel probably was participating.[2]

2:23–25 *See how you behaved in the valley.* The term "valley" probably refers to the Valley of Ben Hinnom. In 7:30–31 God describes the detestable sins that the people of Judah were committing in this valley: they were sacrificing their sons and daughters to pagan gods.

You are a swift she-camel . . . a wild donkey . . . in her heat. This is perhaps one of the most graphic and insulting passages in Jeremiah. God's analogy for the people of Judah moves from the unfaithful bride (2:2–8) to the prostitute (2:20) to camels and donkeys in heat (2:23–25).

2:32 *Does a . . . bride [forget] her wedding ornaments?* Just as a wedding ring today identifies a new bride and thus becomes a source of pride for her, so in the ancient world brides had certain jewelry that marked them as such. No doubt this jewelry was a source of pride for them, just as wedding rings are cherished by new brides today. Thus God asks, somewhat sarcastically, whether a new bride is likely to forget the jewelry that identifies her as a married woman. Not likely!

2:33 *How skilled you are . . . Even the worst.* Again, somewhat sarcastically God declares that the people are not just occasional prostitutes; they are skilled, practiced prostitutes. A wordplay underscores the irony, for the words translated as "skilled" (*yatab*) and "worst" (*ra'*) are antonyms, meaning, respectively, "to be good" and "to be bad."

Theological Insights

The phrase "I am the LORD, who brought you up out of Egypt," alluded to in 2:6, is a foundational and central statement of Old Testament soteriology (theology of salvation). As the central paradigm of deliverance in the Old Testament, the exodus event is analogous in some aspects to the crucifixion of Christ, the central paradigm of deliverance in the New Testament. The exodus provided deliverance from slavery to blessing in the promised land, while the cross provides deliverance from sin to blessing in the kingdom of God.

The fact that God uses an analogy of a jilted husband with an unfaithful wife indicates that when his people are unfaithful to him, it is a very personal issue. God is not some distant and detached monarch or emotionless supercomputer. He loves us as a good husband loves his wife. When we reject him and abandon him, he feels the pain of betrayal and spurned love. It is rather shocking to realize that when God enters into a close, loving relationship with us, he becomes vulnerable. Ironically, his love toward us gives us the ability to cause him pain through our sinful rebellion against him or even by ignoring him.

Teaching the Text

Jeremiah 2 introduces and summarizes the charges/indictments of covenant breaking that dominate the entire book of Jeremiah. In this unit God formally announces the covenant lawsuit against the people in Jerusalem and Judah. But God is not an emotionless set of law codes. Some people suppose that sinning against God is like getting a speeding ticket. The police catch you speeding, and the government forces you to pay a penalty for breaking the law. But in this illustration no one gets hurt. The police certainly do not take your offense personally, and their feelings are not hurt. The unfaithful wife analogy in Jeremiah 2, however, underscores that sinning against God, especially when we abandon him and turn to other things in his place, is more like cheating on your spouse than getting a speeding ticket. It is a betrayal of the relationship, and it sets off a whole range of painful emotions. This presents us with the stark realization that because God loves us so much, we are in a position to hurt him (just as we can hurt our spouses, the ones who love us the most). Sin against God by his people is not emotionally neutral. Likewise, when we abandon him and replace that relationship with other things, God hurts. This puts a whole new perspective on sin and disobedience.

This unit also illustrates how foolish or stupid it is to reject the life that God offers and to chase after cheap substitutes. God had saved the Israelites from Egypt and offered them a wonderful and blessed life, but they rejected this and walked away from the good life that God had laid out for them. How can people make such a foolish decision? Yet we see it happen frequently. The life and the relationship that God offers are wonderful, meaningful, and fulfilling. Life without him is lonely and meaningless and ultimately ends in disaster.

There is a stark lesson here for those who grew up in the church but then later walked away from the faith. "Really?" Jeremiah seems to ask them, pointing out that the conscious decision to turn away from God and the blessings that come with that relationship is the dumbest decision one can make in this life. Surely there is enough clear, logical evidence before us to show that chasing after the so-called American dream or hoping that an entertainment-filled life will somehow give us peace and purpose is foolhardy.

Likewise, today it is a huge mistake to assume that God is somehow "soft on sin" or does not still insist on repentance. The obstinate refusal to acknowledge sin and to repent, then as now, is particularly aggravating and enraging to God. No matter how serious the sin, God is always willing to forgive and to restore the relationship if only people will acknowledge their sin and repent. But when people refuse even to acknowledge their sin as sin, especially when it is repeatedly pointed out to them, God gets especially angry.

This message certainly applies to our wider Western secular culture, which has consciously rejected most of its Christian heritage and abandoned biblical criteria as the basis for right and wrong in favor of what is popularly favored. But there is a message for those in the church as well, for there is always the temptation to use the culture's definition of what sin is rather than God's definition of sin. When the proclamation of biblical truth convicts us of our sin, will we take it to heart, repent, and turn back to God? Or, like Jeremiah's audience, will we reject the message in favor of lies, even hardening our hearts against the message and thus bringing on the anger of God?

Illustrating the Text

It breaks God's heart when we turn our backs on him.

Theater: One of the classic betrayals of history was the assassination of the Roman emperor Julius Caesar in 44 BC. He and the Roman senate were involved in an escalating dispute that ultimately culminated in the savage attack and death of Caesar. The betrayal was so iconic that in 1599 William Shakespeare wrote a play about it, *The Tragedy of Julius Caesar*. In the play a beggar who turns out to be a soothsayer or fortune-teller issues an ominous warning to Caesar, "Beware of the Ides of March" (the Roman way of referring to March 15), foretelling the day of his upcoming death.

The climax of the betrayal comes when Caesar, surrounded by knife-wielding senators, sees his friend in the crowd of attackers and utters the iconic (if historically doubtful) line, "Et tu, Brute?" ("You too, Brutus?").

We can all connect with this classic tale because the pain of betrayal is so common. Ask the members of the congregation to think of a time when they were betrayed. Give them examples to help trigger their memories. Say something like, "Perhaps you were betrayed by a politician, or a friend, or a teacher, or a loved one. How did that feel?" That is how God feels when we betray him. The prophet reminds us that God is wounded emotionally and takes it personally whenever his people forsake him for something less.

God does not make idle threats.

Human Experience: Almost everyone has heard a parent say, "If I have to pull this car over, you'll be sorry." The problem is that too often this is simply an idle threat. The parents have no intention of following through, and as a result their unwillingness to discipline only leads to more misbehavior.

We can relate the interaction between parent and child to our relationship with God. As our Father in heaven, God does not wish to invoke punishment, but he cannot stand idly by and witness injustice and unrighteous behavior forever. Out of his great love for us, he issues repeated warnings in his word. But we should not confuse his patience with apathy. God does not make idle threats. Forsaking God's law is foolish and will eventually result in consequences.

God Calls His Unfaithful Bride to Return

Big Idea

God calls on his wayward people to acknowledge their sin, return to him sincerely, and enjoy his blessings.

Key Themes

- Even though Judah is like a prostitute, God begs her to return to him and be restored.
- Unfaithful Judah has failed to learn from the fate of her unfaithful "sister," Israel.
- God wants to restore the relationship with his people.
- God describes what true repentance looks like.

Understanding the Text

The Text in Context

In Jeremiah 2 God presents the basic covenant lawsuit against his people in Judah, comparing them to an unfaithful wife who has become just like a prostitute. Idolatry is the central charge. In this unit (3:1–4:4) God pleads with the people to repent and turn back to him. As in many places in the book of Jeremiah, these two units overlap to a certain degree. The earlier unit closes by underscoring that the people refused even to acknowledge their sin (2:33–35), though they were steeped in it. Thus it underscores their lack of repentance. Jeremiah 3:1–4:4 stresses the call for repentance and continues to use the imagery of husband and wife introduced in Jeremiah 2. If they fail to repent, God warns, judgment will fall on them (4:4). This warning will transition into the next unit (4:5–31), where the terrible judgment is described. So in these three sections we move from indictment, to instruction, to judgment.

This unit contains a complicated mix of poetic sections (3:1–5, 12–13, 19–25; 4:1–4) and prose sections (3:6–11, 14–18) that unfolds as follows: God observes that a man would hardly take back his wife if she became a prostitute (3:1–5; poetry). He then points out that Judah did not learn anything from the judgment that fell upon her "sister" Israel because of her adulteries over one hundred years ago (3:6–11; prose). Next God calls on the northern kingdom, Israel (destroyed over one hundred years earlier), to return to him (3:12–13; poetry). He then calls both Judah and Israel to repentance, describing the wonderful future restoration (3:14–18; prose). Yet the people still will not return to him (3:19–20; poetry). Continuing in poetry (3:21–25) is an ambiguous cry of repentance, followed by a poetic description of what true repentance looks like (4:1–4).

Historical and Cultural Background

The historical background for this unit is important to recall. After Solomon's death (late tenth century, three hundred years before Jeremiah) a civil war split the nation into two countries: Israel (in the north) and Judah (in the south). The northern kingdom, Israel, immediately abandoned the true worship of God in Jerusalem, replacing it with idol worship (see 1 Kings 12:25–33). Israel never worshiped the true God of its forebears but instead embraced the idolatry of the Canaanites (Baal, calf images, etc.), despite warnings from prophets such as Elijah, Elisha, and Amos. Therefore, in 722 BC the Assyrians invaded, destroyed the northern kingdom, and exiled its inhabitants (see 2 Kings 17:1–41). At the time of Jeremiah only Judah remained. In Jeremiah 3 God refers to these two kingdoms of Judah and Israel as two sisters. (Ezekiel uses a similar "sister" analogy for the two nations in Ezek. 23.)

Interpretive Insights

3:1 *Would not the land be completely defiled?* This concept is repeated in 3:2, 9. When God's presence in the tabernacle moved into the promised land with the Israelites, the land itself picked up a certain "holy" or "sanctified" status. Thus in the Old Testament there is often a close connection between holiness/sin, the people, and the land. That is, the actions of the people and the ensuing consequences had associated repercussions on the land. The word translated as "defiled" means "to pollute" or "to contaminate." It is used especially of ruining or contaminating holy things so that they can no longer be used for their holy, sanctified purpose. The widespread practice of idolatry on the hilltops all across the land had changed the "holy" nature of the promised land into something "defiled." The Hebrew grammar places a strong stress on this act: "Will not the land most certainly be defiled?"

you have lived as a prostitute with many lovers—would you now return to me? The Hebrew verb translated as "lived as a prostitute" (*zanah*) stresses the repeated act of sexual unfaithfulness more than the professional occupation, although it probably always carries at least some connotations of the occupation as well. The same verb is used in 3:6, 8, where it is translated as "committed adultery." The noun form of this verb occurs in 3:3 and also in 2:20, where it is translated as "prostitute." Deuteronomy 24:1–4 specifies that if a man divorces his wife and she marries another man, he is not allowed to take her back. How much more unlikely it is for the "husband" (God) to take back his wayward wife (Israel) in this case, where the wife has left on her own and then slept with many other men. Humanly speaking, this is next to impossible. But God will in fact plead with her to return. The section closes with his plea (4:1). This parallels the story played out in the book of Hosea.

3:3 *the showers have been withheld.* Baal, one of the false gods that the people of Judah worship, is a "fertility-god" they trust to bring the necessary rain for crops to flourish. The tight connection between worshiping Baal and the hope of good agricultural production was deeply entrenched in Canaanite culture and religion, and the Israelites had bought into this thinking as they succumbed to the influence of Canaanite culture. With clearly intended "poetic justice," one of the disciplining actions that God uses to warn the wayward people is the sending of drought and famine.

you have the brazen look of a prostitute; you refuse to blush with shame. Just as a harlot eventually grows hard and accustomed to what she does, so these sinful people no longer even acknowledge that what they are doing is sin. God is trying to call them to repent, but they think that they have done nothing wrong.

3:6–7 *faithless Israel . . . and her unfaithful sister Judah.* Israel, the northern kingdom, which was conquered and exiled over one hundred years earlier, is called "faithless [*shb*] Israel" several times (3:6, 8, 11). The nuance is that of "Israel, who has turned away." The term used for Judah, however, is different

Which Way to Turn?

One of the most important usages in the book of Jeremiah is the Hebrew root word *shub*, which Jeremiah uses over one hundred times. Basically, *shub* means "to turn." Yet it can also mean "to turn to something" or "to turn away from something." Thus in Jeremiah it can refer to "repentance" (turning to God) or "apostasy" (turning away from God). As a noun, it usually means "the one who turned away" and in this usage is generally translated by the NIV as "faithless." Jeremiah loves wordplays, so he uses all these meanings in close proximity. The root word *shub* plays a critical role in 3:1–4:4, occurring thirteen times in various forms in these verses. In this unit the NIV translates the various forms of *shub* as "Return!" indicating a call to repentance (3:12, 14, 22; 4:1 [2x]); "faithless," referring to the fact that the people had turned away and abandoned God (3:6, 8, 12, 14); and "return," in the sense of a wife returning to her husband or a husband returning to his wife (3:1 [2x], 7 [2x]).

(*bagad*), and it carries a connotation of malicious deceit or treachery (3:7, 8, 10, 11).

3:10 *her unfaithful sister Judah did not return to me with all her heart, but only in pretense.* The word translated as "pretense" (*sheqer*) is often translated as "deception" or "deceptive" (Jer. 3:23; 7:4, 8) and is the same word used in Exodus 20:16: "You shall not give false [*sheqer*] testimony against your neighbor."

3:14 *Return, faithless people.* A more literal rendering of the words translated as "faithless people" is "sons of turning." After addressing the northern kingdom and the southern kingdom separately in the previous verses, God now seems to lump them together as he anticipates the future restoration.

3:16 *"The ark . . ." will not be remembered . . . it will not be missed, nor will another one be made.* The ark of the covenant in the temple in Jerusalem, which in the Old Testament represented the presence of God, was still at the center of the ritualistic and syncretistic worship of the Judahites. They probably treated it like a fetish that would protect them. In the future restoration, God declares, the ark will be gone, and no one will even miss it. Indeed, it appears that the Babylonians destroyed it when they captured Jerusalem.[1] From a New Testament perspective, the presence of God as represented in the ark of the covenant will be replaced with the indwelling Holy Spirit, so indeed, in the coming restoration, no one even misses the ark.

3:17 *all nations will gather in Jerusalem.* In Jeremiah's call God appointed him "over nations and kingdoms," both in judgment and in restoration (1:10). Thus, as Jeremiah paints the picture of the future restoration, he includes not only Judah and Israel (destroyed over one hundred years earlier) but also all the nations of the world gathering in Jerusalem to worship God. Several aspects of this restoration picture reflect back to the Abrahamic promise (increased numbers, blessings on the nations, the land [see Gen. 12:1–3]).

3:22 *Return, faithless people; I will cure you of backsliding.* In Hebrew this line only has five words, and three of them come from the root word *shb*. In a wooden, overly literal rendering, this could be translated as "Turn, you sons of turning! I will cure you of your turning!"

4:2 *in a truthful, just and righteous way.* Literally, this reads, "in truth, in justice, and in righteousness." In contrast with the treacherous and deceitful behavior of Judah (3:7–10), true repentance must not only be truthful but also be accompanied by acts of justice and righteousness.

4:4 *circumcise your hearts.* In the Old Testament the "heart" is the place where one makes decisions. Thus throughout Jeremiah the "heart" is closely connected with the decision that one makes to obey or disobey. Circumcision was a physical and personal mark that the Israelites were to use to identify themselves as God's people. True repentance, God explains, includes identifying oneself with him, not only by hidden, private circumcision, but also with external obedience. A true decision to repent and follow God will be evidenced more by active and public obedience than by hidden physical marking.

Theological Insights

In this passage God compares himself to a jilted husband who is grieving and hurting over his wife's betrayal. This is not a minor metaphor in Jeremiah but one that occurs numerous times, suggesting that God wants us to include this image of him in our understanding of his character. Sometimes in our theological attempt to magnify and elevate God, we tend to paint his character as distant and emotionless, as carrying out his decrees with justice but without feeling. But this is not the way God has revealed himself to us in the Old Testament Prophets, especially in Jeremiah. Like a faithful and loving spouse, God loves his people and becomes vulnerable, and if they reject him and are unfaithful to him, he grieves and suffers.[2]

Teaching the Text

This text provides rich insight into the nature of repentance. First of all, no matter how sinful or how far removed one is from God today, and how hopelessly ruined the relationship is from a human point of view, God continues to plead with us to turn back to him (repent) and be restored. This is as true today as it was in the time of Jeremiah.

A life of continual sin, however, tends to produce a hard-hearted attitude toward God and the call to repentance. This is especially true when accompanied by a defiant attitude, even when we know better. Sometimes people today who grew up in the church or who have been influenced by Christians know in their hearts that they are living sinfully. But each time they reject the call to repent, their hearts harden, making repentance more and more difficult. Thus there is a certain urgency in the need to proclaim the gospel and to call these people to repentance. The longer they wait, the more difficult it will be. This underscores the importance of children's ministry and youth ministry. Once people reach adulthood, it is much more difficult for them to repent and turn to Christ, precisely because their hearts have hardened through the years.

Likewise, repentance that leads to a true conversion to Christ cannot be merely superficial; it must be sincere and truthful, marked with an obedient heart that leads to a transformed life. "Walking the aisle" or accepting Christ in some other public manner is an important part of repentance. But it is only one part. The other critical component is to live out the commitment to publicly obey God and to strive to have the same concerns that he has (justice, righteousness, truth).

Yet if there is no repentance, and if people merely harden their hearts more each time they are confronted with the truth, then eventually terrible judgment most certainly will come. God offers salvation to those who repent and come to him in faith. But if people refuse him and rebuff his gracious offer, then the consequence is judgment. This is a reality that we need to include in our proclamation of the gospel, along with the truth of Jesus's love for us and the promise of eternal life for all who believe.

Illustrating the Text

To stop going in the wrong direction, we need to turn around.

Parenting: Whenever we see a two-year-old running toward the street, our first reaction is to say, "Stop! Turn around!" because we know that the child is about to step into harm's way. If you have raised children, tell about a time when you firmly but lovingly stopped a little one from doing something that could have led to injury or harm. Describe some of the consequences that children might face if their parents or guardians do not love them enough to teach them wisdom and self-control in these moments. Then reinforce how God is a loving Father who will always seek to protect his children, even if it means using firm discipline.

Technology: Anyone who owns a GPS (global positioning system) knows that when you are headed in the wrong direction, a gentle voice will automatically chide you by saying something like, "Recalculating route. Make a U-turn as soon as it's safe to do so." According to the owner's manual, this is simply a warning that you have deviated from the preferred route, and unless you turn around, you are in danger of failing to reach your desired destination. Unfortunately, when we are lost, and our emotions are beginning to boil over, it can sound as if the device is really saying, "You just missed the exit, you nitwit. Turn around before it's too late." Sometimes when God's prophet calls us to repent, it can feel the same way. But really, like the father of the prodigal son (Luke 15:11–32), God stands at the end of heaven's driveway, hoping that we will return to him and ready to welcome us with open arms.

Story: A pastor was counseling a couple whose marriage was headed in the wrong direction. The wife had been having an emotionally inappropriate relationship with a man at work, and it was escalating. She was texting him so frequently that even her eleven-year-old daughter could not help but notice. During one of the back-and-forth texting sessions, the daughter walked by and said, "Texting your boyfriend again?" The mother broke down in tears, knowing that she had to turn her life around and end the inappropriate relationship immediately.

Share this story, or one like it (being cautions, of course, to preserve privacy). Talk about how all of us have moments when, in a situation with someone we love and care about, we realize that if our love is genuine, we must challenge that person to stop, turn around, and head in the right direction.

The Coming Babylonian Invasion

Big Idea

Those who reject a relationship with God and refuse to repent of sin will experience the terrible wrath of God.

Key Themes

- Jeremiah "sees" the coming Babylonian invasion and describes the horror of it.
- The coming judgment is compared to a reversal of the creation story.
- The visions of judgment are so horrific that Jeremiah can hardly bear them.
- Once the judgment comes, there is no escape.

Understanding the Text

The Text in Context

In 2:1–37 God describes the terrible sin that the people of Jerusalem and Judah have committed. They have shattered their relationship with him. In 3:1–4:4 God pleads with them to repent and return to him. But they do not repent; they become more entrenched in their sin and rejection of him. Thus 4:5–6:30 describes the consequent wrath of God, the inevitable judgment that will be carried out through the imminent Babylonian invasion. The boiling pot tilting from the north described back in 1:13–15 has finally tipped over, and now the brutal Babylonian army pours out all across the land of Judah.

Jeremiah 4:5–6:30 has three sections. It opens (4:5–31) and closes (6:1–30) with live (present tense) descriptions of the Babylonian invasion. Both of these sections start with "Sound the trumpet!" and a statement about disaster (*ra'ah* [see the discussion below]) coming out of the north (4:5–6; 6:1). These two invasion descriptions form bookends around the middle section (5:1–31), which underscores how guilty Jerusalem is and how well deserved is its judgment.

The root word *shb* ("to turn to, turn away"), which played a prominent role in the previous unit 3:1–4:4, forms a strong connection to 4:5–31. Since the people will not *shub* (turn away) from their sin and *shub* (turn to) God in repentance (3:1–4:4), God will not *shub* (turn away) from his wrath (4:8, 28). This section opens with a trumpet sounding the alarm as the Babylonian invasion begins (4:5) and closes with the dying scream of Daughter Zion (4:31).

Historical and Cultural Background

The term "Zion" is used in 4:6, 31. Originally, when David captured Jerusalem, "Zion" referred to the mount or hilltop just to the immediate south of the space where the temple would be built. After the temple was built, the entire hilltop that the temple sat upon was called "Zion." In Jeremiah, as in the other prophetic books, "Zion" can still refer literally to this hilltop, but more commonly it is used figuratively to refer to the temple itself, the entire city of Jerusalem (as in 4:6), the inhabitants of Jerusalem (especially when called "Daughter Zion," as in 4:31), or to a blurred mixture of all three.[1]

Interpretive Insights

4:6 *Raise the signal to go to Zion!* These signals probably are not fire or smoke but rather banner-like flags hoisted up on tall poles that alerted people in surrounding areas that an invading army was approaching.[2] People would seek safety from the invaders inside the fortified cities of Judah (i.e., those

The Babylonian Invasion

There is a sense in which the Old Testament prophets sometimes stood "outside time" and viewed the future as if it were happening now. In this unit Jeremiah appears actually to "see" (perhaps as in a vision) the future Babylonian invasion that he describes vividly as happening now. In his vision, as the Babylonian invasion begins, alarms are sounded and signals fired so that people can flee to the fortified cities (4:5–9). Although the false prophets had proclaimed "peace" in the name of God, Jeremiah explains that God is bringing judgment instead (4:10–12). The Babylonian chariots and cavalry rapidly advance (4:13–17), and Jeremiah cries out in anguish as he sees the Babylonians destroy the land (4:18–21). God interrupts with a declaration of how foolish the people have been to bring this disaster on themselves (4:22). In fact, the destruction is so bad that God uses figurative language from Genesis 1 and describes the judgment as a reversal of creation—a return to the chaos of Genesis 1:2 (4:23–28). The description of the invasion continues. There is no safety in the towns, and people desperately flee into the countryside, attempting to hide from the invaders (4:29). In trying to survive the invasion, personified Jerusalem once again plays the harlot, seeking to seduce the invaders and thus save her life. It does not work. The Babylonians kill her (4:30–31).

with walls, gates, towers, etc.). "Zion" refers to Jerusalem, the largest and best fortified of Judah's cities.

For I am bringing disaster from the north. The word translated as "disaster" is *ra'ah*. This is a central word in Jeremiah, occurring over 120 times. This word is used frequently in regard to both the actions of sinful people and the judging actions of God. When it is used of people, the NIV generally translates it as "evil" or "wickedness," but the term can refer to a very wide range of negative situations and does not just imply "moral evil." When it is used of God, the NIV generally translates it as "disaster." Jeremiah uses it repeatedly in an extended wordplay. Because the people of Jerusalem have done *ra'ah* to God and to others, God does *ra'ah* to them. The *ra'ah* of the people of Judah and Jerusalem is cited in 4:4, and the consequent *ra'ah* of God is recounted in 4:6, the terrible invasion by the Babylonians.

4:7 *A lion has come out of his lair.* This is a reference to Nebuchadnezzar, the king of Babylon (see also 50:17; cf. Lam. 3:10–12). In an age before electricity, cars, and rifles, lions were terrifying. In the Old Testament the lion metaphor is often used to create a feeling of terror before a powerful, fierce, and deadly foe.[3]

4:8 *lament and wail.* A repeated theme in Jeremiah is that if the people will not be sorrowful in repentance (lamenting over their sins), then they will be sorrowful over the death and destruction of Jerusalem that the Babylonians will bring.

the fierce anger of the LORD has not turned away from us. Once again *shub* ("to turn") is used. Jeremiah 3:1–4:4 makes it clear that the people have no intention of turning away (*shub*) from their sin, so God does not turn away (*shub*) his anger from them.

4:10 *you have deceived this people.* Commentators have disagreed widely on how to understand this verse. It probably refers to the word of peace that the false prophets have been giving in God's name (5:12; 14:13–14). Although God himself will disavow any connection to the message that these false prophets proclaim, Jeremiah seems to be giving his own personal (but incorrect) opinion that God may have sent this message of "peace" intentionally to mislead them as part of his judgment on them (cf. Ezek. 14:1–11).

4:14 *Jerusalem, wash the evil from your heart and be saved.* A last-minute appeal for repentance is given, even as the Babylonian army descends. Using figurative language, Jeremiah calls on Jerusalem to "wash" away the "evil" (*ra'ah*) from its heart. Remember that in the Old Testament it is with the heart that one decides whether to obey.

4:15 *from Dan . . . from the hills of Ephraim.* Dan is the northernmost part of Israel, the area closest to Babylonia and the first to be invaded. Ephraim is a region of Israel just to the south of Dan. So this verse portrays a north-to-south invasion route.

4:17 *because she has rebelled against me.* The Hebrew grammar stresses "against me." The sense of the text is "against *me* she has rebelled." On the surface, it is true that Judah's rebellion against Babylon has brought about the terrible invasion that Jeremiah is describing. Yet God is clarifying that the real cause for this disastrous invasion is Judah's rebellion against him (cf. David's statement in Ps. 51:4).

4:19 *my anguish, my anguish!* The Hebrew term used here actually refers to one's inward parts—that is, one's stomach. It probably implies that sick feeling that one gets in the stomach when confronted with awful, heartbreaking tragedy.

4:23–26 *I looked . . . I looked . . . I looked . . . I looked.* Each of these verses starts identically with "I looked," probably serving to remind the reader that this vision is in graphic first-person language.

the earth . . . was formless and empty. This alludes directly to Genesis 1:2: "formless and empty" (*tohu wabohu*) is the exact same phrase used in Genesis 1:2. This text suggests that in similar fashion to the great flood (Gen. 9), the destruction of Judah and Jerusalem will be like a reversal of creation and a return back to the precreation time of "nonorder" or "uncreation."

4:27 *though I will not destroy it completely.* The concept of a remnant that is saved in the midst of the judgment echoes quietly but persistently throughout Jeremiah. Here it is inserted into one of the chapters with the strongest and most vivid descriptions of the destruction and judgment.

4:30 *Why dress yourself in scarlet . . . put on jewels of gold . . . highlight your eyes with makeup?* As the Babylonian cavalry pours into the towns and cities, the inhabitants of Judah are fleeing for their lives (4:29). It is rather shocking, therefore, when Jeremiah seems actually to see in this vision a woman dressing up and even putting on makeup (4:30). Apparently, she hopes to save herself by once again playing the harlot and embracing the invaders or by relying on her "lovers" to rescue her. It does not work, and the invaders kill her.

Theological Insights

It is a terrible thing to fall under the wrath of God. Sin and the rejection of God ultimately result in judgment, and 4:5–31 describes how terrible the judgment on Jerusalem will be. Jeremiah is trying to paint a very honest picture of the consequences of the people's refusal to repent. The overriding purpose of revealing these horrific scenes of invasion and destruction is to urge the people to reconsider and repent. In fact, even as Jeremiah describes the judgment, he continues to intersperse the judgment scenes with repeated last-minute calls for repentance and clear explanations of the direct connection between the people's sin and this judgment. This tension between the description of imminent judgment and the call to repent continues throughout Jeremiah. God's wrath and his gracious love are always equally present. Because of God's justice and holiness he judges sin and rebellion, but because of his love and his grace he continually pleads with people to repent so that he will not have to judge them.

Teaching the Text

The description in Jeremiah 4 is more than just a vision of what might happen in the future. In all probability God actually shows Jeremiah what happens in the future invasion, showing Jeremiah the real destruction of people and places that he knows, and it tears him up.

In the church today the wrath of God is a topic that we often shy away from. Usually we try to focus on the positive side of the gospel, stressing eternal life and forgiveness of sins. The book of Jeremiah in general, however, and 4:5–31 in particular, forces us to see that unrepentant sin, open defiance of God, and refusal to listen to him ultimately result in experiencing the terrible wrath of God.

Although Jeremiah will soon add social injustice and religious ritualism to his list of indictments against Jerusalem, the main charge that he has made against it so far is idolatry. It is the sin of idolatry that lies behind the analogy of the unfaithful wife that God uses so frequently in Jeremiah. In some quarters of contemporary Christianity, a certain "universalism" movement is afoot that purports that all peoples of all religions will be saved. Jeremiah 4:5–31 is a clear and unambiguous declaration from God that "alternative" approaches to "gods" that are outside his special revelation and his particular manner of relationship with people are unequivocally rejected by him, and those who fail to repent and to accept his specific terms (as revealed) will experience his terrible wrath. The inhabitants of Judah and Jerusalem could not just choose on their own which god they would worship and how they would worship and live without suffering the consequences of rejecting the one true God.

Although this text gives us a stark and clear picture of the wrath of God, it is also instructive to note that God continues to plead for repentance, even as the judgment unfolds. This theme will also continue throughout Jeremiah. So even as we preach the wrath of God against those who rebel and refuse to repent, we must continue, as God did in Jeremiah's day, to plead for repentance down to the final hour and final breath.

Illustrating the Text

Those who reject the love of God will suffer the wrath of God.

Science: To do this experiment you will need a two-liter bottle of diet cola, a 3 x 5 index card, a very large tarp, a roll of Mentos candy, a six-inch piece of plastic pipe slightly larger than the roll of candy, and a brave volunteer. Spread the tarp out on the stage, set the bottle of diet cola in the center, remove the cap, and place the index card on top. Ask the congregation for a volunteer, preferably someone around twelve years old who is fast.

Tell the volunteer that there is a cause and effect in life, and in order to prove it, you would like him or her to be part of a demonstration. Tell the volunteer that you have heard that putting Mentos into an open bottle of cola will result in an enormous eruption.

Ask the volunteer if he or she believes you, but either way, tell the person that he or she has been selected to help you prove it. Have the volunteer unwrap the Mentos, vertically stack them in the tube, and set them on top of the index card. Tell the volunteer to hold the pipe in one hand, pull out the index card with the other, and then run as if his or her feet were on fire. The result will be that the cola will erupt like Old Faithful.

When the laughter and pandemonium die down, tell your volunteer that you have a second experiment involving a stick of dynamite. Instruct the volunteer to bite down hard on it while you light it, but this time you will be the one doing the running. Of course, the volunteer will refuse, and you can say just as there will be consequences for lighting dynamite, so too unrepented sin will one day result in the wrath of God. (In many settings it will not be practical to do this experiment during a sermon or lesson. But you could have some students in your church do it and make a video of it.)

God redeems the unredeemable.

Film: *Saving Private Ryan.* Jeremiah is overwhelmed by the horror of the Babylonian invasion. One of the most graphic portrayals of the horror of war is the epic 1998 movie *Saving Private Ryan*, starring Tom Hanks. The film includes a graphically realistic portrayal of the brutality that took place during the invasion of Normandy in World War II. Although much of the scene depicting the landing on Omaha Beach is too intense and graphic to be shown on a Sunday morning, a short clip of Tom Hanks in the landing craft nervously anticipating what is about to take place will certainly bring back terrifying memories to anyone who has seen the film. It might also be helpful to give a short summary of the film to set up the clip for those who might not have seen it. What Jeremiah "sees" is similar to the scene on Omaha Beach, except that in Jeremiah's story the people never get off the beach.

Deserved Judgment

Big Idea

The coming judgment on those who refuse to obey God and instead embrace immorality, social injustice, and dishonesty is a well-deserved one.

Key Themes

- The sinful behavior of Jerusalem is compared to that of Sodom and Gomorrah.
- Immorality, social injustice, and dishonesty characterize the leaders and the people of Jerusalem.
- God provides hope through a brief glimpse of a future remnant.
- The refusal to obey God is indeed very foolish, for even the sea obeys God.

Understanding the Text

The Text in Context

Jeremiah 1 describes the call of the prophet. Jeremiah 2 charges Judah and Jerusalem with idolatry, a serious breach of the Mosaic covenant. Jeremiah 3 calls for repentance, but there is none, so 4:5–6:30 proclaims the consequent and inevitable judgment.

Remember that 5:1–31 lies in the middle of the larger unit (4:5–6:30). The stress of the larger unit as a whole is that the coming judgment is inevitable. The opening (4:5–31) and closing (6:1–30) sections describe in present tense the horror of the coming Babylonian invasion. Sandwiched between these two invasion descriptions is 5:1–31, which highlights the culpability of Jerusalem and underscores how everyone in the city is guilty and deserving of the judgment.

This section breaks down as follows: God tells Jeremiah to search the streets of Jerusalem and try to find one person who "does justice" and seeks truth (5:1–9). Because of rampant lies and dishonesty, Jerusalem will be stripped of its branches like a vineyard (5:10–13). Furthermore, because of the lies, the Babylonians will come and devour Jerusalem like a fire burning up wood (5:14–19). Even the mighty sea obeys God, so it is extremely foolish for people to refuse to obey him (5:20–25). Yet the entire society of Jerusalem is characterized by social injustice; the leaders and the people are all in it together (5:26–31).

Interpretive Insights

5:1 *If you can find but one person.* This is an obvious allusion to Abraham's negotiations with God regarding judgment on the city of Sodom in Genesis 18:16–33. After arguing down from fifty righteous people, Abraham is able to get God to agree that if ten righteous people are found in Sodom, then God will not destroy the entire city because of the sin of the others. Ironically, in Jeremiah 5:1 God challenges Jeremiah to find even one person who "deals honestly and seeks the truth." The implication is that Jerusalem is as bad as, or worse than, Sodom was.

who deals honestly. The NIV translation is a bit unusual here. The key Hebrew word is *mishpat* ("justice"). Literally, this verse reads, "If you can find one person who does justice and seeks the truth, I will forgive this city." In this verse justice and truth are the two characteristics that God is looking for. Not only is "justice" a central theme throughout Jeremiah, but also the term occurs four times in this particular unit (5:1, 4, 5, 28 [*mishpat*]).

5:2 *Although they say, "As surely as the LORD lives," still they are swearing falsely.* The people are using an oath formula with God's name in it but then telling lies. "Falsely" translates the word *sheqer*, which was used of Judah's "fake" repentance in 3:10 and also of the prophets' lies in 5:31. *Sheqer* ("lie, falsehood") is a major theme in Jeremiah, occurring in thirty-four different verses.[1]

5:4 *They are foolish.* The word translated as "foolish" carries a nuance of "thick-brained" or "stupid." Jeremiah probably is referring to their lack of education. Without the discernment and insight that come from education, he seems to ask, how can the poor really be expected to know the "way [lit., "road, path"] of the LORD" or "the requirements [*mishpat* = justice] of their God"?

5:5 *So I will go to the leaders.* The word translated as "leaders" literally means "the great ones" or "the big ones," and it is the contrasting opposite of the word translated as "poor" in 5:4, which means "the insignificant ones" or "the small ones."

surely they know the way . . . the requirements. These are the exact phrases used in 5:4 regarding what the poor could not be expected to know.

But with one accord they too had broken off the yoke. Jeremiah concludes that it is not an issue of information, education, or understanding but rather one of basic obedience. None of the leaders of Jerusalem even recognize God's right to rule over them anymore. The theme of "yoke" will resurface in greater detail in Jeremiah 27–28, with the Hebrew word for "yoke" occurring in 27:8, 11, 12; 28:2, 4, 11, 14. There the yoke is not the rule of God that they reject but rather the rule of the Babylonians.

5:6 *a lion . . . will attack them . . . a wolf . . . a leopard.* In the ancient world, long before high-powered rifles were invented, it was a terrifying danger to be caught out in the open by a wild animal. The results were gruesome. This figurative language probably also applies to the Babylonians.

for their rebellion is great. Literally, "for many are their rebellions."

and their backslidings many. The word translated as "backslidings" is a plural form of *shb* ("to turn"). That is, they have numerous "turnings away from God."

5:8 *stallions . . . neighing for another man's wife.* Not only was the city guilty of idolatry (5:7), but sexual immorality, especially adultery, was also rife. Common norms of morality, such as honoring marriage, had disappeared.

5:9 *Should I not punish them for this?* God states this twice, once here and again in 5:29. The exposé of the depth and ubiquity of their sin leads to but one conclusion: God should punish them for their sin.

5:10 *do not destroy them completely.* Both here and in 5:18, God states that he will not totally destroy them. This quietly leaves the door open for the remnant theme, developed in more detail later in the book.

for these people do not belong to the LORD. At the very heart of God's covenant relationship with Israel in the Old Testament was the formulaic statement, "I will be your God, and you will be my people." To say that these people no longer belong to God is to imply that the covenant relationship is no longer valid.

5:11 *utterly unfaithful to me.* This is the same word (*bagad*) used of Judah in 3:6–14, and it carries a strong nuance of treachery, or "treacherous dishonesty." Lies and dishonesty tie verses 11, 12, and 13 together.

5:14 *the* LORD *God Almighty.* Literally, this reads, "Yahweh, God of the hosts," with "hosts" referring to armies. It is the name that God frequently uses in contexts of war, stressing his power in battle.

5:15 *I am bringing a distant nation against you.* The "distant nation" is Babylon.

5:22 *I made the sand a boundary for the sea.* In the biblical world the "sea" often represented the forces of "chaos" or of "nonorder," the rebellious challenge in nature to God's order and decrees. Yet God has decreed how far the sea can go and where it must stop, thus indicating that even the most rebellious elements of nature obey his authority and power. Therefore, it is quite ridiculous that mere people would rebel against him (5:23–25) and not fear him (5:22).

5:27 *their houses are full of deceit; they have become rich and powerful.* Extortion and unjust manipulation of the economic system have enriched the crooked leaders in power.

5:28 *They do not promote the case of the fatherless . . . the just cause of the poor.* The book of Deuteronomy demands that God's people care for those who are weak in the socioeconomic system. Deuteronomy stresses especially the care for orphans, widows, foreigners, and the poor. Jeremiah 5:28 probably is including all these groups by mentioning orphans and the poor. Social injustice is one of the main sins of which Jeremiah accuses the leaders in Jerusalem.

5:29 *Should I not punish them for this?* Repeating the question in 5:9 for strong emphasis, God summarizes the main point of this unit. God's justice demands that sin and rebellion like this be dealt with.

5:30–31 *A horrible and shocking thing . . . The prophets . . . the priests . . . and my people love it this way.* Those who had the responsibility of keeping the people faithful to God (by obeying the book of Deuteronomy) were the prophets and the priests. Yet they were the very ones leading the people astray. The prophets were telling lies, and the priests were leading by their own authority (i.e., without following Deuteronomy, God's word). Worst of all, the people did not even mind; in fact, they loved it. The leaders and the people were in this rebellion and sin together. Thus the coming judgment is well deserved.

Theological Insights

Throughout Scripture judgment is presented as a righteous and just response by God to defiant rebellion and sinful rejection of God's gracious covenant. God judges people not because he is vindictive or petty but because he is just and righteous. Not only is this part of his character, but also he wants us to understand this to be part of his character. That is, it is important to God that we do not view him as vindictive or capricious and that we understand the righteous necessity of his judgment.

The imagery of a tree with the branches (symbolizing Israel) stripped off in judgment (5:10) is an image that Paul will pick up in Romans 11:17–21. Here in Jeremiah, as in Romans 11, there is stress on the loss of Israel's identity as God's people, while still maintaining hope for a remnant.

The book of Deuteronomy makes it clear that the true worship of God and obedience to him involve two components: a vertical component (how people relate to God) and a horizontal component (how people relate to one another). Jesus explicates this clearly when he identifies the greatest commandment as "Love the Lord your God with all your heart . . ." and the second as "Love your neighbor as yourself." These two components are inextricably connected. As people abandon their vertical connection of obedience to God, they will undoubtedly soon abandon their love for their neighbor.

Teaching the Text

In Jeremiah's day the people of Jerusalem and Judah had abandoned their relationship with God and gone after idols (thus failing the vertical component). Consequently, since they were now bereft of ethical moorings, they abandoned the horizontal component as well and fell into an "every man for himself" mode of selfish behavior.

True worship today likewise involves both the horizontal and the vertical components. We must love the Lord our God and also love our neighbors as ourselves. The failure to do one generally leads to a failure to do the other. As people today reject the authority of God as expressed through his Scriptures and thus rebel against obedience to him, they soon construct their own morality, driven by self-interest. Issues of justice and concern for others (such as the poor) are usually ignored except in cases where the appearance of concern helps one's public image.

This passage also clearly teaches how foolish or stupid people are to ignore God and/or to rebel against him. This is as relevant today as it was in Jeremiah's day. God commands the sea, and it obeys him. Who do people think they are when they disobey God and believe that they can get away with it? To think that they know better than God what is right and what is wrong is completely absurd.

Illustrating the Text

Refusal to obey God will result in deserved consequences.

Human Experience: Develop a list of potential examples of people getting what they deserve. Parenting certainly provides numerous episodes in which parents can "foresee" how things are likely to play out. And when children choose to disobey the wise instruction of their parents, the consequences are often appropriate to their chosen action. The best illustrations are often the most personal, so if possible, talk about how you felt when you or someone you know got what he or she deserved. One example might be to share your feelings about seeing another driver zoom past you on the interstate going 100 mph and then a few minutes later seeing that person pulled over by the police. One might think, "Duh! What did that driver think was going to happen?" Another may be a child losing a favorite stuffed animal because they insisted on carrying it with them around or outside of the house despite instructions to the contrary. A parent may sadly see a brokenhearted child dealing with the consequences of their unwise and disobedient choice.

Personal Stories: Another way to approach this issue is by personal example either as a parent or as a child. If a child playing in the front yard approaches the curb of the street, a parental warning is almost always issued. "Stop! Don't go any farther," says the parent, hoping to keep the child from harm's way, but if the child continues moving toward the street, most of us will quickly react, forcibly stopping the child on the spot and immediately issuing some kind of consequences, such as a time-out for not heeding our warning. Although the child might not realize it at the time, the discipline being received is well deserved.

Bible: "Because of your stubbornness and unrepentant heart, you are storing up wrath against yourself for the day of God's wrath, when his righteous judgment will be revealed" (Rom. 2:5).

Painful comparisons

Popular Culture: The sinful behavior of Jerusalem was compared to Sodom and Gomorrah. It is easy for people in one culture to point a finger and highlight what is wrong with other cultures, both modern and ancient. Yet before we point a finger at ancient cities steeped in sin, maybe we should look at the reality we face as a world today. Social injustice is widespread and deeply entrenched. Dishonesty certainly hasn't gone away. Likewise, sexual brokenness and sexual sin pervade our culture. And opportunities for these sins are often far more accessible today, from the treatment of the homeless or undernourished around us to the truthfulness of a post or profile on the internet to the websites we can access with a few clicks.

Take some time to visit the Covenant Eyes website and look over the annual report posted there with current statistics on pornography use.[2] Covenant Eyes is a Christian ministry and resource that helps people resist and turn away from pornography. Challenge your listeners with the sobering reality that sexual sin takes many shapes and forms, and God is just as concerned with this sin today as he was in the days of Jeremiah. Share some statistics provided on this site. They are painfully sobering.

You might want to challenge your listeners to use the accountability software provided by Covenant Eyes or other Christian organizations.

The Vision of Jerusalem under Siege

Big Idea

There are serious consequences for those who rebelliously replace the word of God with lies.

Key Themes

- Judgment is coming on Jerusalem because of its continued sin and rebellion.
- The sin of Jerusalem is like a sickness or wound that cannot be healed.
- The lying priests and false prophets deceitfully promise peace instead of judgment.
- Judgment comes on those who do not listen to the word of God.

Understanding the Text

The Text in Context

Jeremiah 2 accused the inhabitants of Judah and Jerusalem of breaking the Mosaic covenant. It focused on idolatry as the central and foundational sin. In Jeremiah 3 God called on the people to repent, to acknowledge their sin, and to turn back to him so that he could restore his relationship with them. They did not repent. They rejected his offer for a renewed relationship; in essence, they spit in his face, continuing full speed ahead in their idolatry and rebellion against God. "What else can I do?" God seems to ask as he describes the terrible punishment that is about to descend on Jerusalem. Jeremiah 4:5–6:30 describes the imminent Babylonian invasion, the means that God will use to pour out his wrath.

Jeremiah 6:1–30 is the third and closing section of 4:5–6:30. In many regards it parallels the opening section (4:5–31). Both passages contain live (present tense) descriptions of the Babylonian invasion. Both start with "Sound the trumpet!" and a statement about disaster (*ra'ah*) coming out of the north (4:5–6; 6:1). Jeremiah 4:5–31 ends with the death of Daughter Zion. This prophetic reality is proclaimed by God again at the beginning of 6:1–30 (in 6:2). These two invasion descriptions form bookends around the middle section (5:1–31), which interrupts the picture of the invasion to recite again the culpability of Jerusalem and Judah, thus underscoring how well deserved is their judgment.

Although both the opening section (4:5–31) and the closing section (6:1–30) describe the Babylonian invasion, the opening section views the entire land under attack as the Babylonians stream in from the north. The closing section, however, focuses on the siege of Jerusalem itself. While 4:5–31 describes the rapid advance of the Babylonian chariots and cavalry, 6:1–30 describes the Babylonian tents surrounding Jerusalem and the construction of siege ramps.

The chapter develops as follows: The Babylonians have Jerusalem under siege and are anxious to get on with the attack (6:1–8). Israel will be gleaned as a vine is gleaned of its grapes, for its sin is great (6:9–15). This disaster is coming because the people have refused to listen to God and to walk in his ways (6:16–21). The people of Jerusalem are terrified as the cruel Babylonian army approaches (6:22–26). Using the analogy of smelting (purifying various metals), Jeremiah gives a concluding summary of the corruption and rebellion practiced by Jerusalem and Judah (6:27–30).

Interpretive Insights

6:1 *Flee . . . people of Benjamin . . . from Jerusalem!* As mentioned above, in 4:5 the people are exhorted to flee *to* Jerusalem, while here they are exhorted to flee *from* Jerusalem. Jeremiah is from the region of Benjamin, so he seems to be warning his neighbors to run away from Jerusalem rather than to it.

Tekoa . . . Beth Hakkerem. These are towns in Judah, south of Jerusalem.

disaster looms out of the north. As in 4:6, God is bringing disaster (*ra'ah*) from the north (i.e., the Babylonians).

6:2 *I will destroy Daughter Zion.* As in 4:31, the term "Daughter Zion" refers to Jerusalem and its inhabitants, along with the temple. Although the Babylonians will be the direct instruments of punishment, God is not ambiguous about his role in the judgment. He is the one who is bringing the Babylonians to destroy Jerusalem.

6:3 *Shepherds with their flocks . . . their tents.* The Babylonian king and his lords ("shepherds") will come and besiege Jerusalem. In an analogy rich with irony, God compares the thousands of enemy tents surrounding Jerusalem to flocks of sheep, the latter usually being a sign of peace and prosperity.

6:4 *Prepare . . . Arise, let us attack at noon!* The irony continues. The three verbs used here are words often used in regard to worship and for temple activities. In a worship setting these would be translated as "make holy" (or "sanctify"), "rise up," and "let us go up." Here they are used not to call worshipers but to call the Babylonian troops to destroy Jerusalem rather than to worship there. The reference to attacking at noon is an indication that the Babylonians are anxious to get on with it. They have no intention of delaying the attack.

6:6 *the* LORD *Almighty.* Literally, this reads, "Yahweh of the hosts," with "hosts" referring to armies. It is the name that God frequently uses when he is going to war. See also 5:14 ("Yahweh, God of the hosts") and 6:9 ("Yahweh of the hosts").

6:7 *As a well pours out its water, so she pours out her wickedness.* The word translated as "pours out" carries the nuance of being cold, cool, or fresh. The word translated as "wickedness" is *ra'ah*, which we have seen repeatedly throughout Jeremiah; "bad stuff" or "bad deeds" are suggested translations. The idea of the verse is "Just as well waters stay cool and fresh, so do her [Jerusalem's] bad deeds."

6:8 *Take warning, Jerusalem, or I will turn away from you.* The word translated as "take warning" carries the nuance of "accepting discipline." The word translated as "will turn away" is not the expected *shub* but a different word altogether. The word used here has the meaning of "a sudden jerking or wrenching." It is used in other places in reference to dislocated bones. It probably implies a painful ripping or tearing away. Also, God states that it is his *nepesh* (his "being," or his "essence") that will be wrenched away. "Accept this discipline," God cries out, "or my very being will be torn away from you." The continued sin of Jerusalem eventually will drive the presence of God right out of the temple and the city. Ezekiel 8–10 describes this departure in some detail.

6:10 *Who will listen to me? Their ears are closed . . . The word of the* LORD *is offensive to them.* Jeremiah 6:9–15 is a dialogue between Jeremiah and God. The word translated as "closed" literally means "uncircumcised." The word translated as "offensive" implies not only something that offends but also something that one scoffs at or ridicules, as if it is an embarrassment. These two ideas are connected, for it is the "uncircumcised ears" (i.e., pagan ears, outside-of-the-covenant ears) that consider the word of God an embarrassment, something to mock or scoff at.

6:11 *I am full of the wrath of the* LORD. This is still Jeremiah talking. The trivializing and scoffing attitude of the people toward the word of God leads to his wrathful response.

Pour it out on the children . . . and on the young men . . . and the old. The speaker seems to have changed from Jeremiah to God. Jeremiah says that he is full of God's wrath and cannot hold it in. God tells him to go ahead and pour it out on everyone in Jerusalem. The terrible judgment carried out by the Babylonians will fall on everyone.

6:13 *prophets and priests alike, all practice deceit.* The prophets and the priests were the ones who were in charge of theological matters. Yet they all were deceitful (lit., "all of them are doing falsehood [*sheqer*]"). As mentioned above, the word *sheqer* occurs thirty-seven times in Jeremiah.

6:14 *They dress the wound of my people as though it were not serious . . . "peace," they say, when there is no peace.* The "sickness/wound" analogy for deep and serious sin was introduced in 6:7. It will occur frequently in Jeremiah. Here the sinful situation of the people in Jerusalem is said to be a deep and serious wound (like a sword wound). The priests and prophets, however, say that it is nothing to worry about. Then they proclaim that the future will be one of "peace," in strong contrast to the message of Jeremiah, which is one of terrible judgment through the invading Babylonians.

6:19 *Hear, you earth.* As in 2:12, God calls on the earth as one of the witnesses of the covenant between Israel and God (cf. Deut. 30:19; 31:28; see also Isa. 1:2).

I am bringing disaster. The word used here is once again *ra'ah*, as in 4:6; 6:1.

6:20 *Your burnt offerings are not acceptable; your sacrifices do not please me.* The people of Jerusalem thought that they could cover over all their sin and disobedience with the rituals of syncretistic worship. God rejects this religious ritualism when it is devoid of obedience (6:19).

6:27–30 *a tester of metals . . . rejected silver.* In 6:27 God makes Jeremiah a "tester of metals." In 6:28–30 he uses the analogy of impure metal in the smelting process to state that, like useless ore, the people have been impossible to purify and are now to be rejected. Ezekiel 22:17–22 expands on this image in some detail.

Theological Insights

Ironically, in this passage that focuses on judgment, God twice refers to Jerusalem with the intimate and relational loving term "Daughter Zion." Thus God appears to be revealing to us an ongoing tension that he feels as he announces the impending destruction of his people. "Daughter" is an emotionally packed term that captures the parental love that God feels for his people. At the same time, his righteousness and justice demand that he bring judgment on Jerusalem for its sin. His wrath is very real and emerges from his righteous character. Likewise, his compassion for his people is very real and emerges from his loving character. Throughout Jeremiah these two aspects of God's character stand in tension, a tension that is not resolved until the death of Christ in the New Testament.

Teaching the Text

One of the major points of this unit is that sin has its consequences. Although God pleads with people and waits patiently with open arms for them, if they continually reject him and "spit in his face," so to speak, then eventually he unleashes his terrible wrath on them. This truth is consistent in both the Old Testament and the New Testament.

Sin is like a serious sickness or fatal sword wound. Without the saving intervention of God, it will result in death. False and deceitful religious leaders, writers, or popular media personalities may say that sin is not serious, or that God will not punish sin, but that is like saying that a fatal sword wound or deadly disease is really nothing to worry about. God does indeed hold people accountable for their sin, and without repentance, sin will lead to death.

The people of Jerusalem were hiding behind their ritualistic religious practices in order to ignore the true ethical and theological mandates of the word of God. This is a danger for people in the church today as well. That is, sometimes today people hide behind the "rituals" of Christianity, rituals such as going to church or singing in the choir, using these rituals to cover up or whitewash their refusal deep in their heart to truly listen to God's word and obey him in critical areas of life (love for one another, unity in the church, justice in society, adherence to God's moral standards, etc.).

Likewise today, the lying voices in our world are numerous and powerful, telling us to rely on the nonbiblical moral views held by our society rather than on the word of God in determining right and wrong. This is particularly true of the persistent message coming from television, movies, and popular music, mediums that regularly ridicule biblical concepts of sin and in the name of "tolerance" advocate a morality that flies in the face of what God has revealed as right and wrong.

The destruction of Jerusalem was tragic and heartbreaking, even for God, whose fellowshipping presence was "wrenched away" because of the people's sin. And the tragedy is that if only they had turned to God and repented of their sin, they could have averted the judgment and enjoyed a wonderful life with God. Likewise today, because of his great love, God is heartbroken over those who rebel against him and reject him, but his justice and righteousness will nonetheless cast them away from his presence into judgment.

Illustrating the Text

There are serious consequences for lying.

History: On June 17, 1972, five men working for the committee to reelect the president were caught breaking into the Democratic headquarters in the Watergate building in Washington, DC. The result was a series of lies and cover-ups that ultimately led to the resignation of then-president Richard Nixon. On numerous occasions and with apparent sincerity, Nixon announced to the American public that he was innocent, but he ultimately resigned in the face of an impending impeachment. The reality of what had happened hit many of his supporters hard. For them, Nixon's resignation was a cold wake-up call to the truth of what had really happened. (Here, the brave may choose to invoke a response by repeating Nixon's infamous line, "I am not a crook.") Many young people became disillusioned with the US government due to Nixon's blatant lying to the public.

Film: *Pinocchio*. A clip from this 1940 animated Disney classic could be used to show the consequences of lying. In the film, Pinocchio's nose grows longer when he tells a lie. As a humorous side note, according to a study conducted by a researcher at the University of Leicester in the United Kingdom, Pinocchio's neck would have broken from the weight of his nose after he told thirteen lies.[1]

Science: Researchers from the Department of Experimental Psychology at the University of Granada discovered something interesting while running experiments using thermography. Using a temperature-sensitive camera, scientists found that when a test subject lied, there was an increase in the temperature in the tissue around the nose. They have dubbed it the "Pinocchio effect."[2]

Scenarios: Imagine a doctor who refuses to tell her patients that they are seriously sick, because she does not want to upset them. How would you feel about her as a doctor? Imagine a police officer who sees crimes unfolding right in front of him and looks the other way because he does not want to deal with the conflict. Imagine a schoolteacher who has good evidence that a child in her class is being abused but keeps her mouth shut because she does not want to make waves with the parents or administration. Imagine parents who have a child who is acting out but ignore the bad behavior because they do not want to "upset" their son or daughter. Imagine a pastor who avoids teaching the hard passages in the Bible because of a desire to stay popular with church members. Sometimes the worst lies are garbed in silence and inaction. If we cry "Peace, peace" when judgment is on the horizon, our lies are costly.

The Temple
and False Religion

Big Idea

A life of unrepentant, continuous idolatry and social injustice results in separation from God.

Key Themes

- In order to remain in God's presence, the people in Jerusalem must put away their idolatry and injustice.
- The people in Jerusalem refuse to "hear the voice" of God and heed his warnings.
- The extent of the idolatry in Jerusalem is widespread and shocking.
- Because of their sin, God will destroy the temple and drive the people away from his presence.

Understanding the Text

The Text in Context

In Jeremiah 2–6 God clearly points out the terrible sin that Jerusalem and Judah are constantly committing, and then he calls on them to repent. Since they defiantly reject his word and refuse to repent, he then describes the frightening and inevitable judgment that is coming (the Babylonian invasion). The next unit, 7:1–10:25, is loosely connected around the theme of false, perverted religion and its consequent, just punishment. This unit opens with a "sermon" delivered by Jeremiah at the temple gates. The hostile reaction to this sermon is recorded in Jeremiah 26.

Jeremiah 4:5–6:30, the previous unit, is almost entirely in poetry. In 7:1 the form of the text switches to prose, and it continues in prose throughout this passage (7:1–8:3), switching back to poetry in 8:4 as the next section begins.

Jeremiah 7:1–15 is typically called the "Temple Sermon," and it has three distinctive subsections: 7:1–8 (only if the people change their ways, putting away their incessant social injustices, will God allow them to stay in Jerusalem in his presence); 7:9–11 (how can they, God asks, continually violate the Ten

Commandments and then believe that they have a "safe hideout" from God in the temple, right in front of him?); and 7:12–15 (just as sin brought the destruction of Shiloh, where the presence of God formerly dwelled, so sin will bring the destruction of Jerusalem, where the presence of God currently dwells). The next three subsections (7:16–29; 7:30–34; 8:1–3) are not part of the actual sermon that Jeremiah delivers in the temple but are closely related in that they describe in more detail the corruption of the worship system and the consequences of such perverted worship. In 7:16–29 God tells Jeremiah to cease interceding for the people. Since they saw fit not to listen to him, he will no longer listen to any petitions regarding them. In the next subsection God explains that since the people are worshiping idols right in the temple and sacrificing their children right outside the temple, the judgment on them will be devastating (7:30–34). Finally, in 8:1–3 God proclaims that since the leaders and the people of Judah and Jerusalem chose to worship the sun, the moon, and the stars, their bones will lie exposed to these "gods" they have worshiped.

Historical and Cultural Background

The Queen of Heaven (7:18) is most likely a syncretistic mix of the Mesopotamian astral deity Ishtar, goddess of love, sexuality, and war, and Asherah, consort to El and "Mother of the gods" in the Canaanite pantheon. The mention of cakes for the Queen of Heaven (7:18) probably refers to the practice of baking cakes using a mold resembling the image of this goddess and using these cakes in worship.[1] Later in the story of Jeremiah, even after God has destroyed Jerusalem for such idolatry, some of the survivors who fled to Egypt are still worshiping the Queen of Heaven (Jer. 44).

Interpretive Insights

7:2 *Stand at the gate of the LORD's house.* God sends Jeremiah right to the temple to proclaim judgment on the perverted worship taking place there. The consequences of this Temple Sermon are related in Jeremiah 26.

7:3–5 *the LORD Almighty.* In Hebrew this is literally "Yahweh of hosts." This is the name that God uses when he is going to war (i.e., it is his "battle name"). It also occurs in 7:21.

Reform your ways . . . If you really change your ways. Both of these phrases use the word *yatab*, which means "to make/do good." It is the opposite of the word *ra'ah* ("to do bad, evil, to bring disaster"), which we have seen throughout Jeremiah. In this unit *ra'ah* occurs in 7:12, 24, 26.

deceptive words. Literally, this is "words of the lie [*sheqer*]." See also 7:8.

the temple of the LORD, the temple of the LORD! An explanation of what "deceptive words" ("words of the lie") refers to, this probably is a chant built on the ritualistic belief that the presence of God in the temple would always protect the people no matter what they did.

If you really . . . deal with each other justly. The verb form used here is emphatic and could be translated, "if you really, really do justice." Justice (*mishpat*) will be defined in the next verse in terms of social justice.

7:6 *if you do not oppress the foreigner, the fatherless or the widow.* True religion, as defined by God throughout the Old Testament but especially in the book of Deuteronomy, includes strong ethical actions and a strong stand for social justice, particularly in regard to those who were the weakest in the culture socioeconomically.

do not shed innocent blood in this place. This implies that the leaders in the temple had actually executed innocent people there. Jeremiah 7:30–31 describes the horrific sacrifice of innocent children in the valley adjacent to the temple. Jeremiah 26, which is the continuation of the Temple Sermon in Jeremiah 7, recounts how King Jehoiakim executed the innocent prophet Uriah.

7:9 *steal and murder, commit adultery and perjury . . . follow other gods.* The Ten Commandments lie at the very heart of the covenant relationship between God and Israel. The sins listed stress the wide-ranging extent to which the people had disobeyed these commandments and thus violated the most basic components of the covenant relationship.

7:10–11 *"We are safe" . . . den of robbers.* The irony expressed here is that these people have committed serious sins against God and then gone to the temple (God's house) for safe haven, like a band of robbers going to their "den" or hideout. Yet it is God himself whom they need to worry about the most, for such action infuriates him, and he will not protect them but rather will destroy them. Thus it is rather stupid for them to come into his very presence and think that they will be safe there. When Jesus cites this verse in the temple (Matt. 21:13; Mark 11:17; Luke 19:46), he is making the same point and predicting the coming destruction of Jerusalem and the temple by the Romans, just as Jeremiah predicted the coming destruction of Jerusalem and the temple by the Babylonians. In both cases the people mistakenly think that the temple is a place of safe refuge without any accountability to God. They fail to understand that God maintains the temple not to meet his own needs or to have a place to stay but rather for the gracious purpose of having a relationship with his people, a relationship that requires holiness.

But I have been watching! The stress is on "I." Literally, this reads, "Behold! *I* see you."

7:12 *Shiloh.* Earlier in Israelite history, Shiloh was where the ark of the covenant resided, which represented the presence of God (see 1 Sam. 1–4). Apparently, the Philistines destroyed Shiloh when they captured the ark (recounted in 1 Sam. 4). God says that he will do to Jerusalem what he did to

Shiloh. There is nothing "magical" or fetish-like about the presence of God that can be manipulated to serve sinful interests.

7:15 *I will thrust you from my presence, just as I did . . . the people of Ephraim.* Shiloh was located in the tribal area of Ephraim. Although Shiloh probably was destroyed by the Philistines in the episode described in 1 Samuel 4, in this verse (Jer. 7:15) God is likely referring to the total dispersion and exile of those in Ephraim carried out by the Assyrians in 722 BC. Whatever the case, when Jeremiah proclaimed his Temple Sermon, Shiloh was nothing but ruins, and the people of Ephraim were scattered to faraway regions.

7:16 *I will not listen.* The word translated as "listen" is *shama'*. Literally, it means "to hear," and figuratively it can often mean "to obey"—that is, to hear and to respond to the hearing. It is used repeatedly in this unit: 7:23, "obey me" (lit., "hear my voice"); 7:24, "they did not listen or pay attention" (lit., "listen or incline their ear"); 7:26, "they did not listen to me"; 7:27, "they will not listen to you"; 7:28, "the nation that has not obeyed the LORD" (lit., "has not listened to the voice of Yahweh").

7:22–23 *not . . . commands about burnt offerings and sacrifices . . . Obey me, and I will be your God.* God is stressing the fact that the essence or heart of the covenant was not about offerings or sacrifices but rather about obedience and relationship. It was not that offerings and sacrifice were unimportant (7:22) but that the practice of these rituals paled in comparison to the fundamental call to obedience and relationship (7:23).

7:24 *They went backward.* They "turned their backs" to God, an action that in the presence of a king or ruler expressed contempt.[2]

7:30 *detestable idols in the house that bears my Name.* Idols had been set up right in the temple. See further details of this in Ezekiel 8.

7:31 *Valley of Ben Hinnom.* This was the small valley (ravine) on the south side of Jerusalem.

to burn their sons and daughters. Child sacrifice was associated with the worship of Molek and Chemosh, the gods of Ammon and Moab (see 2 Kings 23:10, 13). The "detestable gods" mentioned in 7:30 probably included Molek and/or Chemosh, for the Old Testament repeatedly refers to these two gods as particularly "detestable."

Theological Insights

One of the things that seems to infuriate God is that while the people of Jerusalem were worshiping other gods and encouraging all manner of social injustices, they believed that they could come to his house (the temple) for safety and protection (like the hideout for a "den of robbers"). What audacity! God is the very one whom they should fear most, and their total lack of reverence and respect for his righteous presence angers him immensely. They have no fear of him whatsoever, and this irritates God, insulting both his righteousness and his power. We see this same anger reflected in Jesus when he encounters the corrupt money changers right in the temple courtyard. Jesus lashes out at them, connecting them with Jeremiah 7 by accusing them of making the temple a "den of robbers" (Matt. 21:13 // Mark 11:17 // Luke 19:46), thus implying a coming judgment on Jerusalem similar to that which Jeremiah proclaimed. God is particularly offended when people treat him as if he is not really concerned with sin or as if he has no real power to punish anyone for disrespecting and defying him. If we come into God's presence to worship with repentant hearts and an awareness of our sin and his righteous power to judge us, he forgives us and accepts us into his presence. If, however, we seek to worship him with an attitude of arrogance, justifying and embracing our sinful behavior and snubbing our noses at his word, his righteousness, and his power, he gets angry.

Teaching the Text

This passage teaches us that true worship of God allows for no idolatrous competitors. We must be on guard against the "idols" that our society pressures us to worship in addition to God or instead of God. Idolatry for us today is represented by substitutes for God that we trust to take care of us or provide for us, substitutes that take our zeal and attention and teach us an erroneous message of what is right and wrong. Closely attached to truly worshiping God alone is the understanding that such worship involves caring for the weak and vulnerable in our society and advocating justice, especially in regard to these weak ones. Being in right relationship with God, and thus listening to his word, leads us to right relationship with one another and thus creates in us a desire to correct the injustices around us and to defend those who are weak. Idolatry, on the other hand, cuts the moral guidelines from God and encourages us to seek our own well-being instead of that of others.

As in Jeremiah's day, true worship today involves listening carefully to God's word and then obeying it. This is much more important than mindlessly practicing religious rituals, all the while ignoring the call for ethical behavior. Unfortunately, sometimes Christians in the church today seem much more concerned with the issue of worship style (our rituals) than with issues of ethical behavior and social justice (our obedience).

Finally, there is no true worship of God without his presence. The sin and hypocrisy of the people in Jeremiah's day had become so pervasive that he removed his presence from them, allowing the temple to be destroyed and the people to be exiled from the land he had given them. Although as Christians we experience the presence of God differently today, primarily through the indwelling of the Spirit, it is still true that a hypocritical life characterized by modern cultural "idolatry" and social injustice creates a distance between us and God, diminishing or even extinguishing our so-called worship of him. And clearly, at the very least, it upsets him and displeases him, the very opposite result of what worship should do.

Illustrating the Text

Unrepentant disobedience results in separation from God.

Scripture: We receive the same warning from Paul in 2 Thessalonians 1:8–9 and from Jesus in Matthew 7:21–23.

Object Lesson: Explain and demonstrate how the similar poles of two magnets will repulse each other when placed in proximity with each other. Likewise, sin and disobedience are repulsive to God's holiness.

Scripture: Using the story in Genesis 3, talk about Adam and Eve's expulsion from the garden of Eden. Ask your listeners how they think Adam and Eve felt as they exited the east gate of Eden. Would they have wanted a second chance? Would they have taken it if God had offered?

Archaeology: Show an aerial photo of the Temple Mount in Jerusalem. Explain that in Jeremiah's day the temple, which was constructed by Solomon, was a visual reminder that God was ever present with the people of Jerusalem. But because of their unwillingness to repent, God allowed the Babylonians to so thoroughly destroy the temple that scholars have not been able to find enough archaeological evidence to state with certainty exactly where it stood.

Deceit, Deceivers, and the Just Consequences

Big Idea

Those who refuse to repent of their sin, choosing instead to trust in counterbiblical lies taught by influential people, will be judged and will perish along with the ones who taught the lies.

Key Themes

- For personal profit the leaders have deceived the people by proclaiming peace and healing.
- Judgment will come on those who have mishandled God's word and misled the people.
- Believing in lies impacts one's character.
- Believing in lies undermines any chance of repentance; thus judgment is coming.
- Because his people embrace such lies, Jeremiah mourns over their fate.

Understanding the Text

The Text in Context

The larger unit of 7:1–10:25 is loosely connected around the theme of false, perverted religion and its consequent, just punishment. At the center of this large unit is a subunit (8:4–9:26) that can be summarized as follows: because the people of Jerusalem and Judah have foolishly listened to lies rather than the voice of God, what they will now hear is wailing. Within this subunit, 8:4–9:11 focuses on the first half of that summary statement, explaining how pivotal and pervasive the lies and deceitfulness were within the beliefs of those in Jerusalem, and thus how deserving they are of the coming judgment.

Starting at 8:4, the text switches from prose to poetry. All of this passage (8:4–9:11) is in poetry. This section is very much like an anthology, and the subsections are only loosely connected, primarily around the theme of deceitfulness. Jeremiah 8:4–12 opens (8:4) and closes (8:12) with a metaphorical use of the word "fall." Jeremiah 8:4–7 describes the people as stubbornly clinging to deceit, and 8:8–12 focuses on the leaders who are doing the deceiving. Jeremiah 8:13–17 opens (8:13) and closes (8:17) with "declares the LORD." In 8:13 God says that he will take away their crops and in 8:17 that he will send venomous snakes among them. In between these two judgment statements the people speak of fleeing to the fortified cities, where they believe they will perish, for now they understand that the prophecies of peace were false. In 8:18–9:1 Jeremiah cries out in sorrow over the grim situation in Jerusalem; God points out that this punishment is due to their idolatry. Next God (and Jeremiah?) bemoans the fact that the people are characterized by lies and deceitfulness (9:2–6). Finally, because of the constant and widespread deceitfulness of the people, God will completely devastate and make desolate Jerusalem and the towns of Judah (9:7–11).

Interpretive Insights

8:4 *When people fall down, do they not get up?* The point here is that people usually learn from their mistakes and try to correct them. Jerusalem, however, does not learn from its mistakes because the people cling to the lie that nothing is wrong (8:5–7).

8:5 *Why does Jerusalem always turn away?* In earlier units we have seen how frequently Jeremiah uses the term *shub* ("to turn away, backslide, turn to, repent"). *Shub* is used twice in 8:4, three times in 8:5, and once in 8:6. Jeremiah 8:5 literally says that Jerusalem is an "everlasting" or "eternal" "turner" who refuses "to return."

They cling to deceit. The word translated as "cling" means "to firmly grab hold of something with strength." The people have latched on to this lie and will not let go.

8:6 *like a horse charging into battle.* The people are not tentatively or cautiously contemplating this lie. Rather, they show as much thought and reflection as an excited horse, already thundering ahead in a frenzied charge.

8:8 *we have the law of the LORD.* God stresses that the mere possession of his law (*torah*, which can mean "teaching" but here probably refers to the book of Deuteronomy) means nothing if one lies about what it contains and interprets it falsely, as the literary leaders (the scribes) in Jerusalem had been doing.

8:10–11 *From the least to the greatest.* God is stressing the culpability of the entire nation. *All* have sinned. Jeremiah uses this phrase "from the least to the greatest" several other times (6:13; 31:34; 42:1, 8; 44:12).

prophets and priests . . . practice deceit. They dress the wound . . . as though it were not serious. "Peace, peace," they say. These two verses are practically identical to 6:13–14. The leaders have explained that sin such as idolatry and social injustice is insignificant and minor. The future, they teach, will bring peace and healing. This is a false worldview, but the people embrace it. This is the deceit that Jeremiah stresses.

8:12 *they will fall.* The deceiving leaders (prophets and priests) will be punished for their role in Jerusalem's apostasy.

8:14 *Let us flee to the fortified cities and perish there! For the* LORD *our God has doomed us to perish.* Jeremiah speaks here as a hypothetical Judahite, who at some point in the Babylonian invasion realizes with despair that he has no chance against this invading enemy.

given us poisoned water to drink. Water supplies during invasions and sieges were critical. Once a besieged city's water supply became contaminated, the city would soon fall.

because we have sinned against him. Along with words earlier in the verse, this predicts that time of despair when the people of Judah and Jerusalem realize they have been putting all their hope and trust in a lie. The great lie was the trivializing or minimizing of the severity of their sin. At some point, as the Babylonians destroy them and devastate the land, the people will realize the truth, but it will be too late.

8:16 *The snorting of the enemy's horses . . . from Dan . . . the whole land trembles.* As mentioned in 4:15, the Babylonians invade from the north. The region of Dan is the first Israelite territory they enter. Their cavalry is terrifying. Their horses are so numerous that the ground shakes as they advance.

8:17 *I will send venomous snakes.* This probably is a figurative reference to the Babylonians, who cannot be stopped. But the point of reference might well be Numbers 21:6–9, when God sent venomous snakes as a punishment on Israel. In Numbers 21:8–9 the people have the chance to be delivered by looking at the bronze snake on a pole. For Jeremiah's audience, however, there will be no such deliverance.

8:19 *Listen to the cry of my people.* In sorrow, Jeremiah cries out for the people, questioning why this has happened. God will answer in the second half of the verse, pointing once again to their idolatry as the root cause for this disaster. The phrase translated as "my people" is literally "the daughter of my people." The use of "daughter" carries emotional impact, and Jeremiah uses "daughter of my people" throughout this section (8:11, 19, 21, 22; 9:1, 7). Recall the use of "Daughter Zion" in earlier texts (4:31; 6:2, 23).

8:22 *Is there no balm in Gilead? . . . no healing for the wound of my people?* Gilead was the region just to the east of the Jordan River, apparently known for its medicinal "balm" (probably extracted from a certain type of tree). Jeremiah is referring to the balm figuratively, crying out that the wound of the people is so serious that no balm or doctor can cure them. This image will be reversed in Jeremiah 30–33, when "healing" will characterize the coming time of new covenant and restoration (e.g., 30:17; 33:6). Also note the important role that healing plays in the ministry of Jesus in the New Testament.

9:3 *They make ready their tongue like a bow, to shoot lies.* This figure of speech compares the tongue to a bow, as these deceitful people fire arrows (lies) out at people. The word for "lie" used here is *sheqer*, which we have seen used repeatedly in previous passages of Jeremiah to refer to lies and deceit (3:10; 5:2, 31; 6:13; 7:4, 8, 9; 8:8, 10).

9:9 *Should I not punish them for this?* This verse is practically identical to 5:9, 29. God is concerned to show that his punishment of Jerusalem and Judah is just, even necessary, because of their deceitfulness and unfaithfulness.

Theological Insights

God states clearly that leaders who use their influence to convince people to trust in counterbiblical lies and turn away from true worship of God will face severe judgment. But God also holds accountable the people who were duped. This reflects the theological reality that God holds individuals responsible for discerning the truth about sin and repentance even as their leaders actively and persistently present them with lies. Of course, often it is not merely that people are gullible or ignorant but rather that they are rebellious and simply want to believe that they can get away with their sin.

Teaching the Text

Basically this is a text about "worldviews" and the issue of who establishes what is right and what is wrong. Led by selfish and corrupt leaders, the people in Jerusalem had embraced the idea that the God of their ancestors no longer had any say over their behavior or what sin was. With impunity, therefore, they felt they could ignore the guidelines of Deuteronomy and worship pagan gods along with the true God. Also, they felt completely free to follow the pattern of immoral living associated with their pagan neighbors. This "big lie" or foundational "deceit" permeated all of their life and thinking. With this as their basic theological framework, they were never going to repent, for this lie kept them from even acknowledging that they were sinning and needed to repent.

The similarity between this situation and our culture today is strong. In general, much of our culture has rejected the basic idea that it is God who has the prerogative to determine what is right and what is wrong. Our culture is pushing hard to redefine what sin is, and often it downplays or trivializes social sin and various forms of "idolatry" or false worship. Powerful voices in the media and especially in the entertainment industry (television, movies) are propagating the lie that Christian faith is hypocritical, narrow, and intolerant. Christian faith, they argue, is morally archaic, and only narrow and cold people would ever adhere to it. Once the biblical standard for sin is removed, people no longer feel the need to repent.

The gospel offers people today salvation and deliverance from sin through Jesus Christ, but in order to accept this they must acknowledge that they are, indeed, sinners according to God's definition. Many in our culture, undergirded with the postmodern "big lie," simply do not believe that they are sinners in need of saving. A challenge for Christians today in engaging unbelievers is to proclaim the biblical message about sin and to refuse to let the culture redefine sin.

Jeremiah sounds a clear warning for those influential people today who propagate such false teaching about sin and likewise for those people who believe it.

Illustrating the Text

Relying on influential people does not absolve us of our responsibility.

History: At the Nuremberg trials many Nazi officers tried to say that they were not responsible for their actions because they were "just following orders." They repeatedly used the phrase "Befehl ist Befehl" ("orders are orders"). In the end, it was decided that although such circumstances might reduce punishment, they were not enough to eliminate it, and the officers were found culpable along with their superiors. As a result, many were imprisoned or executed for their war crimes.[1]

Analogy: Set up several chairs on stage and solicit a volunteer to sit in each chair. Then slowly recite Jeremiah 8:4 into the ear of the person in the first chair and instruct that person to repeat the verse to the next person. Explain that they are to do the same until the message is whispered to the person in the last chair. When the exercise is complete, ask the person in the last chair to recite what he or she was told. Tell the congregation that unless they are willing to read God's word for themselves, they may not get the information right, but they will be held responsible for every word of Scripture on the day of judgment.

Knowing God's word has the power to change your life.

Personal Testimony: This is the perfect opportunity to use video testimonies. Invite several members of the congregation to describe the impact reading the Bible regularly has had on their lives. Have someone prerecord and edit these testimonies, as well as your own, and salt them in throughout the message.

Statistics: According to a recent study by the Barna Group, nearly nine out of ten Americans own a Bible, and the average number of Bibles per household is 4.7. The problem is that while 62 percent of respondents said that they wished they read the Bible more, only 37 percent said that they read the Bible once a week or more.[2] The result is that we have abdicated our biblical training to someone else. We have given the job to those who claim to speak for God on television or radio or to our local pastor in the Sunday morning sermon.

Regardless of all the misinformation about what Scripture says, some day we will be held accountable for the things that God requires. For this reason, all of us should read the words of Scripture for ourselves. We have resources at our disposal, and we fail to use them at our own peril.

Wailing Women and the Character of God

Big Idea

The truly wise person knows God's character and understands the necessity of judgment.

Key Themes

- The wise person understands that judgment stems from God's justice and righteousness.
- The people will not "listen" and obey God's word, so instead they will "listen" to wailing.
- Understanding God's character in regard to judgment and righteousness is more important than acquiring wisdom, strength, or riches.

Understanding the Text

The Text in Context

As mentioned earlier, 7:1–10:25 is loosely connected around the theme of false, perverted religion and its consequent, just punishment. At the center of this large unit is a subunit (8:4–9:26) that can be summarized as follows: because the people of Jerusalem and Judah have foolishly listened to lies rather than the voice of God, what they will now hear is wailing. Jeremiah 8:4–9:11 develops the first half of that summary statement, explaining how pivotal and pervasive the lies and deceitfulness are within the beliefs and practices of those in Jerusalem, and thus how deserving they are of the coming judgment. The current passage (9:12–26) stresses the second half of that summary, ironically calling on the women to wail and to teach their daughters how to wail.

Indeed, wailing provides the link between 8:4–9:11 and 9:12–26. At the end of 8:4–9:11 Jeremiah wails because of the desolation of the land (9:10). Then 9:17–21 (the central section of 9:12–26) picks up the theme of wailing and elaborates upon it.

References to the "wise" also tie the sections together. In 8:8–9 God declares that no one who rejects the word of God or handles his law (*torah*) falsely can possibly consider himself or herself to be wise. In 9:12–26 two subsections dealing with "the wise" (9:12–16; 9:23–24) frame the central subsection on wailing, where the word "wise" (*hakam*) is used ironically in regard to being "skilled" in wailing (9:17).

This passage opens with a prose subsection (9:12–16) and closes with a prose subsection (9:25–26). The middle two subsections are poetic in structure. Jeremiah 9:12–16 explains that one who is wise will understand that the judgment on the people of Jerusalem is just and well deserved. Next, using a wordplay that seems to suggest a sense of "poetic justice," God declares that since the people refuse to listen to his voice, they will now listen to wailing (9:17–22). Next the text explains that knowing God in the context of his love and his justice is more important than wisdom, strength, or riches (9:23–24). Finally, 9:25–26 adds a footnote: the coming judgment is actually broader than that described so far, for it will also fall on Judah's unrighteous neighboring nations.

Interpretive Insights

9:12 *Who is wise enough to understand this?* The terms "wise" (*hakam*) and "understand" (*bin*) are closely associated with the "wisdom tradition" as reflected in the book of Proverbs. Ironically, and somewhat sarcastically, both terms will be used again in 9:17. The demonstrative pronoun "this" refers to the coming judgment on Jerusalem. God wants people to understand exactly why this judgment came on Jerusalem. He explains why in 9:13–14.

9:13 *they have forsaken my law.* The word translated as "forsaken" (*'azab*) means "to leave" or "to abandon." Jeremiah uses this word frequently (25x). In previous units we have already encountered it several times (1:16; 2:13, 17, 19; 5:7, 19), used to express how the people of Judah and Jerusalem have forsaken/abandoned God (like a wife abandoning her husband). Here it expresses how they have forsaken/abandoned God's law (*torah*), most likely a reference primarily to the book of Deuteronomy, which God had given them to describe the terms by which they could live in the promised land and be blessed.

which I set before them. The word translated as "before" means "in the presence of." God presented Israel with the guidelines of Deuteronomy in a very public manner, before all of them. The agreement (Mosaic covenant) between God and Israel was very clear and very public (see especially Deut. 30:15–16, where the same word "before" is used).

they have not obeyed me or followed my law. Literally, this verse reads, "they did not listen to my voice and they did not walk in it [i.e., the law]." This theme of "listening/hearing" will connect to the next section, where the "voice of wailing is heard" (9:19).

9:14 *Instead, they have followed the stubbornness of their hearts . . . the Baals.* The word translated as "followed" is the same word used in 9:13. Instead of "walking in God's law," they "walked" according to two other ways: the way of their stubborn heart and the way of Baal. Remember that in the Old Testament "heart" is often used as the center of volition—that is, where one makes decisions. Baal was the primary god in the Canaanite pantheon. Ironically, the word *ba'al* can refer to the Canaanite god, but it can also mean "husband," "lord," or "owner of the house," thus adding to the intricate metaphor and wordplay on Israel/Judah as the unfaithful wife.

9:17 *Consider now! Call for the wailing women . . . for the most skillful of them.* As mentioned above, the words translated as "consider" (*bin*) and "skillful" (*hakam*) are terms normally used when speaking of "wisdom," and they clearly connect back (in a sarcastic wordplay) to 9:12. If the people fail to show wisdom (*hakam*) and understanding (*bin*) in regard to the reason the judgment is coming (9:12–16), then once the judgment comes, the wise (*hakam*) and understanding (*bin*) thing to do is to wail over the judgment. In the ancient biblical world, funerals generally were characterized by the presence of women from the community who wailed loudly for the dead person. No doubt some women were better at it than others. Here God says to call for those women who are the best—that is, "the most skillful" (*hakam*; the "wisest")—at public mourning.

9:19 *The sound of wailing is heard from Zion.* Literally, this reads, "the voice of wailing is heard (*shama'*) from Zion." As mentioned above, the point is that if they refuse to listen to the voice of God, then they will listen to the voice of wailing.

9:20 *you women, hear the word of the LORD.* Once again (sarcastically this time) God calls on people to hear (*shama'*) his word. This time, however, it is not a call to repentance or a call to listen to God's law but rather a call to teach their daughters how to wail and sing funeral dirges over the desolation of Jerusalem.

9:21 *Death has climbed in through our windows.* Death is personified, and even though the doors are bolted and the fortress gates closed, death is still able to get in and kill even the children and young men.

9:23 *their wisdom . . . their strength . . . their riches.* These are probably the primary attributes that royalty or nobility desired to acquire.

9:24 *boast about this: . . . the understanding to know me.* Do not boast about acquiring the attributes or accomplishments of the royal or noble classes, God says. Rather, boast about understanding and knowing God. The word translated as "understanding" is also a wisdom term. The word translated as "know" has strong connotations of both knowledge and relationship/familiarity.

the LORD, *who exercises kindness*. "Kindness" is a very weak translation of the word *hesed*, which carries the idea of "loyal love" or "faithful love." This verse underscores the great tension in Jeremiah: God is the one who practices or exercises faithful, loyal love toward his covenant and his covenant people, but he is also the one who is characterized by "justice" and "righteousness." A truly "wise" person will "boast" in understanding how God holds these attributes together continuously, even as he judges and destroys Jerusalem.

Theological Insights

God's judgment on Jerusalem and Judah is neither capricious nor arbitrary, but rather it is appropriate, even necessary, in accordance with true justice and righteousness. But God is still one who is characterized by his loyal, faithful love. There is no bifurcation in the Bible whereby the Old Testament God is a God of wrath and the New Testament God is a God of love. Both Testaments present the character of God as loving but also righteous and just. Judgment on sin, such as the destruction of Jerusalem in the time of Jeremiah, is required by God's justice and righteousness. The truly wise person will understand this and grasp that God is both loving and righteous, even in his judgment. These two aspects of God's character—his great love and his righteous judgment on sin—stay in tension throughout the Old Testament and then merge together in ultimate expression in the substitutionary atonement of Jesus Christ.

Teaching the Text

This passage gives us a glimpse into some interesting aspects of the character of God. First, we see that God is stoutly committed to presenting very clear argumentation establishing that his acts of wrath against Jerusalem and Judah were absolutely necessary, acts of justice and righteousness. Furthermore, it seems to be quite important to him that his people understand this. He wants to be very sure that the people, including us, do not misunderstand his acts of judgment and erroneously view him as capricious or unnecessarily vengeful.

Second, an aesthetic, artistic characteristic of God surfaces here, even in his judgment and wrath, a feature seen elsewhere in the Old Testament as well.[1] Since the people refuse to listen to his voice calling them to repentance, they will listen to the voice of wailing, which mourns the terrible judgment he has brought upon them. Since they have not exercised any "wisdom/skill" at understanding their sin and the call to repentance, they will show "wisdom/skill" at wailing and mourning. This is an example of God's colorful "poetic justice" in Jeremiah. God has not changed over the years. Sometimes we try to portray him as emotionless and without any personality, as if somehow that is more befitting to his majesty. But it is better to understand him and worship him as he has revealed himself to us in Scripture, as in the book of Jeremiah. God has a definite poetic, "artsy" flair for how he brings about his plan, both in how he blesses and in how he judges. Often his punishment is fitting to the crime.

Third, God stresses that the goals of kings (wisdom, strength, riches) are nothing in comparison to understanding and knowing him. In particular, God declares that the important thing is to know and understand that he is a God who is characterized by loyal, faithful love perfectly balanced with his justice and righteousness. This is as true for us today as it was in Jeremiah's day.

Illustrating the Text

God's judgments are just.

Popular Culture: We live in a highly litigious society. People are quick to sue when they think that they have been wronged in any way. The cry of our generation is "That's not fair!" The problem is that when we demand justice, what we really want is equal opportunity, equal housing, and equal pay as long as it works to our advantage. But when it does not, then justice is quickly tossed out the window. With God, justice is meted out based not on what is to our liking but rather on his standard of righteousness.

True Story: There is a concept known as poetic justice that appears again and again in Scripture, literature, and life. Sometimes we refer to this as someone "getting their just deserts" or by saying, "What goes around comes around."

To illustrate this point, you could use the following story (or one of your own). An Ohio newspaper reported the sad story of a nineteen-year-old man who was killed in a car accident in September 2012 after running a stop sign. Ironically, the officer who investigated the accident discovered that there were three stop signs in the back of the young man's pickup truck. It appears that just prior to the crash, he had been stealing the stop signs along Route 20.[2]

Scripture: In Matthew 7:2 Jesus says, "For in the same way you judge others, you will be judged, and with the measure you use, it will be measured to you."

Television: In the Road Runner and Wile E. Coyote cartoons there is a running gag where the crafty coyote orders some elaborate trap from the Acme Corporation to capture or kill the road runner, but in an ironic twist of fate, the trap always seems to backfire, and the coyote ends up being the victim of his own snare. Like the coyote, if people devise evil or ungodly plans that may harm others, the plans can turn back on them such that they end up suffering the fate that would have befallen their victims.

Film: *The Man in the Iron Mask.* In the 1977 made-for-TV movie Richard Chamberlain stars as King Louis XIV and his twin brother, Philippe. The cruel Louis has his brother taken prisoner and put in an iron mask to hide his true identity as a potential rival for the throne. In a twist of fate, Philippe is rescued, Louis is put in his brother's mask and jail cell, and Philippe is secretly made king.

Human Experience: In life we want to believe in the concept of poetic justice, at least for the other guy. For example, Bernie Madoff bilked numerous people of their life savings with his Ponzi scheme, and later he was sentenced to prison by a federal court and ordered to forfeit all his personal wealth and assets, leaving him penniless.

Will You Follow the All-Powerful God or Ridiculous Human-Constructed Idols?

Big Idea

Devastating judgment will come on those who foolishly trust in powerless human-constructed idols instead of the all-powerful God of creation.

Key Themes

- It is foolish to follow the ways of the world and worship worthless, impotent idols that have been made by human hands.
- God, the living, eternal, and all-powerful Creator of the heavens and the earth, is the only one worthy of worship.
- The consequences of replacing the true all-powerful God with worthless human-constructed gods are destruction and exile.

Understanding the Text

The Text in Context

The central theme of the larger unit of 7:1–10:25 is false religion and its punishment. This large unit opens with Jeremiah's proclamation in the temple, "Reform your ways [*derek*] and your actions, and I will let you live in this place [i.e., Jerusalem]" (7:3). Obviously, the people of Jerusalem do not "reform their ways," and consequently the unit closes with God telling them to gather up their belongings because he is about to throw them out of the city and the land (10:17–22).

Also, the wisdom theme running throughout the previous sections (8:4–9:11; 9:12–26) connects and continues in 10:1–25 as wisdom terms are used frequently (see *hakam* in 10:7, 9, 12).

Practically all of 10:1–25 is in poetic form. Connecting the opening and closing subsections is the word *derek* ("road, way, path"), which is translated as "ways" in 10:2 and "lives" in 10:23. In 10:1–5 God exhorts the people to avoid following the valueless ways of the other nations, especially in regard to worshiping their impotent gods that have been made by human hands. Next, Jeremiah declares that it makes much more sense to fear (worship) the all-powerful, living God than to worship worthless, human-constructed idols (10:6–10). All the worthless, false idols, which did not create the world, will perish. God, on the other hand, is the all-powerful Creator of heaven and earth, the one who actually controls the thunderstorms and rain (10:11–16). In 10:17–22 God declares that he will hurl the people of Judah out of the land because of their continued idol worship. Finally, Jeremiah prays again to God, acknowledging God's sovereignty and calling on God to pour out his wrath on the unbelieving nations while showing mercy toward him (10:23–25).

Historical and Cultural Background

Idols played a central role in the polytheistic religions of Israel's neighbors throughout the ancient Near East. Within these religions it was commonly believed that the gods themselves initiated the construction of the idol. After the construction of the idol was completed, special rituals were carried out to transfer the god from the spiritual world to the physical world. The idol then functioned as the mediator of the divine presence. The idol mediated presence and revelation from the god to the people and then likewise mediated worship from the people to the god.[1]

Interpretive Insights

10:3 *For the practices of the peoples are worthless.* The word translated as "worthless" is *hebel*, which occurs three times in this passage (10:3, 8, 15). It has connotations of something that is not only worthless but also illusionary. It is used of things such as cloud vapor—something that looks like it has essence but which in reality does not. The idols look impressive, but that "look" is a deception, for in reality, since they are human-constructed, they are impotent and powerless. *Hebel* occurs thirty-eight times in Ecclesiastes, where it is usually translated by the NIV as "meaningless" (e.g., Eccles. 1:2).

10:5–7 *Like a scarecrow in a cucumber field.* The word translated as "scarecrow" simply means "palm tree" or "post," but the context could suggest a scarecrow-like function. The word translated as "cucumber" may refer instead to melons. This text could be referring to the impotence of the idols (like scarecrows that do not really keep the birds away), or, more likely, it draws a sarcastic analogy between people bowing down to an idol and melons/cucumbers "bowing down" to a post or palm tree in the middle of a field.

Do not fear them . . . Who should not fear you . . . ? The word translated as "fear" in 10:5 and 10:7 carries connotations similar to the English nuances of "fear," but it also reflects ideas such as "reverence" and even "worship" (cf. NIV 1984: "Who should not revere you?"). The point is that it is stupid to "fear/revere/worship" a human-constructed idol. In contrast, however, everyone should "fear/revere/worship" God.

10:11 *Tell them this: "These gods . . . will perish."* Curiously, this verse is written not in Hebrew but in Aramaic, the language of the Babylonians and the international language of diplomacy at the time of Jeremiah. Scholars are widely divided over the significance of the Aramaic usage, but most likely the pronoun "them" in 10:11 refers back to the "nations" in 10:10. God declares to the nations that all their worthless idols will perish, and God states this in the language that they can all understand. On the other hand, if "them" in 10:11 refers forward to "these gods" in the same verse, then God is perhaps mocking the inability of the pagan "gods" to understand a different language like Hebrew, so he addresses them in their own language.

10:12 *But God made the earth . . . founded the world . . . stretched out the heavens.* This verse has three parallel lines stressing that, in contrast to the impotent idols, God created the heavens and the earth. The word translated as "stretched out" is normally used of pitching tents.

by his power . . . by his wisdom . . . by his understanding. This triad stresses the strength/power of God and the wisdom of God, in contrast to the impotent and stupid idols (they cannot even walk, speak, or stand up by themselves [10:4–5]).

10:13 *When he thunders.* Literally, this reads, "at his voice."

the waters in the heavens . . . clouds . . . lightning . . . rain . . . wind. It is God who brings thunderstorms and rain, not Baal, the central god in the Canaanite pantheon, who was worshiped as the "storm-god" who supposedly controlled the rain and thunderstorms.

10:14 *Everyone is senseless.* The word translated as "senseless" refers to the difference in mental capacity between people and animals, especially cows. It occurs three times in this section (10:8, 14, 21). In contrast to God, who formed the world through his wisdom (10:12), the people who "create" idols are particularly dumb (i.e., "dumb as cows"), since they worship what they themselves made.

The images he makes are a fraud. The word translated as "fraud" is *sheqer,* which literally means "a lie." *Sheqer* occurs in thirty-four different verses of Jeremiah (see comments at 5:2). Deception is part of false religion.

10:16 *the Portion of Jacob . . . Israel, the people of his inheritance.* The word translated as "portion" refers to one's share of something (food, plunder, land). It is frequently used of land, and often it carries the idea of "inheritance." Thus there is a double concept of inheritance being expressed here. God is Jacob's (i.e., Israel's) "inheritance," and, as his people (like sons), they normally would receive the "inheritance" that he gives them (i.e., the land). Yet note the contrast in 10:17–18. Instead of inheriting, they will be kicked out of the land. All these terms (portion, Jacob, people, inheritance) are also grouped together in similar fashion in Deuteronomy 32:9.

the Maker. This term normally is used of potters and pottery (i.e., the one who forms all things like a potter shapes his pottery).

the Lord *Almighty.* The Hebrew is *yhwh ts^{e}ba'ot*, which carries a strong nuance of God as the leader of the armed hosts in battle (i.e., this is his "battle name") and thus provides a transition to 10:17–18, where God drives the people of his inheritance right out of the land.

10:21 *The shepherds are senseless.* The image of shepherd is used regularly in Jeremiah to represent the leaders of Jerusalem and Judah. Here they are said to be "senseless." This is the same word that was used in 10:14 that has connotations of being "dumb as an animal" (i.e., not very smart). Using "shepherds" with this word creates a pointed wordplay: the "shepherds" (who are supposed to be leading and protecting) have become as dumb as their sheep.

and do not inquire of the Lord*; so they do not prosper.* The word translated as "inquire" has the nuance of "to seek" and often is used particularly in the context of inquiring for oracles from God. That is, the leaders of Judah and Jerusalem (i.e., the "shepherds") do not look for God or his leading. They have no interest in his guidance. Thus they become as dumb as their sheep. The word translated as "prosper" is actually another wisdom term. It refers to being wise or prudent and thus doing well because of one's wise actions.

Theological Insights

It is foolish to worship or fear idols made by human hands. They cannot walk or talk, and they must be supported just to stand up. Their "glory" or beauty is a fraudulent illusion because it is created by human artisans who should know better than to worship what they themselves have built. Sometimes in the Old Testament the idols of the nations (e.g., Baal, Dagon) are treated rhetorically as real entities, as if they were really there, just infinitely less than the God of Israel. Here, however, Jeremiah mocks them and designates them as nothing more than the work of human hands. They can neither help nor hurt people, since they are only human-constructed. Yet God is also probably addressing them rhetorically in 10:11 as if they were real. Whether they are real or not, the God who created the entire universe will destroy them.

Teaching the Text

God underscores how stupid it is to fear and worship an idol that is human-constructed. These idols have no real power; they cannot walk or talk or even stand up by themselves. When people bow down to them, they are like melons in a field "bowing" down to a palm tree. The appearance of glory or grandeur projected by the idols is a huge deception, created by clever artisans (who are, nonetheless, quite dense themselves for worshiping this very deception that they themselves have created). The idols cannot help and cannot hurt; they have no power to do anything.

God, however, is altogether different. He is the one who created all things by his power and his wisdom. He is the living God, the true God, the eternal King, the maker of all things, and mighty in battle. Unlike manufactured gods, God has the power to help—to deliver, to sustain, and to bless. Yet he is also a battle God who gets angry when he is betrayed and provoked, and thus, also unlike the human-constructed idols, he has real power to pour out his wrath and judgment on those who foolishly spit in his face and turn to worshiping their own creations.

These principles are extremely relevant to us today. When people turn away from God, they inevitably turn to something that they (or the culture) have created to take his place (i.e., the "way of the world/nations"). Whether it is consumerism, the great American dream, Zen Buddhism, or carnal sensuality, people today often put something in the place of God and then "worship" it instead of worshiping God. Jeremiah tells us that this is stupid for two reasons: (1) These human-constructed "gods" cannot really do anything to help us; they do not have the power to bless or to sustain; like the mist, it appears as if something real is there when it is not. (2) Worshiping these idols is a betrayal of God, and it offends him, the one who does have the power to bring judgment on those who thumb their noses at his rights and status as King and Creator.

So, do not follow the way of the world. Do not fear what the world fears, and do not worship what the world worships. Fear and worship the God and Father of our Lord Jesus Christ, who is the Creator of the world and the mighty King.

Illustrating the Text

The choices we make will determine the direction that our lives take.

Statistics: If you go into a convenience store or a gas station to get a gallon of milk, you might end up waiting in line behind someone who is buying a lottery ticket, hoping to win the Mega Millions jackpot. You can tell the person that his or her chances are quite slim. In October 2013 the pool of numbers available for the Mega Millions lottery was increased, which in turn lowered the chances of winning from 1 in 176 million to 1 in 259 million. To help put that into perspective, according to figures compiled by a researcher for *National Geographic*, the odds of being struck by lightning in your lifetime are 1 in 3,000, the odds of being murdered in the United States are 1 in 19,000, and the odds of being killed by a shark are 1 in 3.7 million.[2]

Theological Reference: According to the answer to the first question in the Westminster Shorter Catechism, "Man's chief end is to glorify God." This means that we are born with a desire and a need to worship God, so when we turn away from him, we inevitably turn to something else. In our culture false gods can be found everywhere. The pursuit of possessions, position, power, and personal pleasure has taken God's place as the chief desire of too many of our hearts, and ultimately there will be a price to pay for that. Here Jeremiah reminds us that life is about choices, and who or what we choose to worship will have eternal ramifications.

Popular Music: "Gotta Serve Somebody," by Bob Dylan. In this 1979 bluesy hit song singer/songwriter Bob Dylan captured the spirit of what the prophet Jeremiah is saying. In the song Dylan reminds us that no matter what our station in life, we all must serve someone, and Dylan says that "it may be the devil or it may be the Lord." If possible, as part of the worship service, play source recording or have church musicians play the song as a special music number.

The Broken Covenant

Big Idea

Intercession before God is possible only within a valid covenant relationship.

Key Themes

- The covenant relationship between Judah and God required obedience from Judah.
- God's patience has limits, yet his love continues.
- Judah's continued refusal to obey God shatters the Mosaic covenant.
- Intercessory prayer is not effective without a valid covenant relationship.

Understanding the Text

The Text in Context

Remember that Jeremiah 1–29 as a whole deals primarily with the broken covenant and the consequent judgment. Jeremiah 1 recounts the call of the prophet. Jeremiah 2 presents the formal, legal lawsuit. Jeremiah 3:1–4:4 is an unsuccessful call for Judah to repent and to return to the covenant. Jeremiah 4:5–6:30 describes the consequent judgment: the Babylonian invasion. Jeremiah 7:1–10:25 zeroes in on false religion (primarily idolatry) and its punishment. Idolatry is at the heart of the broken covenant and the broken relationship with God.

Jeremiah 11 opens a new, large subunit within Jeremiah 1–29 that continues to the end of Jeremiah 29 and focuses on Jeremiah's role as God's prophet in conflict with the kings of Judah and their false prophets, who oppose God's word and prophesy counteractive lies in God's name. In 11:1–17, the opening section, God instructs Jeremiah to proclaim to the people of Jerusalem that they have shattered the covenant, and thus their relationship with God is over. This proclamation sets the stage for all the coming conflict and hostility that Jeremiah will experience from the major institutions of power in Jerusalem (the kings, the court prophets, the priests), one of the central themes in the following chapters.

The passage unfolds as follows. In 11:1–5 God tells Jeremiah to remind the people of Judah and Jerusalem of the curses and blessings spelled out in the covenant (i.e., Deuteronomy). However, God continues in 11:6–8, these people have repeatedly disobeyed; thus the curses in Deuteronomy have now started to fall upon them. The continued disobedience of the people of Judah, especially their idol worship, has actually annulled the covenant, and therefore God will no longer listen to their cries (11:9–13). So since the covenant relationship has ended, God tells Jeremiah himself not to intercede for the people (11:14). But in the end, God laments over this terrible tragedy, that his beloved people have done such terrible things that they must now be destroyed (11:15–17). The entire section is in prose, except for God's lament and the following verses (11:15–16), which are in poetry.

Historical and Cultural Background

A covenant is basically a legal contractual agreement between two individuals or other entities. The formalized covenant was not unique to Israel; it was a common legal structure throughout the ancient Near East. Structurally, for example, the book of Deuteronomy is similar in many regards to ancient literary Hittite treaties between the Hittite suzerain (king) and his vassals.[1]

Through the exodus event and his spectacular revelation on Mount Sinai (Exod. 19–24), God enters into a special covenant relationship with Israel, often referred to as the Sinaitic or Mosaic covenant.[2] The book of Deuteronomy is at the heart of this covenant relationship, defining the terms by which Israel could live in the promised land and be blessed by the presence of God living in their midst. Deuteronomy 28 spells out the terrible consequences for Israel under this covenant if it rejects God and refuses to "listen" and obey the terms in Deuteronomy. It is this covenant relationship that Jeremiah proclaims as shattered, implying that the terrible curses of Deuteronomy 28 will soon descend on Judah.

Interpretive Insights

11:2 *Listen to the terms of this covenant.* The literal sense of this phrase is "hear the words of this covenant." The word translated as "listen" is *shama'*, a word that Jeremiah uses frequently (see comments at 7:16). Literally, this word means "to hear," but figuratively it means "to respond to" or "to obey." It is used repeatedly in this section (11:2, 3, 4, 6, 7, 8, 10, 11, 14). Likewise, throughout this section, the NIV often uses "terms" to translate what is literally "words" (11:2, 3, 6). "This covenant" refers to the covenant that God made with the Israelites at Sinai after he delivered them from Egypt. The covenant was restated in the book of Deuteronomy just before Israel entered the land. References to "covenant" throughout Jeremiah 11 (vv. 2, 3, 6, 8, 10) have a primary reference to the book of Deuteronomy.

11:3 *Cursed is the one who does not obey the terms of this covenant.* This is a direct allusion to Deuteronomy 28:15 and the verses that follow, where God spells out the specific curses that will fall on Israel if it does not obey ("listen"; *shama'* is used in Deut. 28:15, 45). A "curse" in this context carries connotations of a judgment; it is the opposite of blessing.

11:4 *you will be my people, and I will be your God.* This is the standard, relational, oft-repeated Old Testament formula that lay at the heart of the covenant.

11:10 *Both Israel and Judah have broken the covenant I made with their ancestors.* The word translated as "broken" is *parar.* This word does not mean "to transgress against" or "to violate" as when someone today "breaks" the law; rather, it means "to annul" or "nullify" (cf. Num. 30:8–15; 1 Kings 15:19; Ezek. 17:15). It cannot mean "to transgress against" because Jeremiah uses it in regard to God in 14:21 ("Remember your covenant with us and do not *break* it").

11:11 *I will bring on them a disaster.* The word translated as "disaster" (*ra'ah*) is a central term in Jeremiah, occurring frequently throughout the book. When the word is used of people, the NIV usually translates it as "evil" (e.g., 11:8, "evil hearts"; but "wickedness" in 11:15), but when the word is used of what God does, the NIV usually translates it as "disaster" (11:11, 12, 17). As in numerous other places in Jeremiah, here there is a wordplay. Because of the people's *ra'ah* hearts (11:8), God will bring *ra'ah* upon them.

Although they cry out to me, I will not listen to them. As mentioned above, the word *shama'* ("to hear, listen, obey") is used frequently throughout this section. Because the people of Judah and Jerusalem have repeatedly refused to "listen" to the words of the covenant, God will not "listen" to their cries when the consequent judgment falls on them. This is a consequence of the "broken" covenant.

11:14 *Do not pray for this people.* God tells Jeremiah not to intercede anymore for the people. The time for intercession has passed. The covenant is shattered, and there is no longer any relational basis by which God will listen to them. This theme will reemerge in Jeremiah 14–15.

11:15 *my beloved.* The Hebrew word for "beloved" occurs eight times in the Old Testament, usually used for people whom God loves (Pss. 60:5; 108:6; 127:2; Isa. 5:1). Although singular in form, this word is often used, as it is here, to refer to Israel/Judah as a corporate entity. Note the sad poetic irony of this verse as God watches his beloved (i.e., the people of Jerusalem and Judah) actually rejoice over the wickedness (*ra'ah*) that they do right in the temple. The consequences are then poetically described in 11:16.

11:16 *he will set it on fire, and its branches will be broken.* God is describing poetically the destruction of Jerusalem and Judah. Paul appropriates this same imagery in Romans 11:17–21.

Theological Insights

In the Old Testament, under the Mosaic covenant, there were sins "within the covenant"—that is, individual shortcomings and failings that could be dealt with through sacrifice and atonement. But there were also sins "against the covenant," sins that shattered the covenant relationship and removed the basis for God's acceptance of sacrifice and atonement. The people in Jerusalem had been practicing an ongoing and blatant idolatry, thus in effect rejecting their covenant relationship with God. This was a sin against the covenant, one that rendered the covenant null in regard to forming a means of relating to God. Thus they could not expect to use the sacrifices and intercessory methods of the covenant, since it was no longer in effect. (See the discussion on covenants in the "Theological Insights" section for Jeremiah 30:1–24.) Therefore, God tells Jeremiah not to pray or intercede for these people (11:14.) There is no longer any covenant basis by which God can honor a request from Jeremiah to forgive them. Intercessory prayer is valid and effective only when a valid covenant relationship between God and people is in place. In this context, it is impossible to overemphasize the importance of the "new covenant" (see Jer. 31) that is inaugurated by Jesus Christ, for it reestablished a valid covenant relationship within which God can forgive people, based on the sacrifice of Jesus Christ.

Note the frequent reference to the "people of Judah and those who dwell in Jerusalem." While the judgment certainly falls on the entire nation of Judah, there is a special focus on Jerusalem, the personification and representation of the nation. This same emphasis will be repeated in the New Testament when, in the Gospels, Jesus travels to Jerusalem, speaks to a personified Jerusalem, proclaims coming judgment on Jerusalem, and brings his earthly ministry to a climactic conclusion in Jerusalem.

Teaching the Text

The people of Jerusalem and Judah just assumed that they could do whatever they wished and God would still accept them and bless them within his covenant relationship. Yet God emphatically rejects this notion. Those outside his covenant will not receive the blessings of his presence. Likewise today, people cannot assume that God will bless them and take care of them even if they are hostile to him and have no covenant relationship with him. Jesus Christ, however, establishes the new covenant, and it is under this covenant that we have a relationship with God. Yet those who remain disobediently outside this covenant cannot expect to approach God as if they were part of that covenant. Covenant relationship with God comes only through Jesus Christ, whose blood established the new covenant.

Also, while the new covenant is characterized by grace instead of law, obedience is still a factor. People must put faith in Jesus Christ and "obey" by coming to God through Christ. They cannot just worship whatever and however they want. It is not that God does not "hear" at all the cry of those outside Christ but that he will hardly bless and care for those who have belligerently chosen to reject Christ and who spurn his invitation for this covenant relationship. He will always welcome those who cry out to him through Christ and who enter into the covenant relationship that Christ provides. But he will not respond to those outside Christ who simply expect God to bless them in their sinful lives outside the covenant.

God was extremely patient with the people of Judah and Jerusalem, but at some point his patience ran out, and his wrath was unleashed on them. Likewise today, God often is extremely patient with those who repeatedly hear the gospel and yet reject it again and again. But eventually the time comes when those who have chosen to defy him and reject him will have to answer for their rejection of him and their sin. At some point in everyone's life, the day of reckoning comes. Either they are under the new covenant and in Christ, destined for eternal life, or they are not and thus destined for judgment.

Yet right in this same context of ended relationship and intercession, God still refers to this sinful, evil people as "my beloved." Even as the wrath of God and the necessary judgment fall on Jerusalem and Judah, God reveals how this breaks his heart because of his love for them. God loves people today and does not desire that any of them perish. Nonetheless, his justice will be carried out, painful as it is for him.

Illustrating the Text

Answered prayer is dependent on our relationship with God.

Scripture: The eleventh chapter of Luke's Gospel begins with the disciples asking Jesus to teach them how to pray, and he instructs them to begin by saying, "Father." Then a few verses later Jesus says, "Which of you fathers, if your son asks for a fish, will give him a snake instead?" When the words are read in context, we can see that Jesus is reminding us of the important role that our relationship plays in soliciting a response.

When we refuse to obey God, we damage our relationship with him.

Cultural Institution: Wedding vows are intended to be in force "until death do us part," but the court is more flexible. An annulment (a legal declaration that the marriage never existed) is granted if one or more parties can demonstrate that the marriage should not have been legally allowed.

For example, Renee Zellweger and Kenny Chesney were married in May 2005, and just four months later Zellweger filed for and was granted an annulment. This was marital bliss compared to Britney Spears, whose marriage to Jason Alexander was annulled just fifty-five hours after they exchanged their vows.

Of course, Roman Catholic annulments are more difficult to obtain than those from a secular court, but here too the numbers are staggering. For example, according to statistics compiled by the Vatican, 49,233 marriages were annulled worldwide in 2006, and more than 27,000 of those were in the United States. The number has increased dramatically in the last several years, and as a case in point, in 1968 the number of annulments granted by the Roman Catholic Church in the United States was 338.[3]

As sad as these statistics are, they pale in comparison to the number of people who have nullified their covenant relationship with God by refusing to obey him.

God's patience has a limit.

Economics: In most loans there is something called a "grace period." This is a provision in the contract, set by the lender, that allows payments to be made for a certain period of time (usually fifteen days) after the actual due date of the loan without incurring a late fee or penalty.

In the case of a federal government Stafford Loan for students, the grace period is generously extended to six months after graduation, or when the student drops below a half-time credit load. When that time expires, the payment is due.[4]

Those who have trusted in Jesus Christ already have their sins paid for in full. For those who have not trusted in Christ, however, God has set an undisclosed due date to get right with him during this grace period. Yet even his patience has a limit, and the day is coming when payment will be demanded in full for their sins.

Facing Persecution

Big Idea

In the midst of persecution, God exhorts his people to endure, trust, and wait.

Key Themes

- Proclaiming the word of God brings hostility from those who want to stifle the message by silencing the messenger.
- God protects his prophet during times of betrayal and persecution.
- Jeremiah questions God about why evil people who oppose him are allowed to prosper.
- God mildly rebukes the prophet, implying that he is to "wait and endure."

Understanding the Text

The Text in Context

The larger unit of Jeremiah 11–29 is united by the theme of the prophet in conflict. The previous section (11:1–17) introduces the unit by stressing the broken covenant and thus the betrayed and shattered relationship between God and his people. In this present section (11:18–12:6), as Jeremiah proclaims that message, he himself is betrayed by his own people (i.e., his neighbors and relatives in his hometown), so he calls for justice and judgment on them. God, however, tells him that the betrayal and persecution will get even worse. Then in the following section (12:7–13) God speaks of judgment on the people of Judah, even as he repeatedly uses relational terms stressing that these are his own people ("my house," "my inheritance," "the one I love"). That is, the betrayal and rejection of Jeremiah by the people of his hometown parallel the betrayal and rejection of God by the people of Judah and Jerusalem.

This unit is a mix of prose (11:18–19a; 21–23) and poetry (11:19b–20; 12:1–6). Jeremiah's complaint to God in 12:1–4 is very poetic, and it is interesting to see that God responds to him in colorful poetry as well (12:5–6).

Interpretive Insights

11:18 *the LORD revealed their plot to me.* The pronoun "their" is clarified in 11:21 as the "people of Anathoth." Jeremiah 1:1 introduced Jeremiah as one of the "priests at Anathoth." Thus it appears that Anathoth is his hometown. It was located near Jerusalem.

he showed me what they were doing. A more literal translation reads, "He caused me to see their evil deeds [i.e., what they were plotting]." Although Jeremiah does not tell us how God revealed this plot to him, he is very explicit about the fact that he would not have suspected this plot against him had God not shown it to him.

11:19 *I had been like a gentle lamb led to the slaughter.* The Hebrew grammar suggests a contrasting stress on "I." The sense is that "*they* were plotting evil deeds . . . but *I* was like a lamb led to the slaughter." Jeremiah was completely unaware of the plot and would have walked right into the trap just as an unsuspecting lamb goes clueless to the sacrifice.

destroy the tree and its fruit . . . that his name be remembered no more. Jeremiah's fellow townspeople want not only to kill him but also to erase any memory of him. To die without any descendants and therefore be forgotten was viewed as a curse; thus these plotters were conniving to do more against Jeremiah than just kill him. This probably also reflects their desire to remove both the prophet and the discomforting message that he had been proclaiming. To forget Jeremiah would be to forget his message as well. Note the irony of the fact that more than 2,500 years later we are still remembering and studying the words of Jeremiah.

11:20 LORD *Almighty.* Literally, this translates as "Yahweh of the hosts," with "hosts" referring to armies. It functions as the "battle name" for God, who uses it for himself frequently in contexts of going to war. Here, as Jeremiah calls on God to bring vengeance on his enemies who plot to kill him, he addresses God by his "battle name."

11:21 *Do not prophesy in the name of the* LORD *or you will die.* The Hebrew negative form used in "do not prophesy" is a strong prohibitive form implying a total and complete cessation. Jeremiah's hostile neighbors in Anathoth foolishly believe that only when Jeremiah speaks the word of the Lord does that word become "activated" and start to unfold. They suppose that if they can silence Jeremiah, this would restrain the word of the Lord.

11:22-23 *young men . . . sons and daughters . . . Not even a remnant will be left to them.* God's judgment reflects a strong sense of poetic justice. In 11:19 the people of Anathoth plotted to erase Jeremiah and all memory of him, including any descendants. In response, God declares that his judgment will completely destroy these people, and none of them will survive. Thus it will be they who are "cut off" (cf. 11:19), not God's prophet Jeremiah.

12:1 *Why does the way of the wicked prosper?* As played out in the book of Job, there was a common line of popular thinking among the Israelites that we call the "retribution principle," which assumed that people get what they deserve. Jeremiah knows that God is righteous and just, so he is puzzled that these people can plot evil against him and yet God does nothing about it. He seems to be hoping that if he points this out, God will be spurred to action on his behalf.

12:2 *You are always on their lips but far from their hearts.* Literally, this could be translated as "Near are you in their mouth, but far from their inner feelings." These people plotting to kill Jeremiah speak religious language and mention God often. No doubt they believe that silencing Jeremiah is the correct theological thing to do. But in reality, Jeremiah points out, God is far from "their hearts." The word used here is not the regular term used for "heart" but rather one that refers literally to one's inner organs. Some dictionaries suggest a translation of "kidneys." This term is used figuratively of one's "seat of emotion." That is, although these people speak of God, they have no deep emotional love for him or any loyalty to him that might result in obedience.

12:3 *Drag them off like sheep to be butchered!* In calling on God to judge them, Jeremiah uses imagery that contrasts directly with his own situation that he described in 11:19: "I had been like a gentle lamb led to the slaughter." The word translated as "butchered" in 12:3 is from the same root word translated as "slaughter" in 11:19. Yet while Jeremiah says that he was "led," he calls on God to "drag them off." The Hebrew word used here is a strong one with connotations of violence.

12:5 *If . . . men on foot . . . have worn you out, how can you compete with horses?* God has clearly stated to Jeremiah several times that he will indeed judge the wicked. Jeremiah's objection in 12:1–4 is in regard to God's timing (why the delay?) and seems to arise from the fact that people were now specifically plotting to kill Jeremiah himself. In his answer to Jeremiah, God does not address the timing of his judgment but rather addresses the attitude and strength of Jeremiah in the face of this persecution. God seems to imply that this plot from Anathoth is a minor incident in light of what will transpire later. Indeed, as we read through the story of Jeremiah, especially in chapters 26 and 37–38, we see kings, nobles, false prophets, and priests all scheming against him. He is accused, beaten, imprisoned several times, and threatened with death; indeed, he comes close to death. So in reality this threat from the people of Anathoth is slight in comparison to the threat Jeremiah will later experience from the central power structures of Jerusalem (the monarchy, the nobility, the priesthood, etc.), people who are much more powerful and thus much more dangerous.

12:6 *Your relatives, members of your own family . . . have betrayed you.* More literally, this reads, "Your brothers and the house of your father . . . have betrayed you." The term "house of your father" refers to the most basic clan unit in Israelite society. It was the most powerful emotional and sociological source of an Israelite's self-identity and community connection. This reference to Jeremiah's family ("house of your father") also provides the connection to the next section, where God will describe the people whom he is going to judge as "my house" and "my inheritance." Judgment will come on those from Jeremiah's family (Anathoth) who betrayed him at the same time that it falls on those in God's family (i.e., Judah and Jerusalem) who betrayed him. This parallel is hardly coincidental.

Theological Insights

Jeremiah's question of why the wicked and rebellious ones seem to prosper while those who obey God suffer (or are persecuted) is one that surfaces frequently in the Bible, often voiced directly by characters in the story or by the narrative itself (e.g., Job's complaints, David's laments in Psalms, the Joseph narratives). Yet throughout the Scriptures we observe that, as is the case for Jeremiah, God always has his plan, and ultimately he will judge everyone and everything with justice. However, he will not be manipulated into revising his plan just to accommodate the short-term understanding of one of his servants. In the case of Jeremiah, God does not remove Jeremiah from his suffering but instead exhorts him to stay steadfast in his proclamation of God's word, trusting in God for protection and strength. The Babylonians are indeed coming to destroy those who have rejected God and persecuted Jeremiah, but God will bring this about in his own good time.

Another theological theme introduced in this unit is that of the persecuted prophet serving as the symbol and focal point of the people's rejection of God and his word. In this sense, the rejection of Jeremiah parallels and symbolizes the people's rejection of God. This connects very tightly to the issue discussed above. Jeremiah sees his persecution only from his own personal perspective. In the big picture, however, the treatment of Jeremiah by the people of Jerusalem also represents their hostile attitude toward God. So the timing of Jeremiah's deliverance and vindication is tied to God's judgment on the people of Jerusalem for rejecting the covenant and their God. Yet God is patient and long-suffering. He continues to plead with Jerusalem to repent and turn back to him. This is the aspect that Jeremiah does not seem to understand yet. It is interesting to note the New Testament parallels, especially in the Gospels and in Acts, as God's messengers and his word proclaimed through them are rejected and met with dangerous hostility in a fashion very similar to what Jeremiah experiences. As in the case of Jeremiah, God gives the leaders and people of Jerusalem several chances to repent, but then eventually, a similar and terrible judgment falls on them. In both cases Jerusalem is destroyed (587 BC by the Babylonians; AD 70 by the Romans), and those leaders who opposed God's word by persecuting his prophets are killed.

Teaching the Text

Jeremiah will face much hostility and opposition throughout the book. It is interesting that the first actual plot against him comes from his own clan ("the house of his father"). The text does not tell us why they were so opposed to Jeremiah being the prophet who proclaimed the message from God. Perhaps they were worried that his identification with them as clan member would hurt the reputation of the clan because the powerful authorities in Jerusalem despised him and rejected his message. He was an embarrassment to them, and they wanted to distance themselves from him. Likewise, for us today it is perhaps easier to endure opposition and hostility from strangers and outsiders than from family members and lifelong neighbors and friends. Yet God calls on us to be strong and to trust in him, even if our faith or our calling to proclaim God's word is opposed by those who are close to us or leads to their rejection or "distancing themselves" from us.

God informs the naive Jeremiah of the danger he is in, yet God seems to chide Jeremiah after the prophet overreacts to the crisis. God's plan at this time seems not to be to crush Jeremiah's opponents immediately (as the prophet requests) but rather to warn him and to sustain him in the midst of opposition. Jeremiah's suffering and endurance of the hostility, however, play an important role in God's plan, something that Jeremiah does not seem to understand. For us today, God does not directly bring suffering or persecution on us just for the sake of our suffering, but sometimes when such difficult times do fall on us, he uses such circumstances to further his plans, which often are not apparent to us. As in the case of Jeremiah, he calls on us to endure and to trust in him as he works out his long-range plan, a plan that might include, as a critical component, the difficult situation we are enduring.

Also, as God informs Jeremiah, this small crisis introduced from the small town of Anathoth is but a warm-up exercise for the huge crisis shaping up in Jerusalem. So for us, as God calls on us to endure and to trust him during our current difficulties, we need to remember that he may have in mind a much bigger task for us in the future for which our current trying situation is but a warm-up exercise to prepare us.

Illustrating the Text

God expects us to be patient.

Sports: There is an art to fly-fishing. You need to become familiar with the feeding habits of the trout, the weather patterns of the season, the dynamics of the rapids on the river that you intend to fish, and the exact time the fish will spawn. Then, if you go at the right time of day, to the right location in the river with the right line and the right fly, maybe, if you are lucky, you will get a bite. But even if you do everything right, there are no guarantees. These things take time. You must be doggedly persistent, and even then the line could snap, the fish could spit out the hook, the net could break, or you could slip, fill your waders with water, and be dragged under.

One reason so many anglers go home with an empty creel is impatience. After ten minutes, after an hour, or two hours, or three hours a voice in your head says, "They're not biting today. You might as well go home." At that moment the question is simply this: How committed are you? Are you a true believer or not?

And the same thing is true of life. Doubting ourselves, doubting our circumstances, and, worst of all, doubting God in the face of uncertainty are default responses that all of us must learn to fight. We must discipline our hearts to trust God, and wait for his time to come.

The preacher/teacher could come dressed in waders, a fishing hat, and a vest, and cast a line (with no hook!) around the congregation while giving this talk.

Christians patiently endure persecution.

Church Missions: An Ethiopian Christian evangelist from the region of Wolayta traveled to a predominately Muslim town in a nearby region and tried to proclaim the gospel there. The Muslim residents of the town beat him severely until he was near death and then cast him out of town. His colleagues carried him back to Wolayta. Years later (in the mid-1980s) a terrible famine gripped this part of Ethiopia, leading to the death of thousands Ethiopians. As part of the famine relief efforts, SIM (an evangelical mission organization) organized relief teams to go into hard-hit areas and distribute food. The evangelist from Wolayta volunteered to work for one of these teams. To his surprise, his particular famine relief team was assigned to the very same Muslim town where he had been beaten. As he sat at the table in the center of town registering families for grain distribution, several of the townspeople recognized him. Amazed and overwhelmed, they said to him, "You are the man we beat and left for dead. How is it that you have returned to save the lives of our starving children?" Several people in that town turned to Christ.[1]

The Broken Relationship and the Agony of God

Big Idea

God agonizes over the terrible consequences of the broken relationship with his people, but he still offers hope for the future.

Key Themes

- God mourns Judah's hostile, insulting rejection of his loving relationship.
- God expresses anger as well as profound sorrow at the broken relationship.
- Due to the broken relationship, God will withdraw his protective hand, and enemies will devastate his beloved people.
- After a time of judgment, restoration is possible, even for the enemies of God's people.

Understanding the Text

The Text in Context

The central theme running throughout Jeremiah 1–29 is the broken covenant and the consequent judgment coming on Judah for abandoning and rejecting God and his gracious covenant. Within this larger theme, Jeremiah 11–29 zeroes in on the hostility directed at God's prophet Jeremiah because he is the "point man" in highlighting Judah's sin and proclaiming the coming judgment. Jeremiah 11:18–12:6 has the prophet bemoaning the fact that his own people, even those from his hometown, have rejected him and are openly persecuting him. Jeremiah 12:7–17, our current passage, parallels that text in that it presents the hostility and rejection of God by his own beloved people, the people of Judah and Jerusalem.

This passage is composed of two parts, 12:7–13 and 12:14–17, united by the repeated use of the term *nahal*, "inheritance" (12:7, 8, 9, 14, 15). In 12:7–13 the "inheritance" is from God's perspective ("my inheritance" is repeated three times), and in 12:14–17 the "inheritance" is from the perspective of both Judah and the surrounding nations. Jeremiah 12:7–13 focuses on the painful loss of God's inheritance, while Jeremiah 12:14–17 underscores the offered future restoration of Judah's and the nation's inheritance.

Historical and Cultural Background

The reference in 12:14 to the "wicked neighbors who seize the inheritance I gave my people Israel" probably alludes to the neighboring nations (Syria, Ammon, Moab, Edom, Tyre, and Sidon), several of which opportunistically allied themselves with the Babylonians and raided Judah either during the Babylonian invasion of 598 BC (2 Kings 24:2) or during the Babylonian invasion of 588–586 BC (Ps. 137:7; Lam. 4:21–22; Obad. 10–14). The specific charge against these nations is that they "taught my people to swear by Baal" (Jer. 12:16). Baal was the central Canaanite storm/fertility-god that posed the most central challenge to Israel's monotheistic worship of Yahweh during the Israelites' history from the time they entered the promised land until they were exiled away from the land. Jeremiah repeatedly mentions the worship of Baal by the people of Jerusalem and Judah as one of the central sins that they were committing against God and the covenant (2:8, 23; 7:9; 9:14; 11:13, 17; 19:5; 23:13, 27; 32:29, 35). Of Judah's neighboring nations, Tyre and Sidon are most closely associated with Baal.

Interpretive Insights

12:7 *I will forsake my house, abandon my inheritance . . . give the one I love.* God's people have rejected him and broken the covenant, and he responds by describing his separation from them with three parallel statements. "House" can refer to the people of Israel as God's family or, more likely, to the temple. Likewise, when used of God, "inheritance" can refer to the land of Israel or to the Israelites themselves. "The one I love" is feminine in gender and is a personification of the people of Judah as God's beloved wife (cf. 11:15). All three terms connote strong relational, even kinship, ties. Jack Lundbom suggests that there is a progressive accumulation here: God's abandonment of the temple, the land, and the people.[1]

12:8 *My inheritance has become to me like a lion in the forest.* The word translated as "inheritance" (*nahal*) refers to the concept of permanent family property. Unlike the connotations of our English word "property," *nahal* has strong connotations of kinship connection and permanence. For the Israelites, *nahal* referred to their share in the promised land. God refers to "my inheritance" in regard to either the land or his people (or both). While in 12:7 it seems to refer to the land, here in 12:8 it appears to refer to the people, who ironically have turned against God like a violent wild lion in the woods.

therefore I hate her. The essence of the word translated as "hate" (*sane'*) can be seen in the actions in 12:7 of forsaking, abandoning, and giving into the hands of enemies.

12:9 *a speckled bird of prey.* There is some uncertainty about how to translate this phrase. The NIV, NLT, and KJV translate this phrase as "bird of prey" or "vulture." The NRSV, ESV, and HCSB, however, follow the translation tradition in the Septuagint and translate it as "hyena" or "hyena's lair." Either way, the meaning is clear and similar to 12:8. God's people now oppose him with hostility like a wild scavenger animal (whether it be a vulture or a hyena).

other birds of prey surround . . . gather all the wild beasts. Here the tables are turned, and the same imagery of the wild animal is used for judgment on the people who had opposed God. Thus, because the people of Judah snarled at God like a wild lion and acted toward him like hostile birds of prey (or hyenas) (12:8), so birds of prey will feast on them, and wild beasts will devour them (12:9).

12:10 *Many shepherds will ruin my vineyard . . . my field . . . my pleasant field.* The threefold reference here to "my vineyard . . . my field . . . my pleasant field" connects figuratively to the concept of inheritance and parallels the threefold reference in 12:7 ("my house . . . my inheritance . . . the one I love"). The term "shepherds" is often used, as it is here, to refer to kings and other leaders. Thus "many shepherds" connects back to the "wild beasts" in 12:9 and refers to Nebuchadnezzar and his staff, along with the kings of other nations who joined him. Note the irony in using the figurative term "shepherd" in referring to those who will absolutely destroy the promised land. Usually shepherds are caring for their sheep and not destroying the good pastureland of the sheep.

12:12 *the sword of the LORD will devour.* Earlier references to the antagonists who destroy Judah (birds of prey / wild animals [12:9]; shepherds [12:10]; destroyers [12:12]) are allusions to King Nebuchadnezzar and the Babylonians. As God removes his protective hand, the enemies of the people of Judah will destroy them (12:7). But here in 12:12 God underscores the ultimate and terrible consequence of the broken covenant and the insulting hostility that the people of Judah have shown him: he himself will fight against them. The Babylonians become like a sword in God's hand.

no one will be safe. The word *shalom* connotes more than just being safe; it encompasses the entire spectrum of well-being. *Shalom* was what characterized the life of the people of Judah when they were in covenant relationship with God. Now that he has moved away from them and removed his protective hand, indeed, even raised his sword against them, all traces of *shalom* are gone with the wind.

12:14 *I will uproot them.* The Hebrew term translated as "uproot" and the image of pulling up a plant by the roots and casting it aside occur frequently in Jeremiah. God's call to Jeremiah in 1:10 defined his work in just these terms (uprooting in judgment and then replanting in restoration). Here in 12:14–17 there is a certain degree of conditionality (as in 18:7–8, where the same word for "uprooting" is used). Both the people of Judah and the nations that destroy them will be "uprooted" (in judgment), but afterward there will be an opportunity for those nations to be reestablished along with God's people (i.e., as part of God's people) if they turn to God.

Theological Insights

We are comfortable with statements that God loves his "inheritance" (the people of Israel [12:7]). Love is one of the most central virtues that define the character of God. Yet as these same people reject God to the extent that they are likened to hostile lions roaring against God in aggression, God declares that he "hates" them. Is "hate" part of the character of God? Can God both love and hate at the same time? The word translated as "hate" (*sane'*) "expresses an emotional attitude toward persons and things which are opposed, detested, despised and with which one wishes to have no contact or relationship. . . . Whereas love draws and unites, hate separates and keeps distant."[2] God uses this term in Hosea 9:15, in similar fashion, to describe the shift in relationship due to Israel's terrible sin (see also Mal. 1:2–3). Throughout the book of Jeremiah we see that God loves his people and feels pain when they reject him. But he is not passive, and he responds negatively to their insulting, dishonoring, hostile rejection of him. Likewise, he feels passionately negative toward their disgustingly sinful behavior (idolatry, oppression, etc.). In this passage God replaces the associated actions of "love" (drawing near, uniting, caring for) with the associated actions of "hate" (separating, creating distance, leaving, removing support and care). Lundbom notes that the terminology in 12:7–13 reflects the language of divorce.[3] Indeed, the human experience of divorce may provide our best (although obviously imperfect) analogy for understanding the "love-hate" paradox reflected in this text. If one spouse has repeatedly cheated on the other and has now openly rejected the faithful spouse with hostility and verbal abuse, the latter's response of "I hate you" (i.e., "I hate what you have done") is not an inappropriate or unexpected outburst, even if the faithful spouse does indeed still love the one who has caused the injury. As the people of Judah reject God and the relationship that they once had with him, God does not stop loving them, but the relationship definitely changes. The separation, distancing, and removal of care and protection are best described by the word *sane'*.

Teaching the Text

This passage opens with ironically poignant and painful statements by God: "I will forsake my house, abandon my inheritance, give up the one I love." Both the rejection of God by his people and the ensuing judgment upon them are painful and very personal for God. This is not just any country and any people; this is his land and his people, and it grieves him to bring judgment on them. God is neither a passionless supercomputer nor a cold, cynical old man on a throne callously meting out judgments on people. He loves his people and their land, and he wants to be in a loving relationship with them. It grieves him when this relationship is rejected and he is spurned, resulting in judgment. This is as true today as in the time of Jeremiah.

The fact that God's own beloved people have now become like hostile wild animals toward him is another huge irony of this passage. Indeed, God seems to underscore how ridiculously shocking this is. The people whom he has lovingly cared for are now snarling and growling at him. How can this be? Yet we see the same phenomenon today. Often in their rejection of God people today turn hostile toward him and blame him for all their misfortunes. This hostility is quite irrational, but nonetheless it brings pain to God.

Yet for all God's patient love and understanding, he is still the omnipotent God, sovereign Lord, and Creator of the universe. Can he be betrayed, rejected, snubbed, belittled, and treated disrespectfully without consequences? As happens with a jilted husband, bubbling up around God's love is anger and rage. Do people today think that they can sinfully spurn God and his call for righteous living or make fun of God without any reaction from him? He is the same God today as he was in the days of Jeremiah, and his anger is a terrible thing.

God wanted to be in a personal covenant relationship with the people of Judah. In this relationship he would care for them and bless them. When they rejected this relationship, they lost his care and his blessings on them. Thus they became vulnerable to all the hostile dangers of the world, and their enemies soon devastated them. Today, although God does not promise the easy life here and now for those who enter into relationship with him, there still are wonderful blessings and provisions in store for those who enter into relationship with him through Christ. To walk away from this relationship with God, along with its blessings, provisions, and promise of eternal life, and to trust instead our chances alone in the world or to cast our hopes on the shallow and deceitful promises of the world is foolish, even tragic.

Finally, in spite of the pain and rejection, and in spite of God's anger at Judah and its neighbors for their sinful behavior, God speaks of a future restoration, a time when the people of Judah and those foreign peoples who attacked them will both be united under his care as his people. He leaves this promise as one with a condition: there must be a truly repentant turn to God. Today this restoration promised by God is ultimately fulfilled in Christ. All peoples, regardless of their sinful pasts, can come to God through Christ and be made part of his special people, entering into a wonderful relationship with God.

Illustrating the Text

God must be the center of all our relationships.

Children's Games: Juxtaposing two childhood games might illuminate the importance of focusing people's attention on God as the center of human response. A "treasure hunt" consists of following various clues to locate a prize at the end of the game. Players begin with a single clue that leads them to the next clue and to the next, with the final clue leading to the treasure. This kind of game has a transactional quality to it. The person to find all the clues first wins the prize. The game "follow the leader" is quite different. In it, the leader is the focus throughout. There is no mapping of clues to get to a prize; instead, to be successful, the players must keep their focus on the leader and do what that person does. This game has a more relational quality to it and provides a better illustration of what it means to keep God at the center.

Rejecting God's love could cost us everything.

News Story: Mel Gibson's divorce from Robyn, his wife of nearly thirty years, began in 2009 and was finalized in 2011. It cost him $425 million. Human divorces can be costly. "Divorcing" God, that is, rejecting his love and spurning his desire for a relationship, is even more costly.

Shame and Judgment for Trusting in "the Lie"

Big Idea

God will bring shame and disgrace on those who arrogantly refuse to listen to his word.

Key Themes

- Jerusalem and its leaders replace the glory and renown of God with their own pride and arrogance.
- God is particularly offended by human pride and arrogance.
- God holds the leaders of Jerusalem particularly responsible for the sin and arrogance of the people.
- Arrogance leads to trusting in human lies rather than God's word of truth.

Understanding the Text

The Text in Context

In Jeremiah 12 God explains how his very own people living on his land not only had rejected him but also had turned into hostile enemies. Furthermore, God seems to be saying in Jeremiah 13, they (led especially by their leaders) have also rejected his glory and his honor, replacing it with prideful arrogance, boasting in the glorious things of the promised land but not acknowledging that it was God who gave it to them. Thus part of his judgment on them will be to shame them, removing everything that they boasted in and totally humiliating them by invasion and exile.

The first half of this section (13:1–14) is in prose, the second half (13:15–27) is in poetry. This is one of the more peculiar "anthology-like" sections of Jeremiah, in which the subsections are only loosely connected by one or more central themes. The central theme of this section is how the pride, arrogance, and boasting of Judah and Jerusalem will be turned into shame and disgrace. Uniting this section within this broad theme is the repeated usage of symbols and metaphors that employ clothing. Thus the section opens with the symbolism of a rotted and decayed linen loincloth and closes with the shameful image of a skirt being pulled up over the face of a woman. Uniting the subsection of 13:15–27 is the repeated use of feminine singular verbs and pronouns. That is, although the king is mentioned in 13:18, most of this poetic subsection is presented as if spoken to a woman, perhaps the personified Jerusalem but more likely the queen mother, also mentioned in 13:18.

Historical and Cultural Background

"Perath" (13:4) is the name of a small town not far from Jerusalem, only three miles northeast of Jeremiah's hometown of Anathoth. Ironically, however, it is also the Hebrew word used to refer to the Euphrates River, the primary river of Babylonia, which flows right through Babylon. In fact, several English translations translate *perat* in this verse as "the Euphrates" (ESV, NASB, NRSV, KJV). Yet in almost all instances where *perat* refers to the Euphrates River the word for "river" is included. Here the text has *perat* only. Also the Judahite town of Perath is only a few miles from Jerusalem, where Jeremiah is when God speaks to him, while the River Perath (i.e., the Euphrates) is seven hundred miles away. A trip by Jeremiah to and from the Euphrates River probably would have taken about eight months. For these two reasons, most scholars conclude that in this verse "Perath" refers to the town near Anathoth.[1] On the surface, "Perath" in this verse probably does refer to the small Judahite town. But certainly the dual possibility of meaning for this word is no accident, and there is probably a not-too-subtle wordplay taking place here, one that would be obvious to Jeremiah and his audience. The mention of the small town of Perath certainly brings to mind, or perhaps even symbolizes, the River Perath (Euphrates River) in Babylonia, where the people of Judah soon will be exiled.

Interpretive Insights

13:1 *Go and buy a linen belt.* This probably is a "loincloth" (NRSV) that covered from the waist to the knees. It generally served as an undergarment. There are several different Hebrew words used for "linen" in the Old Testament, the difference probably relating to the quality or grade of the material. The word used here is for the more common linen cloth and not the extremely high-priced, bleached-white kind of linen.

13:7 *I went to Perath and dug up the belt . . . but it was ruined.* Cast off from regular use as an undergarment and buried in the ground, the linen loincloth quickly deteriorates and becomes worthless. Just as this loincloth leaves its owner (Jeremiah) and becomes ruined near Perath (a town near Jerusalem), so the people of Judah and Jerusalem, like God's loincloth, will be cast off near the River Perath (i.e., the Euphrates River in Babylonia) and ruined.

13:9 *I will ruin the pride of Judah and the great pride of Jerusalem.* The word translated as "ruin" is the same word used in 13:7. The word translated as "pride," when referring to nations and cities, connotes the things that the nations take pride in: their wealth, their power, the magnificence of their buildings and fortifications. Jerusalem, in particular, with its spectacular temple and powerful fortifications, was a source of great pride.

13:11 *For as a belt is bound . . . so I bound all the people of Israel and . . . Judah to me . . . to be my people for my renown and praise and honor.* Speaking figuratively, God states that the people of Israel and Judah were to him like a loincloth, very close and intimate, and in a position to be part of the great glory and honor that surround God, the one who wore the loincloth. But they rejected this great honor, sought pride and glory from themselves, and thus were ruined altogether.

13:12 *Every wineskin should be filled with wine.* This probably is a well-known proverb. The meaning of the word translated as "wineskin" is uncertain, but the reference likely is to special clay pots (rather than "skins") made specifically to hold wine.

13:13 *I am going to fill with drunkenness all who live in this land.* In 25:15–38 wine is used as a symbol of God's wrath. Making the people drink this wine is analogous to having them experience God's wrathful judgment. The imagery here in 13:13 is similar. God will pour out so much wine (his wrath) that they will all be very drunk.

the kings who sit on David's throne, the priests, the prophets, and all those living in Jerusalem. This list introduces and summarizes all those who will oppose Jeremiah and the word of God in the chapters to come. In the midst of this harsh judgment text, the mention of David's throne provides an allusion to God's covenant with David (2 Sam. 7), a primary basis of hope beyond the judgment. In the ancient Near East, prophets usually were in the employment of the king, and as such they normally tried to please the king. Thus it was highly irregular for a prophet to condemn his king.

13:14 *I will smash.* The word translated as "smash" means "to shatter" or "dash to pieces."

I will allow no pity or mercy or compassion. This underscores the seriousness of the sin and the certainty of the coming judgment.

13:15 *do not be arrogant.* The word translated as "arrogant" means "to be high or exalted." This continues the theme of pride and arrogance versus shame and dishonor.

13:16 *darkness.* Darkness is frequently used in Jeremiah to describe the coming judgment. Several descriptive terms relating to darkness are used in this poetic verse (darkness, darkening hills [lit., "hills of the evening twilight," perhaps a reference to shadows], utter darkness, deep gloom [lit., "a heavy cloud"]).

13:17 *I will weep in secret . . . because the* LORD'*s flock will be taken captive.* Jeremiah is the speaker in this verse. The imagery of the king as shepherd and the people as his sheep was a fairly common one both in the Bible and throughout the ancient Near East. Jeremiah points out, however, that the flock is really the Lord's (13:17) and yet has been entrusted to the ruling monarch (13:20).

13:18 *the king and . . . the queen mother.* This probably refers to King Jehoiachin and his mother, Nehushta. Jehoiachin came to the throne at the age of eighteen. He and his mother were taken into exile by the Babylonians in 597 BC (2 Kings 24:8–17; Jer. 22:26; 29:2). Several mothers of kings are mentioned in 1–2 Kings, suggesting that they continued to be powerful individuals after their sons came to the throne.

13:20 *Look up and see.* As in this verse, most of the verbs and pronouns in 13:20–27 are feminine singular, probably referring to the queen mother in 13:18 or, less likely, to Jerusalem.

13:21 *special allies.* At various times during Jeremiah's ministry the kings of Judah thought that both Babylon and then Egypt were "special allies." In fact, first Egypt and then Babylon subdued Judah to their control.

13:22 *your skirts have been torn off.* The terrible fate of Jerusalem at the hands of the invading Babylonians is compared to a woman being raped. Remember that God frequently compares Jerusalem's idolatry to marital unfaithfulness, even prostitution (13:27).

13:23 *Can an Ethiopian change his skin?* The word translated by the NIV as "Ethiopian" is *kush*. This proverb is thus referring to people from the African kingdom of Cush. This kingdom straddled the Nile River, to the immediate south of Egypt in what is now modern Sudan. It is not the same region as that occupied by Ethiopia today. The people from Cush were Africans with dark skin. The noticeable presence of Cushites in Jerusalem of Jeremiah's day is evidenced by the heroic actions of Ebed-Melek the Cushite in 38:7–13; 39:15–18. The point in 13:23 is that Cushites cannot change their characteristic black skin, and leopards cannot change their characteristic spots. It is equally impossible for the people of Judah and Jerusalem to change from their characteristic evil ways to good ways.

13:25 *you . . . trusted in false gods.* Literally, this reads, "you trusted in the lie [*sheqer*]." The word *sheqer* occurs thirty-seven times in Jeremiah (e.g., 7:4; 23:14, 25). It is a singular noun, but probably it is used here to personify the complex of lies and deceit common in Jerusalem. While idolatry certainly is a central part of the lies and falsehood being taught and believed in Jerusalem, the deception is much broader than that, and this word suggests a wide range of lies—for example, that Jerusalem could never be conquered and destroyed; that the weak could be oppressed with impunity; and that adultery, child sacrifice, and pagan worship were acceptable.

Theological Insights

God often instructs Jeremiah, as well as other prophets (cf. Ezek. 4), to communicate to the people through symbols and acted-out dramatic lessons. Besides the linen belt, for example, Jeremiah also smashes a pot (19:10) and wears a yoke (27:2). This kind of presentation of God's word does not happen just because God is a visual and effective communicator; rather, it seems that he also has a powerful but poetic sense of justice and likes to describe his judgments as memorable "punishments that fit the crime." Jesus often follows in this tradition. In Mark 11:12–14, for example, he destroys a fruitless fig tree as a symbol of judgment on fruitless Jerusalem.

Also from this text (and throughout the Bible) we see how consistently God opposes human arrogance. He simply does not like prideful people. This particular sin seems to irritate God in a special way, and it sorely tries his patience.

Teaching the Text

Note the power of God's loincloth imagery. The people of Judah and Jerusalem had been in close, intimate relationship to him. He compares them to his inner garments. The stress in this image is on closeness. As part of God's wardrobe, the people would get to participate in and help to magnify God's great name and his glory. Yet they rejected this fantastic relationship in order to seek their own glory and honor. Thus they became like an old, rejected, and rotted cast-off garment, totally ruined. This has direct relevance for Christians today. Do we seek our own glory through our relationship with God? Do we arrogantly look for glory and honor through our own status and accomplishment? Are we flippant and nonchalant about the wonderful close and intimate relationship that we can have with God? Do we treasure this as our most highly prized possession, or do we casually cast it aside?

It is also important to note that arrogance and pride are most clearly evident when people decide that they have the power to determine what true religion is and how they should behave ethically. There are many today, even some under the umbrella of Christianity, who look to themselves, along with accepted cultural norms, to define what kind of "god" they choose to worship and how they choose to behave. They reject the revealed word of God as an appropriate guideline and embrace the "lie" of our age: that each person can determine alone what is true in regard to religion.

Even within the church, it is critical to realize how much God despises pride and arrogance, especially in regard to how church members treat one another. From this text in Jeremiah, we see how influential leaders are in this regard. Within churches today leaders set the tone for godly and proper humility or for pride and arrogance. The leaders in the church will serve as models for the members.

Illustrating the Text

Pride goeth before a fall.

Scripture: "Pride goeth before a fall" is a cultural expression derived from Proverbs 16:18.

History: South of Fredericksburg, Virginia, on a grassy field in the town just outside Spotsylvania, is a plaque commemorating the spot where Major General John Sedgwick was killed by a bullet from a Confederate sharpshooter. As the general examined the line of Union soldiers, he was repeatedly warned not to stand in that location because he might be shot by Confederate sharpshooters concealed in the woods some five hundred yards away. "I'm ashamed of you," scolded Sedgwick. "They couldn't hit an elephant at this distance." Shortly thereafter a bullet struck him in the face and killed him instantly.

News Story: Lance Armstrong was the golden boy of professional cycling after winning the Tour de France a record seven times, as well as overcoming stage-three testicular cancer. On numerous occasions he was asked if he had ever used performance-enhancing drugs, and he repeatedly denied it. "I have never doped," Armstrong insisted in 2012. "I have competed as an endurance athlete for 25 years with no spike in performance, passed more than 500 drug tests and never failed one."[2]

Then, in January 2013, in an interview with Oprah Winfrey, he came clean, admitting to having used banned substances to enhance his cycling performance throughout his career. He was subsequently stripped of his medals.[3]

Following False Prophets Can Be Fatal

Big Idea
Devastating judgment will fall on false prophets and those who listen to them.

Key Themes
- A terrible drought and famine will be part of the judgment coming on Judah.
- God will not accept shallow religious ritual in place of true worship and obedience.
- God will judge the false prophets who mislead people in his name.
- God holds the people accountable for listening to the false prophets, and both will experience the same severe judgment.

Understanding the Text

The Text in Context

In light of the broken covenant proclaimed in Jeremiah 11, Jeremiah's role as prophet and intercessor now has to be reclarified. This theme will dominate the next two sections (14:1–16; 14:17–15:9) as Jeremiah and God dialogue over the issues of deserved judgment and prophetic intercession. The intercession of Moses to save Israel from God's wrath after the episode of the golden calf (Exod. 32) hovers in the background of both sections.

This passage is composed of two parallel subsections, the first one in poetry (14:1–10), the second in prose (14:11–16). These are two dialogues between Jeremiah and God, both covering the same basic topic. The first dialogue exchange is done poetically; that is, God and Jeremiah exchange poems. The second dialogue exchange is a more normal prose dialogue, complete with conversation markers such as "the LORD said." Connecting the two subsections is the repetition of "this people" in 14:10, 11. The parallel structure of the two dialogues can be illustrated as follows:

Dialogue Content	Dialogue 1	Dialogue 2
God gives a description of the coming judgment.	14:1–6	14:11–12

Dialogue Content	Dialogue 1	Dialogue 2
Jeremiah pleads for a reprieve for the people.	14:7–9	14:13
God answers with strong reasons for judgment.	14:10	14:14–16

Historical and Cultural Background

Both the Bible and nonbiblical historical records from the ancient Near East indicate that court "prophets" (numerous different technical terms are used for these prophet-like "advisers") who functioned as intermediaries between the pagan kings and their gods were fairly common in royal courts throughout the region. In anticipation of this, God had given clear guidelines requiring that false prophets be put to death (Deut. 18:14–22),[1] but the stipulations of Deuteronomy had received little concern from the people of Jerusalem since the death of Josiah early in Jeremiah's ministry. Instead, the royal court in Jerusalem now included numerous "court prophets" according to the model set by its neighboring pagan kingdoms.

Interpretive Insights

14:2 *Judah mourns . . . a cry goes up from Jerusalem.* Judah and Jerusalem are personified. They are mourning and crying out because of the great drought, described in the verses that follow.

14:3 *The nobles send their servants for water.* Neither the regular Hebrew word for "noble, lord" nor for "servant" is used in this verse. The word translated as "nobles" literally means "the majestic ones," and the word translated as "servants" literally means "insignificant ones" or "little ones." The term "majestic ones" probably reflects a little sarcasm from God, as there is not much that is majestic about them once the drought brings them to their knees.

they cover their heads. This exact same phrase is also used of the farmers in 14:4. In the ancient world a common posture for mourning was to cover one's head with one's arms.

14:7 *Although our sins testify against us.* Several similar-sounding Hebrew words are placed together in this phrase (*'awonenu 'anu banu*). The Hebrew word for "sin" used here connotes not so much the idea of "rebellion" or "falling short" as the nuance of "iniquity." The word translated as "testify" is a very common one that simply means "to answer, respond." In a court or trial setting, it would mean "to testify."

do something, Lord, for the sake of your name. Jeremiah knows that he is on flimsy legal ground asking God for a reprieve from his judgment, since the covenant is broken. He mentions God's "name" twice (14:7, 9). Jeremiah seems to be implying that perhaps God's name or his glory will be diminished if Judah, which bears his name, is destroyed. In 14:10 God responds by saying no, and then in 14:11 he admonishes Jeremiah not to intercede for these people in this way anymore.

14:9 *You are among us . . . do not forsake us!* Jeremiah knows that the presence of God in their midst is a critical component of their relationship with God. The word translated as "forsake" often carries the nuance of "to rest," but it can also mean, as it does here, to "leave behind," "to abandon and walk away from." In 14:7–9 Jeremiah pleads for God to save them and not leave them, in spite of their sin.

14:11 *Do not pray for the well-being of this people.* The word translated as "pray" carries strong connotations of "intercessory prayer." Since the covenant is broken, judgment is inevitable, and God tells Jeremiah to cease interceding for the people, a theme that will carry over into Jeremiah 15. "Well-being" is a translation of the word *tob*, a word with a wide range of meaning, but basically meaning "good." This word is quite frequently used as the opposite of *ra'ah* ("disaster, calamity, bad stuff"), a word that we have seen repeatedly in Jeremiah. These opposites open (14:11) and close (14:16) God's answer to Jeremiah. Do not pray for their *tob* ("good"), God tells Jeremiah in 14:11, because God is going to pour out their own *ra'ah* ("bad stuff"; NIV: "calamity") back upon them.

14:12 *Although they fast . . . offer burnt offerings and grain offerings.* One of the themes running throughout Jeremiah is the fact that religious rituals do not cover over serious violations of the covenant such as idolatry and immorality. Rituals are to be the means to enhance the relationship with God. Once the relationship is shattered and the very basis of the relationship is violated, the rituals of the covenant are meaningless.

sword, famine and plague. This triad occurs frequently in Jeremiah and summarizes the coming judgmental events. Droughts, invading and ravaging armies, and long sieges all produce famine and plagues. The Babylonians, to be sure, will kill thousands with "the sword" as they destroy the cities of Judah, but the consequences of war (famine and plague), exacerbated by drought, will also take their toll. All these terrible judgments are predicted in the "curses" of Deuteronomy 28:15–68.

14:13 *The prophets keep telling them, "You will not see the sword or suffer famine."* Repeatedly in the book of Jeremiah the false prophets deny the serious sin of the people. Thus they also deny the coming judgment on that sin, as they predict peace instead (e.g., 5:12). This is part of the great "lie" (*sheqer*) that Jeremiah mentions so frequently (14:14).

14:16 *And the people they are prophesying to . . . no one to bury them . . . their wives, their sons and their daughters.* In 14:13 Jeremiah seems to try to say that it is not the fault of the people, because the false prophets have been misleading them. God, however, will have none of this blame-shifting. The false prophets were merely saying what the people wanted to hear, and it was the people's inclination to believe what they wanted to believe that drove this downward spiral. Listening to the false prophets' promise of peace was simply a way of denying the reality of their sin and guilt.

I will pour out on them the calamity they deserve. As mentioned above, the word translated as "calamity" is *ra'ah* ("disaster, calamity, bad stuff"), used frequently throughout Jeremiah. Literally, this verse reads, "I will pour out upon them their *ra'ah*." The implications of how God uses this word in this verse, as in several other places in Jeremiah, are that if the people choose to break the covenant by doing *ra'ah*, then God will do *ra'ah* to them. Some translations will often render *ra'ah* as "evil," but since this word is used frequently of both the people's actions and of God's actions (often in wordplay), a more consistent translation would be something like "bad stuff" or "bad-consequence action." Also, as mentioned above, *ra'ah* is the opposite of *tob* ("good, well-being"), and thus this verse parallels 14:11 and concludes this subsection.

Theological Insights

The judgment of famine and drought, so graphically depicted in 14:1–6, had been clearly presented to Israel in Deuteronomy 28:22–24 as a certain consequence if the people abandoned the Mosaic covenant and turned away from God. Thus Jeremiah is not introducing a new concept or new theological doctrine to them. There was nothing fuzzy or ambiguous about the responsibilities of Israel under the Mosaic covenant. In Deuteronomy 28 God had been redundantly clear to the Israelites about the terrible judgments that would fall on them if they rejected him and ignored his covenant guidelines. Throughout the book of Jeremiah practically all the aspects of God's wrath and judgment that Jeremiah describes come directly from Deuteronomy 28. There is nothing arbitrary or confusing about why judgment comes and how terrible it is. This is a continuous theological theme running throughout the Old Testament and into the New Testament, climaxing in the book of Revelation, where many of these same judgments reappear.

Teaching the Text

Throughout Jeremiah the people of Judah and Jerusalem have consistently and repeatedly defied God and rejected his gracious offer of restoration and deliverance. The notion that God will judge such people is not some new or mysterious doctrine. It is a standard, consistent message of God proclaimed throughout both Testaments and preached by the church for two millennia. There is no ambiguity about this. Jeremiah merely restates with unmistakable clarity what had already been made clear in Deuteronomy. Likewise today, as a critical part of the gospel, we need to be very clear in regard to the consequences of continued sin against God.

God tells Jeremiah that even though these people are fasting and offering sacrifices, he will not listen to them or accept their sacrifices. Now as then, people cannot ignore God, live willfully rebellious and sinful lives, and then think that by observing some simple rituals on the day of worship they will be all right. For those within the covenant, who have trusted Christ and now walk with God in obedience, religious ritual is a means to enhance their relationship, a means to worship and fellowship. For those without a covenant relationship with God, however, religious ritual is meaningless. It certainly does not cover up or "offset" rebellion and sin against God. Shallow and hypocritical ritual will not avert the coming judgment.

As repeated several times in Jeremiah, God expresses how furious he becomes when people teach lies in his name. This is a strong reminder to all who preach, teach, or write about God and his word that God absolutely insists that we represent his word accurately and without any distortion based on our personal agendas or illusions. God is very emphatic about this. Preachers, teachers, and writers should prayerfully and studiously strive to understand his word and what he wants to say through it.

Jeremiah suggests to God that perhaps the people cannot be blamed for their sin, since their leaders have been misinforming them. God, however, rejects this line of argumentation completely. The people are not excused for believing the lies propagated by their leaders, and their judgment will be fair and deserving, even as it is devastating and terrible. The world today certainly abounds with false teachings and false religious ideas, and for people growing up in contexts where these lies are widely accepted, it can appear difficult for them to navigate clearly to the truth. But God reminds us that leading them to the truth must be our goal. People who are taught false religious ideas by their parents and/or religious community leaders are still responsible for their sin and will perish in their sin, unless we lead them to repentance and faith in Christ.

Illustrating the Text

Religious ritual on its own is meaningless to God.

Prayer: We teach our children to pray by saying simple prayers such as "Now I lay me down to sleep . . ." or "Lord, bless this food and drink." Such prayers begin to teach our children that no matter what happens, we are under the watchful loving care of our Father in heaven. The problem is that rather than growing and maturing in their faith, too many adults ritualistically mouth the prayers they learned as children without realizing that what God wants is a relationship, not ritual.

Analogy: Magicians often use magic words such as "abracadabra" or "hocus pocus" before they complete their tricks, giving the illusion that there is some special power in the words themselves. In the same way, some people believe that if they just say the right words, or do the right thing, or jump through the right religious hoop, they can pacify God and avoid the coming judgment.

In Jeremiah's day the people of Jerusalem believed that they could appease God's wrath by following the temple rituals. They saw God as the eternal scorekeeper, and therefore they wanted to do the things that they thought would win God's favor.

The Limits of Old Covenant Intercession

Big Idea

God mourns for unrepentant people, who must be judged.

Key Themes

- God suffers and weeps over the terrible destruction that falls on Jerusalem.
- Jeremiah tries to intercede for the people, but God tells him that no one can intercede for them now.
- God has been patient with the sinful behavior of Jerusalem for a long time, and now judgment can no longer be averted.
- Bereavement will be widespread because Jerusalem has rejected God and will not repent.

Understanding the Text

The Text in Context

This passage is similar to the preceding one (14:1–16) in that both contain intercessory pleas from Jeremiah on behalf of the people, followed by God's explanation that it is too late for any human intercession. In Jeremiah 11 God proclaimed that Judah had shattered and annulled the covenant relationship. In the present section Jeremiah pleads with God to keep the covenant intact and not to annul it (14:21). But the covenant is broken, and one of the consequences of the broken covenant is that there is no longer any basis for intercessory prayer from Jeremiah the prophet. There is no intercessor who can smooth things over and avert the judgment. The judgment is coming, and it is inevitable. This is the central theme of Jeremiah 14–15.

In 14:17–18 God weeps over the terrible tragedy that falls on his beloved people. Jeremiah speaks next, confessing the sin of the nation and pleading with God to keep the covenant intact and to deliver them (14:19–22). God, however, tells Jeremiah that it is too late for intercession; not even Moses or Samuel could avert this grisly judgment. God then addresses personified Jerusalem, telling her that since she has rejected him and turned away from him, he will bring terrible bereavement and destruction on her (15:5–9).

This passage opens and closes with parents anguishing over the tragic loss of their children. God is the "parent" at the beginning (14:17), and the mothers of Judah and Jerusalem are the ones anguishing at the end (15:8–9).

Historical and Cultural Background

Manasseh (reigned 687–642 BC) was the son of Hezekiah, a fairly good king, and the grandfather of Josiah, also a good king. According to 2 Kings 21:1–18, however, Manasseh was one of the very worst kings ever in Judah. He initiated and popularized many of the terrible pagan practices that Jeremiah preaches against still in his day (pagan altars in the temple, child sacrifices, etc.). Judah never recovered theologically from the pagan stamp that Manasseh left on the country. His grandson Josiah could only delay the judgment by his valiant attempt to reform the nation. The negative momentum could not be reversed, and upon Josiah's death Judah reverted right back to the idolatrous worship popularized by Manasseh, and thus God promises to destroy Judah and exile the people from the land (2 Kings 23:26–27).[1]

Interpretive Insights

14:17 *Let my eyes overflow with tears.* Using strong anthropomorphic language, God says literally, "Let tears go down from my eyes night and day."

for the Virgin Daughter, my people, has suffered a grievous wound. The phrase "my people" implies that God probably is the speaker in 14:17–18. This verse can be translated as it is here ("the Virgin Daughter, my people"), where daughter and people are equated, or it can be translated as "the virgin daughter of my people," in which case the "daughter" probably is a reference to Jerusalem. Either way, note the fluidity of God's figurative imagery. Throughout Jeremiah God describes Jerusalem and the people of Judah as a cold-hearted, unfaithful, and betraying prostitute. Here, however, he speaks as a sorrowful parent who remembers the innocence of his child.

14:18 *sword . . . famine . . . a land they know not.* There are three terrible components of the judgment running throughout Jeremiah 14–15. The Babylonians will invade and kill thousands of people (sword). Between the drought that God sends and the complete destruction of agricultural production due to the invasion (along with long city sieges), famine will also take thousands of lives. Finally, most of those who survive the sword and the famine will be taken into exile. These same judgments are underscored in 15:2.

14:19 *Have you rejected Judah completely? Do you despise Zion?* The speaker is now Jeremiah, and he cries out to God regarding the judgment. "Zion" is a reference to Jerusalem.

14:20 *We acknowledge our wickedness . . . we have indeed sinned against you.* Jeremiah offers a prayer of confession on behalf of the people. The problem is that this confession is only Jeremiah's. The people never confess their sins and repent. Jeremiah cannot cover their sin with his intercessory prayer.

14:21 *For the sake of your name do not despise us.* This is the same argument that Jeremiah used in 14:7–9. Jeremiah is implying that destroying the "people of God" will somehow tarnish God's name.

Remember your covenant with us and do not break it. The covenant mentioned here is the Mosaic covenant, which God made with the Israelites when he saved them from Egypt. The heart of this covenant is expressed in the book of Deuteronomy. The word translated as "break" is *parar*, the same word used in 11:10. It means "to annul, render invalid." The people of Jerusalem and Judah have already annulled and shattered this covenant (11:10), but here Jeremiah pleads with God to continue to honor it.

14:22 *Do any of the worthless idols of the nations bring rain?* Baal, one of the primary gods in the Canaanite pantheon, was the god of thunderstorms and rain. As part of his "confession" on behalf of the people, Jeremiah alludes to the fact that only God can bring rain, not Baal or any other god. The word translated as "worthless" is *hebel*. It has connotations of something that looks real but is only an illusion, like cloud vapor. It is used of the idols three times in Jeremiah 10 (vv. 3, 8, 15).

15:1–2 *Even if Moses and Samuel were to stand before me.* Several times during the exodus, Moses interceded effectively on behalf of the disobedient people (see especially Exod. 32:11–14). Likewise, in 1 Samuel 7:9 Samuel "cried out to the Lord on Israel's behalf, and the Lord answered him." Yet things are different now. God has patiently endured Israel's blatant apostasy for years and years. He has given the people repeated gracious opportunities to repent and be restored, all of which they have rejected with hostility. The time for any possible intercession is over, and the time for judgment has arrived.

Send them away . . . "Where shall we go?" . . . ""to death . . . to the sword . . . to starvation . . . to captivity."" The language used in 15:1 suggests an ironic allusion to the exodus. Here, however, they will not be "sent away" (same word as in "let my people go") to the wonderful promised land, but rather "sent away" to death or exile. The three grim options listed in 14:18 (sword, famine, exile) are repeated here.

15:3 *four kinds of destroyers.* Ironically, the word translated as "kinds" means "families" or "clans." In the Old Testament the number "four" often conveyed the nuance of "completeness." Thus the four horrible fates described in 15:2 (death, sword, starvation, and captivity) and the four terrible destroyers in 15:3 (sword, dogs, birds, and wild animals) serve to stress the total completeness of the coming destruction.

15:6 *You have rejected me.* There is a strong grammatical stress on "you." Throughout 15:5–6 the pronouns "you" are feminine singular, referring to Jerusalem.

I am tired of holding back. The word translated as "holding back" means "to relent" or "to change one's mind." A more literal reading is "I am weary of relenting." God has delayed and postponed the judgment repeatedly, and this delay in justice has "wearied" him.

15:8 *I will make their widows more numerous than the sand of the sea.* In Genesis 22:17 God uses the sand of the sea as an image of how numerous Abraham's descendants will be. It was part of the tremendous blessing that God promised Abraham. This verse no doubt alludes to that promise, but in ironic contrast the image is now used of the judgment instead of the blessing. It is now "widows" who are as numerous as the sand.

Theological Insights

Not surprisingly, the portrayal of God's character in the book of Jeremiah is complex and deep. On the one hand, we hear God expressing his anger and pouring out his wrath on Judah and Jerusalem for their terrible and cold-hearted betrayal of him. Yet God goes to great lengths to underscore how deserved this judgment is; in fact, his justice demands that this judgment occur. Then here in this passage we see God weeping over the fate of the people. It is almost as if God himself, even in his empathy for the people, cannot back away from bringing judgment because of his justice. Therefore, as he explains to Jeremiah, since God's own love and compassion will not avert the judgment, it is unlikely that Jeremiah's empathy will be able to do so.

Furthermore, the character of God revealed in Jeremiah is in strong contrast to the portrayal of other gods in the ancient Near East of Jeremiah's day. It would be very unusual for a god to destroy his people, since they were the ones who cared for his needs through the rituals of the temple. Likewise, there is no precedent in the ancient Near East of a god who cared so much for his rebellious people that he would weep over them.

Teaching the Text

In the opening verses we see God weeping over his people as they suffer the inevitable consequences of their sin. The book of Jeremiah is dominated by images and oracles of judgment, but here God opens up and shares how much he suffers for his people even when they turn against him and experience his wrath. This emotional side of God—hurting when he is betrayed and weeping when his people are punished—is an important part of his eternal character, and since he reveals it to us repeatedly in Jeremiah, it seems to be something that he wants us to grasp. God is not an emotionless entity, like a great supercomputer or like "the Force" in the *Star Wars* movies. He is like a parent with a wayward child or like a husband with an unfaithful wife, one who is hurt because of our sin and then who suffers with us if we continue obstinately to disobey and thus to receive the necessary punishment. This is part of God's character revealed to us consistently both in the Old Testament and in the New Testament.

Jeremiah tries his best to intercede effectively for the rebellious people, but since the covenant basis for intercession has been ended, and since the judgment on these people is long overdue, his intercession is invalid and ineffective. The intercession of Jesus Christ for people today, however, is absolutely effective because Jesus is not only the perfect intercessor but also the one who establishes a new covenant relationship between God and estranged people. Yet in order for people to enter into this new covenant relationship and to enjoy the blessings of Jesus's intercession on their behalf, they must repent and accept his offer. In this sense, the situation is similar to that in Jeremiah's day. Even though he tried, Jeremiah could not repent on behalf of the people in Jerusalem. God required that each of them personally repent of his or her sins and turn to him. Likewise today, neither parents, friends, nor pastors can repent on behalf of wayward people. They must repent of their sins themselves and then turn to Christ and accept his offer of salvation.

An ironic side issue to note is that Jeremiah's repeated attempts to intercede come in the middle of a larger unit (Jer. 11–20) that stresses the persecution and hostility that he receives from the leaders and people of Jerusalem. He tries to save them and pleads to God on their behalf, but at the same time they plot against him. As seen in the New Testament, Jesus will face a similar reaction from many of the Jews, particularly the Jewish leaders, even as he tries to save them. Likewise today, it is sad and tragically ironic that those Jesus came to save often reject him, ridicule him and his followers, and frequently take his holy name in vain. Often we will face severe opposition and ridicule from the very people we are trying to lead to salvation.

God underscores once again that when people reject him and choose a life of rebellion and sin, they will experience terrible judgment that will affect everyone. It will be sorrowful beyond imagination. The consequence of rebelling against God is not only the loss of his blessing but also trading in that blessing for a terrible judgment. This general principle continues to be true for everyone today who with hostility rejects God's great offer of salvation through Christ. This principle appears to be true not only for individuals but also for nations. If, for example, we analyze the United States in this context, the results are ominously negative.

Illustrating the Text

Now is the time to get right with God, before it is too late.

Object Lesson: For this lesson, you need a clear-glass bowl, some water, and two eggs, one fresh and one old. Some foods, such as meat and milk, develop a bad smell when they have gone bad. Other foods, such as bananas, turn a different color. But eggs smell and look the same even when old. So the best way to tell if an egg is edible is the water test. Put the egg in a bowl filled with water at least two inches deep. The fresh egg will sink, meaning that it is good to eat; but the old egg will float, meaning that it has gone bad and should not be eaten.[2] Not only foods but also things such as treasury bonds, automobile warranties, concert tickets, prescription medications—almost everything—has an expiration date. So do we. Now is the time to get right with the Lord, before it is too late.

History: There were fears that a problem in the coding of computers would create a major meltdown at midnight on December 31, 1999. Until the early 1990s, computer programmers abbreviated the four digits of the year using only the last two in order to save space in the computer memory. For this reason, many believed that when the year turned to double zeros at the year 2000, computers would understand it as 1900 and shut down.

This fueled widespread speculation that almost everything computer-related—banks, stock exchanges, elevators, telephones, medical equipment, government defense systems, and more—would simply shut down. Because the chaos was projected to begin the second the year 2000 began, it was referred to as the Y2K problem. Interestingly, because so many people believed that the Y2K problem would bring chaos that signaled the end of the world, there was a measurable uptick in church attendance on the last Sunday of December 1999. When the first day of 2000 arrived, and the predicted chaos did not happen, people lost their newfound sense of urgency to get right with God.

How would you live for the next month if you knew that Jesus was returning and the world would end in thirty days?

God's heart breaks for the lost.

Parenting: Ask the parents in the congregation if they have ever said the words "This is going to hurt me more than it hurts you" to their children. Did they mean it? Did their children believe it at the time? Sometimes disciplining our children is necessary despite the fact that it hurts us to do it.

Dealing with Discouragement

Big Idea

God dispels discouragement with his promise of deliverance and his empowering presence.

Key Themes

- Because of hostile opposition, Jeremiah cries out to God in discouragement.
- Jeremiah accuses God of misleading him into thinking that he would always be protected from such difficult times.
- God gently rebukes Jeremiah, telling him to be more careful about what he says.
- God reassures Jeremiah that those who oppose him will not triumph over him.
- God promises that his powerful presence will result in the prophet's protection and deliverance.

Understanding the Text

The Text in Context

The larger unit of Jeremiah 11–29 is connected by various themes that focus on Jeremiah's role as God's prophet in conflict with the rulers of Judah and Jerusalem as they turn hostile toward God's word and his spokesman. The point of connection between the preceding section (15:1–9) and the two that follow (15:10–21; 16:1–21) is the reference to "widows/wives" and "mothers." Jeremiah 15:1–9 closes by portraying how terrible the coming judgment will be from the viewpoint of wives and mothers (15:8–9). "Speaking of mothers," Jeremiah seems to say as the book moves to the next section (15:10–21), in which he cries out in discouragement, "I wish mine had never given birth to me." Then in 16:1–21 God picks up on the wife theme, forbidding Jeremiah to marry.

This passage is basically a dialogue between Jeremiah and God. Feeling overwhelmed by his opposition, Jeremiah cries out in despair that everyone hates him (15:10). God responds by telling Jeremiah that he has "good" planned for him (15:11). In the midst of the dialogue, God turns to address Judah (15:12–14), but his words to Judah are for Jeremiah's benefit; that is, his words to Judah are part of his answer to Jeremiah. In 15:15–18, apparently not satisfied with God's answer, Jeremiah complains about how hard his life has been, and then he accuses God of not giving him the support that he promised. Apparently, Jeremiah crosses over the line of appropriate lament, for God rebukes Jeremiah for questioning his faithfulness and then reminds the prophet that he will be sustained by God's own presence (15:19–21).

Interpretive Insights

15:10 *Alas, my mother, that you gave me birth.* The word translated as "alas" is *'oy*, which can carry the connotations of "alas" but more commonly means "woe." Literally, this text reads, "Woe to me, my mother, because you gave me birth." In similar fashion, Job in his despair cursed the day he was born (Job 3:1–3).

the whole land strives and contends! "The whole land" refers to the nation of Judah. Jeremiah speaks figuratively with mild hyperbole.

I have neither lent nor borrowed. There is humor here. It must be something of a universal principle that when neighbors loan things to each other, tension can arise. Sarcastically, Jeremiah asks how he could have alienated everyone in the country when he has not even borrowed anything from them or loaned anything to them.

yet everyone curses me. "Everyone" parallels "the whole land" in the first half of the verse. The word translated as "curses" means "to make light of," "to treat as small or insignificant," or "to belittle." It is the opposite of "to honor."

15:11 *Surely I will deliver you.* The word translated as "deliver" means "to loosen" or "to set free." In Job 37:3 it is used of God unleashing (setting free) the lightning.

for a good purpose . . . in times of disaster. "Good purpose" is a translation of *tob*, which basically means "good." "Disaster" translates *ra'ah*, which means "bad stuff, evil, disaster, calamity." These two words are opposites and are used together frequently throughout Jeremiah. It will be "good" for Jeremiah and "bad" for his enemies. Jeremiah will be "turned loose" or "set free" for "good" (i.e., to do good and to experience good), while when the "bad" comes, his enemies will plead with him for deliverance.

15:12 *iron from the north—or bronze?* "Can a man break iron . . . from the north?" is a clear reference to the fact that Judah will be unable to defeat the Babylonians. "Bronze" could also be a reference to the Babylonians, placed in parallelism with "iron." However, in light of the fact that later in this same passage God tells Jeremiah that he will make him as a "fortified bronze wall" to the people (15:20; see also 1:17–19, Jeremiah's call), the "bronze" reference seems to refer to Jeremiah. That is, the people of Judah cannot stand up against either the Babylonians (iron from the north) or Jeremiah the prophet (a bronze wall).[1]

15:13 *Your wealth and your treasures.* Jeremiah 15:13–14 bears strong similarity to 17:3–4 and 20:5. Conquering nations typically carried away the wealth of the defeated nation as plunder. Ironically, here God declares that he will give away Jerusalem's wealth for free. The fulfillment of this prophecy is described in detail in 2 Kings 24:13 (which appears to allude to the book of Jeremiah), as well as in 2 Kings 25:13–17 and Jeremiah 52:17–23.

15:15 Lord, *you understand.* There is grammatical stress on "you." A literal translation is "You, you know, O Yahweh." The word translated as "understand" has the basic meaning of "to know," and its occurrence here provides a strong contrastive connection to the same word in 15:14 ("in a land you do not know").

15:18 *You are to me as a deceptive brook, like a spring that fails.* The verb form here is emphatic, "Surely, you are to me" or "Most certainly, you have been to me." The word used here is not an actual Hebrew word for "brook" or "spring" but rather only the ambiguous term "waters." In this figure of speech Jeremiah is comparing God to a stream of water that looks as though it will always flow but then dries up and disappears (common in the arid areas around Israel). Literally, the ending phrase could be translated as "waters that are not faithful" or "waters that cannot be trusted." These are strong words that God does not take kindly to.

15:19 *If you repent, I will restore you . . . Let this people turn to you, but you must not turn to them.* The word *shub* ("to turn, return, repent") is used four times in this verse. The NIV translates it once as "repent," once as "restore," and twice as "turn."

that you may serve me. The concept of "serve" may be implied here, but this text literally reads, "that you may stand before me." In Israel, as throughout the ancient world, the prophets were believed to have direct access to the divine council chambers, where they would actually listen to the planning and receive messages and instructions from God. It is Jeremiah's role as the prophet (one who stands in the presence of God) that is in jeopardy here.

15:20 *a fortified wall of bronze.* Well-fortified cities in Judah at this time often had walls of stone, but frequently the top layers of the wall were mud brick. Archaeological excavations reveal the vulnerability of these walls. Their ruins testify to their inability to stop either the Assyrians or the Babylonians, who easily breached such walls by tunneling underneath them until they collapsed (called "sapping"). Using hyperbole, God tells Jeremiah that he will be like a wall made of bronze—something almost unimaginable, a wall infinitely strong and unassailable, one that could not be breached by battering with a ram or sapping. God seems to be encouraging Jeremiah by saying, "They will not topple you."

Theological Insights

At first it might seem surprising that God saw fit to include in the Bible this account of Jeremiah's struggle with discouragement and his doubting of God's faithfulness. Yet this theme is expressed in numerous places throughout Scripture. As in the book of Job, the implication is that in times of pain and confusion God's people can express their questions, doubts, and discouragements honestly to God, as long as they listen to his answer and move on. Likewise, in many of the individual lament psalms David cries out in discouragement, but he uses the lamenting process to work through his discouragement and to end up with a strong affirmation and declaration of praise for God's faithfulness to him.

Teaching the Text

Jeremiah is not a mythical superhuman hero; he is a real man with real fears, one who struggles with discouragement. Likewise, there are often difficult times in our lives when we can certainly relate to Jeremiah in this area. Like Jeremiah, even the strongest of us undergo discouragement sometimes and feel the need to cry out to God in pain or frustration. Sometimes the work that God has called us to do does not go as well as we thought it would. Likewise, as in Jeremiah's case, sometimes the "grind" of the work—the continued day-after-day struggle in a difficult situation—takes its toll and wears us down, causing us to doubt God or to wonder why he is not providing us with more direct help. Jeremiah teaches us that this is not to be completely unexpected. It is not evidence of particularly weak or immature faith but simply a reality of human frailty. Likewise, we should be alert to moods of discouragement in the lives of fellow servants of God, especially those whom we work with. We should try hard to encourage them and help them through those challenging times, supporting them and pointing them to God for strength.

The ministry of Jeremiah and his times of discouragement point out to us dramatically that serving the Lord faithfully does not always lead to popularity and success (from a human perspective). Often today those in ministry can get discouraged or have feelings of inadequacy if their ministry flounders or moves very slowly. It is important for us to remember that almost no one ever really listened to the message that Jeremiah preached. Humanly speaking, his ministry of reconciliation and his call to repentance were basically a flop. Yet he was carrying out the work that God had assigned to him. This underscores a very important lesson from Jeremiah. Sometimes God calls people to a service or ministry that will not be successful in human terms. Those who are faithfully serving God and doing the work to which he has called them should not grow discouraged if they see no significant evidences of success, as measured by human means (conversions, church numerical growth, etc.). They should stay focused on doing the work that God called them to. Obedience to the task that God has called us to is the measure of our success or failure.

It is perhaps also helpful to note that God responds rather strongly to Jeremiah's accusations. God seems to be willing to listen patiently to Jeremiah's complaints, but God does not tolerate Jeremiah's accusations of unfaithfulness and unreliability. The teaching here is similar to that in the book of Job and in many of the psalms of lament. The Scriptures seem to encourage us to pour out our hearts to God and speak honestly about our doubts, fears, and frustrations. But there are limits to this privilege, and accusations against God's faithfulness (Jeremiah) or his justice (Job) draw strong clarifying responses from God.

At the heart of God's reaffirmation to Jeremiah is his promise to sustain and empower him with powerful divine presence. Likewise, this is God's answer to our doubts, fears, and discouragement. It is God's powerful presence through the indwelling Holy Spirit that enables us to be strong and to do the tasks that he has assigned to us. It is also his powerful presence that reassures us and comforts us.

Facing serious discouragement, Jeremiah feels the pressure either to capitulate to the prevailing popular views or to withdraw from the conflict altogether. God, however, calls on him to stand his ground and see it through, drawing strength and encouragement from God's powerful presence. Similarly, in difficult times today we are not to give in to the difficulties and challenges, nor are we to run away and withdraw from the ministry to which God calls us. Rather, like Jeremiah, we are to carry on. Encouraged and sustained by God's presence, we are to endure the difficulties that face us and persevere in faithful service.

Illustrating the Text

Encouraged by God's presence, we can endure any difficulty.

Personal Experience: When my children were young, they were afraid to go out to my detached workshop in the backyard when it was dark, but they would gladly go if I went with them. My presence calmed their fears. Relate a similar experience from your own children or from your own childhood.

Bible: Many of the psalms of lament are communal complaints of Israel, but there are also individual laments, a few of which are considered protests of innocence such as Psalms 5; 7; 17; and 26. Here David cries out to God, protesting his innocence and challenging the fairness of the way he is being treated. For us, like David and Jeremiah, one of the best ways to work through our discouragement is to pour out our hearts to God while we remember his faithfulness in the past.

Bible: When Jesus taught his disciples how to pray, one petition that he taught them, now enshrined in what we know as the Lord's Prayer, is "Lead us not into temptation, but deliver us from evil" (Matt. 6:13). This petition can apply to those in ministry (either pastors or laypeople) who, like Jeremiah, go through times of discouragement and are tempted to quit or to do something that would be considered evil in the eyes of the Lord. The weight of ministry can be heavy particularly when we struggle with feelings of inadequacy. At such times, Jeremiah reminds us, God has not promised us success, but he has promised to be with us.

God challenges us to be faithful in the face of opposition.

Sports: The oldest continuously run road rally in North America is called "Press On Regardless." It began in 1949 as an event sponsored by the Detroit Region of the Sports Car Club of America. It is a TSD (time-speed-distance) event, which means that the winner is not the first person to cross the finish line but rather the one whose odometer and time stamps show that he or she drove the proper route at the right speed.[2]

It is the job of the driver and the navigator to figure out the correct speed and route of a predetermined course that covers over five hundred miles of unpaved roads in northern Michigan by interpreting the clues from various checkpoints along the way. The challenging nature of the event often results in the competitors getting lost or their vehicles breaking down, or both, which explains why the rally is called "Press On Regardless." The event is much like the walk of faith, which is often fraught with challenges and obstacles that must be overcome.

Weddings, Funerals, and the Future Multinational New Exodus

Big Idea

Even though some people will reject God and experience uncomforted and terrible judgment, others throughout the world will find a spectacular and wonderful salvation, even greater than the exodus.

Key Themes

- God tells Jeremiah not to marry, symbolizing the "end of joy and gladness" in Judah.
- God tells Jeremiah not to attend any funerals, symbolizing the end of comfort and consolation.
- Because the people have forsaken God, he withdraws his compassion and promises to expel them from the land.
- In the future there will be a great new exodus in which God restores his people along with the nations of the world.

Understanding the Text

The Text in Context

As mentioned earlier, the larger unit of Jeremiah 11–29 finds unity in the various aspects of Jeremiah's role as God's prophet in difficult times of conflict. In this current section (16:1–21), Jeremiah's role is to live out symbolically certain aspects of the dreadful coming judgment. Thus he is prohibited from marrying, attending funerals, or attending any festive gatherings, especially weddings. This is a rather ironic decree from God, especially in the context of the preceding passage (15:10–21), in which Jeremiah cries out in lonely discouragement. But note that at the end of this current section (16:1–21), Jeremiah reaffirms his trust in God as his strength and protection, while looking optimistically toward the time when even the nations will turn and recognize God.

The wife/widow/mother theme running throughout 16:1–9 connects this text to the two preceding passages. In 15:1–9 Jeremiah proclaims how terrible the coming judgment will be on wives and mothers. Then in 15:10–21 Jeremiah bemoans the day that his mother gave birth to him. In 16:1–9 God declares the end to joy and gladness, especially as exemplified in new marriages. Thus Jeremiah is ordered not to marry. Likewise, God tells Jeremiah not to attend funerals, for there will be no comfort for those who lose loved ones, even their fathers and mothers.

This coming judgment is a result of the people's abandonment of God and their embrace of other gods, actions that will result in their expulsion from the promised land (16:10–13). God then declares that in the future he will regather his people back into the promised land, an event that will overshadow the original exodus (16:14–15). In the meantime, however, since the people have so defiled God's land, they will be hunted down and punished (16:16–18). Jeremiah then prays to God, reaffirming his trust in God as his strength and protection (16:19–20). God affirms Jeremiah's statement, adding that he will teach the nations about his power and might so that they will know that he is the Lord (16:21).

Interpretive Insights

16:2 *You must not marry and have sons or daughters.* Hebrew has two different ways to make negative commands (prohibitions). The form used here reflects a permanent, long-term prohibition (as opposed to an immediate and specific prohibition). This is the same form used in the Ten Commandments.

16:4 *They will not be mourned.* The word translated as "mourned" refers to loud wailing or lamenting. This same word occurs in 16:5, 6.

will be like dung lying on the ground. A proper and respectful burial with an appropriate time of mourning was very important to the people of Israel and throughout the ancient world. Part of the judgment on the people of Judah was the fact that they would die without any proper burial (unburied bodies scattered across fields like cattle dung in a pasture; vultures, jackals and hyenas eating the bodies).

16:5 *because I have withdrawn my blessing.* The word translated as "withdrawn" means "to gather up and remove." It is used especially in regard to harvesting crops. The word translated as "blessing" is *shalom*, a term often translated as "peace." However, it carries a wider meaning and includes the totality of well-being. What God is about to gather up and carry away like a harvested crop is the entire peaceful and blessed situation that Israel has enjoyed in the promised land. Remember, ironically, that the false prophets had been promising continued "peace" (6:14; 8:11; 14:13), but God declares that he will remove his "peace," and in its place will be dead bodies lying in the fields like dung.

my love and my pity from this people. This is a devastating verse. God is also gathering up "the loyal, faithful love" (*hesed*, with a definite article) and "the compassions" (the Hebrew word is a plural of intensity). *Hesed* ("loyal, faithful love") is the primary term used to describe God's covenant relationship with his people. The implications of this withdrawal are reflected in God's calling them "this people" instead of "my people."

16:6 *Both high and low will die in this land.* The words translated as "high" and "low" in 16:6 are also used together in 6:13 and 8:10, where the phrase is translated as "from the greatest to the least." In 6:13 and 8:10 the range "high and low" or "greatest to least" is stressing that all the people, from the rich to the poor, are greedy and are implicated in the great "deceit." Here in 16:6 Jeremiah uses the same terms, recalling those indictments, to describe the extent of the upcoming massacre.

16:9 *I will bring an end to the sound of joy . . . gladness . . . voices of bride and bridegroom.* In 16:2 Jeremiah was told not to marry. Here in 16:9 God explains that joyful times such as weddings will cease as the judgment descends on Judah. Thus Jeremiah's actions (not marrying, etc.) become prophetic signs of judgment.

16:11 *your ancestors forsook me . . . They forsook me.* The twofold repetition of this phrase ("they forsook me") in this verse stresses how foundational and how serious this action was. The word translated as "forsook" means "to abandon" and implies the end of the relationship. The pronoun "me" is stressed.

16:12 *But you have behaved more wickedly than your ancestors.* The stress here is on "you." The verb translated as "have behaved more wickedly" is related to the noun *ra'ah* ("bad stuff, wickedness, disaster"). As in numerous other texts in Jeremiah (e.g., 11:1–17), there is a wordplay on *ra'ah* in this passage. The word is used in 16:10 ("Why has the LORD decreed such a great *disaster* against us?") and then twice in 16:12 ("you *have behaved more wickedly*" and "following the stubbornness of your *evil* hearts"). As in 11:1–17 (and elsewhere), it is the *ra'ah* of the people in Judah and Jerusalem that brings God's great *ra'ah* down upon them.

16:14 *who brought the Israelites up out of Egypt.* The primary salvation formula and divine relational statement in the Old Testament is "I am the LORD, who brought you up out of Egypt." Certainly the exodus event is the central paradigmatic saving action of God in the Old Testament. The promise here in 16:14, however, declares that the great future restoration will overshadow even the exodus and will thus become the new paradigmatic statement of deliverance and God's new relationship with his people.

16:15 *I will restore them.* Literally, "I will cause them to return" (from *shub*, "to turn, return").

16:19 *my strength and my fortress.* "Strength" (*'oz*) and "fortress" (*ma'oz*) translate words from the same Hebrew root.

to you the nations will come from the ends of the earth. In 16:15 God speaks of restoring the Israelites to their land in the future. Here that "new exodus" image is broadened to include all the nations (or "peoples") from the very ends of the earth, who come confessing that their gods are false. Thus Jeremiah mixes the restoration of Israel with the inclusion of the nations.

16:21 *Therefore, I will teach them.* "Them" refers back to the nations in 16:20.

they will know that my name is the LORD. The comparison with the exodus continues. In the book of Exodus the phrase "that they may know that I am the LORD" is repeated numerous times.

Theological Insights

Throughout the Old Testament the story of Moses and the exodus from Egypt serves as the paradigm or the synthesizing picture of salvation. This passage of Jeremiah includes numerous references to the exodus event that have theological significance. In 16:14–15 God reveals that the future regathering and restoration will actually replace the great exodus event as the paradigm of God's saving action. Then in 16:21 God declares that "they [i.e., the nations] will know that my name is the LORD." One of the central themes that God repeats throughout the book of Exodus is that everyone will "know that I am the LORD." He declares that the Israelites (and the foreign peoples who exit with them) will know him as the Lord in deliverance, while the Egyptians, who oppose him, will know him as the Lord in judgment. In contrast, here in 16:19–21 the nations are pictured as coming to God as part of the great restoration, and thus they will be taught of his great saving power and will know him as the Lord (in deliverance instead of judgment), while judgment will fall on Judah and Jerusalem, which will know him as the Lord in judgment.

Teaching the Text

In his role as God's prophet, Jeremiah is asked by God to carry out certain difficult actions (do not marry, do not attend funerals) that symbolize the coming judgment on the people in Jerusalem and Judah. The prophets Ezekiel and Hosea also carried out difficult symbolic actions that spoke to the people in their context (Ezek. 4:1–5:4; 12:3–7; 24:15–27; Hosea 1:2–9; 3:1–4). The revelation of God's message and the unfolding of God's plan certainly take priority over Jeremiah's personal life and the comforts that most people would expect. Likewise today, Jesus calls us to deny ourselves and take up our cross and follow him. Answering God's call and obediently serving him do not come with promises of a comfortable life. God often requires that sacrifices be made by those who serve him. It is his plan, not our comfort, that takes priority.

As highlighted in Jeremiah 11, the coming judgment is not simply a disciplinary event but rather a change in the relationship between God and Israel. The covenant is broken. Israel will lose not only the land but also God's presence and his loyal love, a devastating consequence. Likewise today, the rejection of Christ does not lead to a mere disciplinary action followed by "Plan B." It results in total alienation, judgment, and eternal separation from God.

In the midst of this, Jeremiah is able to look beyond the immediate disaster to see that time in the future when God's glorious deliverance will unfold. This deliverance will be even greater than the spectacular exodus event in the time of Moses. Even the foreign nations will recognize God and know him. Likewise, it is important for our encouragement to keep things in proper "big picture" perspective. There certainly are areas of the world today (including the United States) that are hostile to God and show no signs of repenting anytime soon. Yet there are numerous other regions of the world where Christianity is flourishing and spreading rapidly. When the hard, unresponsive regions tend to discourage us, we need to remind ourselves that God is moving powerfully in many other areas of the world. We should rejoice and find encouragement in that fact and maintain a global perspective of God's work in the world.

Illustrating the Text

Judgment and restoration are both part of God's promise.

Contrasting Concept: Rob Bell, the author of *Love Wins*, suggests in his book that even after we die, we will get a chance to repent and be welcomed into heaven.[1] This is merely a new spin on the concept of purgatory, and it was the subject of a striking debate between Bell and journalist Martin Bashir, which can be viewed on YouTube.[2] A clip showing portions of this debate might clarify what the Bible actually teaches about hell and judgment, and it would make a good teaching moment for this text. After the clip is shown, the observation can be made that there is no shortage of prophets in every generation who promise "peace" when God is promising "justice."

For those who want to explore this in more detail, a more in-depth study of what the Bible says about hell can be found in Francis Chan and Preston Sprinkle's book *Erasing Hell*.[3]

God promises to return and restore Israel.

History: During World War II the Nazis systematically set out to confiscate the priceless artwork of every nation that they conquered. An untold number of treasures were taken, many of which were lost or damaged, but thanks to a coalition of allied art experts, most of the stolen treasures were recaptured, repaired, and returned to their rightful owners. As late as February 2014, one of these stolen artifacts was returned to its rightful owner when US officials were made aware that the painting *St. Philip Baptizing a Servant of Queen Kandaki,* by eighteenth-century artist Johann Conrad Seekatz, was being sold by a New York auction house. The painting had been stolen from the Polish National Museum in Warsaw during World War II.[4] Since 2007, more than 7,150 artifacts have been returned to twenty-seven different countries. Just as the government continues to keep its promise of restoration, so too God will one day restore his people. It may take time, but God's promise of restoration will be realized.

Film: ***The Monuments Men.*** This 2014 movie, based on the book of the same name, narrates the story of the heroic men and women who risked their lives during World War II to restore artwork stolen by the Nazis to their rightful owners.

In Whom Do You Trust?

Big Idea

Trusting in God results in victory and blessing, whereas trusting in oneself results in defeat, God's wrath, and the loss of everything.

Key Themes

- The sin and rebellion of the people of Judah are engrained in their lives as permanently as inscriptions in stone.
- Trusting in one's own deceitful heart results in judgment and separation from God.
- Trusting in the power and faithfulness of God results in blessing.
- Jeremiah trusts in God by turning to him in times of persecution.
- Trusting in God includes faithfulness in money matters.

Understanding the Text

The Text in Context

This section in Jeremiah draws heavily from Exodus 31–34 (the Sabbath, the Ten Commandments etched on stone tablets, and the idolatry of the golden calf). At the very end of the preceding passage (16:21), God states that in the future restoration the nations "will know that my name is the LORD." As we noted in that section, the phrase "to know that I am the LORD" is tightly tied to the book of Exodus. Yet in Exodus 31:13–18 the concept of knowing the Lord is also directly connected to keeping the Sabbath. Thus the subsection in our present passage that deals with the Sabbath (17:19–27) probably is springing off that phrase, along with the other related references to Exodus in the previous section. Likewise, the Sabbath warning in Exodus 31 ends with a reference to the two tablets of stone, written by the finger of God (31:18), a text that is, no doubt, closely connected to the opening verse in Jeremiah 17.

There are numerous other aspects of the story in Exodus 31–34 that find parallels in Jeremiah 17. These include Sabbath instructions (Exod. 31:12–17; Jer. 17:19–27), inscribing on tablets (Exod. 31:18; 34:1, 4, 28–29; Jer. 17:1), negative attitude of the people toward God's spokesman (Exod. 32:1; Jer. 17:15–18), worship of idols (Exod. 32:2–6; Jer. 17:2), intervention of God's spokesman to save the people (Exod. 32:11–14; Jer. 17:15–16), references to the burning anger of God (Exod. 32:10–11; Jer. 17:4, 27), and references to altars and Asherah poles (Exod. 34:13; Jer. 17:2).

In Jeremiah 16:18 God declares, "They have defiled my *land* . . . and filled my *inheritance* with their detestable idols." Then God connects these same two terms inversely in 17:4, "You will lose the *inheritance* I gave you. I will enslave you . . . in a *land* you do not know."

The first two subsections (17:1–4, 5–11) are connected by the theme of "heart."

The opening (17:1–4) and the closing (17:19–27) subsections have several parallels that tie the unit together. As mentioned above, both of these subsections allude to Exodus 31:12–18. Also, "Judah's sin" is mentioned in 17:1, and then the people/kings of Judah are mentioned numerous times in 17:19–27. Also, references to "fire" open and close this section. The first subsection (17:1–4) ends with God saying, "You have kindled my anger [lit., "you have kindled a fire in my nose"—"nose" being a Hebrew idiom for anger], and it will burn forever." Then the final subsection (17:19–27) ends with "I will kindle an unquenchable fire in the gates of Jerusalem."

The first three subsections (17:1–18) are in poetry, while the closing subsection (17:19–27) is in prose. In 17:1–4 God declares that just as the Ten Commandments were etched in stone, so the idolatrous sin of the people of Judah is etched on their hearts. Then God explains that trusting in him results in blessing, whereas trusting in one's own strength and one's own deceitful heart will result in being cursed (17:5–11). Jeremiah speaks in 17:12–18. For him, trusting in God means exalting him and calling on him for protection from persecutors. Then God tells Jeremiah to stand in the gates of Jerusalem and declare that continued Sabbath violation will result in the destruction of the city's gates and occupation by foreign rulers (17:19–27).

Historical and Cultural Background

Asherah poles (17:2) were wooden poles that represented Asherah, the fertility "mother-goddess" and consort of Baal. They were often placed next to altars of Baal or syncretistically next to an altar of God. They were strictly forbidden, not only in Exodus (34:13) but also in Deuteronomy (12:3; 16:21).[1]

Interpretive Insights

17:1 *engraved with an iron tool, inscribed with a flint point.* These two phrases are in synonymous parallel. The word translated as "engraved" is the common Old Testament word for "to write" (the identical word used of

God writing the Ten Commandments), but the reference to the iron tool as the writing instrument indicates that this writing is done on stone or other very hard surface (i.e., their hard hearts). The word translated as "inscribed," however, is the primary word used in the Old Testament to refer to plowing. In Proverbs it is used several times with the word "heart" to mean "to devise, plan." Here it is used figuratively to mean "to inscribe," but when applied to the word "heart," it no doubt carries some added nuance of "devising" or "planning."

hearts. In the Old Testament the "heart" is the place where one makes decisions. It is not so much the center of emotion (as in English usage) as the center of decision making.

17:2 *Even their children.* The grammatical construction that the NIV translates as "even" often carries a temporal (time) nuance of "as" or "when," thus tightly connecting 17:1 and 17:2. The sin of the people of Judah is etched on their hearts (permanent) when their children (lit., "sons") participate in idol worship. That is, the permanence of their sin is established as they incorporate the next generation into the same idolatrous disobedience to God.

remember their altars and Asherah poles. One of the most central sins that Jeremiah proclaims against Judah is that they have "forgotten" God (2:32; 3:21; 13:25; 18:15; 23:27). In contrast, their children are "remembering" pagan altars and Asherah poles.

17:4 *my anger . . . will burn forever.* The "permanence" of God's anger (lit., "until forever") metaphorically matches the permanence of Judah's sin in 17:1.

17:5–8 *Cursed is the one who trusts in man.* This psalm-like passage (17:5–8) is very similar to Psalm 1, which likewise connects trusting in God with the most foundational aspects of well-being in life.

17:9 *the heart is deceitful . . . and beyond cure.* This connects back to the usage of "heart" in 17:5, where the one whose heart turns away from God is cursed. In Hebrew thought the heart was the center of volition, where one decides to obey or disobey. The word translated as "deceitful" comes from a fairly rare word that can mean "heel," "rough or treacherous ground," or "deceitful." The patriarch Jacob's name is based on a wordplay of this word: "the one who grasps the heel; the one who deceives" (Gen. 25:26; 27:36). The word translated as "beyond cure" occurs several times in Jeremiah (15:18; 17:9, 16; 30:12, 15). It means "to be seriously sick or injured."

17:10 *search the heart and examine the mind.* The Hebrew connotations of these two terms are the inverse of the connotations in English. That is, the "heart" is the seat of volition, where one makes decisions. The other term, although translated as "mind," literally means "kidneys" and is used to refer to the seat of emotion and affection.

17:13 *the spring of living water.* This same expression occurs in 2:13. "Living water" simply means that this is a flowing spring that bubbles up to the surface, in contrast to water in a well or cistern. Jesus uses this same analogy in John 4:14.

17:21 *Be careful not to carry a load on the Sabbath.* The word translated as "load" probably refers to sacks or jars of grain. Thus from the surrounding fields people probably were carrying in loads of grain to sell at or near the gate (17:21, 24, 27). The city inhabitants were carrying their empty jars from their houses to go buy the grain and then return to their houses (17:22). A similar violation was encountered later by Nehemiah (Neh. 13:15–19). Such commercial and work activity was a blatant violation of the Sabbath. Keeping the Sabbath was more than just one of the Ten Commandments; it was a sign of the relationship between God and Israel (Exod. 31:13, 17). That is, under the Mosaic covenant, keeping the Sabbath was synonymous with acknowledging that the Lord was Israel's God, and that Israel was in covenant relationship with him. It also lay at the heart of trusting in God for Israel's well-being.

17:25 *kings who sit on David's throne.* This alludes to God's covenant promise to David in 2 Samuel 7:1–17. God seems to patiently endure the extended idolatrous behavior and repeated disastrously poor leadership by the kings of Judah because of his promise to David.

17:27 *I will kindle an unquenchable fire.* In the opening section (17:1–4), the idolatry of the people of Judah kindles a figurative "fire" in God (his anger). Now, at the end of this passage, God's anger (kindled by Judah) results in a real fire that burns Jerusalem's gates and fortresses. This destruction was literally carried out by the Babylonians.

Theological Insights

The opening verses of this passage are part of an important theological sequence. In Exodus and Deuteronomy, God writes the Ten Commandments on tablets of stone. This is mentioned repeatedly (Exod. 24:12; 31:18; 32:15–19; 34:1–29; Deut. 4:13; 5:22; 9:9–17; 10:1–15). This establishes the Mosaic covenant. In Jeremiah 17:1, however, it is Israel's sin that is written on the tablets of the people's hearts, in effect shattering the covenant. God's great solution to this problem comes in Jeremiah 31:33, where as part of the new covenant he will write his law directly upon his people's hearts (instead of on stone tablets). One of the great characterizing features of the new covenant in Jeremiah 31 is forgiveness (31:34). Under the new covenant, God will forgive his people and empower them to be faithful, replacing the heart etched in sin with a heart etched with God's great Torah, the teaching about himself.

Teaching the Text

This passage is about trusting in God. One of the most foundational decisions that every person must make in life is whether his or her decisions will emerge from trust in God or from trust in self. This includes both mundane, day-to-day decisions and momentous, life-changing decisions.

Jeremiah 17:1–4 starts off with one of those momentous decisions. The tragedy of Judah's decision to worship idols is that the people were transmitting this apostasy down to the next generation and thus creating a permanent failure to trust in God. Through participation, the children will remember the idolatry (misplaced trust) of their parents and will in turn embrace this practice themselves, thus bringing God's wrath upon them. To learn from this negative example, we should be asking, "What will our children remember and emulate regarding where we place our trust?"

Next Jeremiah presents us with a wisdom-like psalm that gives sound, broad, generic advice about the wisdom of trusting in God and the foolishness of trusting in oneself (17:5–11). These are the general principles underlying the specific examples in the other three subsections of this passage. Living a life characterized by trust in God leads to a blessed life rather than a "cursed" life. Droughts (difficult times) will still come, but the person who trusts in God will be sustained by him during those tough times. This is solid wisdom for us today too.

Pulling us away from the wisdom of trusting in God is the basic deceitfulness of our hearts, which defiantly and arrogantly tells us that we can rely on ourselves. Such self-centered arrogance leads us to disobedience, falsely assuming that we know better than God does.

For Jeremiah, trusting in God meant relying on God, even exalting and praising God, during difficult and frightening times of persecution (17:12–18). The same holds true for us. It is precisely in difficult times that reliance on God and trust in him are the most critical.

For the people of Judah, Sabbath observance meant trusting in God to provide their livelihood even though they worked on only six days instead of seven. It was an economic trust. God apparently draws a tight connection between their failure to trust him in regard to money and income (i.e., work on the Sabbath) and their complete lapse into unbelief. Likewise today, if we refuse to trust God in areas of money and income, this is likely to affect other areas of faith and our life of obedience to God.

Under the new covenant that Jesus inaugurated, trusting in God is still a critical component. Yet God has now forgiven us, replacing the engraved sin on our hearts with the knowledge of him. Jesus also redefined and dismissed the legalistic aspect of Mosaic covenant Sabbath observance. But trusting in God is a constant exhortation, even in the New Testament. Likewise, the general lessons from the psalm of Jeremiah 17:5–11 still hold. Those who trust in God will have no need to worry in the time of drought, and they will never fail to bear fruit.

Illustrating the Text

Trusting God versus trusting ourselves

Humor: In a very heavy section of the Scriptures with serious themes, it is sometimes helpful to make a biblical point with some lightness. Here is a true story you can tell that contrasts trusting God with trusting ourselves.

Harold and Lillian were snowbirds. They lived in the Midwest but headed south to Florida every winter to escape the cold and snow. One spring, as they prepared to head back north, the news predicted a late-season blast of cold weather with possible snow and hail. They decided to make the drive and pull their trailer anyway because they were eager to get back to their home church, family, and friends.

Before pulling out of the trailer park in Florida, they prayed for protection, for safety, and for God's hand on them. In their own words, they asked for "traveling mercies." Well, God was with them, and although the roads were icy and treacherous in spots, they navigated the fifteen hundred miles with relative ease.

As they were pulling off the highway onto the country road just two minutes from their home, Harold prayed this simple prayer: "Lord, thanks for keeping us safe. I'll take it from here!" A short time later, as Harold turned into his own driveway, they hit black ice, and their truck and trailer slipped off the road and into a ditch right next to their home.

From that time on, whenever Harold told this story, he finished by saying, "We need to learn to trust God all the way into the driveway!"

Trust in the Lord.

Hymn: "Jesus, I Am Resting," by Jean Sophia Pigott. It is God's sovereign reign that generates our trust. Pigott (1845–80), an Irish composer, wrote about resting in the joy of discovering the greatness of Christ's loving heart. A story is told about Hudson Taylor, missionary to China, who, during the Boxer Rebellion at the end of the nineteenth century, sat at his desk, knowing that other mission stations had been destroyed, singing Pigott's words:

> Jesus, I am resting, resting,
>   in the joy of what Thou art;
> I am finding out the greatness
>   of Thy loving heart.

Thou hast bid me gaze upon Thee,
and Thy beauty fills my soul,
for by Thy transforming power
Thou hast made me whole.[2]

Popular Culture: The Stratosphere Hotel in Las Vegas boasts an extreme ride called "Insanity." The ride extends 68 feet over the edge of the 1,149-foot Stratosphere tower, not only providing a great view of the city but also challenging the faint of heart. The maximum speed is 40 miles per hour, with a 70 degree seat angle, and includes a spin up to three Gs.[3] There are many people who would look at this ride and say, "No way would I ride Insanity!" But there are others who would gladly pay the fee and enjoy every moment of the ride. What's the difference? Unless there is a related health issue, it may have to do with confidence in the designer and those who ensure that the ride is safe (government agencies and the hotel). If we trust the design and maintenance of the ride, then we know there is nothing to fear. When it comes to life in this world, there will be times when we will feel like we are on Insanity, times when life is frightening and we do not feel as if we are in control. It is in these times that we must remember we can trust the One who designed us and maintains our lives. Our ability to live with joy in these moments is a function of how well we know and trust God.

The Plans of the Great Potter

Big Idea

Like a great potter, God reshapes his plans for people in accordance with their response and obedience to him.

Key Themes

- If the people of Jerusalem will listen and repent, God will cancel the judgment plans that he has for them.
- The people of Judah and Jerusalem reject God's offer and embrace their own "plan."
- The rejection of God's offer of grace and mercy is stubborn and irrational.
- The people's rejection of God's offer of grace is accompanied by hostility toward God's prophet, the very one who is trying to intercede for them.

Understanding the Text

The Text in Context

The broader unit of Jeremiah 11–29 is tied together by the theme of conflict and hostility against Jeremiah as the messenger of God. In Jeremiah 18 God offers to revise his plan of judgment against the people of Judah if only they will repent and obey. Instead, they reject God and his offer and opt to follow their own evil "plan," one that includes silencing God's messenger, Jeremiah.

There are also several connections to the previous passage. In 17:19–27 there are repeated references to the "heart" of the people (17:1, 5, 9, 10). In 18:12 it is from their "evil heart" that the people determine to reject God's plan for their own evil plan. Another probable connection to the previous passage (17:19–27) is that both 17:19–27 and 18:1–11 present conditional situations.

The following passage, Jeremiah 19, is likewise closely connected. While in Jeremiah 18 God uses an analogy of a potter shaping and reshaping a soft clay pot according to his plans, in the very next chapter God tells the prophet to take a hardened pot and shatter it. The time for shaping and reshaping does eventually come to an end.

Jeremiah 18:1–23 is composed of three narrative sections and two poetic sections. Note that the three narrative sections are united by the catchword "plans." In 18:1–11 (a narrative) God tells the people that just as a potter changes his plans for a clay pot, so he will change his plans regarding the judgment that he has for them, if they will only listen, repent, and obey. Continuing in narrative, God predicts their negative response (18:12). Next is an emotional and poetic response from God to their rejection. Who has ever heard of such a stupid thing? Thus God promises to scatter them (18:13–17). In narrative again, God predicts that the people will also turn against Jeremiah and make plans to destroy him (18:18). In 18:19–23 Jeremiah reacts, likewise speaking poetically and calling on God to punish the people for still seeking to kill him, the very one trying to intercede on their behalf.

Interpretive Insights

18:1 *This is the word that came to Jeremiah from the* Lord. The Hebrew term *dabar* (the noun literally means "word," and the verb means "to speak") occurs throughout this passage and is translated in various ways: "word" (18:1), "message" (18:2), "word" (18:5), "announce" (18:7), "spoke" (18:8 [untranslated in the NIV]), "announce" (18:9), "says" (18:18), "spoke" (18:20).

18:2 *Go down to the potter's house.* The noun "potter" (18:2, 3, 4, 6) is from a verb meaning "to form" or "to make," and thus the noun literally means "the one who forms/makes (pots)." This is important because God will use this same verb in a wordplay in 18:11, "I *am preparing* a disaster for you" (i.e., as the potter makes the pot, so God makes the coming judgment on Judah).

18:3 *at the wheel.* Literally, this reads, "at the two stones." Presumably a lower round stone was worked by the potter's foot while the upper round stone held and spun the clay.

18:4 *so the potter formed it into another pot.* Literally, the Hebrew reads, "the potter turned [*shub*] and made it into another pot." The word *shub* is a frequent and important term used throughout Jeremiah to mean "to turn, return" and "to repent." It will be used several times in this passage in ironic wordplay (18:4, 8, 11).

18:7 *If at any time.* God introduces two major conditional situations, one here in 18:7 (the announcement of judgment on a nation) and one in 18:9 (the announcement of restoration and blessing on a nation). The conditionality of these two contrasting announcements of God is central to the passage.

a nation or kingdom is to be uprooted, torn down and destroyed. These are the same terms that God used when he first called Jeremiah and described his ministry to him (1:10). Jeremiah is the one whom God has used to make "the announcements" that he speaks of in this passage (18:7, 9). In essence, this passage is a symbolic summary of Jeremiah's ministry.

18:8 *if that nation I warned repents of its evil.* "Repents" is a translation of *shub* ("to turn, return, repent"), mentioned above in 18:4. "Evil" translates *ra'ah*, likewise a favorite term of Jeremiah's that can mean "disaster, bad stuff" or "evil things that people do."

then I will relent and not inflict on it the disaster I had planned. The word translated as "relent" implies changing one's mind. It is not that God is fickle or indecisive. Yet in the divine mix of God's omniscience, sovereignty, and grace, he reveals in this chapter that he will always respond graciously to repentance, and the "inevitable" judgment can always be averted if one will only repent. The sovereignty and omniscience of God do not imply fatalism. "Disaster" translates *ra'ah*, picking up the terms from the first half of 18:8 in a wordplay. If this nation "turns from" (*shub*) its *ra'ah* (bad stuff that it does), God will change his plans regarding the *ra'ah* (bad stuff) that he was going to do to it.

18:9 *a nation or kingdom is to be built up and planted.* As in 18:7, this terminology reflects 1:10. Note that "built up" and "planted" are inverse opposites of the terms "uprooted" and "torn down" in 18:7.

18:10 *if it does evil . . . does not obey . . . I will reconsider the good I had intended.* Using several of the same terms, this verse reflects the opposite action/reaction presented in 18:8. If the nation does *ra'ah* (evil things that people do; bad stuff), then God will "reconsider" (i.e., "change his plans") for it. The word translated as "reconsider" is the same word translated as "relent" in 18:8.

18:11 *I am preparing a disaster.* As God moves from the hypothetical nations discussed above to zero in on Judah and those in Jerusalem, he employs the same terminology, continuing the wordplay. "Am preparing" translates the Hebrew verb for "making a pot" used above in the potter analogy. "Disaster" translates *ra'ah*. Just as the potter shapes a pot, so God is shaping a terrible judgment of "bad stuff, disaster" (*ra'ah*) for them. God is not speaking of a "natural" disaster such as a tornado or tsunami. He is speaking of the coming Babylonian invasion and destruction of Jerusalem, a very specific and well-deserved judgment.

and devising a plan. The same Hebrew root is used twice here (lit., "planning" a "plan"). The word connotes devising a well-thought-out plan by careful thinking and calculating. Just as the potter carefully shapes the pot, so God carefully shapes the coming judgment on Judah (the Babylonian invasion).

So turn from your evil ways. Once again, using the terms from 18:8 in a wordplay, God calls on them to "turn" (*shub*) from their "evil" (*ra'ah*) way.

18:12 *our own plans . . . the stubbornness of our evil hearts.* The word translated as "plans" is the same word used for God's plan and his planning in 18:8, 11. Here it is used in mockery of God's plan. The people will follow their own plans, which come out of their evil (ra'ah) hearts. In Hebrew thought the heart is the seat of volition, where decisions are made.

18:18 *let's make plans against Jeremiah . . . let's attack him with our tongues.* The people's "evil plans" of 18:11–12 are picked up here as they plan (i.e., plot) against Jeremiah to counteract his words. The word translated as "attack" means "to strike violently." Often this word is used of killing someone, but here it seems to refer to a well-planned, vigorous, and violent verbal attack, as in a propagandistic smear campaign. On the other hand, Jeremiah indicates that their plots also include his murder (18:22–23).

18:20 *Should good be repaid with evil?* Once again, "evil" translates *ra'ah*. "Good" (*tobah*) is the opposite of *ra'ah*.

I stood before you and spoke in their behalf. Jeremiah has been the one interceding for the very people who now seek to kill him. Literally, this could be translated as "I stood before you to speak good for them." This is the same word for "good" as used earlier in this verse.

Theological Insights

Although the book of Jeremiah regularly affirms God's sovereignty and his ability to know and control the future, here in Jeremiah 18 the text stresses conditionality (and thus flexibility) in how God fulfills his plans, based on how people do or do not respond. As also reflected in the book of Jonah (which uses terminology very similar to that in Jer. 18), if God proclaims imminent judgment but people repent, then he will change his mind regarding this judgment. This is the mercy and grace of God. That is, if people listen and repent, he will "reshape" his plans for judgment into plans for salvation.

In Romans 9:21 Paul states that just as a potter has the right to make whatever he wants to out of his clay, so God has the right to determine what will become of Israel. Paul probably is alluding to Jeremiah 18, implying that the future for Israel is contingent on whether they respond to the gospel with repentance and belief.

Teaching the Text

This passage revolves around the potter imagery. But we must make sure to catch the central point and not deviate into other "potter" analogies that, while true, are not the meaning that Jeremiah intends. For example, sometimes this text is preached as an example of how God, like a great potter, shapes us and forms us, smoothing off the rough edges to shape us into the person he wants us to be. Thus the sermon is about discipleship and the challenge to be malleable in God's hands. This is not the meaning of Jeremiah 18.

Jeremiah 18 is, first of all, about Israel. God had devised a wonderful plan for Israel, but his people had abandoned him and turned against him, doing "evil." So now he is devising a judgment plan for them, a terrible invasion by the Babylonians that will scatter the inhabitants of Judah and Jerusalem to the wind. But these judgment prophecies of Jeremiah's are not fatalistic or set in stone. God continues to stress that if his people will but listen to him, repent, and obey, the plan of judgment will be replaced by a "reshaped" plan of restoration and blessing. Thus the prophecies of judgment in Jeremiah are stronger than warnings but still short of fatalistic, unstoppable prediction. If the people refuse to repent and continue to sin (and every indication is that they will), then the judgment is indeed imminent and unstoppable. But if only they will repent, then the judgment prophesied against them will not happen. The repentance of the Ninevites in the book of Jonah provides a good illustration of this very possibility. In fact, much of the same terminology found in Jeremiah 18 is used in Jonah 3–4.

Thus this passage finds relevance primarily in regard to unbelievers who defy and reject God and his message. Such a rejection of the gospel will result in God's judgment. That is his plan and his right as the potter and owner of the clay. Yet regardless of how entrenched the defiance and disbelief are, it is not too late to listen to God and repent. For God will change his plans for judgment if only the unbeliever will turn to him and repent.

Yet frequently, in the time of Jeremiah as well as today, people under judgment do not "get it," and they continue to believe rather foolishly that they can make their own plans apart from God. Unfortunately, the driving source of their "plans" will be their own corrupt hearts, and rather than accept God's gracious offer, they are more likely to reject both his offer and him; indeed, they frequently turn hostile toward his messengers who proclaim his gracious offer.

When the people in Judah of Jeremiah's day turn against him and plot to kill him (the very one trying to save them through his intercession with God), Jeremiah calls on God to destroy them. Jeremiah sees this as fitting and just. In contrast, in the New Testament when the people in Judah later turn against Jesus (a much greater intercessor) and plot to kill him, he says, "Father, forgive them, for they do not know what they are doing" (Luke 23:34). It is the model of Jesus that we are to embrace, forgiving those who oppose us and persecute us on account of our obedience to God.

Jeremiah 18 also teaches us that there is no deterministic "fatalism" in God's plans. To be sure, and as stressed throughout the book of Jeremiah, judgment will eventually come on those who reject his gracious offer of deliverance. In the meantime, however, God continues to plead for repentance, and he remains ever willing to reshape his judgment plan into a plan of blessing.

Illustrating the Text

It is foolish to reject God's grace.

News Story: In 2014 and into 2015, the world grappled with the terrible outbreak of Ebola. Widespread concern raced across the United States as infected medical missionaries Dr. Kent Brantly and Nancy Writebol were allowed to return home for treatment. They were successfully treated, but then Thomas Eric Duncan, a Liberian who was visiting relatives in Texas, came down with the disease, was hospitalized, and ultimately died.

All of these individuals submitted to the best treatments available in this life-or-death situation. Describe for the congregation a scene in which doctors have a treatment for a terrible virus, but the infected patients refuse the care and decide instead to put their trust in local religious superstitions.

God graciously offers forgiveness for those who repent.

Christian Music: "Drinking from My Saucer," by Michael Combs. In the first verse of this song Combs defines grace as "reaping better than I've sown." In the song he drinks from his saucer because his cup has overflowed—the result of God's grace.

Hymn: "Amazing Grace," by John Newton. This hymn, perhaps the best-known hymn of all time, captures the essence of our need for grace in the first verse. The 2007 film *Amazing Grace* conveys some of the backstory of why John Newton wrote the lyrics.

Statistics: Rejecting God is as prevalent in our day as it was in Jeremiah's. According to a 2011 poll by the Barna Group, 25 percent of American born-again Christians (those who believe that they are going to heaven because of their confession of sins and acceptance of Jesus Christ as their Savior) also believe in universalism (the belief that all people will ultimately be saved or accepted by God because he loves them too much to condemn them to hell).[1] The same poll indicates that 40 percent of Americans believe that they are going to heaven regardless of how they live or what they believe. Like Judah, these people have rejected God's offer and foolishly embraced their own plan of salvation.

Theological Book: *The Cost of Discipleship*, by Dietrich Bonhoeffer. In this classic book, first published in 1937, Dietrich Bonhoeffer defines "cheap grace" as "the preaching of forgiveness without requiring repentance, baptism without church discipline, Communion without confession, absolution without personal confession."[2] He goes on to say that what people want is grace without the cost of Christ on the cross. In other words, like the people in Jeremiah's day, so also in our day what people want is the benefit of God without paying the price.

Jerusalem to Be Shattered like a Clay Pot

Big Idea

Some sinful behavior is so bad that God is enraged and responds with terrible judgment.

Key Themes

- Jeremiah smashes a clay pot, symbolizing the coming destruction of Jerusalem.
- Idolatry, especially child sacrifice, will bring the wrath of God in judgment on Jerusalem.
- God describes the coming destruction of Jerusalem with "poetic justice" style punishment that fits the crime.

Understanding the Text

The Text in Context

In Jeremiah 18 God tells the people of Judah and Jerusalem that if only they will repent and turn back to him, then like a potter with soft clay he could reshape them into something good and useful. But they do not repent, and in Jeremiah 19 the pottery theme continues as God tells Jeremiah not to reshape a soft pot but rather to shatter a hard one. Jeremiah's symbolic demonstration and the message that went with it will lead to his imprisonment (20:1–6), followed by his last poetic lament to God in the book in 20:7–18.

Jeremiah 19 repeats much of the same content of Jeremiah 7:30–8:3 (Valley of Ben Hinnom renamed as Valley of Slaughter; child sacrifice; astral worship; burial in Topheth). The difference is that in 7:30–8:3 the overall focus is on the theme of false, perverted religion and its consequent, just punishment. Jeremiah 19 sits in a broad unit (Jer. 11–29) that stresses conflict and hostility against Jeremiah the prophet as the messenger of God. Thus Jeremiah 19 is the setup and background for the arrest and imprisonment of Jeremiah in Jeremiah 20.

The entire chapter is in prose, and the narrative actually continues from 19:1 to 20:6. Jeremiah 19:14–15 is transitional and could be included with either this section (Jer. 19) or the next section (Jer. 20).

Historical and Cultural Background

Topheth (19:6) is apparently a specific area in the Valley of Ben Hinnom, near a gate known as the Potsherd Gate. The Valley of Ben Hinnom runs from west to east for several hundred yards along the south of Jerusalem until it intersects with the north-south running Kidron Valley. Probably right outside the gate was the trash dump of broken pottery (and dung). Beyond this trash dump (or farther up or down the valley), but well within view, was the region of Topheth, where pagan altars had been constructed. The Hebrew word actually has a definite article, "the Topheth."

Additional background material can be found in 2 Kings. King Manasseh had rebuilt the high places, offered child sacrifices, and worshiped astral deities (2 Kings 21). As part of his reforms, King Josiah had removed these high places and stopped the child sacrifices (2 Kings 23). Josiah even desecrated Topheth, in the Valley of Ben Hinnom, to keep people from practicing child sacrifice there (2 Kings 23:10). Apparently, after the death of Josiah, the people returned to all these terrible practices.[1] God's pronouncement of judgment in Jeremiah 19:3 is very similar to the judgment he proclaimed in 2 Kings 21:12 ("the ears of everyone who hears of it will tingle").

Interpretive Insights

19:1 *buy a clay jar from a potter.* The word translated as "jar" is a fairly rare term. It refers to an expensive flask or decanter type of pot, usually four to ten inches high, with a rounded bottom section and a long, narrow neck and a ring-shaped handle. The mention of the "potter" (lit., "the one who forms things") connects back to Jeremiah 18.

elders of the people and of the priests. The "elders of the priests" are the senior priests. Jeremiah will be addressing specific idolatrous worship practices, presumably led by these priests.

19:2 *the Potsherd Gate.* Potsherds are pieces of broken pottery. Presumably, it was just outside this gate that ruined or broken pottery was thrown away. Clay pottery does not decompose, so over time quite an accumulation could pile up. Thus this area perhaps was similar to a modern trash dump. There is no other reference to a "Potsherd Gate" in the Old Testament, but this probably is the same gate called the "Dung Gate" in Nehemiah 2:13; 3:13–14; 12:31, indicating that it was not only broken pottery that people discarded into the valley here.[2]

19:4 *a place of foreign gods . . . burned incense in it to gods.* Both in this passage and in 7:31 reference is made to the worship of foreign gods in the Valley of Ben Hinnom. Burning incense and the sacrifice of children are specifically mentioned. Likewise, the mention of "high places" (probably altars) in 19:5 suggests that there were other sacrifices and worship practices taking place here as well. These practices were well entrenched in the religion of Judah when King Josiah came to the throne, and 2 Kings 23:4–14 describes the many pagan worship sites that Josiah destroys in and around Jerusalem, including in the Valley of Ben Hinnom. All indications are that after the death of Josiah the nation returns to the pagan practices that he tried to eliminate, and thus the description of the sites and practices described in 2 Kings 23:4–14 is probably a good overall picture of what was happening in the Valley of Ben Hinnom and elsewhere in and around Jerusalem.

the blood of the innocent. This is a reference to the practice of child sacrifice, further described in the next verse.

19:5 *to burn their children in the fire as offerings to Baal.* This practice is also mentioned in 7:30–31; 32:35. Usually in the Old Testament child sacrifice is associated with the Ammonite god Molek (Lev. 20:2–5; Jer. 32:35), but pagan religious practice was quite syncretistic and fluid, and the title "Baal" (lit., "Lord") was fluid and could be applied to several deities.

I did not command or mention, nor did it enter my mind. Child sacrifice is prohibited frequently (Lev. 18:21; 20:2–5; Deut. 12:31; 18:10).

19:7 *in this place I will ruin the plans.* The word translated as "ruin" (*baqaq*) is similar in sound to the word for "jar" (*baqbuq*) used in 19:1, 10.

carcasses as food to the birds and the wild animals. Note also 19:11, "They will bury the dead in Topheth until there is no more room." God paints a horrific picture of the aftermath of the Babylonian invasion. The area of Topheth will become the mass grave for those slaughtered, but there will not be enough space, so the wild animals will feed on the bodies. Thus it will be renamed the "Valley of Slaughter" (19:6). In the New Testament the Valley of Ben Hinnom is known as Gehenna, a place where garbage was dumped and burned. In the New Testament the term "Gehenna" also became a symbol or an image of the place of final judgment.

19:9 *eat the flesh of their sons and daughters.* During long sieges of cities often the inhabitants ran out of food. Faced with starvation, sometimes they turned to cannibalism (cf. 2 Kings 6:28–29). God tells them that this is what will happen during the upcoming Babylonian siege of Jerusalem. Note the poetic irony: this is the consequence of having sacrificed some of their children to pagan gods. The fulfillment of this horrible prophecy is bemoaned in Lamentations 4:10.

19:11 *just as this potter's jar is smashed and cannot be repaired.* Several analogies merge together in the act of smashing the potter's jar. Likewise, the connection to Jeremiah 18 is implied. No longer is the potter able to re-shape the pot. Furthermore, Jeremiah probably stands on the top of a slope and throws the pot down the slope, where it shatters and scatters in pieces, perhaps on top of other old broken bits of pottery. Throughout this passage God seems to be saying that those slaughtered in the siege of Jerusalem will likewise lie in this valley like these broken pieces of pottery.

19:13 *The houses . . . will be defiled like this place, Topheth.* The word translated as "defiled" is used frequently (especially in Leviticus and Numbers) in reference to being ceremonially unclean. Contact with a corpse made a priest or a sacred place "unclean" (Lev. 5:2–3; 21:1; 22:4; Num. 5:2; 19:13; 2 Kings 23:14–20) and thus unfit to serve or to be in the presence of God. When Jerusalem is destroyed, Topheth will become the mass grave, filled with so many bodies that the survivors will not be able to cover them all. These dead bodies "defile" the area, in essence desecrating this pagan "holy place." Likewise, God states, the houses of Jerusalem, with pagan "holy places" on their rooftops, will be just as defiled (filled with dead bodies).

where they burned incense on the roofs to all the starry hosts. The rooftops were flat, and the people were using them to hold incense burners and to burn incense to astral deities, probably at night. This same phrase "starry host" is mentioned in Zephaniah 1:5. It may be the same deity referred to as the Queen of Heaven (Jer. 7:18; 44:15–25).

19:15 *on this city and all the villages . . . every disaster I pronounced against them.* Wordplay runs throughout this verse. The Hebrew words translated as "villages" (lit., "her cities") and "against them" look and sound very similar. "Disaster" is translated from *ra'ah*, a word used throughout Jeremiah both for the bad things that people do (usually translated as "evil") and for the "bad stuff" that God will do to them in judgment. Here he promises "every disaster" (lit., "all the bad stuff") that he has spoken against them.

Theological Insights

The horrific consequences of abandoning God and worshiping idols were outlined clearly as a warning for Israel in Deuteronomy 28, where even the unthinkable act of cannibalism is predicted in gruesome detail (Deut. 28:53–57). Jesus also preaches words of warning against Jerusalem in Mark 13 and Luke 21, a judgment that was carried out in horrific fashion by the Romans in AD 70. Obviously, judgment on sin cannot be viewed as merely a feature of the Old Testament; rather, it as an overarching biblical theme. The rejection of God's message and his messenger, followed by the destruction of Jerusalem, are central events that happen twice, uniting both

Testaments thematically and serving as a strong warning for all people today as well.

The macabre poetic justice running throughout this passage should also be noted. The people were worshiping pagan gods and sacrificing their children at Topheth. God turns Topheth into a mass grave where birds and wild animals feed. Indeed, during the terrible Babylonian siege of Jerusalem those who had sacrificed some of their children will be forced to eat their other children. The very houses with rooftops used for astral deity worship will be made into rubble like the clay pot. All the pagan sacred worship areas (Topheth and the rooftops) will be desecrated by the dead bodies of those in Jerusalem whom the Babylonians slaughter. God does seem to favor sending judgment that accords with the sin that he is judging, a characteristic of God that likewise seems to be reflected in Romans 1:18–32.

Teaching the Text

In Jeremiah 18 God as the potter reshapes the pot in accordance with how the people respond to his message. In Jeremiah 19, however, the implication is that the sin of the people in Jerusalem has so hardened their hearts that the time for reshaping has passed. Now is the time for judgment. Certainly today God continues to call people to repent. He promises to "reshape" the pot that defines their life into something meaningful and everlasting if they will turn to him and repent. God pleads and waits patiently, but for those who continually reject him and refuse his offer, the time eventually does run out; their hearts harden, and God's terrible judgment falls on them.

Once again we see the grim consequences of sin. Rebelling against God and abandoning his love and relationship have very terrible consequences. These texts are shocking! Indeed, that probably is the intention of this passage. As in the time of Jeremiah, if people today refuse God's gracious offer of forgiveness and eternal life through Christ, choosing sin and rebellion instead, they will face a terrible, unimaginable time of judgment. In this passage God seems to be almost screaming, "Don't you realize what will happen?" This text in Jeremiah is an old-fashioned "fire and brimstone" sermon, where the fire and brimstone were real and imminent, soon to be brought on by the savage Babylonian army.

It is bad enough that the people are worshiping other gods, and God is angered by their idolatry because it involves a rejection of him, his covenant, and his love. Yet he seems to become especially enraged over the practice of child sacrifice, particularly because of the "innocent blood" involved. The modern-day practice of abortion seems to be a valid and relevant parallel, which obviously likewise involves "innocent blood." We should take note of the fact that this is not just a violation of God's law but is a practice that particularly angers, even enrages him. Jeremiah 18 indicates that God will not stand by and watch this indefinitely but will respond with terrifying judgment.

Illustrating the Text

God will be hardest on those who take advantage of the innocent.

Statistics: The statistics of children being mistreated by adults in the United States are staggering: over a million abortions take place each year; half of the pregnancies in the United States are unintended and of those pregnancies, four out of ten end in abortion;[3] more than six million cases of child abuse are reported every year.[4]

The wages of sin is death.

Scripture: In Romans 6:23 the apostle Paul clearly agrees with the poetic justice of God's punishment of sin, but he also sees, like Jeremiah, that God's grace is available to those who will repent.

Classic Sermon: In his unforgettable sermon "Sinners in the Hands of an Angry God," Jonathan Edwards used vivid imagery, typical of the Great Awakening, to awaken his hearers to the horrible reality that awaited them if they did not get right with God. It was preached on July 8, 1741, but like Jeremiah, the message is timeless.

Perhaps it would be beneficial to read a portion of Edwards's message when preaching on this chapter, emphasizing that the sermon begins with three timeless observations about sin: (1) God is not just disappointed but angry; (2) the unrepentant deserve what they will get; (3) even though they do not realize it, they are condemned already.

This sermon and this section of Jeremiah are intended to be a wake-up call. So it would have an interesting effect to place several alarm clocks around the auditorium set to ring at a certain point in the service.

God takes sin seriously, and so should we.

Object Lesson: Hold up a clay jar as you talk about the destruction of Jerusalem. (You can explain what the "jar" Jeremiah used looked like by reviewing the teaching notes in this section.) Talk about how fragile clay is, and how difficult it is to repair. Take the jar and wrap it in a towel (for safety and easy clean up), lay it on a small tabletop, and then take a hammer and strike the jar. If you can have a microphone near the towel so that people can hear the clay shatter, this could heighten the effectiveness of the image. Slowly unwrap the towel and show the shattered clay.

Use this to demonstrate that there are times when slight adjustments are needed in our spiritual lives and hearts. However, there are also times when God brings real judgment on those who defiantly refuse to repent and turn to him. There is a breaking, a shattering, and a crushing that God's justice demands. This was such a time for the people of Judah and Jerusalem. You might want to linger here, or point to the return and restoration that came seventy years later at the end of the exile. In either case, let this vivid image wake people up to the fact that sin demands judgment, and God is perfectly just.

The Cost of Being a Prophet of God

Big Idea

Faithful servants of God who experience hostile opposition and times of discouragement should still continue to trust in God.

Key Themes

- Jeremiah is beaten and imprisoned for proclaiming God's message to Jerusalem.
- Jeremiah pronounces judgment on those responsible for this hostility.
- Discouraged by the persecution, Jeremiah cries out to God in despair.
- Jeremiah also affirms his trust in God, calling for judgment against those who persecute him.

Understanding the Text

The Text in Context

The larger unit of Jeremiah 11–29 deals primarily with opposition and hostility toward Jeremiah, God's prophet. This passage underscores that theme. Numerous times in the book Jeremiah cries out to God in poetic "laments" or "complaints" (11:18–12:6; 15:10–18; 17:14–18; 18:19–23). In 20:7–18 we find his last "lament" or "complaint" in the book. This lament of Jeremiah's is very similar to the individual laments found in the psalms (e.g., Pss. 3; 5; 7; 22), yet while the lament psalms typically end on a final note of trust and confidence in God, Jeremiah's lament in 20:7–18 ends on a cry of despair and discouragement (cf. Ps. 88).

Jeremiah 20:1–6 is in prose and continues the narrative from the previous chapter. The rest of Jeremiah 20 is in poetry and is composed of three "songs" of Jeremiah. It starts with a negative lament (20:7–10) and ends with a negative lament (20:14–18). Sandwiched in the middle is a strong contrasting statement of trust in God (20:11–13). The poetic section (20:7–18) has several allusions to Jeremiah's call in Jeremiah 1.

Interpretive Insights

20:1 *Pashhur . . . the official in charge.* "Pashhur" is a common name in Judah at this time. This official is a different person than the Pashhur in 21:1. The Pashhur here is a priest in the temple, but with some type of oversight responsibility, perhaps the head of a type of temple "security."

20:2 *he had Jeremiah the prophet beaten and put in the stocks.* The inclusion of Jeremiah's title "the prophet" adds to the irony and the coming indictment. The word translated as "beaten" (NRSV: "struck") is a strong one that in many cases is used to describe fatal blows (Exod. 2:12; Jer. 20:4; 21:6; 26:23). This was probably not a mild slap on the face but rather a terrible beating. The meaning of the Hebrew word translated as "stocks" is uncertain. The large wooden "block" that holds the head and hands is a later European invention and so is not in view here. This could have been some type of uncomfortable binding device, or it could have been just a small confined prison. It is mentioned again in 29:26.

20:3 *The LORD's name for you is . . . Terror on Every Side.* Jeremiah wastes no time in pronouncing judgment on Pashhur. As soon as Jeremiah is released, he tells Pashhur that God has renamed him "Terror on Every Side" (*Magor Missabib*), an allusion to a terrifying situation from which there is no escape, such as will happen when Jerusalem falls to the Babylonians. This same phrase is used in Psalm 31:13; Jeremiah 6:25; 20:10; 46:5; 49:29; Lamentations 2:22. The terror that Pashhur will see is further described in 20:4. He will see all his friends fall by the sword.

20:4 *put them to the sword.* The word translated as "put" is the same word translated as "beaten" in 20:2 (lit., "strike"). Pashhur, a leader of Judah, "strikes" Jeremiah the prophet and puts him in the stocks; thus God "strikes" the people of Judah and exiles them to Babylon.

20:7 *You deceived me, LORD . . . you overpowered me and prevailed.* Jeremiah is alluding to his call in Jeremiah 1. The NIV's translation of "deceived" misses the gist of the Hebrew word used here. In Jeremiah 1 God is not "tricking" or "deceiving" Jeremiah into anything, for God tells him clearly that his ministry will be difficult, and that he will face terrifying opposition (1:8, 17–19). The word used here in 20:7 can also mean "to entice, seduce, persuade," and these concepts reflect the more likely connotations intended here. The next two words relate to strength ("overpowered") and power/ability ("prevailed"). Taken together, what Jeremiah is saying in this verse is that he did not volunteer for this job; he was chosen by God, who did not really give him any choice about it. In Jeremiah 1 God swept away any objections that Jeremiah tried to make and insisted that Jeremiah become his prophet. So Jeremiah is griping to God about this, saying something like, "You forced me to be your prophet, and now I am being ridiculed, mocked, and threatened all the time."

20:8 *the word of the* Lord *has brought me insult and reproach.* Jeremiah's primary task as God's prophet has been to proclaim the coming judgment. As 4:5–6:30 (and elsewhere throughout Jeremiah) illustrates, the coming Babylonian invasion will be a nightmare. But the people of Judah do not want to hear this message, and they respond with hostile criticism. The word translated as "insult" means "taunting" or "mocking with scorn." The word translated as "reproach" connotes "ridiculing" or "making fun of." Proclaiming God's word has not brought Jeremiah respect; instead, people have laughed at and mocked him.

20:9 *But if I say, "I will not mention his word."* Literally, this last phrase translates as "I will not remember him/it." The pronoun in question ("him/it") can refer back to either the Lord himself (20:7) or the "word of the Lord" (20:8). But the meaning is similar. For Jeremiah, remembering God is also remembering that God has commissioned him to proclaim his word.

his word is in my heart like a fire. The Hebrew literally reads, "It/he is in my heart like a burning fire." As mentioned above, this can refer to either the Lord himself or to the "word of the Lord."

I am weary of holding it in; indeed, I cannot. The phrase translated as "I cannot" literally reads, "I am not able to" or "I do not have the power to." This is the same term Jeremiah uses in 20:7 when he says that God "prevailed." There is a wordplay taking place, for this same word will also occur in 20:10, 11 (used of Jeremiah's opponents). Because of the ridicule described in 20:8, Jeremiah apparently has tried to keep quiet and to stifle the word of God, but the word of God burns in his heart like a fire, and even if he tries, he is unable to keep the word of God to himself.

20:10 *Terror on every side!* Jeremiah has pronounced this as judgment on Pashhur (20:3), but now, ironically, his enemies are trying to create this terror for him.

Perhaps he will be deceived . . . we will prevail . . . and take our revenge on him. The three words translated as "deceived," "prevail," and "revenge" connect to several verses in this passage through word repetition. In 20:7 God "deceived" (enticed, persuaded) and "prevailed" over Jeremiah. When Jeremiah tried to stay quiet, he was unable to "prevail" (20:9). His opponents hope that Jeremiah will be "deceived" so that they can "prevail" over him and take "revenge" (20:10), but Jeremiah declares that God, like a mighty warrior, will not allow them to "prevail" (20:11) and will instead enact "revenge" (NIV: "vengeance") on them (20:12). The context for this verse probably reflects the situation described in 20:1–3. A very deadly game of royal court intrigue and power was taking place. Being a prophet and of a priestly family provided

Jeremiah with a certain amount of status and protection, but his many foes plotted against him, desiring to have him either beaten and silenced or executed.

20:11 *The* LORD *is with me like a mighty warrior.* The statement of God's comforting and empowering presence alludes to God's promise in 1:8. The English word "mighty" does not quite capture the nuance of this Hebrew word. It carries connotations of "dreaded" or "terrifying." God is not just a "strong" or "mighty" warrior standing beside Jeremiah; he is such a fierce and powerful warrior that he instills terror in those who oppose him.

20:12 *probe the heart and mind.* As in 11:20 and 17:10, the terms are literally "heart" (the place of decision making) and "kidneys" (the center of emotion).

20:18 *Why did I ever come out of the womb?* The entire final section (20:14–18) of Jeremiah's lament bemoans the day he was born (cf. Job's similar lament in Job 3). Indeed, in the last two verses (20:17–18) Jeremiah uses the Hebrew word for "womb" three times. No doubt Jeremiah is alluding to his call recorded in Jeremiah 1. Remember that part of God's overpowering argument when he "called" Jeremiah was "Before I formed you in the womb I knew you, before you were born I set you apart" (1:5). These are the first words that God speaks to Jeremiah. Taken with Jeremiah's opening statements in 20:7–10 of how God prevailed over him, Jeremiah seems to be saying here (poetically) that the only way he could have resisted God's call was never to have been born.

Theological Insights

God frequently sends his "prophets" into situations where they will be persecuted. Likewise, he has expectations regarding how they are to respond to the situation. The leaders and people of Jerusalem reject Jeremiah and persecute him. Because of this, the Babylonians come and destroy Jerusalem. The New Testament story of both Jesus and his apostles, especially as told in Luke-Acts, is very similar, with the judgment on Jerusalem carried out by the Romans in AD 70. Indeed, Jeremiah is the prototypical "persecuted prophet" alluded to several times in Luke-Acts (Luke 4:24; 13:33; Acts 7:52). An interesting story comparison and stark contrast can be observed between Jeremiah in Jeremiah 20:1–18 and Paul (and Silas) in Acts 16:16–40. Both Jeremiah and Paul are arrested, beaten, and placed in some sort of stocks. Both are released the next day. Jeremiah proclaims judgment on his "jailer" or the one responsible. Paul and Silas, however, lead their jailer to the Lord. Jeremiah ends his lament with a cry of discouragement. Paul and Silas, however, sing praises to God from within the jail. Both passages speak to persecution and times of discouragement, but Paul and Silas, strengthened by the Holy Spirit, give us a much better model to follow than Jeremiah in his discouragement.

Teaching the Text

One of the myths of the Christian life that many perpetuate is that if we are living in obedience to God, his blessings will shower down in a way that gives us a wonderful and happy life, without difficulty, tragedy, and heartache. Yet God tells Jeremiah from the beginning that his ministry will be difficult, and that he will face hostility. It is precisely because Jeremiah is obedient to God that he faces such hostility from the entire nation. We may face hostility and opposition precisely because we are faithfully carrying out God's will.

This passage also speaks to the challenge of bearing up under hostility and difficult situations over extended periods of time without becoming discouraged. Likewise, it is much more difficult to praise the Lord in all things if you have just been beaten as Jeremiah was. At times he affirms his faith in God and at times he slides into despair and discouragement. Our experience probably will be the same. God, however, never gives up on Jeremiah, and he will never give up on us either.

Hostility from unbelievers toward God's message and his messengers, accompanied by rebellion against his word, results in terrible judgment. This is as true today as it was in the day of Jeremiah. God's judgment will come; that is certain. But he does not promise to come in judgment just to ease our suffering or to immediately vindicate our message. He has his perfect timing. In the meantime he calls on us to be faithful and to endure.

It is easy to say that if we are truly trusting in the Lord, we should always be upbeat and optimistic. Jeremiah perhaps gives us a picture closer to reality. Faithful servants of God do in fact experience discouragement, even as they serve God obediently. In this particular passage (Jer. 20) there is no immediate response from God. But the answer from God comes in the chapters that follow and throughout the rest of the book. Jeremiah is vindicated. His prophecies do come true. Jerusalem is destroyed, and all those who oppose him are either killed or taken into exile. Likewise, when we find ourselves discouraged due to hostility from those who oppose God's words, we need to keep in mind that this is a temporary situation, and that God will eventually establish his kingdom in power and justice and bring an end to all opposition.

Illustrating the Text

Those who speak for God should expect opposition.

Spiritual Biography: *William Tyndale: A Biography*, by David Daniell. A case study could be made of the great Reformer William Tyndale. His translation of the New Testament from the original Greek text into English ultimately cost him his life because it represented such a challenge to the Roman Catholic Church. He was put to death by being strangled and burned at the stake after being convicted of heresy in 1536.[1] Some 90 percent of the King James Version New Testament and 75 percent of the Revised Standard Version New Testament are based largely on Tyndale's translation. For this reason, he is often called "the father of the English Bible." You might ask people how many Bibles they have at home, and remind them that that privilege came at a cost.

Spiritual Biography: *Through Gates of Splendor,* by Elisabeth Elliot. Missionary Jim Elliot, whose life was taken by the very people he was trying to save, is another example of the cost of speaking for God. On January 8, 1956, he and four others were killed while trying to bring the good news to a remote tribe in Ecuador. In light of his sacrifice, Jim became famous for writing, "He is no fool who gives what he cannot keep to gain that which he cannot lose." The story is told in detail by his wife, Elisabeth, in her book *Through Gates of Splendor.*[2]

Church History: In the mid-second century AD, after already executing several other Christians, the authorities in the city of Smyrna (modern Izmir, Turkey) finally captured the eighty-six-year-old Polycarp, who was the bishop and spiritual leader of the Christians in the region. In AD 156 he was brought into a stadium filled with hostile people calling for his death. The governor called on him to recant his faith in Christ and to declare, "Caesar is Lord," or else be burned alive. The feisty Polycarp refused and warned the governor of the eternal fire that awaited the ungodly. The governor ordered his execution, but after the fire failed to kill him, the executioner killed the elderly Christian with a dagger. A complete account of Polycarp's death can be found in Bryan Litfin's *Early Christian Martyr Stories.*[3]

Sometimes even the strongest Christians cry out to God.

Quote: In his book of daily meditations *God's Message for Each Day,* Eugene Peterson reminds us, "The language of prayer is forged in the crucible of trouble."[4] Prayer is simply the believer crying out to God, trusting that he will answer.

Help You? I'm Going to Attack You!

Big Idea

Those who spurn God and embrace a life characterized by injustice will come to know God as attacker rather than defender.

Key Themes

- It is not ethnic heritage but rather covenant relationship and covenant obedience that determine whether God delivers or judges.
- God reveals himself as furiously outraged and exploding with anger because of social injustice.
- Deliverance will come only for those who accept and submit to God's plan.
- God holds leaders especially responsible for social justice.

Understanding the Text

The Text in Context

The larger unit of Jeremiah 11–29 is united by the theme of Jeremiah the prophet of God in conflict with the king and other leaders of Jerusalem. Jeremiah 11–20 stresses the tragic reality that instead of obeying God's gracious call to repentance, these leaders have responded with hostility and active persecution against Jeremiah, God's messenger. Then Jeremiah 21–29 focuses on God's response, particularly to these leaders, delineating the judgment that is coming specifically on them and their ruling institutions. Numerous specific individuals are mentioned by name in these chapters, and the fate decreed for most of them is quite grim.

Jeremiah 20 ends with Jeremiah the prophet feeling rather discouraged and overwhelmed by the opposition against him. That chapter ends without any response from God. Jeremiah 21 and the chapters that follow, however, are filled with judgment on those people who have persecuted Jeremiah; perhaps this judgment is God's response.

This passage opens with Zedekiah asking Jeremiah to seek God's deliverance for them from the Babylonians (21:1–2). God's response to Zedekiah comes in

143

21:3–7: God will not deliver them because it is actually God himself who is the one fighting against them. Furthermore, God continues (21:8–10), addressing the people of Jerusalem, their only hope of survival is to surrender to the Babylonians (since God is fighting on the side of the Babylonians). The root cause of all of this, God explains in 21:11–14, is the lack of justice in their ruling practices.

Chronologically, the story introduced in Jeremiah 21 continues in Jeremiah 38 as a lead-in to the actual fall of Jerusalem. Pashhur, son of Malkijah, one of the messengers mentioned in 21:1, is one of the hostile leaders who later arrests Jeremiah, argues for his execution, and then throws him into the cistern of Malkijah to die, as described in 38:1–6.

Historical and Cultural Background

Historically, the events in this unit take place around 589–588 BC. The current king of Judah is Zedekiah, who has been hostile toward Jeremiah and has continued to be a champion of idolatry and social injustice. Ignoring Jeremiah's advice, Zedekiah has rebelled against Babylonian rule, and thus Nebuchadnezzar, the Babylonian king, is now angrily advancing against Judah with a powerful army.

Interpretive Insights

21:1 *Pashhur son of Malkijah and the priest Zephaniah.* This Pashhur is a different individual from the Pashhur who has Jeremiah beaten in 20:1–6. As mentioned above, this Pashhur (son of Malkijah) is the one who will accuse Jeremiah of treason and then throw him into a cistern. The "priest Zephaniah" appears again in 29:25–29. He is also specifically mentioned as being among the leaders that the Babylonians execute in 52:24–27.

21:2 *Inquire now of the LORD for us.* The word translated as "inquire" is often used specifically of seeking or requesting a word or oracle from God. Note the irony of this request. Jeremiah has been preaching the word of God to the people of Judah and Jerusalem for nearly forty years; now, with the Babylonians at the gates, they finally want to hear what God has to say.

Perhaps the LORD will perform wonders for us as in times past. The word translated as "wonders" means "to be extraordinary, surpassing, wonderful, marvelous." It connotes actions that are beyond human ability, actions associated with the heavenly realm. The powerful wonders worked by God during the exodus may be in mind here, but more likely they are thinking of God's deliverance of Jerusalem from the Assyrians during the reign of Hezekiah (2 Kings 19:35–37; Isa. 37:36–38).

21:4 *the Babylonians.* The word used here is *kasdim* ("Chaldeans"). Technically, this word refers to those from a region in southern Babylonia, where the current ruling dynasty originated, but in Jeremiah this term is used inter-changeably with "Babylonians" in reference to the larger country. This is the first usage of the term *kasdim*, which occurs 46 times in Jeremiah, as opposed to 162 occurrences of "Babylonia/Babylonians" throughout the book.

21:5 *I myself will fight against you with an outstretched hand and a mighty arm*. The phrases "outstretched hand" and "mighty arm" are used of God frequently in various combinations to describe his powerful and miraculous deliverance of Israel from Egypt. That is, his "hand" and his "arm" were the poetic instruments by which God crushed the Egyptians and delivered the Israelites (e.g., Exod. 3:20; 6:6; 7:5; 13:9–16; Deut. 4:34; 5:15; 6:21). Ironically, and in a reversal of Israel's great salvation story, now God is using this same power against the king and the people of Jerusalem.

in furious anger and in great wrath. Three very strong and emotional Hebrew terms are used here in hammer-like repetitive stress, combining to express connotations of the most furious rage imaginable.

21:7 *the plague, sword and famine*. These three terms are used together repeatedly throughout Jeremiah to describe what will happen during the siege and fall of Jerusalem (14:12; 21:9; 27:8, 13; 32:24; 38:2).

he will show them no mercy or pity or compassion. Note the parallel rep-etition of triads in 21:6–7: anger, fury, and wrath; plague, sword, and famine; no mercy, no pity, and no compassion. This tripling of terms produces strong emphasis.

21:8 *I am setting before you the way of life and the way of death*. Literally, this reads, "I am giving to you the road of the living ones and the road of the dead one." This is an ironic allusion to Deuteronomy 30:15, where this same terminology is used in regard to keeping the Mosaic covenant and having life or disobeying the covenant and dying. The word translated as "way" literally means "road" or "path," but it is frequently used figuratively to mean "way" or "manner of life." In this case there is an ironic interplay of figurative and literal. In order to survive and live, one had to take the literal road out of Je-rusalem. This was the "way" of life.

21:10 *I have determined to do this city harm and not good*. A literal trans-lation of this clause could read, "I have set my face against this city for bad stuff [*ra'ah*] and not for good" (both of these terms are also used in Deut. 30:15). In the New Testament, Luke probably is pronouncing judgment on Jerusalem by alluding to this verse in 9:51, which literally reads, "Jesus set his face to go to Jerusalem."

21:12 *Administer justice every morning*. The call for social justice, especially judicial justice from the king and other leaders of Judah, is foundational to the message of Jeremiah. One instance of "justice" is described in the second half of 21:12: "rescue from the hand of the oppressor the one who has been robbed." The phrase "every morning" probably alludes to the practice of holding court in the mornings.

or my wrath will break out and burn like fire. Literally, this translates, "lest the fire of my wrath go forth and burn without ever being extinguished." The word translated as "wrath" (also in 21:5) carries connotations of "heat, fury, anger," and thus the colorful "fire" imagery for judgment is rather appropriate.

21:14 *I will punish you as your deeds deserve.* The word translated as "punish" can mean "to visit" or "to appoint." It is a favorite word of Jeremiah, occurring forty-nine times. It is within the poetic context of "to visit" that it carries the idea of punishment, a usage frequent in Jeremiah. Literally, this verse could be translated as "I will visit against you according to the fruit of your actions."

I will kindle a fire in your forests. In the next chapter the wood paneling in the king's palace will be compared to forests (22:6–7). Thus the reference to "fire in your forests" probably poetically alludes to burning the palace.

Theological Insights

Here, as continually throughout Jeremiah, we see how crucially important justice is to God. In fact, justice is an integral part of God's character, and when people oppress the weak and practice injustice, it seems to offend God's basic nature. That is, even though he is patient and loving, his love for justice and his care for the weak underclass cause him to become extremely angry when they are unjustly oppressed. Jeremiah underscores what a terrible thing it is to be the object of such wrath. Likewise, one truth that emerges throughout Jeremiah is that the wrath of God toward sin and injustice is just as much a central part of his character as his love is.

Teaching the Text

Zedekiah and the inhabitants of Jerusalem thought that because of their ethnic identity as Israelites, because of their association with God and his temple, and because he had protected and delivered their ancestors in the past, God would protect and defend them now no matter what. They lived a life of spiteful, rebellious disobedience, characterized by continuous social injustice toward others, and then they erroneously assumed that God would still save them. In similar fashion today, we sometimes encounter people who may have grown up in the church or around the church but who have never repented of their sin and committed to following Jesus. Instead, these people rebel against the truth that they know and ignore God's call to follow him and to live in accordance with his commands. Can they trust in the faith of their parents or in the close proximity of the church, especially back in their childhood, and thus assume that they will be delivered by God and given eternal life? Absolutely not!

Likewise, in this passage once again we gain insight into the character of God in regard to sin. God is not neutral toward sin; neither is he flippant or dismissive. He gets angry when people spurn him and chase after other gods instead. But he gets equally angry when people ignore his call to enact justice in situations around them, choosing instead to live only for self, wielding whatever socioeconomic power they have to oppress the socioeconomically weak underclass and to gain profit for themselves. In particular he holds leaders accountable to care for those in the society who are weak and to establish social justice for them. Today is no different. God expects the leaders of his church to lead his people in standing against social injustice and to be defenders of those who are socioeconomically weak and vulnerable. This does not detract from the proclamation of the gospel but rather is part and parcel of it.

God's words and actions in the passage (as elsewhere in Jeremiah) teach us much about the seriousness and depth of sin, along with a graphic picture of what punishment for sin looks like. This understanding thus helps us also to see the depths of grace. Jesus does not save us from some kind of easily dismissed, trifling sin (there is no such thing); rather, he saves us from the same kind of sin that results in the explosive rage of God seen in this passage. Grace is not cheap; Jesus endured this wrath and punishment on the cross in our place. But in order to find deliverance, we must come to God on God's terms; we must submit to his plan. Salvation by grace through faith in Jesus Christ is his plan. There is no other way to be delivered.

We have noted several parallels between judgment on Jerusalem during the time of Jeremiah and judgment on Jerusalem prophesied during the time of Jesus and the apostles and fulfilled shortly afterward. Just as Jeremiah tells the inhabitants to leave Jerusalem when the Babylonians besiege it, so Jesus also warns the inhabitants of Jerusalem to flee when they see armies (the Romans in AD 70) surrounding it (Luke 21:20–21). Then, in a probable allusion to Jeremiah, Jesus states, "For this is the time of punishment in fulfillment of all that has been written" (Luke 21:22). Thus in both the Old Testament and the New Testament the rejection of God's gracious call to repentance and active hostility and persecution against God's messengers who deliver his word do eventually bring on God's judgment. Finally, we see that God holds the leaders of his people particularly responsible to lead those people to strive to establish justice throughout the society. This does not negate the call to proclaim the gospel but rather is integral to it. Leaders in the church today should lead with passion both for the proclamation of the gospel and the establishment and operation of biblical justice, especially for those who are socioeconomically weak and vulnerable.

Illustrating the Text

God holds us responsible for justice in the world.

Quote: Dietrich Bonhoeffer stood up to challenge the atrocities of Adolf Hitler and the Nazis in a time when most of his fellow clergy sat in silence. In 1939 he was safe and secure in the United States teaching the lessons of his book *The Cost of Discipleship* and passionately challenging the status quo of Christianity. Many at the time urged him to continue his work here to avoid what appeared to be certain persecution.

Bonhoeffer felt that as Christians it was our duty to confront the Nazi brutality against the Jews head-on, and so, embracing his call, he bravely decided to return to Germany to take on Hitler and the Third Reich. As a Christian pastor and author with a notable reputation, he felt it was his duty to do so. "Silence in the face of evil is itself evil," he said. "God will not hold us guiltless. Not to speak is to speak. Not to act is to act." In the end, Bonhoeffer's decision cost him his freedom and ultimately his life. To this day, his actions remind us that as Christians God demands that we stand up for what is right no matter what the cost.[1]

Scripture: Micah 6:6–8 and Amos 5:24 are two of the many prophetic Old Testament texts that underline God's call for justice.

God is both defender of the innocent and attacker of the unjust.

Christian Literature: *The Lion, the Witch and the Wardrobe*, by C. S. Lewis. In this novel, first published in 1950, Lewis uses Mr. Beaver to describe the great Aslan ("Aslan" is Turkish for "lion"), the son of the Emperor-beyond-the-Sea. "Aslan is a lion," he says, "*the* Lion, the great Lion." "Ooh!" says Susan, "I'd thought he was a man. Is he—quite safe? I shall feel rather nervous about meeting a lion." "Safe?" says Mr. Beaver. "Who said anything about safe? 'Course he isn't safe. But he's good. He's the king, I tell you."[2]

Aslan, of course, is symbolically Jesus, the Lion of Judah, and Lewis is reminding us that he is anything but tame. He will fiercely fight for those who are being treated unjustly.

Quotes: Martin Luther King Jr., in his "Letter from Birmingham Jail," wrote, "Injustice anywhere is a threat to justice everywhere."[3]

Physicist Albert Einstein said, "In matters of truth and justice, there is no difference between large and small problems, for issues concerning the treatment of people are all the same."[4]

Justice in the Palace?

Big Idea

God demands that his people stand for justice, especially in caring for the weak and vulnerable ones in the society.

Key Themes

- God demands that the leaders of Judah establish and maintain social justice.
- God wants his people to care for those who cannot care for themselves.
- Justice includes eliminating the death of innocent people.
- Social injustice and idolatry are interrelated sins.

Understanding the Text

The Text in Context

The primary theme of Jeremiah 11–29 is the conflict between Jeremiah the prophet and the leaders of Jerusalem. Within this larger unit Jeremiah 21–29 zeroes in on the consequent judgment that will fall on these leaders for shattering God's covenant, worshiping other gods, living unjustly, and persecuting his prophet Jeremiah.

Within 22:1–12 the flow of thought is as follows. In 22:1–5 God instructs Jeremiah to go to the palace of the king and deliver a prophecy of warning to the king and his officials, especially in regard to justice given to the weak and oppressed. If they fail to obey, the palace will be destroyed. Then in 22:6–9 God pronounces judgment on the king's palace and on Jerusalem because they have forsaken the covenant and served other gods. In fact, one of the kings (Shallum/Jehoahaz) is already in exile and will never return (22:10–12).

There are numerous connections and similarities between 22:1–12 (the prophecy in the "house of the king") and 7:1–34 (the prophecy in the "house of the LORD"), especially the call for justice; the call to care for orphans, widows, and foreigners; the demand to end the shedding of innocent blood; and the demand to end idolatry.

One of the clearest background texts for the indictment regarding foreigners, orphans, and widows is Deuteronomy 24:17–22. Twice in that passage God tells the Israelites to remember that they were once slaves in Egypt (24:18, 22). He stresses this in order to motivate them to be compassionate to other unfortunate people (orphans, widows, foreigners, etc.). It is interesting to note that in Jeremiah 22 God announces judgment on Judah for ignoring these laws on social justice from Deuteronomy 24. Then inserted awkwardly into Jeremiah 22 is a passage about Shallum (Jehoahaz), the king who was exiled by the Egyptians back to Egypt (recalling their time of slavery there), where he will die (22:10–12). Thus poetic justice is carried out in this "exodus reversal" event, the consequence of failing to obey Deuteronomy 24.

Historical and Cultural Background

Recall that the final kings of Judah (in chronological order) are Josiah, Jehoahaz (also called "Shallum"), Jehoiakim, Jehoiachin, and Zedekiah. The two with whom Jeremiah collides repeatedly are Jehoiakim (reigned 609–597 BC) and Zedekiah (reigned 597–586 BC).

In Jeremiah 21–22 God continues to use Jeremiah to pronounce his judgment on these rebellious and disobedient kings of Judah. There are several sections in a row that contain prophecies against the kings of Judah, but these are not in chronological order. Thus 21:1–7 focuses on Zedekiah, the last Judahite king to rule before the Babylonians conquered Jerusalem and destroyed it. Then 22:1–9 addresses the kings of Judah as a generic group and not as individuals ("you, king of Judah, you who sit on David's throne"). In 22:10–12 Jeremiah refers to Shallum (Jehoahaz), who ruled only for a few brief months and then was taken into exile in 609 BC to Egypt. Next (22:13–23) Jeremiah indicts Jehoiakim (reigned 609–597 BC) and then finishes the chapter by describing the fate of Jehoiachin (reigned briefly in 597 BC).

Interpretive Insights

22:1 *the palace of the king of Judah.* The word translated as "palace" literally means "house." The identical phrase is repeated in 22:6.

22:2 *you, king of Judah.* The generic reference implies that the address is to all the kings of Judah.

who sit on David's throne. Although the northern kingdom, Israel, experienced several different non-Davidic royal dynasties, all the kings of Judah were descendants of David. Up to this point God has honored the "throne" of Judah precisely because of his promise to David in 2 Samuel 7. The Davidic covenant is implied in the term "David's throne," mentioned here and in 22:4. It is not Jehoiakim's throne or Zedekiah's throne. It is the throne (rule) and the house (dynasty) promised to David. The current kings of Judah will be allowed to continue to sit on this throne (ruling Judah) only if they follow the decrees of God (social justice, etc.).

22:3 *Do what is just and right.* Literally, this translates, "Do justice and righteousness." The demand for justice (*mishpat*) is a central theme in the book of Jeremiah, and this word occurs thirty-two times. The dual terms "justice" and "righteousness" embody the totality of what is fair, just, and right. The rest of 22:3 provides the context for the specific things God has in mind when he says, "Do justice and righteousness."

Rescue from the hand of the oppressor the one who has been robbed. This same command occurs in 21:12. It is also associated with justice in that passage. The word translated "rescue" can also mean "to deliver." It is used frequently of God's deliverance of Israel from slavery (e.g., Exod. 3:8; 6:6). Since the nation of Judah had abandoned the social and moral guidance of Deuteronomy, economic extortion and oppression were now widespread. Those at the top (i.e., the royal house) were the ones profiting the most from this corruption.

the foreigner, the fatherless or the widow. A critical component of the Mosaic covenant, especially as presented in Exodus and Deuteronomy, is the command to see that justice is enforced and special care provided for foreigners, orphans (the fatherless), and widows (Exod. 22:21–22; Deut. 10:18; 24:17–21; 26:12–13; 27:19). These three groups represented those who did not have enough socioeconomic clout to fend for themselves in an "every man for himself" kind of society; they were particularly weak and vulnerable and lacked many basic rights and privileges that the rest of the society enjoyed. Deuteronomy makes it crystal clear that to be in right relationship with God involves taking care of the weaker ones in the society. This is important to God.

and do not shed innocent blood in this place. The phrase "innocent blood" occurs also in 19:4, and in that context it refers to child sacrifice in the Valley of Ben Hinnom. Here in 22:3 the phrase seems to be broader and tied to acts of extortion and oppression against the powerless in the society (foreigners, orphans, and widows). Probably foreigners, orphans, and widows (since they were without family connections and family power) who tried to oppose or stop the institutionally approved acts of extortion and stealing were simply killed. In 7:6 Jeremiah makes the same accusation in the temple.

22:4 *if you are careful to carry out.* The Hebrew grammatical construction is very emphatic ("if you really, certainly carry this out").

kings who sit on David's throne will come. Jeremiah is proclaiming that only if the mandates for social justice are carried out will descendants of David continue to rule over Jerusalem.

22:5 *declares the* LORD, *I swear by myself.* The insertion of the phrase "declares the LORD" (lit., "oracle of the LORD") into the middle of the sentence and the powerfully binding "I swear by myself" oath both stress the certainty of this promise: "this palace/house will become a ruin."

22:6 *Gilead . . . Lebanon.* Both of these regions were heavily forested. With figurative language God is comparing the cedar-paneled interior of the king's palace to dense forests.

22:7 *I will send destroyers . . . each man with his weapons.* Ironically, this verse uses Hebrew terms normally used of temple worship to describe those who will destroy and burn the king's palace. The word translated as "I will send" is literally "I will set apart, sanctify," and the word translated as "weapons" often refers to the "vessels" (pots, pans, incense burners, etc.) used in temple service.

cut up your fine cedar beams and throw them into the fire. The analogy from 22:6 continues. The palace, lined with so much fine cedar that it resembles a forest, will be cut up and burned like a forest fire.

22:10 *Do not weep for the dead king.* The "dead king" is Josiah, who was killed by the Egyptians in 609 BC as they marched north to fight the Babylonians.

weep bitterly for him who is exiled. After the Egyptians defeated Judah and killed Josiah, they appointed Shallum (Jehoahaz) as a puppet king. After a few months, however, they changed their minds, exiled him to Egypt, and replaced him with Jehoiakim.

Theological Insights

The call for care and social justice regarding the societal "underclass," defined in the Old Testament as foreigners, orphans, and widows (sometimes the "poor" are added), runs consistently throughout the Bible and appears to flow right out of the character of God. That is, just as God calls on his people to be holy because he is holy, so he also calls on his people to have a heart for justice and compassion just as he has a heart for justice and compassion. Indeed, God presents this as a foundational part of the law in Exodus and Deuteronomy, the prophets repeatedly indict Israel and Judah for violating this requirement, and the New Testament makes this a normal feature of obedient Christian living (James 1:27).

The Old Testament dual requirement presented in Jeremiah of worshiping God alone while also living justly and compassionately with one another is paralleled in the New Testament by the interaction of faith and works. You cannot have one without the other. Obviously, faith is critical in our relationship with Christ; but the call to follow Jesus is also a call to live justly and compassionately, particularly in regard to those who are weak socioeconomically.

Teaching the Text

True worship of God involves two components: a vertical relationship between humankind and God, and a horizontal relationship between fellow human beings. God demands that his people worship him and him alone, but he also demands that we love and care for one another, and in particular that we care for those who are weak and vulnerable. One of God's defining terms in his demand to treat one another correctly is "justice."

In our day and time many tend to draw a sharp distinction between the seriousness of idolatry and the seriousness of social injustice, viewing idolatry as really bad and social injustice as less so. Historically, many churches have been very slow in recognizing and responding to economic injustices due to race and ethnicity. Often white middle-class and upper-middle-class Christians assume that because the legal system and the economic system work fairly for them, these systems work fairly for everyone, even though consistent statistical data state otherwise. Yet throughout Jeremiah social injustice is just as serious a crime against God as idolatry is. God demands that his people worship him and him alone, and he also demands that we live with one another justly, caring for those who do not have the power or opportunity to care for themselves. Failure to do either is a serious sin. Furthermore, a breakdown in one area usually leads to a breakdown in the other.

Indeed, often today Christians are more concerned about going to heaven than they are about reflecting the character of God in their lives. On the other hand, as we identify ourselves more and more as "in Christ" and become more and more focused on being like Christ, we will take on the heart and character of God and, like him, be outraged at social injustice.

Yes, we should worship God alone through Jesus Christ and proclaim the gospel boldly. But we should also be concerned with protecting, defending, and caring for those in our society who have difficulty adequately caring for themselves—the elderly, the unborn, immigrants, battered women, exploited women and children, those who are ill, those with mental instabilities, addicts of all kinds, the unemployed, and the list goes on. God expects his people, and especially the leaders of his people, to take the lead and to make the implementation of justice a high priority. Of course, these are not the things that save us, but they are the things that show we are the true people of God.

Illustrating the Text

If we do not provide justice, we cannot expect justice.

Object Lesson: Invite someone, preferably a child, to come up and help you make your grandma's favorite recipe for chocolate-chip cookies. Here is a list of ingredients (or use a recipe of your own):

    1 cup   butter, softened
    1 cup   white sugar

1 cup   packed brown sugar

2 eggs

2 teaspoons vanilla extract

3 cups all-purpose flour

1 teaspoon baking soda

2 teaspoons hot water

½ teaspoon salt

2 cups semisweet chocolate chips

Have your assistant read the recipe out loud, one ingredient at a time, while you combine the ingredients. As the ingredients and amounts are read, purposely disregard the recipe. Use four eggs instead of two, gummy bears instead of chocolate chips, a ½ cup of salt instead of a ½ teaspoon, all the while insisting that everything is okay. Then have someone who is known for making great cookies interrupt you and explain that things are not okay. This person can explain that you will not get the desired outcome because you did not do the recipe justice.

God demands that we stand up to injustice.

Literature: *To Kill a Mockingbird,* by Harper Lee. In this Pulitzer Prize–winning novel, two young children, Scout and Jem, are growing up in the South during the 1930s. Their father, Atticus Finch, the town lawyer, is a strong believer in fairness and justice. He lives by a biblical code that requires him and his children to turn the other cheek and to stand up for what is right. As the movie unfolds, the children's innocence is lost as they are exposed to the racism, poverty, and evil that exist in their town.

Atticus defends a black man, Tom Robinson, who is accused of raping and beating a white woman. During the trial the children and their father bear the brunt of numerous racial slurs and unfounded accusations. Ultimately, Atticus proves that Tom could not have committed the crime, but he is convicted anyway.

History: In the story of Rosa Parks it is not so much a case of standing up for justice as one of sitting down. In December 1955, in Montgomery, Alabama, Parks defiantly refused to give up her seat when the bus driver asked her to move so that a white person could sit down. Her act of civil disobedience violated Alabama's segregation laws, and her subsequent court case thrust the civil rights movement into the national spotlight.

Literature: In his book *Pursuing Justice,* Ken Wytsma challenges us to pursue the dreams of justice and fairness that God has for his world instead of chasing after the ultimately unsatisfying dreams of affluence.[1]

A second resource is the critically acclaimed *Half the Sky*, by husband-and-wife team Nicholas Kristof and Sheryl WuDunn. This book probes the widespread oppression of women and girls in the developing world, including the horrors of human trafficking and sexual violence worldwide against women, and challenges us to make a difference.[2]

The King, Injustices, and Knowing God

Big Idea

Those who oppress the poor and needy instead of caring for them simply do not know God.

Key Themes

- Great leadership is measured not by building projects but by justice and righteousness.
- Those who truly know God will stand for social justice and defend the rights of the poor.
- Righteous and just leaders will treat their workers fairly.

Understanding the Text

The Text in Context

In Jeremiah 11–29 the central, unifying theme is opposition to Jeremiah the prophet of God by the king of Judah and other leaders. In the second half of this unit (Jer. 21–29), the focus is on the consequent judgment that falls on these leaders because of their opposition to God's message and their blatant rebellious violation of God's covenant. Throughout Jeremiah 21–29 numerous individual leaders of Judah are mentioned specifically by name in the context of judgment. The previous passage (22:1–12) ended by declaring that King Shallum (Jehoahaz), exiled to Egypt by the Egyptians in 609 BC, will never return to Judah. Our present passage, 22:13–30, addresses Jehoiakim and Jehoiachin, the next two kings (609–597 BC). Jehoiakim, in particular, opposes Jeremiah vigorously and harasses him repeatedly throughout his reign, explicitly ignoring the word of God that Jeremiah delivers to him. Against Jeremiah's advice, Jehoiakim rebels against the Babylonians, who control the region at this time. As the Babylonian army advances toward Jerusalem, Jehoiakim dies, presumably assassinated by someone unhappy with his foreign policy. The young Jehoiachin becomes king, promptly surrenders to the Babylonians, and is carried off into exile, paralleling the fate of Jehoahaz in the previous unit (22:11–12); one king is exiled south to Egypt, and one king is exiled north to Babylon.

The story in 22:13–30 unfolds within this historical context. In 22:13–19 God declares judgment on King Jehoiakim because of his oppression and extortion, particularly through his palace building projects. Consequently, Jehoiakim will not even receive a decent burial but instead will be thrown outside the gates of Jerusalem like a dead donkey. Connecting to the mention of Jerusalem at the end of 22:19, God next addresses the city as a person (using feminine verb endings and feminine pronouns), proclaiming judgment on her and her leaders (22:20–23). Then he declares that just as King Shallum (Jehoahaz) was exiled to Egypt (22:11–12) in the recent past, so King Jehoiachin will be exiled to Babylon in the near future, and, like Shallum, he will never return to his homeland (22:24–30).

The theme of "palace" (lit., "house") also connects 22:13–30 with the previous passage (22:1–12). In 22:1–12 Jeremiah goes to the palace ("house") of the king to pronounce judgment against that palace ("house") for its social injustice. Ironically, in 22:13–17 a specific example is presented: Jehoiakim has literally carried out construction on his "house" using unjust forced labor.

The mention of King David also ties the two sections of Jeremiah 22 together. Jeremiah opens the chapter by mentioning "those who sit on David's throne" (22:2, 4), and then he concludes the chapter by prophesying that no descendant of King Jehoiachin will sit on the throne of David.[1]

Our text also alludes to Jehoiakim's father, King Josiah (reigned 640–609 BC), the last good king of Judah. Jeremiah paints a strong contrast between the just and righteous rule of Josiah and the injustices of Jehoiakim, who reversed all the good reforms that Josiah had implemented.

Interpretive Insights

22:13 *Woe to him.* The Hebrew word translated as "woe" is an interjection, similar to "Ah!" or even "Argh!" in English. It conveys a lamenting tone of sorrow or sadness due to something terrible and tragic, such as death. This same word is used four times in 22:18, where it is translated as "alas." In 22:13 it implies that something terrible and tragic is going to happen to the one addressed. The context of this passage helps us to identify "him" as King Jehoiakim.

who builds his palace. This term translated as "palace" literally means "house." It can refer to the actual structure that someone lives in. Thus "house of the king" usually refers to his "palace" (22:1, 6), and "house of the LORD" usually refers to the temple (7:2). It can also refer to the "household" or all the people who are part of the house (i.e., the entire royal court, including officials), as it does in 21:11. Likewise, "house of Israel" or "house of Jacob" refs to the entire nation (3:18, 20). This word can also refer to a family dynasty, particularly a royal dynasty (2 Sam. 7:11; Jer. 21:12). In 22:13 there is probably a subtle double meaning. On the surface, it refers to the actual structure in which the king lives (i.e., "palace"). But the double, tongue-in-cheek meaning probably includes those who make up the royal court bureaucracy and the royal dynasty.

by unrighteousness . . . by injustice. The concepts of "unrighteousness" and "injustice" are formed in Hebrew by placing negative particles before the terms for "righteousness" (*tsedek*) and "justice" (*mishpat*). In 22:3 and 22:15 Jeremiah uses these same two terms (without the negatives) to describe what a good king should do.

22:14 *panels it with cedar.* Cedar had to be imported from Lebanon and was rather expensive. To panel a house with cedar was the height of opulence. Jeremiah uses the word "cedar" four times, all in this chapter (22:7, 14, 15, 23), all in negative contexts.

22:15 *your father . . . did what was right and just.* Jehoiakim's father was Josiah, the last good king of Judah. Also note that the text stresses "doing" what is right (*tsedek*) and just (*mishpat*) and not just "being" right and just. The same verb for "do" is used in 22:3.

22:16 *Is that not what it means . . . ?* "That" refers back to doing what is right and just, and defending the poor and needy.

to know me. The word translated as "know" is a noun form of the verb *yada'*. It carries connotations not only of cognitive "knowledge" but also of an ongoing and close relationship.

22:17 *your eyes and your heart.* "Eyes" represent one's desire, and "heart," the seat of decision making. Jehoiakim's desires, along with his criteria for making decisions, were set not on righteousness or justice but rather on selfish and dishonest acquisition, even if that required extortion or murder.

22:19 *the burial of a donkey.* Proper burial was extremely important to people in Israel and throughout the ancient Near East. To die and not be buried properly was viewed as a curse. Dead donkeys, of course, received no real burial at all. They were thrown into an area like a garbage dump just outside the city gates, where scavenger birds and animals ate them. Notice the movement in the passage from the opulent cedar-lined upper rooms of the palace to the garbage dump outside the city walls.

22:20 *Go up.* The Hebrew verbs used here are feminine, referring figuratively to Jerusalem.

all your allies are crushed. The word translated by the NIV as "allies" usually means "love/lovers" (also in 22:22), and it is translated that way in several versions (NRSV, NASB, ESV). It can also mean "covenant friends" or "allies," as it probably does here, but no doubt the ironic wordplay on the normal nuance of "lovers" is intentional (cf. Jer. 2:2, 33; 8:2; 20:4, 22; 30:14; Lam. 1:2). Jehoiakim had formed an alliance with the nations around him and then rebelled against the Babylonians. This "alliance" quickly unraveled as the Babylonian army drew near.

22:22 *The wind will drive all your shepherds away.* There is a clever wordplay here. The Hebrew verb translated as "will drive" basically means "to shepherd." It is the same root that the noun "shepherds" comes from. Literally, this verse reads, "The wind will shepherd all your shepherds" (cf. NRSV). The term "shepherds" is used figuratively to refer to Jerusalem's leaders, a theme picked up again in Jeremiah 23. Rather than lead, they will be scattered, as illustrated by the fate of Jehoiachin (22:24–30) and Jehoahaz (22:11–12).

22:24 *signet ring.* This probably was the ring with the royal seal, and it signified who had the authority to continue the royal dynasty. God is saying that descendants of Jehoiachin will not be involved in the ongoing dynastic succession of David, a promise stated even more clearly in 22:30.[2]

22:26 *I will hurl you.* The word translated as "hurl" indicates the act of throwing something as far or as hard as one can. It is often used in the Old Testament of "hurling" spears (e.g., 1 Sam. 18:11; 20:33). It is used again in 22:28.

Theological Insights

Because God is so concerned with justice and the well-being of people, those who seek to obey him will discover that theology and economics are closely intertwined. For example, it is important to God that his people pay their workers a just wage on time. This is stressed not only here in Jeremiah but also in Deuteronomy 24:14–15 and Malachi 3:5, and obedience to this desire of God is inseparable from other central theological tenets about knowing God. In contrast, widely accepted capitalistic principles often lead Christian business leaders today to seek to minimize pay to workers as much as possible in order to increase profits. God, however, seems to be quite concerned with justice and what is fair in the workplace. "Is this a fair and just wage?" is the question that Christian business owners and managers ought to be asking. This is an issue that God is very much concerned about as he looks at our businesses.

Likewise, "knowing God" (22:16) is tied to the following: doing what is right and just (22:15), and defending the cause of the poor and needy (22:16). Knowing God means to know his moral character and to live accordingly. The connection between justice and righteousness and knowing God is also emphasized in 9:24. Many Christians today would list "knowing God" as one of the top priorities in their life. But "knowing God" is not just an inner spiritual feeling that one gets in secluded quiet time alone with God; rather, it involves living in the manner that God desires for us, and that clearly includes doing justice and defending the poor and needy in the nitty-gritty world we live in.

Teaching the Text

God is adamant throughout the book of Jeremiah that being in right relationship with him also includes relating properly to one another. This is not an issue of "works righteousness" or legalism but rather a reality that God wants in our lives that emanates directly from his own character. Thus, for God's people there is an interconnected vertical relationship (between us and God) and a horizontal relationship (among ourselves). These are inextricably connected. God is righteous and just, and he expects those who know him and serve him to live righteously and justly within the world. In this passage, as well as throughout the book of Jeremiah, God provides us with some clear examples of what righteous and just living involves. He makes it quite clear that at the heart of righteous and just living is caring for the poor and needy. This is a timeless truth, just as true today as in the time of Jeremiah. Anyone who truly knows God will care for the poor and needy. Failure to care for those who need help is just as unacceptable for Christians as is idolatry; that is, the violation of the horizontal relationships is viewed by God as seriously as violation of the vertical relationship. Some Christians erroneously assume that if they pay taxes and the government uses those taxes to care for the poor, then they have fulfilled this responsibility. Our tendency in many churches today is to stress proper worship, soteriology, and doctrine of God but to leave issues of social justice as optional or at least as secondary in importance. Yet clearly this is a distortion of how God wants us to live. This truth is likewise clearly presented in the New Testament, where the book of 1 John emphasizes this same theme.

Another specific issue of social justice raised in this passage that has contemporary relevance for us is in regard to fair wages for workers. King Jehoiakim was forcing workers to build his palace without paying them properly. Based on the standards of other kings and other countries, this was well within the normal practices of kings. But God adamantly rejects this practice, both in Deuteronomy and in Jeremiah. For Christians today in ownership or management positions, the determination of "fair wages" or other benefits should be something that is weighed against the expectations of God and not the profit-driven market (i.e., what the "other kings" are doing). This should also influence our perspective and our vote regarding the minimum wage.

Leadership is a central issue in this passage. Because of their influence (and their opportunity), God holds leaders responsible for the behavior of their people and for how well they implement social justice in their sphere of influence. Obviously, the situation concerning leaders in ancient Judah in the time of Jeremiah does not find exact parallel in the church today (e.g., we are not a monarchy), but nonetheless some basic principles do apply. Leaders in the church today should be actively involved in helping their parishioners to mature in the faith, in both the vertical and the horizontal relationships. Integrating the passion for social justice into the life of the church should be a high-priority task for church leaders today. "Knowing God" continues to be at the top of the priority list for Christians today, but God makes it perfectly clear that to know him includes embracing his heart and his attitude toward helping those in our society who need socioeconomic assistance.

Illustrating the Text

The godly are willing to make sacrifices for the sake of the poor.

Quote: Regarding the teaching of Paul in 2 Corinthians 8:8–15, John Stott writes,

> Let me try to sum up these instructions, in the reverse order, applying them to the world situation today. (1) God has provided enough for everybody's need (adequate resources in sun and rain, earth, air and water); (2) any great disparity between affluence and want, wealth and poverty, is unacceptable to him; (3) when a situation of serious disparity arises, it ought to be corrected by an adjustment, in order to secure "equality" of "justice"; (4) the Christian motive for desiring such "justice" is "grace," loving generosity, as in the case of Jesus Christ . . . ; (5) we are to follow his example in this, and so prove the genuineness of our love. Just how a worldwide equalization could or should be effected is another question. Economists differ. Whatever the method, however, the motivation for seeking equality or fairness is love.[3]

Scripture: In Micah 6:8 we are told that the Lord requires us "to act justly, and to love mercy, and to walk humbly with our God." The church of Jesus Christ would be a much greater force to be reckoned with in the world if it would better learn and act on this lesson. In Luke 10:25–37 Jesus tells the story of the good Samaritan to remind the religious people of his day (and ours) that it is our duty as God followers to be willing to make sacrifices to help those in need, especially those who are different from us. As Jesus said in Matthew 25:40, "Truly I tell you, whatever you did for one of the least of these brothers and sisters of mine, you did for me."

Leadership is measured by the way it treats people.

News Story: The Enron Corporation, which went bankrupt in December 2001, claimed that it had a profit of $101 billion in 2000. The company had over twenty thousand employees, most of whom believed that they were working for a hugely successful company. They were as shocked as anyone when the story broke that members of the upper-management team had secretly collaborated in an elaborate scheme to show a profit where there was none. The accounting fraud sent ripples through the New York Stock Exchange and eventually led to a criminal trial that ended with the arrest and conviction of several of Enron's top executives.[4]

Righteous leaders treat their workers fairly.

Quote: In his book *Christians in an Age of Wealth*, Craig Blomberg writes,

> Materialism, the worship of the god "Mammon" as the greatest good on earth, may well be the biggest competitor with the God of Jesus Christ for the allegiance of human hearts in our world today. . . . Like the Israelites of old who believed they could still worship Yahweh under the guise of a golden calf, Christians in more well-to-do nations or parts of the world think they can serve Jesus while still worshiping money and material possessions even more. They quickly deny that their attachment to those possessions comes anywhere close to worship, but when one compares the time and energy expended in working for it, managing it, protecting it, longing for more of it, . . . with the time and energy put into kingdom activity, the denials often ring hollow.[5]

The Righteous Shepherd Is Coming

Big Idea

A truly just and righteous messianic king will come and save his people in a new and spectacular way.

Key Themes

- God will replace the current "bad shepherds" with "good shepherds."
- God himself will act as a shepherd for his people.
- The coming messianic king will rule with justice and righteousness.
- The deliverance brought by this messianic king will overshadow even the exodus.

Understanding the Text

The Text in Context

Throughout Jeremiah 11–29 the repeating and unifying theme is that of opposition and hostility against Jeremiah (and God's word) by the leaders of Judah (especially the various kings, their priests, and their court prophets). The consequences of such hostility and opposition are serious, and God frequently proclaims the coming judgment on these leaders in clear and unequivocal terms throughout this section. In the midst of this larger section that is condemning Judah's corrupt and unfaithful kings and prophets, 23:1–8 comes as a shocking but beautiful contrast, for in this passage God describes the coming messianic king. The point of this insertion is to underscore the drastic contrast between the current leadership of Judah and the coming Messiah.

In the previous chapters Jeremiah has critiqued Pashhur the chief officer of the temple (20:1–6), King Zedekiah (21:1–14), the kings of Judah in general (22:1–9), King Jehoahaz (22:10–12), King Jehoiakim (22:13–23), and King Jehoiachin (22:24–30). Jeremiah 23:1 ("Woe to the shepherds who are destroying and scattering the sheep of my pasture!") thus serves as a concluding summary of the previous units, as well as an introduction to our current passage. The interjection translated as "Woe!" which opens this passage likewise connects it back to Jeremiah 22, where this same Hebrew word occurs five times, once in 22:13 (translated as "woe") and four times in 22:18 (translated as "alas").

Jeremiah 23:1–8 contains both prose and poetry; the beginning and ending subsections (23:1–4, 7–8) are in prose, while the center subsection (23:5–6) is in poetry. Jeremiah 23:1–4 opens with "Woe!" as God declares that he will replace the unworthy leaders of Judah with good leaders; in fact, God himself will serve as one of these leaders. The next two sections, united by the opening phrase "the days are coming," elaborate on this promise. First, in 23:5–6 God states that he will raise up a descendant of David to rule over Israel, but in contrast to Judah's current leaders, this one will do what is righteous and just. In fact, God continues in 23:7–8, this new king/shepherd will bring about an entirely new paradigm of deliverance that will even overshadow the exodus (the old paradigm of deliverance).[1]

Likening the king and other leaders to shepherds is a common analogy in the Bible (e.g., Ezek. 34), and Jeremiah uses it for both good kings (like a good shepherd) and bad kings (like a bad shepherd). The shepherd analogy connects this current passage to the mention of shepherds in the preceding passage (22:22). The mention of David and the allusions to the Davidic covenant (22:2, 4, 30; 23:5) also tie these units together. Furthermore, it is no accident that, in a text stressing the fulfillment of the promise to David, God uses the imagery of shepherds as his primary analogy for leadership, for David was the premier shepherd/king in Israel's history.

In Jeremiah 33 God explains the fulfillment of the Davidic covenant in some detail. Jeremiah 23:5–6 is repeated as part of that explanation (33:15–16).

Interpretive Insights

23:1 *Woe.* As mentioned above on 22:13, the word translated as "woe" is an interjection, similar to "Ah!" or even "Argh!" in English. It conveys a lamenting tone of sorrow or sadness due to something terrible and tragic, such as death. In this verse it implies that something terrible and tragic is going to happen to the ones addressed (i.e., the "shepherds").

the shepherds. In 23:1, 4 the Hebrew word that means "shepherding, pasturing, caring for sheep and goats" is used four times in various forms. The participle ("the one who shepherds") is translated as "shepherds" (23:1, 4). The "place of shepherding" is translated as "pasture" (23:1), and the verb "to shepherd" is translated as "tend" (23:4).

23:2 *scattered my flock and driven them away.* God refers to his people as "my flock." The image of the flock being scattered and driven away is a reference to the coming exile, in which the Babylonians will deport most of the people living in Judah to Babylonia. Note that in this text God puts the blame for the exile squarely on the corrupt leaders of Israel.

for the evil you have done. The word translated as "evil" (*roaʿ*) is a form of the word *raʿah*, which Jeremiah uses repeatedly throughout the book to refer to "bad stuff, evil actions." An interesting wordplay takes place here, however, because the word for "shepherding" is also *raʿah*. These are different words, but they often have identical forms. As mentioned above, forms of *raʿah* that refer to shepherding occur twice in 23:1 and twice in 23:4. Sandwiched directly in the middle (23:2) is the *raʿah* that means "bad stuff, evil actions," the poetically appropriate punishment for being a bad (*raʿah*) shepherd.

23:3 *I myself will gather the remnant.* There is a strong grammatical emphasis on the word "I," which the NIV expresses with "I myself." As part of the shepherding analogy, "gathering" is the opposite of "scattering." Several times in Jeremiah God promises that in the future he will "gather" his people back in the land (23:3; 29:14; 31:8; 32:37).

they will be fruitful and increase in number. This full English sentence translates only two Hebrew words. One means "to be fruitful," the other "to become many." These same two Hebrew words occur several times in the early chapters of Genesis (1:22, 28; 8:17; 9:1, 7); thus here in Jeremiah 23:3 God appears to be describing the future regathering in terms of a "new creation." There are also probable allusions to the "numerous descendants" promise made to Abraham and the patriarchs, where the word translated as "to become many" is used several times (Gen. 16:10; 17:2; 22:17; 26:4, 24).

23:5 *a righteous Branch.* The word translated as "branch" literally refers to a "new growth, a sprout, a new shoot." The Hebrew word for "righteous/right" (*tsedek*) is used twice in this verse, once here in describing the "branch" and once in describing actions of the king as doing "what is just and *right.*" Taken together, they form a metaphor for the "rightful heir." Jeremiah is stating that the rightful heir to David is neither Jehoiachin (exiled to Babylon) nor Zedekiah (currently on the throne) but rather one that the Lord will raise up in the future (i.e., the Messiah).[2]

23:6 *he will be called: The LORD Our Righteous Savior.* The Hebrew here simply has "the LORD is our righteousness" (cf. NRSV), and a wordplay is taking place. The final king of Judah is Zedekiah, whose name means "my righteousness is the Lord." But as earlier texts declare, Zedekiah is far from righteous. The coming Davidic king, however, who will actually be righteous, will be called "The LORD is our righteousness," a spoof, so to speak, on Zedekiah's name that at the same time reveals a startling new reality.

23:8 *the descendants of Israel.* The word translated as "descendants" literally means "seed." This Hebrew word for seed is a central term of the Abrahamic covenant, used repeatedly in God's promise to Abraham of "numerous descendants" (Gen. 12:7; 13:15, 16; 15:5, 18; 17:7, 8, 9, 10, 19; 22:17,

18). Note also the interesting shift in terminology from "the Israelites" (lit., "the sons of Israel") in 23:7 to "the descendants of Israel" (lit., "the seed of the house of Israel").

Theological Insights

When Jeremiah looks beyond the coming judgment to describe the future restoration, he draws heavily on the gracious promises (often called "covenants") that God made to Abraham (Gen. 12; 15; 17; 22) and to David (2 Sam. 7). To Abraham God promised a land, blessings, and uncountable descendants (lit., "seed"). At the heart of the Davidic covenant was God's promise of a coming king who would rule forever. Jeremiah 23:1–8 proclaims that the coming Messiah will bring fulfillment of the promises contained in both of these covenants.

Likewise, the shift in terminology from "*sons* of Israel" in 23:7 to the "*seed* of the house of Israel" in 23:8, within the picture of the future restoration brought about by the Messiah, suggests a special and new understanding of the term "seed." In the New Testament Paul will interpret the concept of "seed" (descendant) as referring both to Christ and to those who are in Christ by faith (Rom. 4:13–17; 9:6–29; Gal. 3:15–20, 29). The New Testament will clarify that the messianic "regathering" of the "seed" promised by the Old Testament prophets includes those who are of faith, both Jews and gentiles.

It is difficult to ascertain exactly to what degree of specificity the coming Messiah was revealed to Jeremiah. But certainly Jeremiah knew that this coming Davidic king whom God would raise up would be characterized by justice and righteousness in a special way; indeed, his name would be "The LORD is our righteousness." Yet we probably will have to look to the New Testament and Paul to explain all the theological depth and richness of how Jesus the Messiah becomes "our righteousness."

Teaching the Text

This chapter in Jeremiah teaches us that the coming Messiah will be a king like no other king, a reality we see explained in more fullness in the New Testament. Here in Jeremiah God underscores that the imminent judgment on Judah is coming largely because of the apostasy and unjust rule of the current leaders (kings, priests, and court prophets). Therefore, as God looks to the future and describes the wonderful time of restoration, it is no surprise that he places special emphasis on how radically different the coming messianic king will be. And indeed, the contrast between Jesus Christ, God's prophesied messianic king, and most rulers of the world throughout history is staggering.

In this passage, after declaring how terrible the current "shepherds" are and the judgment that will come because of them, God continues to use the shepherding image as he promises the regathering of "his flock." In describing the future hope and restoration, God presents himself as the shepherd who restores and provides for his flock (see also Ezek. 34:11–16, where God says essentially the same thing). These are precisely the passages and the image that Jesus is connecting to when he declares, "I am the good shepherd" (John 10:11–18). That is, Jesus's self-identification as the good shepherd is a direct fulfillment of this passage (along with Ezek. 34:11–16).

Yet God also refers to other "shepherds" (plural) that he will provide to tend and care for his people. The fulfillment of this promise starts to unfold during the postexilic period through the ministry of godly leaders such as Ezra and Nehemiah. This fulfillment continues in the New Testament through the leadership of Paul and the other apostles and leaders of the early church, and it continues to this day. Thus the New Testament applies the shepherding image not only to Christ but also to his true leaders in the church today (John 21:15–19; 1 Pet. 5:1–4). Godly shepherds gather God's sheep (his people) together, providing and caring for the flock, enabling God's sheep to be fruitful and to multiply (these are strong images of blessing).

The character of the messianic king and the nature of his rule will likewise be in stark contrast to the corrupt leadership of Israel in the time of Jeremiah. The Messiah will be a descendant of David, and he will rule with justice and righteousness, providing deliverance for his people. Jesus, of course, epitomizes this prophetic picture, being completely righteous and providing imputed righteousness for those who follow him and become his people. Yet as prophesied by Jeremiah, Jesus also stresses justice, not just at the theological level but also at the social level (e.g., Matt. 5–7; Luke 18–19).

The salvation brought by this future messianic king will be different and spectacular. In the Old Testament the central paradigm of deliverance/salvation is the exodus. This event, in which God brought his unworthy people out of Egyptian slavery and established them in the promised land with his presence living among them to bless them, defines for the Old Testament what salvation was all about. Thus it was quite radical and dramatic for God to declare through Jeremiah that in the coming days the new messianic king would usher in a time of deliverance that would overshadow the exodus and redefine salvation and the saving character of God. Indeed, just as Jeremiah predicted, the salvation that Jesus provides is bigger, better, longer lasting, and more spectacular (words fail us here) than even the wonderful exodus event led by Moses.

Illustrating the Text

The messianic king will bring a deliverance that will overshadow the exodus.

Personal Experience: I remember growing up in New Mexico and how we frequently saw beautiful ravines and canyons in the mountain ranges there. I appreciated their beauty and their spectacular testimony to the creative power of God. But later I realized that I only *thought* that I knew about the beauty and spectacle of canyons. Later in life I spent six days on a rafting trip covering 190 miles of the Grand Canyon. *Wow!* I thought. *The Grand Canyon dwarfs all other canyons, and its beauty and size are overwhelming.* Thus the deliverance offered by Christ dwarfs the great and spectacular deliverance offered to Israel in the exodus. Here you might be able to share such a moment in your own life.

Learning from shepherds

Theological Book: *A Shepherd Looks at Psalm 23,* by Phillip Keller. This book is a study of Psalm 23 in light of the duties, behaviors, and practices of shepherds.[3] Consider using this book and the lessons in it to draw out two distinct and important aspects of this section of Jeremiah.

First, look at what a good shepherd does and illustrate this as the desired norm. You can then contrast this with what the bad shepherds of Israel were doing.

Second, use the examples of positive and healthy practices of a shepherd in relationship to how God tends his flock, his beloved people.

If you have the capacity to do so, show pictures or video of sheep as you talk about what a good shepherd looks like (both from a human and a divine perspective).

The Grim Consequences of False Prophecy

Big Idea

Those who claim to speak with the authority of God are held responsible for accurately and truthfully proclaiming his word.

Key Themes

- Jeremiah mourns over the lies and deceit that are being proclaimed as the word of God.
- Encountering God's presence and encountering God's word are inseparable.
- The false prophets misled the people by proclaiming peace when God was warning of judgment.
- God gets particularly angry with those who falsely claim to speak in his name.

Understanding the Text

The Text in Context

The common theme running throughout Jeremiah 11–29 is the conflict between Jeremiah and the leaders of Judah. In Jeremiah 11–20 the prophet's message from God was met with active hostility from the leaders in Jerusalem that soon grew into serious and dangerous persecution. The focus of Jeremiah 21–29, not surprisingly, is God's coming judgment on these leaders who have rejected his word and sought to persecute, even kill, his prophet.

Just as the kings rejected God's word, leading the people of Judah away from God, so too did the "religious" leaders (the priests and the court prophets). Although the priests are also mentioned briefly in this passage (23:11, 33–34), the focus is on the court prophets who were contradicting Jeremiah with counterprophecies supposedly coming from God. So after proclaiming judgment on the kings of Judah (21:1–23:8), Jeremiah now brings the judgment of God to bear on the false prophets.

Jeremiah 23:9–40 is a collection of several short "oracles" or messages, first in poetry (23:9–24) and then in prose (23:25–40), all relating to the false prophets in Jerusalem. "Concerning the prophets" (23:9) introduces the entire section. Jeremiah himself speaks in 23:9–10, bemoaning the evil behavior of the prophets. The rest of the passage reflects the direct speech of God, who seems to be responding to and extensively adding to the opening lament-like statement of Jeremiah. Connected by the twice-repeated "declares the LORD" in 23:11–12, the text has God declaring that since these prophets do evil (ra'ah) right in his temple, he will bring evil (ra'ah) right on them. He compares the lying and immoral actions of the current prophets in Jerusalem to the earlier, repulsive prophets of Baal who lived in the northern kingdom, Israel. Indeed, God underscores, they are as bad as those at Sodom and Gomorrah (23:13–14). Next come two subsections, a short one and a longer one, united by the phrase "what the LORD Almighty says." In 23:15 God proclaims coming judgment on these prophets because of their ungodly influence on the entire country. In 23:16–22 he expresses his anger and his judgment on them because they have the audacity to claim to speak in his name. Next comes another two-verse subsection (23:23–24) connected by a twice-repeated "declares the LORD," which parallels 23:11–12. In 23:11–12 God has expressed how offensive it is that these false proclaimers practice their wickedness right in the temple (i.e., in his presence, right in front of him). The parallel passage (23:23–24) notes that God's presence is also throughout all heaven and earth; thus he sees all their wickedness.

The last two subsections are in prose, the first (23:25–32) dealing with false dreams, the second (23:33–40) with false oracles.

The passage opens and closes with references to God's presence. Since Jeremiah has experienced the presence of God and the associated presence of God's word, he is distraught over the sin that pervades Judah (23:9). Throughout the middle of the passage, the false prophets are accused of not having experienced the presence of God; thus they do not know his word either. Consequently, at the end of the passage God proclaims that he will literally expel them even further from his presence.

References to "heart" also tie the section together: Jeremiah's heart (23:9), the stubborn heart of the people (23:17), the Lord's heart (23:20), and the heart of the false prophets (23:16, 26). Likewise, ra'ah ("bad stuff, evil behavior") and related forms are used in numerous wordplays repeatedly throughout the passage (23:10, 11, 12, 14 [2x], 22 [2x]).

Interpretive Insights

23:9 *my heart is broken.* The word translated as "broken" means "to be smashed into pieces."

because of the LORD and his holy words. Literally, this reads, "because of the presence of the LORD and because of the presence of his holy words." In contrast to the false prophets, who had never been in the presence of God or heard his word (23:21–22), Jeremiah has experienced God's presence / God's word, and thus he is distraught and upset at the sin he sees in the land.

23:10 *follow an evil course.* Literally, "their running is evil/bad [*ra'ah*]." The Hebrew word for "run" shows up again in 23:21.

23:11 *even in my temple I find their wickedness.* Literally, "even in my house I find their *ra'ah* [bad stuff/evil behavior]."

23:12 *their path will become slippery.* This imagery picks up the "running according to *ra'ah*" motif of 23:10.

23:14 *They commit adultery and live a lie.* These two charges, adultery and lying, are explained in the next two lines. Literally, "they are strengthening the hands of those doing *ra'ah* [bad stuff/evil behavior] so that they will never turn from their *ra'ah* [bad stuff/evil behavior]." The prophets and priests are not correcting the sinful behavior of the people; rather, they are reinforcing it.

23:16 *visions from their own minds.* The word translated as "mind" here is the word for "heart," but the translation captures the intent of the text because the language reflects the idea common in the ancient world that cognitive processes took place in organs such as the heart.

23:20 *until he fully accomplishes the purposes of his heart.* The word translated as "purposes" usually carries negative connotations—that is, a damaging or judgmental purpose. Likewise, note the ironic use of "heart" connecting back to earlier verses. The false prophets are speaking visions originating from their own hearts (23:16), thus proclaiming peace in God's name even to those who despise God and follow the stubbornness of their own hearts (23:17). Therefore, the anger of God will not be turned back until all the judgmental plans in his heart are carried out against these people.

23:22 *stood in my council.* The word translated as "council" in general refers to a meeting of close confidants. In this context God is using it of his heavenly council. True prophets had access to the heavenly council, and it was there that they listened in on the business, discussions, and decisions of God and received their message to deliver to the people.

23:39 *I will surely forget you.* The Hebrew grammar stresses the certainty of the verb "forget." In 23:27 the false prophets are leading the people to "forget" the name of God. Here in 23:39 God stresses that it is the false prophets who will be forgotten. In Hebrew "forgetting" and "remembering" refer not to mere recollection but rather to action or inaction in their regard.

cast you out of my presence. The word translated as "cast" means "to leave, forsake, abandon." Since the false prophets had ignored God's presence in their false proclamation of his word, he now will make this a literal reality, removing them from his indwelling presence in the temple in the midst of Israel. This verse refers both to the departure of God from the temple and to the exile of the people of Jerusalem from the city.

23:40 *everlasting disgrace—everlasting shame that will not be forgotten.* "Everlasting" (lit., "forever") is repeated twice for emphasis. God says in 23:39 that he himself will forget them (i.e., he will no longer care for them or protect them by his presence), but here, in contrast, he says that their disgrace and shame will never be forgotten.

Theological Insights

An important theological insight from 23:9, 18–22 is that the presence of God is closely associated with the word of God. For Jeremiah, standing in the presence of God is to hear the word of God and vice versa. The two go together. You cannot have one without the other. To encounter God is to encounter his word; likewise, to encounter his word is to encounter him. This theological truth is also stressed in the New Testament (John 1). In Jeremiah's day the false prophets had not been in the presence of God; thus they knew neither God nor the word of God, but only the delusions of their minds. A true encounter with the presence of God is inextricably interconnected with a true encounter with the word of God.

Teaching the Text

Although Christians experience the presence of God through the indwelling of the Spirit and not, like Jeremiah, through standing in the heavenly council, those of us who have been in the presence of God and know his word may find ourselves heartbroken and distraught over the widespread distortion and misrepresentation of the "word of God" in our land, especially as we come to grips with the terrible consequences of this falsehood. This is part of what Jesus is referring to when he says, "Blessed are those who mourn" (Matt. 5:4).

It is bad enough to ignore the word of God. Worse is trying to replace the word of God with one's own self-serving, contradictory agenda, all the while deceitfully dubbing this self-derived message as "the word of God." Few things seem to irritate God more than this, and he has very strong, frightening, and condemnatory words for those who put forth their own ideas as his word. Whether we are pastors, professors, Sunday school teachers, Bible study leaders, or just friends giving biblical advice, it is important that we never put forward our own ideas and beliefs as the "word of God." The worst violators of the third commandment (taking the Lord's name in vain) are not those who treat it as powerless and thus use it flippantly without thought but rather those who know that it is powerful and therefore seek to exploit that power for their own personal agendas.

So why did these "false prophets and priests" proclaim a message that was so contrary to the true word of God? They probably were seeking popularity and affirmation from the king and the people. They were trying to fit in and be accommodating to popular opinion and the desires of the political powers. Likewise, the current "tastes" of our culture and the "political correctness" required for public dialogue today often pressure us to modify, adapt, and distort the word of God to fit in. However, do not miss the end of this passage from Jeremiah. God declares that he will "forget" (i.e., cast out of his presence) those who speak falsely in his name. What will be remembered forever is their shame—the fact that they were responsible for the downfall and destruction of God's people. As our culture moves away from obeying the word of God, if we, the proclaimers of God's word, provide affirmation for that shift, whitewashing the sin involved in it, then we will be held culpable for the consequences that will fall on people who are deceived by it all.

So how can we be sure that we are accurately proclaiming the word of God? Jeremiah 23 connects being in the presence of God and knowing/encountering the word of God. The two are inseparable and, conceptually, simultaneous. In order to enter into the presence of God, we must embrace the word of God (i.e., know it and actively obey it), but only as we experience the presence of God will we truly know the word of God and be able to live it out. Can you see how Jesus pulls all this together for the Christian? He is both the word of God and the manifestation of his presence through the incarnation. Furthermore, we are now "in Christ," and he is "in us" (John 14:20). He also sends the Spirit, who dwells within us and empowers us to live out his word. As teachers called to proclaim the word of God, we should diligently study his word in the context of living obediently in his presence. Serious study of God's word, committed obedience to God's word, and a life of worship and devotion lived in God's presence all go together, empowering us to proclaim accurately God's word to our generation.

Illustrating the Text

God's word and God's presence are inseparable.

Analogy: Some things in life go hand in hand. They just seem to go together. There are many examples. Here are some light and less serious examples: chips and salsa, Paris and romance, country music and trucks. You can add a couple of examples from your own setting.

There are also examples of things that are inseparably linked: fire and heat, snow and cold, sin and judgment, and many other examples. There are things in this world that, by their very existence, demand that something else be present.

In the spiritual world, when God's word is spoken, read, or heard, God is present. In Jeremiah's day the truth of God was being spoken by Jeremiah. Today we have the Bible, the very word of God. Every time we read the Bible, hear a biblical sermon, or meditate on the Scriptures, in a very real way, God is near. He has given his word, and his Spirit helps us understand what it means, convicts, and calls us to action.

Scripture: In the first verse of John's Gospel, he makes a declaration that takes a little thought to understand. Suggest that the congregation might know what it says, but ask if they understand it. Then read it slowly, stopping after the words "In the beginning was the . . . ," asking them, "The what?" Then read the rest of it, pointing out that in the beginning "was" the Word, and it "was with God," and it "was God." John's point is similar to Jeremiah's. There is a very tight connection and association between the "word of God" and God himself.

False prophets mislead people, claiming that they speak for God.

Government: Treaties between countries typically are negotiated by someone such as a secretary of state or an ambassador. These representatives do not have the freedom to simply say whatever they want. They are there to speak for the president or prime minister or monarch and must represent the leader's views impartially and without bias.

Advertising: We are all familiar with advertisements that are designed to mislead. There are commercials that make grand claims for all sorts of products. One of the most prevalent and consistent sources of false advertisement is in the area of weight-loss products. The Federal Trade Commission website provides a list of seven red flags to help you identify false claims for weight-loss products.[1]

It is one thing to speak falsely about a dietary product; it is a far worse thing to speak as if representing God and tell people what they want to hear rather than what they need to hear. Even today we need to be aware that there are people who claim to speak for God but knowingly mislead people with words that are attractive but false. We should also be very careful when we say things like, "The Lord told me." To speak falsely in the name of the Lord is to move into very dangerous territory.

Good Figs—with Hearts to Know God

Big Idea

God restores repentant people to a renewed relationship with him, but he judges those who continually defy him.

Key Themes

- God graciously promises to restore his relationship with a remnant of Israel.
- This remnant will come from those already in exile.
- God will give the remnant a renewed heart to know him truly and to serve him wholeheartedly.
- Those disobedient ones remaining in Jerusalem will not be part of the remnant.

Understanding the Text

The Text in Context

This passage has several connections to Jeremiah 1. In Jeremiah 1 the prophet sees a vision of an almond tree and a boiling pot. In Jeremiah 24 he sees a basket of good figs and a basket of bad figs. These are the only two chapters in which Jeremiah sees visions of such symbolic items. Both chapters include the dual themes of judgment and restoration. Furthermore, the language of restoration in 24:6 (build up and not tear down; plant and not uproot) echoes the commission that God gave to Jeremiah in 1:10.[1] Jeremiah alludes to this "bad fig" analogy again in his letter to the exiles in 29:17–19.

There are also several connections between Jeremiah 24 and Deuteronomy 26, such as the firstfruits offering before God (Deut. 26:1–15), following God "with all your heart" (Deut. 26:16), and the covenant formula "I will be your God; you will be my people" (Deut. 26:17–18).

Historical and Cultural Background

The historical context is critical for understanding this passage. King Jehoiakim of Judah had rebelled against the Babylonians. As the Babylonian army approached in reprisal, Jehoiakim died. His young son Jehoiachin wisely surrendered to the Babylonians and was carried off into exile along with the artisans and leading citizens of Jerusalem. The year was 597 BC, and 24:1 locates the events in this passage as occurring after this "first exile" and yet before the final destruction of Jerusalem and massive exile of 587/586 BC. The two groups that 24:1–10 addresses are those with Jehoiachin already in exile in Babylon (the good figs) and those with Zedekiah still resisting Jeremiah's message in Jerusalem (the bad figs).

This fits well within the major theme of Jeremiah 21–29 that focuses on God's response to the kings and leaders who oppose Jeremiah and reject God's word to them. Jehoiachin surrendered to the Babylonians, in essence accepting the judgment of God as inevitable (as Jeremiah was proclaiming). Thus Jehoiachin survives, and God declares that the future of Israel rests with those who went with him into exile. In contrast, back in Jerusalem Zedekiah refuses to follow Jeremiah's advice and thus does not surrender to the Babylonians. This, along with numerous other defiant and disobedient sins, will lead to his destruction, along with those associated with him.

Interpretive Insights

24:1 *the* LORD *showed me two baskets of figs.* The fig tree is one of the most common and important trees in biblical Israel. Because of the sweet taste of its fruit and the shade provided by its branches, the fig tree often is used as a symbol of peace and prosperity (e.g., Hosea 9:10; Mic. 4:4; Zech. 3:10).[2]

placed in front of the temple of the LORD. The temple reference implies that the figs are part of a firstfruits offering (Deut. 26:1–11).

24:2 *very bad figs, so bad they could not be eaten.* The word translated twice as "bad" in this verse is a variant form of *ra'ah*, which is used repeatedly throughout Jeremiah in reference to the "evil" or "bad actions/behavior" of Israel. There is a wordplay here: these *ra'ah* figs represent the same *ra'ah* people whom Jeremiah has been confronting throughout the book. See also 24:8.

24:5 *to the land of the Babylonians.* The word translated by the NIV as "Babylonians" is *kasdim*, and some versions, such as the NRSV, translate this as "Chaldeans" (see comments at 21:4). This term is used interchangeably with "Babylonians."

24:6 *My eyes will watch over them for their good.* Literally, this translates, "I will put my eyes upon them to bring good." Being in exile in Babylon did not remove them from the caring, watchful "eye" of the presence of God, who will bless them and bring "good" (*tob*, opposite of *ra'ah*) to them.

24:7 *a heart to know me.* In Hebrew "heart" often refers to the place where one makes decisions, especially decisions relating to faithfulness. Likewise, "to know" often has relational or experiential connotations.

that I am the LORD. Various forms of the phrase "to know that I am the LORD" occur throughout the book of Exodus and are best understood from that context. For his people, to know the Lord is to experience his great salvation and the blessings of his powerful and awesome presence. Likewise, it implies understanding the terrible judgment that he brings upon his enemies. "To know that he is the Lord" is to see him in action.

They will be my people, and I will be their God. This statement is a direct allusion to the primary and oft-repeated definition of God's covenant relationship with his people in the Old Testament: "I will be your God, and you will be my people" (cf. Exod. 19:6).

they will return to me with all their heart. This is the sign of true repentance. They will return (*shub*) wholeheartedly. This implies that they will abandon their syncretistic idolatry and worship God alone.

24:8 *or live in Egypt.* This probably alludes to those Judahites who flee to Egypt after murdering the governor Gedaliah (Jer. 41–44). The future does not rest with them.

24:9–10 *reproach . . . byword . . . curse . . . sword, famine and plague.* These judgment terms occur repeatedly throughout Jeremiah.[3]

Theological Insights

There are several probable connections to Ezekiel in this passage. Ezekiel is one of the exiled Judahites taken to Babylon along with Jehoiachin, and he ties his opening vision to the fifth year of Jehoiachin's exile. Indeed, Ezekiel appears to represent these exiles in his opening vision of God's presence (Ezek. 1). In Jeremiah 24:5–7 God promises to watch over the exiles in Babylon with his "eyes" (a promise of presence?) and to bless them with a renewed covenant relationship. Ezekiel describes the new presence of God among the exiles in Babylon (Ezek. 1), a presence characterized by the symbolism of "eyes" (Ezek. 10:12), and a promise of renewed heart (Ezek. 11:19) and covenant, "They will be my people, and I will be their God" (Ezek. 11:20).

Keep in mind that the exiles in Babylon (the "good figs") are in exile because of their sin and disobedience (idolatry, social injustice, etc.), as Jeremiah has been stressing. They are chosen to be the "good figs" not because they are innocent or worthy but solely by the grace of God. All they have actually done correctly is to surrender to the Babylonians. They have not repented or turned back to God yet. He takes the initiative in bringing them to a restored relationship and proclaims confidently that they will turn back to him wholeheartedly.

Although there is considerable disagreement among scholars over this identification, it is probable that from a New Testament perspective the exiles who will be restored as God's people (the good figs) also include the gentiles (Isaiah blurs the two groups repeatedly in his visions), while those remaining in Jerusalem to receive judgment (the bad figs) typologically symbolize those Jews of Jesus's day who rejected him and drove his followers out of the city.

Teaching the Text

God takes the initiative in bringing his disobedient people back to him. Notice the stress in this text on God's actions: "*My* eyes will watch over them . . . *I* will bring them back . . . *I* will build them up . . . *I* will plant them . . . *I* will give them a heart to know me . . . *I* will be their God." That is, the road to restoration is driven by God's compassion and blessing. When we drift away from God, he continually calls us to come back to him in repentance. He wants to change our hearts so that we will truly know him and be able to have a close relationship with him.

The concept of God giving his people a renewed heart is often connected to the themes of repentance, forgiveness, and renewed, closer relationship with God. For example, after David's horrendous affair with Bathsheba, he cries out to God, "Create in me a pure heart . . . a steadfast spirit. . . . Do not cast me from your presence" (Ps. 51:10–11). This theological reality is likewise true today. Repentance includes acknowledging the wayward tendencies of our hearts, and forgiveness includes God's provision of "renewed" hearts that enable us to be more faithful to him.

The renewed heart from God also leads the repentant believer into a better knowledge of God. This renewed, faithful heart gives us a better understanding of God's character, his love, and his will for us. Remember that back in Jeremiah 22:16 God pointed out that knowing him results in active ministry, which in that context meant caring for the poor and needy. This underscores that knowing God and being in his presence bring upon us an insightful understanding of God's character—what he likes and dislikes, what he desires for us to be, the character and actions he desires for us, and so forth. Knowing God results in actions and a changed life. For New Testament believers today, the Holy Spirit plays a critical role in our renewed hearts, helping us to turn to God and to know him.

"They will be my people, and I will be their God" describes the most foundational biblical relationship that we have with God. We are his people, related to him, protected and blessed by him. Likewise, he is our God, demanding and deserving our total allegiance and worship. God's words "for they will return to me with all their heart" stress the call for total, wholehearted commitment to God. He does not give us a renewed heart so that we can merely carve out a small portion of our life for him; rather, he wants all of it. Just as there was no place for idolatry in Israel's worship of God, so there is no room for other "gods" in our life either. God calls on us to serve him "with our whole heart," not just partially or occasionally. There are so many things in life today that try to entice our heart—work, wealth, popularity, success, pleasure, and so on—distracting us from a wholehearted commitment to God. But God desires all of us and all of our heart.

Finally, as we have seen throughout Jeremiah, the wonderful blessings of renewed relationship with God are starkly contrasted with the fate of those who never repent and who continue to defy God and his call to them for restoration. There is no neutral ground. To know that "he is the Lord" is to know him either as the powerful and wonderful Savior who blesses through intimate relationship or as the terrible avenger and destroyer who crushes his defiant enemies. The proclamation of the gospel today likewise carries both sides of this coin. There is wonderful blessing in store for those who turn to God wholeheartedly, but terrible eventual judgment on those who stubbornly and defiantly refuse the call to repent and to turn to him. There is no middle ground.

Illustrating the Text

If we repent, God promises to restore our relationship with him.

Television: The History Channel features a series called *American Restoration*. It gives us a look into the daily operation of a Las Vegas antique restoration company, Rick's Restorations. The owner, Rick Dale, and his crew, consisting of family members and employees, bring old and damaged items back to their original glory. The shop works on everything from antique cars and motorcycles to vintage vending machines—even once on a 1960s hot dog cart for Dodger Stadium.

In the show's opening title sequence, Rick explains what they do: "Remember back in the day when things were made by hand, and people took pride in their work? My name is Rick Dale, and I bring these things back to life. Every restoration has its own challenges. There's no owner's manual for what we do, but there's no job we can't handle."

You could show the opening promo, or you could show before-and-after clips of some of the projects that they have restored. You might also want to have someone role-play Rick's opening segment, saying something like this: "Remember back in the day I made everyone by hand, and I took pride in my work? Then sin entered the world, and perfection was polluted. My name is the Lord God Almighty, and I bring these things back to life. Every restoration has its own challenges. There's no owner's manual for what I do, but there's no job I can't handle."

Restoring broken things is difficult. Restoring our broken relationship with a holy and righteous God is impossible for us, but, thankfully, nothing is impossible with God.

Props: This might also be a great week to invite members of the congregation to bring their antique cars and motorcycles to church and set up a small-scale antique car show in part of the parking lot. People could talk about the complications of their restoration projects but the delight that they took in the process.

Personal Story: Make and show a video of someone telling a personal story about restoring an antique, such as a car, a piece of furniture, or a quilt. Have the subject focus on the delight and joy that he or she took in seeing something transformed over time. Follow up by talking about how God delights and celebrates when our lives are restored and made new by his work in us.

Hymn: "Come Thou Fount of Every Blessing," by Robert Robinson. This beloved hymn, penned in 1757, speaks poignantly and eloquently to the wandering nature of our hearts. The David Crowder Band has an updated version of this classic for those who are looking for a more contemporary rendition.

Seventy Years for Judah and for Babylon

Big Idea
Failure to listen to the prophetic word of God results in judgment.

Key Themes
- Even though God repeatedly sent his word via the prophets, the people of Judah continuously refused to listen.
- Thus in their banishment these people will not hear the sounds of joyful living.
- God will raise up a Babylonian king to judge Judah, but after seventy years God will also bring judgment upon the king of Babylon.

Understanding the Text

The Text in Context

The larger unit of Jeremiah 11–29 stresses the conflict between God's prophet Jeremiah and the leaders (and the people they lead) in Jerusalem. Since these leaders and people have rejected the word of God and turned hostile against his prophet (Jer. 11–20), God now responds with judgment on them (Jer. 21–29).

In this context Jeremiah 25:1–14 oozes with irony. Since the people and the kings of Judah will not listen to God's true servants such as Jeremiah, they will be destined to serve God's new "servant," Nebuchadnezzar, king of Babylon, who in essence replaces the king of Judah.

Both Judah and the surrounding nations, their allies, will now "serve" the king of Babylon for seventy years, a symbolic time of fullness and completion.

Chronologically, Jeremiah 25 is close in time to Jeremiah 26 (both during the reign of Jehoiakim). In both chapters God states that he sent his "servants the prophets, again and again," thus connecting these two chapters by that phrase. The theme of judgment on the nations is introduced in 25:1–14, and this theme flows into the very next section, 25:15–38, connecting the two halves of Jeremiah 25.

Historical and Cultural Background

In regard to historical context, the "fourth year of Jehoiakim" (25:1) was 605 BC. This was the year that King Nebuchadnezzar of Babylon defeated the Assyrian/Egyptian alliance at Carchemish, thus establishing clear Babylonian dominance over the entire region. The geopolitical ramifications for Judah would be dramatic, as Egyptian hegemony over Judah would be replaced with Babylonian control. Jeremiah has repeatedly referred to a coming "foe from the north" (1:14; 4:6; 6:1, 22; 10:22; 13:20; 15:12). The battle of Carchemish in 605 BC clearly identified this "foe" as King Nebuchadnezzar and the Babylonians.[1]

Note that Jeremiah 25 (605 BC) predates Jeremiah 24 (597 BC). As we noted in the introduction, the book of Jeremiah is often organized thematically rather than chronologically.

Interpretive Insights

25:1 *the fourth year of Jehoiakim . . . the first year of Nebuchadnezzar.* This verse reflects a very significant shift in how Jeremiah reckons time. He is transitioning from counting time based on the Judahite kings ("the fourth year of Jehoiakim") to counting time based on the Babylonian king ("the first year of Nebuchadnezzar").

25:3 *For twenty-three years.* The rejection of Jeremiah by the king and the people of Jerusalem was not a one-time event; it stretched over two decades, underscoring their culpability.

again and again. The word translated as "again and again" is also used in 25:4. It means "to rise early and get an early start." It is used idiomatically in the same sense as our English expression "all the day long" or perhaps "from dawn to dusk." It connotes not so much "repeatedly" (the sense conveyed by the NIV) as it does "continuously" or "persistently" (NRSV, ESV). This same phrase occurs in 7:25; 26:5.

25:4 *the LORD has sent all his servants the prophets to you again and again.* Not only had Jeremiah preached for twenty-three years, but also God had sent many other prophets to try to call Israel to repentance, all of whom were ignored. This is very insulting to God, and this phrase is repeated in Jeremiah several times as an indictment (7:25; 25:3; 26:5; 29:19; 35:15; 44:4).

but you have not listened. The word translated as "listen" is *shamaʿ*, which means "to hear," but in this construction it also implies obeying what is heard. In this context "to not listen" means "to disregard and fail to obey." This accusation is repeated throughout the passage (25:3, 4, 7, 8).

25:7 *you did not listen to me.* God is equating the words of the prophets with his direct, personal words. The people of Judah have failed to listen to Jeremiah (25:3), all the other prophets (25:4), God himself (25:7), and God's words (25:8). There seems to be no difference between the word of God and the word of the prophets.

25:9 *my servant Nebuchadnezzar king of Babylon.* For God to call Nebuchadnezzar, the invader and hostile enemy of Judah, his "servant" would have been devastating for those in Judah to hear. God uses the term "servant" in the sense that Nebuchadnezzar will be carrying out God's divine will: the destruction of Jerusalem and the exile of the people of Judah.

25:10 *the sound of millstones and the light of the lamp.* Flour was ground with millstones, usually in the morning. Oil lamps were lit at night. The two represented peace and prosperity, day and night.[2]

25:13 *all that are written in this book and prophesied by Jeremiah against all the nations.* Jeremiah's prophecies against the nations are recorded in Jeremiah 46–51. In the Septuagint (the early Greek translation of the Old Testament), Jeremiah 46–51 is inserted here at the end of 25:13, which then serves as an introductory summary of that unit.

Theological Insights

One of the themes running throughout the book of Jeremiah is that God, not the Babylonians, is in control of history. As the dazed and bewildered Israelites are carried off into exile in Babylon, the words of Jeremiah remind them that this was neither a random tragedy nor an act of power sponsored by the Babylonian deities or the Babylonian monarchy. God brought this tragedy upon them because they did not listen to him. And he used the Babylonians to carry out his plan. The implications, of course, are that since he was the one who orchestrated the exile, he certainly would orchestrate the return and restoration.

Likewise, reflecting God's use of irony, in Jeremiah God uses his "servant" Nebuchadnezzar, king of Babylon, to destroy Jerusalem and to exile the Judahites, and in Isaiah God uses his "shepherd" and his "anointed one" Cyrus, king of Persia (the one who conquers Babylon), to implement the return to the land and the reconstruction of Jerusalem (Isa. 44:28–45:1, 13).

It is interesting to observe that God uses the pagan enemies of Israel (such as the Babylonians) as his instruments of judgment on Israel. This does not imply that God approves of the Babylonians; in fact, judgment on Babylon is the theme of Jeremiah 50–51. Yet he certainly seems to feel free to employ them to carry out his plans, especially judgment. The same thing can be observed in the New Testament era as the pagan Roman armies destroy Jerusalem in AD 70. So what does this imply for today? It would not be out of character for God to use non-Christian forces in the world (repressive regimes, atheists, ungodly government policies, etc.) to judge or chasten his disobedient people if that is part of his plan.

Which Seventy Years?

Jeremiah mentions "seventy years" in 25:11–12 and again in 29:10. He appears to use it in regard to both how long Israel would be in exile and how long it would be until God judged and destroyed Babylon. Jeremiah's seventy years are also cited explicitly in Daniel 9:2 (related to the length of time Jerusalem would lie desolate) and in 2 Chronicles 36:21 (related to the Sabbath rest connected to the desolation of the land). Zechariah 1:12 is also probably an allusion to the seventy years prophesied by Jeremiah. In 538 BC Cyrus, the king of Persia, issued a decree allowing the exiles of Judah to return home. In 2 Chronicles 36:22 this event appears to be associated with the end of Jeremiah's seventy years, but scholars disagree over the precise start and stop dates for Jeremiah's seventy years. Several possibilities have been suggested. The "start" of Babylon is often identified with the fall of Nineveh, the capital of Assyria, in 612 BC. From this "start" of Babylon (612 BC) to the fall of Babylon in 539 BC equals seventy-three years; to the decree of Cyrus (538 BC) equals seventy-four years. If the "start" of Babylon is identified with the decisive victory over the Assyrian/Egyptian alliance at Carchemish (605 BC), then one calculates sixty-six years to the fall of Babylon (539 BC) and sixty-seven years to the decree of Cyrus (538 BC). Others tend to emphasize the length of the destruction period for the temple, calculating from the fall of Jerusalem and the destruction of the temple in 587/586 BC to the reconstruction of the temple in 520–515 BC, which equals approximately seventy years.

On the other hand, some scholars view "seventy years" to be a figurative reference to a complete lifetime; the restoration would begin with the next generation, not with those who went into exile. This seems to be the point of Jeremiah's letter in 29:1–14. Others note the associated symbolism with the number seventy (10 times 7, the number of completeness) and see the number as symbolic only. The number seventy does obviously carry symbolic significance, but this "completeness" nuance can also include the length of a lifetime as well as an approximation of the time Israel would be in exile and the time until Babylon fell from power. Thus in Jeremiah the "seventy years" seem to carry an ironic double nuance: the length of time Israel would be in exile in Babylon and the length of time until Babylon is judged for what it did to Israel.[a]

[a] Hays, *Message of the Prophets*, 169. On the symbolism of seventy, see *DBI* 775–76.

Teaching the Text

There is a strong emphasis in this passage on the extreme importance of listening to the word of God, especially his word as proclaimed by his prophets. God clearly identifies the words of the Old Testament prophets as being the same as his own direct speech, carrying the same absolute authority. In the New Testament, the Gospels and the book of Acts connect Jesus and his apostles with this authoritative tradition, thus giving the same "word of God" power and authority to their words as well.

True "listening," of course, includes taking to heart and obeying. If we truly hear the word of God proclaimed and taught, we will respond with obedience to his word. This text reaffirms the central importance of preaching/teaching the word of God for the healthy life of the church. Likewise, as believers respond to God's word, they will commit to wholehearted service to God. They will put aside all "idolatries" and distractions and focus on serving God and God alone, led in this service by the guidelines and admonitions of God's word itself.

Notice that the Israelites in Jeremiah's day had regular access to the word of God. Jeremiah and the other prophets proclaimed it to them over and over. They simply did not listen seriously to it. As earlier chapters show, they created their own counterprophecy from their own prophets. How many people today go to church week after week but never listen wholeheartedly and obediently to God's word? Or perhaps they filter the word of God only in order to find something that immediately encourages them or uplifts them. That is, they ask, "How can God help me to feel better right now?" God, of course, certainly does uplift and encourage, but as we listen to God's word, we should be asking, "How can I serve God more obediently?" As we listen and obey, we will be uplifted and encouraged.

The consequences of refusing to listen to God's word are serious. For the Israelites in Jeremiah's day it meant experiencing a terrible judgment that included being banished from the good life in the land that God had intended for them. Jeremiah describes their banished life as being devoid of all the happy sounds of the good life. It is only in listening and obeying God's word that we find joy in life.

We can also see the sovereignty of God at work in this passage. He chooses the pagan king of the Babylonians to carry out his plans for judgment on Judah, but then he also brings these same Babylonians under judgment. He is in complete control of history. He can use "bad people" to carry out his will if he chooses to. This does not mean that he approves of them or even accepts them as his own. In this case he judges them (the Babylonians) and destroys them after they have carried out his desired plan.

Illustrating the Text

Failing to listen to God is disastrous.

Sports: When the coach speaks, the team is supposed to listen, but the expectation is even greater. If the coach says something like, "Grind it out, eat up the clock, keep the ball on the ground," and the quarterback decides to pass the ball instead, the quarterback will not be playing that position very long. The expectation of coaches, and bosses, and parents, and teachers, and preachers, and especially God is that those they speak to, as James puts it, "Be doers of the word, and not hearers only" (James 1:22).

Sports: If you have been to a NASCAR race, you know that the noise level makes it almost impossible to hear. For this reason, race officials communicate with the drivers by using brightly colored flags. It is the flagger's job to make sure that the drivers know what is going on around them on the track.

For example, a green flag indicates the start of the race. A yellow flag signals caution, and it usually indicates that there is some kind of debris on the track ahead. A red flag tells drivers to stop immediately because there is an accident ahead. When the caution is lifted, the green flag is waved again indicating that passing is again permitted. A black flag signals that the driver has five laps to make a pit stop and communicate with race officials. A black flag with a white diagonal strip indicates that the driver failed to respond properly to a black-flag warning and has been disqualified. A blue flag with a diagonal yellow stripe is the courtesy flag, and it tells slower drivers to yield to faster drivers on the track. A white flag indicates that the lead driver has started the final lap, and, finally, a checkered flag is waved when the first driver crosses the start/finish line.

The law of God is intended to help us navigate our way through life to the finish line, and we ignore it at our own peril.

Story: A pastor preached a sermon on the call of God to share resources with the poor and needy. He looked at this theme through both the teachings of the Old Testament prophets and the words of Jesus. He called the people in the congregation to examine their hearts and see how generous they were toward the needs of the poor.

After the sermon, while greeting people in the back of the church, an older gentleman shook the pastor's hand firmly and said, "You know, Pastor, when you started talking about giving away money, the battery in my hearing aid wore out, and I couldn't hear a thing you said!" The elderly church member laughed at his own joke and walked out of the church.

We need to beware that we do not plug our ears or let our hearing aid battery wear out when the prophetic truth of God's word is convicting us. There are many ways we close our ears to the needs and cries of the poor; none of them is acceptable to God.

The Nations Drink the Cup of God's Wrath

Big Idea
All people and all nations are accountable to God for their sinful actions.

Key Themes
- God is the judge of all the nations of the earth.
- Not just the sin of Israel but all sin worldwide will be judged.
- God will bring justice to all people and nations.

Understanding the Text

The Text in Context

In the previous passage (25:1–14) Jeremiah introduced the theme that Judah and Jerusalem will not be the only ones judged by God for their sin, but all the nations, including Babylon, will likewise be judged by God. Jeremiah 25:15–38 continues to develop this theme.

The first half of this passage (25:15–29) is in prose and focuses on the metaphor of a cup of wine representing God's wrath. The second half is related, also colorfully depicting the coming wrath of God (25:30–38). Consisting of three short oracles (25:30–31, 32–33, 34–38), this poetic section opens and closes with the figurative portrayal of God as a roaring lion (25:30, 38). In 25:30 the lion's roar is heard; in 25:38 the rampaging lion arrives.

In the first half of Jeremiah 25, the stress is on the repeated failure of Israel to "hear" the word of God (25:1–8). At the end of this chapter (25:30–38), the stress is on the sounds of God's judgment (voice of a roaring lion, shouts, tumult, weeping, wailing, etc.) that Israel, along with all the nations, will now hear.

Jeremiah 25:30–38 echoes much of 4:5–31 (the lion out of its lair, an invading army like a thunderstorm), but in Jeremiah 4 the destroyer is Nebuchadnezzar, and in Jeremiah 25 the destroyer is God.

Historical and Cultural Background

Historically, this section still reflects the geopolitical situation of 605 BC, as identified in 25:1. The Babylonians had just defeated the Assyrian/Egyptian coalition at the Battle of Carchemish, arguably the most important battle that had been fought to date in world history. All the kings and nations in the region, indeed everyone, would be profoundly affected by this event. It is at this precise time that God proclaims his worldwide sovereignty and his authority, indeed, his plan to judge all the nations of the world, not just Israel, for their sin.

Interpretive Insights

25:17 *I . . . made all the nations to whom he sent me drink it.* The NIV correctly ends this verse with a colon, for 25:18–26 contains a list of seventeen nations and kings, the first sixteen of which are direct objects of the verb. Apparently, Jeremiah does this (causing the nations to drink the cup) by his prophetic proclamation of judgment against them, especially as described in Jeremiah 46–51. Jeremiah does not actually go to these nations to present these oracles in person, but his pronouncements of judgment are effective nonetheless. Furthermore, they serve as a testimony to those in Jerusalem who actually hear Jeremiah that God is in control of all history and all nations. God will bring his justice upon all the nations of the world, not just upon Judah. He is not a regional god of just Judah but rather God of the whole world.

25:18 *Jerusalem and the towns of Judah, its kings and officials.* Judgment will come on the entire nation, but the culpability of the leaders (kings and officials) is stressed, not only here but also throughout this larger section of Jeremiah. Note the repetition of "king/kings" throughout 25:18–26.

25:19 *Pharaoh king of Egypt.* The list of nations to be judged includes most of the major nations that impacted the biblical world at the time of Jeremiah. Yet the list starts with Egypt and ends with Babylon. While these two reflect a south-to-north inclusion, the mention of Egypt first also perhaps alludes to the devastating judgment that fell on Egypt in the book of Exodus at Israel's beginnings.

25:26 *the king of Sheshak will drink it too.* "Sheshak" is a kind of cipher or simple alphabet code, called an *atbash* by later rabbis. In this alphabet code the last letter of the alphabet is used to represent the first letter of the alphabet, the next-to-last letter represents the second letter, and so forth. In English Z would represent A, and Y would represent B, and so on. The three Hebrew letters used here (*sh, sh, k*) correspondingly represent *b, b, l* (i.e., Babel, or Babylon). This reference to the king of Babylon is not part of the long list of direct objects in the previous verses. It is set off as a final and climaxing event. This is similar to the list of judgments against the nations in Jeremiah 46–51, which also climaxes with judgment on Babylon.

25:30 *The* LORD *will roar.* The word translated as "roar" refers explicitly to the loud, frightening roar of a lion.

he will thunder from his holy dwelling. More literally, this reads, "from his holy dwelling place he gives his voice." The word "voice" is in parallel to the lion's roar in the first line of this verse. "Thunder" is adequate as a translation as long as the connection to the lion is maintained. This is not a "thunderstorm" analogy but rather one of a roaring, hungry lion. It is the lion's roar that "thunders."

and roar mightily. The same Hebrew word used for the lion's roar in the first line of this verse is used here. It is repeated twice in this line in a grammatical construction that stresses the certainty or severity of the action. The NIV's "mightily" is an attempt to capture this stress. It could also be translated as "he will most certainly roar."

He will shout like those who tread the grapes. The treading of grapes was done by walking on them and trampling them by foot. At the joyful conclusion to the grape harvest, those who treaded the grapes often shouted joyfully or sang as they worked. The shout here, ironically, is a loud, tumultuous, even joyful shout at the conclusion of a successful harvest.[1] In 25:15–29 God commands Jeremiah to make the nations drink the cup filled with the wine of his wrath. Jeremiah 25:30 depicts God as trampling the grapes to produce the wine.

25:31 *The* LORD *will bring charges.* "Charges" is a translation of the Hebrew word *rib*, which refers to a legal case or lawsuit. God's judgment on the nations is not arbitrary but rather is based on evidence; he has a legal case against them. In Jeremiah 50:34 and 51:36 the *rib* against Babylon is based on Babylon's destruction of Jerusalem and the exile of Judah (cf. Isa. 34:5). That is, God will use the Babylonians as an instrument of his judgment but still hold them accountable for the terrible things they do to Judah.

he will bring judgment on all mankind. The Hebrew verb *shapat*, translated by the NIV as "judgment," carries a strong nuance of "justice," especially "social justice." A rendering that captures this nuance is "he himself will bring justice on all flesh."

the wicked. The Hebrew word means "wicked" in a criminal, guilty sense; it refers to someone who has done very wicked things and thus is deserving of serious punishment. This is the same word used four times in Psalm 1 to describe those opposed to God (Ps. 1:1, 4, 5, 6).

25:34 *shepherds.* The numerous kings mentioned in 25:18–26 are called "shepherds" in this text. "Shepherd" was a common figure of speech used to refer to the king, both throughout the Bible and in other ancient Near Eastern literature.

25:38 *because of the* LORD'*s fierce anger.* This can also be translated as "from the presence of his burning anger" or "before his burning anger." Just as the presence of God brings blessing to those who serve him, so his presence, especially the presence of his intense anger, brings terrible devastation to those who sin against him.

Theological Insights

Some may find it puzzling that God raises up nations such as Babylon to judge Judah and then judges Babylon for this very action. Yet note that the Babylonians do not invade and destroy Judah because the Babylonians are righteous or because they are seeking to obey God. They invade because they are sinful (imperialistic, selfish, violent, etc.). God in his sovereignty does not cause their sinful behavior but does allow the actions coming out of their sinfulness (the invasion of Judah) to bring about his plan (judgment on Judah as a consequence of their sin). Thus he still holds the Babylonians (and other nations) culpable for their sinful actions (the terrible things that they did during the invasion of Judah and other countries). For the shattered remnant of Judah (the "good figs" of Jer. 24) who were carried off into exile in Babylon, the promise of God's judgment on their captors and the other nations perhaps would have brought a certain encouragement as they realized that God is sovereign over all these nations and that he had not forgotten them. The power and authority that would soon crush Babylon is the same power and authority that would bring about the restoration of God's people in exile.

Teaching the Text

Throughout Jeremiah God has been accusing the leaders and people of Jerusalem and Judah of idolatry and social injustice, serious violations of the terms of their covenant with God (especially as expressed in Deuteronomy). Because of their sin and their obstinate failure to listen to him and repent, they will experience judgment. Here in 25:15–38 God explains that this principle (that wicked, sinful behavior and defiance against God result in judgment) is universal. All people and all nations stand accountable before God, just as Israel does. The story of Israel is a pattern or paradigm for the whole world and is equally relevant for today.

God is not arbitrary or petty in his wrath. His judgment is based on evidence and a very strong legal case. It is the guilty ones who will experience his wrath. Furthermore, his judgment comes upon the wicked ones of the world in order to bring justice to the earth. God is a just and righteous God.

Widespread acts of injustice, especially when such injustice becomes "normative" for entire nations, make him angry. His wrath against such people is terrible, like a rampaging lion.

God's wrath against sinful behavior is not merely an Old Testament theme; it is a biblical theme. Paul makes the same point in Romans 1:18–3:31, saying that "the wrath of God is being revealed against the godlessness and wickedness of people" (1:18), and "all have sinned and fall short" (3:23). Paul, of course, is using the universality of sin and coming wrath to show that all people, Jews and gentiles alike, need the salvation and justification by faith that Jesus Christ offers. Likewise, the book of Revelation describes the widespread wrath of God poured out on the earth (e.g., the seven bowls of God's wrath in Rev. 16) and then even employs the same image of one who "treads the winepress of the fury of the wrath of God Almighty" (Rev. 19:15).

Although Jeremiah 25 is serious and grim in its picture of judgment on Judah and all the nations of the world, as in the rest of the Bible, the message of Jeremiah does not end here in judgment. He is establishing the clear need for the "new covenant" presented in Jeremiah 31. In regard to the fate of the foreign nations, Jeremiah will provide hope through the story of Ebed-Melek the Cushite (Jer. 38–39), a foreigner who finds deliverance because of his "trust" in God (39:18).

This passage is also about the sovereignty of God.[2] As in the time of Jeremiah, God still has control over all the nations of the world and over all history. He uses the actions of presidents, premiers, and nations to move his plan along. Likewise today, God is committed to justice and righteousness, and in his sovereignty he will move through judgment to establish justice and righteousness on the earth.

Illustrating the Text

The imagery of God roaring like a lion

Science: The roar of a lion can travel over five miles and be as loud as 114 decibels, which is the equivalent of a jetliner taking off.[3] Lions use the startling volume of the roar to disorient their prey. There are several great videos of roaring lions on YouTube (search "lion roaring"), and if your context permits, showing a clip would graphically illustrate Jeremiah's image of the fierceness of the Lord's anger at injustice and sin.

Sin will be judged.

Prop: Take a baseball or softball and hold it up at eye level. Ask the congregation, "What do you think will happen when I let go of this ball?" If you have an eager group, they will tell you, "It will drop and hit the ground." If you have a more timid group, you might have to coax them for a response. Let them know it is not a trick question.

When people have correctly identified the simple law of gravity, agree with them, open your hand, and let the ball go. Then, pick it up and ask the same question. This time the answer should come more quickly. Ask your congregation, "How many times, out of a hundred, do you think the ball will fall and hit the ground?" They will know, and you can affirm, that the ball will drop and hit the ground every time for a hundred or a thousand times in a row. Gravity demands it.

Then, ask this question: "How many times, out of a hundred, will God judge sin?" Assure them that the answer is one hundred times. God will judge sin every time it is committed. This includes the sin of Israel, the surrounding nations, and our sin. God's holiness and justice demand it. The judgment does not always come immediately, but it will always come.

This could be a moment to address the spiritual reality that Jesus washes away sin by his sacrificial death on the cross, but this does not mean that sin has gone unpunished. It means that the sinless Lamb of God has taken the just punishment for our sin. But sin always brings judgment. The question is, "Do we bear the consequences, or does Jesus bear them for us?"

God's Prophets on Trial

Big Idea

The faithful proclamation of God's word can bring persecution upon his messengers.

Key Themes

- God warns the people of Jerusalem to listen to his prophets.
- The leaders of the temple attempt to have Jeremiah executed.
- The defense of Jeremiah is successful.
- Not all faithful prophets survive the persecution as Jeremiah does.

Understanding the Text

The Text in Context

Jeremiah 26 is closely connected to Jeremiah 7. In Jeremiah 7 God sends the prophet to the temple to proclaim judgment against Jerusalem and the temple. Jeremiah 26 follows up on that event, describing the hostile reaction against Jeremiah because of that "temple sermon." Remember that the book of Jeremiah is structured more along thematic than chronological lines. Thus the temple sermon itself (Jer. 7) is placed in the section dealing with false religion and its consequences (Jer. 7–10). Jeremiah 26, however, which deals with the reaction to the sermon and the ensuing attempt to execute Jeremiah, is located appropriately in Jeremiah 11–29, where the central theme is God's prophet in conflict with the king and other leaders of Jerusalem.

Jeremiah 26:1–6 relates God's instructions to Jeremiah, while 26:7–11 describes his arrest and the opening charges of his trial. His defense consists of three different components: his warning to his opponents about killing an innocent man (26:12–16), the citation of Micah the prophet by the elders of the land (26:17–19), and support from the powerful courtier Ahikam (26:24). Sandwiched in between these last two arguments in Jeremiah's defense, and obviously shouting out the very real danger of Jeremiah's situation, is the account of Uriah the prophet's execution for saying the same things that Jeremiah was saying.

Interpretive Insights

26:2 *Stand in the courtyard of the LORD's house.* The temple, referred to as the "house of the LORD" or just "this house," is mentioned numerous times in 26:1–10 for emphasis (26:2 [2x], 6, 7, 9 [2x], 10 [2x]). Much of Jeremiah's specific message addresses the serious misconceptions that these "worshipers" held about the temple (see the larger version of this message in Jeremiah 7). Likewise, proclaiming this message in the temple allowed Jeremiah to reach a wide range of people: priests, false prophets, and temple officials; residents of Jerusalem; and people from the countryside of Judah.

who come to worship in the house of the LORD. Of all the possible audiences that Jeremiah could preach to, this one (worshipers in the temple) should have been the most sympathetic and receptive.

do not omit a word. The word translated as "omit" means "to hold back, diminish, reduce."

26:3 *Perhaps.* See "Theological Insights" below.

they will listen. The word translated as "listen" is *shama'*. It means "to hear," but it often carries connotations of hearing and understanding, or of hearing and then obeying. *Shama'* occurs ten times in this passage (26: 3, 4, 5, 7, 10, 11, 12, 13, 21 [2x]), and the wordplay swirling around this term reveals the irony of the message in this chapter. God connects *shama'* with listening to him and his servants the prophets (26:3, 5), a listening that results in repentance and obedience to God's *torah* (26:3–4). After Jeremiah proclaims God's message, the text states, ironically, that the priests, false prophets, and all the people "heard" Jeremiah (26:7), but rather than repenting or obeying, they seek to kill him (and thus silence his words). The fact that they do indeed "hear" his words underscores their culpability. They cannot plead ignorance. Note their own self-indictment as they proclaim, "You have heard it with your own ears!" (26:11). Likewise, King Jehoiakim "hears" the words of the prophet Uriah but seeks to kill him (26:21). Uriah "hears" of this and flees (26:21), but to no avail. Jehoiakim has him executed (26:23).

each will turn. The word translated as "will turn" is *shub*, used throughout Jeremiah. Here it indicates turning away from (i.e., to quit practicing) sinful behavior.

from their evil ways. "Evil" is translated from the word *ra'ah*, a favorite word for Jeremiah that means "bad things." When used of people, it refers to their bad or evil behavior; when used of God, it means "bad things" (usually translated as "disaster") that he is going to do as judgment. Related forms of the word *ra'ah* appear three times in this verse (translated in the NIV twice as "evil" and once as "disaster"). The word translated as "ways" means "road" or "path."

Then I will relent. The word translated as "relent" means "to change one's mind, one's course of action." Jeremiah 26:3 uses several of the same terms as 18:8. If the people only will turn (*shub*) from their evil (*ra'ah*) ways, God will change the course of action that he was planning and not do *ra'ah* to them. Similar language is used in 26:13.

26:6 *make this house like Shiloh.* Earlier in Israelite history, Shiloh had been the town where the ark of the covenant resided. Apparently, it was destroyed by the Philistines (likely in the battle recounted in 1 Sam. 4). As indicated in Jeremiah 7, the priests and false prophets believed that the temple in Jerusalem could never be destroyed. Jeremiah, however, tells them that God will destroy the temple and Jerusalem, just as Shiloh was destroyed.

this city a curse. The idea here is that the destruction of Jerusalem will be so bad that people will use the name of Jerusalem in curses (i.e., "May your town become like Jerusalem").

26:7 *the prophets.* This is a reference to the "false prophets" who were closely associated with the temple and the monarchy. Throughout the ancient Near East, court prophets regularly served as advisers in the royal courts.

26:8 *all the people.* "All the people" is an idiomatic phrase that refers to lots of people. It does not imply that every single individual is included. This phrase occurs several times in this passage (26:7, 8 [2x], 9, 11, 12, 16). Note the fickleness of the crowd. In 26:8 they seize Jeremiah and call for his execution, but by 26:16 they are arguing for his innocence. Then in 26:24 at least some of "the people" appear to be seeking Jeremiah's execution again.

You must die! The Hebrew grammar stresses the certainty of the verb. Thus it could also be translated as "You will certainly die!" or "You are doomed to die!" It does not necessarily imply the immediacy of the impending death, but rather indicates that the death sentence has been passed.

26:15 *you will bring the guilt of innocent blood on yourselves.* This is Jeremiah's central defense. He is innocent and simply has been following God's instructions. Thus if the people kill him, they will bring God's wrath upon themselves.

26:17 *elders of the land.* These were men from villages and farms outside Jerusalem. Ironically, it is they, not the priests and court prophets, who interpret Jeremiah in light of Israel's earlier venerated prophets such as Micah. There is no indication that their argument from Micah 3:12, used in 26:18, swayed anyone in Jeremiah's trial. But their statements and their quotation from Micah restate Jeremiah's basic message and likewise point to judgment upon Jehoiakim.

26:18 *Micah.* The prophet Micah was a contemporary of Isaiah and prophesied a little over one hundred years earlier. His words apparently were venerated and already well known. This illustrates the power of oral tradition. Although Micah's prophecies probably had been written down, these rural elders were unlikely to be literate, and at any rate they most likely would not have had access to those written documents. Part of an elder's role in the community was to maintain the traditions; thus they probably were drawing from their familiarity with the preserved oral tradition of Micah.

26:19 *Did not Hezekiah fear the* LORD . . . ? Hezekiah listened to the prophets (Isaiah and Micah) and turned to God; thus Jerusalem was saved from the Assyrian invasion (2 Kings 18–19; Isa. 36–37). This reference underscores the glaring contrast between Hezekiah and Jehoiakim, who in the very next verses executes God's prophet.

26:20 *Uriah son of Shemaiah.* "Uriah" was a common name in Israel and Judah. Obviously, this is a different Uriah from the one whom David has killed in 2 Samuel 11–12. Uriah's father's name, "Shemaiah," means "the one whom the LORD hears," an ironic continuation of the wordplay on *shama'*.

26:21 *King Jehoiakim.* The mention of Jehoiakim again (cf. 26:1) indicates that both of these episodes (the trial of the prophet Jeremiah and the execution of the prophet Uriah) occur at very near the same time.[1]

26:23 *Jehoiakim, who had him struck down with a sword.* This is a brutal execution of a true and innocent prophet of God, apparently without any trial at all. Jeremiah's words of warning in 26:12–15 as well as the argument from Micah 3:12 in 26:17–19 apply as well to this execution and scream out judgment against Jehoiakim. That is, the arguments that spared Jeremiah's life should have been equally applicable to Uriah, but apparently they went unheeded by Jehoiakim.

26:24 *Ahikam . . . supported Jeremiah.* In spite of the logical and biblical arguments given earlier in Jeremiah's defense, this story closes with a brief statement indicating that a significant opposition ("the people") still clamored for his death. Only the support of a powerful noble in the court protects Jeremiah from the crowd.

Theological Insights

God's use of the word "perhaps" in 26:3 is intriguing. Some suggest that God is expressing some uncertainty about what the people's response would be. That is, even though he has proclaimed that the judgment is certain, he continues to plead with his people, hoping that "perhaps" they will listen (and thus repent). Others, however, argue that God seems to know quite clearly that the people will not listen and repent; thus his "perhaps" is only a hypothetical or rhetorical "hope" against what he knows will happen. Another option that some suggest is that God is simply being sarcastic.[2] It is probably best to let the word "perhaps" mean "perhaps" even from the mouth of God. Also it is important to keep the conditional aspects of the judgment prophecies suggested in Jeremiah 18 in mind. As the book of Jonah demonstrates, even proclaimed judgment can be averted if true repentance occurs. Although anthropomorphic analogies have their weaknesses, the character of God in Jeremiah seems to be portrayed as God knowing in his head that judgment is indeed coming but hoping in his heart that something can be done even at the last minute to save the people he loves.

Teaching the Text

We live in a fallen world, filled with much evil. This evil is often institutionalized into the power structures of society. Today, as in the time of Jeremiah, as God's people proclaim his prophetic truth that challenges and condemns evil behavior and institutionalized practices, they can expect some hostile "pushback." The pages of church history are filled with the persecution of God's spokespersons and the martyrdom of his people who had the courage to confront the evil and unjust powers of their day with the gospel.

Indeed, this passage is about serious persecution against those who stand up and proclaim the truth of the Bible. When people we know and work with exclude us from their parties because they know we disapprove of what may go on there, this is hardly persecution in the sense that Jeremiah 26 is addressing. Much of what North American Christians label "persecution" is minor inconvenience at best. However, persecution is very real for many Christians in the world. For example, for those advocates of international social justice who are trying to stop the sex-slave trade that is institutionalized in Southeast Asia and elsewhere, there is a very real threat of retaliation, even death. There is also imminent and serious danger for those national Christians who proclaim the gospel in areas where it is not tolerated, such as parts of Indonesia, Pakistan, and northern Nigeria. In the United States Christians rarely experience persecution merely for professing faith in Christ. But even in the United States, if Christians engage and try to change evil social injustices such as poverty, racial discrimination, sexual slavery/prostitution, abortion, and so forth, they can expect some "pushback," even persecution in some cases. Often this persecution is economic, and the forecast seems to be that Christian businesspeople who try to employ Christian principles in their businesses (e.g., refusing to include abortion drugs in their health coverage) may face serious fines and financial penalties.

God promised Jeremiah at his calling (1:17–19) that he would protect him from all opposition. Thus Jeremiah survives all the attacks and trials and imprisonments that the leaders of Jerusalem throw at him. But the grim reality of the execution of Uriah the prophet reminds us that not everyone who is faithful to God will survive persecution. As mentioned above, the pages of church history bear testimony to this, for they are filled with the deaths of faithful martyrs.

Jeremiah 26:1–24

Jeremiah (and Uriah) is the Old Testament paradigm for the New Testament references and allusions to "the persecuted prophet." That is, there is a biblical trajectory of "persecuted prophet" from Jeremiah to Jesus (in the Gospels) to Jesus's followers such as Peter, John, Stephen, and Paul (in Acts). Peter and John and Paul are delivered from their persecutors in Acts, much like Jeremiah. But Stephen is executed, much like Uriah. Serving God wholeheartedly and proclaiming his message in hostile contexts can result in serious persecution. Nonetheless, in both Testaments God calls us to proclaim his truth to those around us, even in dangerous, hostile situations. "Perhaps," he says, "they will listen."

Illustrating the Text

Speaking the truth can often have negative consequences.

Testimony: Saeed Abedini is an American Iranian who converted from Islam to Christianity in 2000. He became very active in Iran as a pastor, evangelist, and church planter. In 2012 the Iranian authorities arrested him on charges of "undermining national security" and sentenced him to eight years in prison. In September 2014, Samaritan's Purse published the letter that he wrote to his eight-year-old daughter from his Iranian prison:

> You are growing so fast and becoming more beautiful every day. I praise God for His faithfulness to me every day as I watch from a distance through the prison walls and see pictures and hear stories of how you are growing both spiritually and physically. Oh how I long to see you. I know that you question why you have prayed so many times for my return and yet I am not home yet. . . . I desire for you to learn important lessons during these trying times. . . . God is in control of the whole world and everything that is happening in it is for His good purpose. . . . I pray God will bring me back home soon. But if not, we will still sing together as Habakkuk [3:17–19] did, Hallelujah, either separated by prison walls or together at home.[3]

Metaphor: Before modern methods of communication were invented, most messages were carried by a human courier from one party to another. When the message contained bad news, it sometimes was the practice to take out one's frustration on the envoy. For this reason, the catchphrase "Don't shoot the messenger" is often added if the messenger knows that the news about to be announced is likely to be received negatively.

As messengers of the gospel we are sometimes put in the position of telling people things that they do not want to hear. If we truly believe that there are eternal consequences for failing to follow the law of God, we will not hesitate to speak the truth, no matter what the earthly consequences.

False Prophets and the Sovereignty of God

Big Idea
Deciding whether to submit to God is a life-and-death decision.

Key Themes
- God's sovereign power was established when he created the earth and its inhabitants.
- God alone controls world events and history.
- Those who ignore God and listen instead to false prophets will perish.
- Those who submit to God and obey his servants will live.

Understanding the Text

The Text in Context

Throughout Jeremiah 11–29 we see God's true prophet in conflict with the hostile leadership of Jerusalem. The second half of this unit (Jer. 21–29) focuses on the consequent judgment that will come upon Jerusalem and these leaders because of this hostility. One of the subthemes throughout this unit is the negative role of the court prophets, those "false" prophets of the king who oppose Jeremiah and give counterprophecies to the leaders and the people, thus giving them "religious" justification for ignoring God's word as proclaimed by Jeremiah. This subtheme is developed in Jeremiah 27–28. These two chapters are closely connected by the exhortation to submit to Nebuchadnezzar (represented by the construction of a real but symbolic yoke) and by the opposition to this command by the false prophets. The words related to "yoke" occur repeatedly throughout Jeremiah 27–28 (27:2, 8, 11, 12; 28:2, 4, 10, 11, 12, 13, 14), as does the name "Nebuchadnezzar" (27:6, 8, 20; 28:3, 11, 14). Likewise, the subjugation of both the nations and the "wild animals" is mentioned in both chapters (27:6; 28:14). Also, in Jeremiah 27 the "false prophets" are generic; in Jeremiah 28 they are represented by one specific individual (Hananiah). One of the false prophecies given by the false prophets was the prediction that the "humiliation" of the Babylonian looting of the

Jerusalem temple a few years earlier (597 BC) would soon be reversed. This false teaching, along with the mention of Nebuchadnezzar, likewise connects Jeremiah 29 with Jeremiah 27–28.[1]

Forms of the phrase "do not listen to the [false] prophets" occur three times in this passage (27:9, 14, 16), declared once to each of the three groups being addressed: the envoys of the neighboring countries (27:1–11), the Judahite king Zedekiah (27:12–15), and the Judahite priests, along with all the people (27:16–22).

There is also a wordplay on *'abad* throughout 27:6–17 (27:6 [2x], 7, 8, 9, 11 [2x], 12, 13, 14, 17) that harkens back to a similar wordplay in the early chapters of Exodus. Various words derived from the root (*'bd*) can mean "serve," "servant," "slave," "slavery," "work," or "worship," and in Exodus there is a lengthy wordplay on this range of meaning. The people of Israel are "serving" Pharaoh, who oppresses them with hard "service." Moses, the "servant" of God, comes to rescue them from "serving" Pharaoh so that they can "serve" (i.e., worship) God and live. Here in Jeremiah things are in reverse (and the great story of Israel's deliverance is also now in reverse). The people have refused to "serve" God, so he is sending his "servant" Nebuchadnezzar (quite a contrast to Moses!). In order to live, they must now submit to "serving" Nebuchadnezzar, just as they used to "serve" Pharaoh. Adding a new dimension to the wordplay is the fact that there is only one small difference in spelling between the word *'abad* (root *ayin-bet-dalet*, "serve") and the word *'abad* (root *alef-bet-dalet*, "perish"), and they sound very nearly the same when pronounced. In 27:10–15 God says that if they listen to the false prophets and refuse to *'abad* (serve) Nebuchadnezzar, then they will *'abad* (perish).

Interpretive Insights

27:1 *Early in the reign of Zedekiah.* Jeremiah 28:1 connects the events of Jeremiah 28 to those in Jeremiah 27 and provides more detail ("the fourth year" of Zedekiah) for dating this episode. Thus the date is 594–593 BC.

27:2 *Make a yoke.* Yokes were used to connect oxen to plows or wagons. Throughout the biblical world the yoke was also used as a symbol of servitude to the king.

put it on your neck. It is not clear whether Jeremiah dons the entire heavy wooden crosspiece or only the straps and connections, but probably it is the entire wooden crosspiece.

27:3 *Edom, Moab, Ammon.* These were the three small kingdoms on the eastern and southern borders of Judah.

Tyre and Sidon. Tyre, the dominant maritime power throughout the Mediterranean region at this time, was the most powerful entity on this list, and it had not yet been subdued by the Babylonians. Sidon, twenty-five miles to the north of Tyre, was likewise a powerful maritime city. Both were inhabited by Phoenicians, the descendants of the original Canaanites who were never completely driven out of the promised land.

Send word to the kings . . . through the envoys who have come. Apparently each of these neighboring kingdoms had sent envoys (lit., "messengers") to Jerusalem for a conspiracy meeting of some kind to plot against the rule of Nebuchadnezzar.

27:4 *the LORD Almighty.* Literally, "Yahweh of the armies," this term for God portrays him as a great warrior at the head of his army. It also occurs in 27:18, 19, 21; thus it frames God's message in this chapter. A favorite name for God in Jeremiah (occurring seventy-seven times), it is used frequently in judgment passages and stresses the sovereign power of God to bring about his plan.

27:5 *I made the earth.* In Hebrew these are the opening words of the verse (and the entire message given to the conspiratorial kings in 27:5–11). Likewise, in Hebrew the use of the independent personal pronoun "I" as the first word in the verse adds a strong emphasis (*"I am the one* who made the earth"). The point of mentioning God as the Creator is not so much the material origins of the creation as God's control of it.

to anyone I please. The word translated in the NIV as "please" has strong connotations of ethical and legal "rightness." A more nuanced rendering is "based on what is right in my eyes."

27:6 *Now I.* Again the independent personal pronoun is used for emphasis, paralleling 27:5. It is the one who made the earth and its inhabitants who is now giving these countries into the hand of Nebuchadnezzar.

my servant Nebuchadnezzar. The Babylonian king is called a "servant" of God because he is carrying out the plan of God. Thus, ironically, he is placed in strong contrast to Zedekiah, who is disobeying God. Although it is doubtful that Nebuchadnezzar ever actually became a true worshiper of the God of Israel, in the book of Daniel he makes several strong statements recognizing the power of God and the authority of God's messengers (Dan. 2:47; 3:28–29; 4:34–37), something that Zedekiah and his court refused to do. Likewise, after conquering Jerusalem, Nebuchadnezzar and his officials treat Jeremiah the prophet with honor and respect (Jer. 39:11–12), in contrast to Zedekiah, the false prophets, and his court, who opposed Jeremiah and tried to kill him.

I will make even the wild animals subject to him. The word translated as "subject" is the same word that is usually translated as "serve" or "servant" throughout this passage (lit., "I will make even the wild animals serve him" [cf. NRSV]). The use of "wild animals" probably is a figure of speech, painting an image of lions and jackals joining in to help Nebuchadnezzar's invasion (compare similar usage of these same Hebrew terms in 12:9). The wild animals may also be figurative of the surrounding nations that join in the invasion (see the use of "wild animals" in 28:14).

27:8 *with the sword, famine and plague.* This triad encompasses the punishment of God brought about by a foreign invasion. This triad (or variations of it using only two of these terms) occurs repeatedly in Jeremiah. Note the repetition of this phrase in 27:13.

27:9 *So do not listen.* In Hebrew this verse begins with the second-person independent pronoun, contrasting "you" (plural) with the "I" in 27:5–6.

27:10 *you will perish.* As mentioned above ("The Text in Context"), the Hebrew words for "serve" and "perish" are very similar, creating an ironic wordplay.

27:12 *to Zedekiah . . . "Bow your neck."* Jeremiah now turns to address his own king, Zedekiah, but Jeremiah uses plural imperatives through this section (27:12–15), indicating that he probably is addressing all of the royal court and even the nation at large.

27:19 *the pillars, the bronze Sea.* These are the Solomonic treasures of the temple that Nebuchadnezzar left behind in Jerusalem just a few years earlier (597 BC), probably due to their unmanageable size. Two gigantic bronze pillars (twenty-seven feet tall and eighteen feet in circumference) stood at the entrance of the temple (1 Kings 7:15–22), symbolizing the power with which God established the temple. The "Sea" was a huge water basin, likewise cast of bronze, fifteen feet in diameter and seven and a half feet high (1 Kings 7:23–26). In the ancient Near East, the sea symbolized the forces of chaos. The bronze Sea in the temple symbolized God's control over the waters of chaos[2] (note that Jer. 52:17–23 describes the removal of these very objects by Nebuchadnezzar in 586 BC).

Theological Insights

One very striking aspect of the book of Jeremiah in general, and this passage in particular, is that God's plan and his revealed word to his people through his prophet are very much at odds with the "national interest" of Judah. God moves forward with his plan, and the country of Judah can get on board (and survive) or continue to oppose the plan (and suffer the consequences). God had no intention of conforming his will to the national interest of any country, even Judah. God was bringing about his plan, and he exhorted his people to detach themselves from blind allegiance to their country (Judah) and to give top priority to obeying his word. The same is true today. Sometimes among Christians in the United States, there is a subconscious assumption that what is best for their country must surely be part of God's will and part of his plan. To think that God would never do anything but bless the United

States, regardless of the country's sinful actions, is a faulty assumption that runs contrary to the message of Jeremiah and the character of God.

Teaching the Text

This passage reminds us that God created the earth and everyone in it. As the Creator of the earth, he has both the right and the power to bring about his plan, whether a plan for salvation or a plan for judgment. God's plan is based upon what is right in his eyes. His plan is certain, and his promises regarding his plan are reliable. Furthermore, he has revealed much of his plan to his prophets and his apostles, who have relayed this message in both oral and written form. So we have the basic outline of God's plan with us today in the Scriptures.

Like the false prophets of Jeremiah's day, there are those today who would reinterpret God's word or even oppose God's word with hostility whenever it runs contrary to their own perceived self-interest or national interest. They proclaim that God will do what is right in *their* own eyes. Pride and arrogance lie at the heart of this approach, for many people today believe that they can decide what is right and what is wrong and that they can decide to reject God's word without consequence. Rather than recognize God's warnings and his call for repentance, they deny the imminent danger and seek to counteract God's word, minimizing issues of sin and disobedience and misleading their audience into thinking that they can avoid the consequences of defying God. This is the nature of American civil religion.

Leaders and the people they lead are thus faced with a choice. They can listen to God's true message as revealed in the Scriptures, submit to his plan, and find life, or they can ignore God's word, listen to their own "false prophets," foolishly try to defy God's plan, and perish. Obviously, this is a profoundly serious decision with eternal consequences—the most important decision an individual (or a nation) can make.

Illustrating the Text

Ignoring God's warnings will eventually be fatal.

Fable: Once there was a railroad that ran through the middle of a cornfield. Two grasshoppers lived in the cornfield, near the tracks. They were arrogant and boastful, and they liked to mock the train as it went by: "That train is mostly just smoke and noise! He has no real power! If you have power, O train, come over here and kill us! Ha! See! Nothing! Just as we thought!" The train just rumbled on through the cornfield, and the grasshoppers felt smug in their belittling of the train. You see, the train was intent on its purpose and destination; thus it ignored the prattle of the insignificant grasshoppers. This went on for many days. But then one day the grasshoppers found themselves up on the tracks as the train approached. In their arrogance they mocked the train again as they had always done, but this time they tried to *stop* the train from reaching its destination. Needless to say, it rolled right over them and squashed them without any effort.[3]

The severe consequences of ignoring true prophets and listening to and following false prophets

Biblical History: In the time of the divided kingdom both the northern and the southern kingdoms had prophets. Some spoke the truth and word of God, and others said what they believed people wanted to hear. Israel, the northern kingdom, ignored prophets such as Elijah, Elisha, Amos, and Hosea. The people of Israel refused to repent of their idolatry and habitual injustice. Ponder the consequences of their decision. In 722 BC ten tribes of Israel were taken into captivity by the Assyrians and, for all practical purposes, disappeared from history. They had received warning after warning, but they ignored God's clear call to repent. The consequences stand in biblical history as a warning to all of us.

The Devastating Results of False Prophecy

Big Idea
Using the name of God to teach what is false is particularly offensive to God and leads to severe consequences.

Key Themes
- False prophets can use biblical language to make their message sound true and appealing.
- Those leaders who persuade people by falsely claiming to speak the word of God are particularly offensive to God.
- Proclaiming lies in the name of God brings serious consequences.

Understanding the Text

The Text in Context

The central theme in Jeremiah 11–29 is the conflict between Jeremiah as God's true prophet and the leaders of Judah, who react to Jeremiah and God's word with hostility. In the latter half of this unit (Jer. 21–29) the spotlight falls on the consequences that these leaders (the king, the priests, the prophets, the nobles) will experience for rejecting God's word and his messenger. Jeremiah 27–28 focuses specifically on the false prophets. The two chapters are closely connected; indeed, Jeremiah 28 is a narrative continuation of Jeremiah 27. Both chapters are in prose.

At the beginning of Jeremiah 27, God tells Jeremiah to construct a yoke and to wear it as a sign that Judah and its surrounding neighbors must submit to the control of Nebuchadnezzar (27:2, 8, 11–12). In Jeremiah 28 Hananiah, one of the court prophets who oppose Jeremiah, breaks this same yoke and uses this action to symbolize a completely contrary prophecy: not only will Judah (and its neighbors) not be subjugated to Nebuchadnezzar, but even those who were exiled to Babylon several years earlier will be released and will return to Jerusalem (28:2, 4, 10, 11). Earlier in Israel's history the prophet Isaiah had used the image of a broken yoke as a symbol of God's great deliverance of

Israel (Isa. 9:4; 10:27; 14:25), but clearly Hananiah is misapplying the image here.¹ God, of course, has the final word, reusing the yoke image by stressing that the wood yoke that Hananiah broke will be replaced with an unbreakable iron yoke (28:12–14), thus emphasizing the solid control that Nebuchadnezzar will indeed have over Judah.

Jeremiah 27 deals with false prophets in general; no particular names are mentioned. In Jeremiah 28, however, we meet a specific false prophet, Hananiah. The movement from general to specific across these two chapters suggests that Hananiah is a representative of the false prophets. In 27:15 God tells Zedekiah that he and those who were prophesying lies to him will perish. In 28:17 Hananiah, the representative of these false prophets, actually dies.

Throughout Jeremiah 28 both Hananiah and Jeremiah are repeatedly and consistently referred to by the narrator of the story (in Hebrew) as "Hananiah the prophet" and "Jeremiah the prophet" (28:1, 5, 10, 11, 12, 15, 17). Thus this chapter is a story of direct conflict between two "prophets." Both God and Jeremiah, however, refer to Hananiah merely as "Hananiah" (28:13, 15), refusing perhaps to give him "prophet" status. Hebrew has no word for "false prophet" so that distinction is often left for the reader to perceive from the details of the story.

Note also that while Jeremiah 26 is from a different historical situation than Jeremiah 27–28, it is quite connected thematically. At the end of Jeremiah 26, as a climax of hostile opposition to God's message, the king of Judah executes Uriah, a true prophet of God. At the end of Jeremiah 28, in contrasting parallel and with poetic justice, God executes the false prophet Hananiah.

Interpretive Insights

28:1 *of that same year.* This phrase opens and closes the chapter (28:1, 17), forming an inclusio.

the fourth year. This refers to the fourth year of Zedekiah's reign (594–593 BC).

28:2 *the* LORD *Almighty, the God of Israel.* Hananiah uses the exact same language in describing God that Jeremiah used in 27:4.

28:4 *I will also bring back to this place Jehoiachin, son of Jehoiakim.* Jehoiakim was the terrible king who ruled from 609 to 598 BC and who opposed Jeremiah with open hostility. After rebelling against the Babylonians, Jehoiakim died mysteriously just as the Babylonian army arrived at Jerusalem. His young son Jehoiachin became king, promptly surrendered, and was taken into exile (597 BC).

and all the other exiles. Along with Jehoiachin, in 597 BC the Babylonians took many of the nobles, military officers, and skilled workers of Judah back to Babylon as exiles (2 Kings 24:8–17).

declares the LORD. In Hebrew this phrase is literally "oracle of Yahweh." This phrase is used frequently by Jeremiah and the other true biblical prophets to stress the origin of the message that they deliver. By using this phrase, Hananiah is claiming that his message is a direct revelation from God himself and carries the authority of God.

28:6 *Amen!* The English word "amen" is a transliteration of the Hebrew word *'amen*. It means "may it be so," "it is so," or something like "truly!"

May the LORD *fulfill the words you have prophesied.* The Hebrew grammar expresses a volitional hope on the part of Jeremiah that God will actually do this. The English "may the LORD" captures the idea fairly well. It is difficult to tell what Jeremiah actually thinks about Hananiah's prophecy. Some scholars suggest that Jeremiah is a bit rattled by this counterprophecy and hopes deep down in his soul that Hananiah's prediction of peace and the quick return of their kin from Babylon is true. Others note that after fighting against these false prophets of "peace" for over a decade, Jeremiah is not likely to be taken in by this. Thus his answer may be satirical.[2]

28:9 *truly sent by the* LORD *only if his prediction comes true.* This is the criteria for determining a true prophet of God that was prescribed in Deuteronomy 18:17–22.

28:14 *control over the wild animals.* As in 27:6, the subjugation of the wild animals (in Hebrew, "beasts of the field") is closely connected to the subjugation of the surrounding nations. Just as God will give Nebuchadnezzar control over wild animals (lions, hyenas, leopards, etc.), so he will give Nebuchadnezzar control over the surrounding nations (Moab, Ammon, Edom, etc.). Ironically, although these nations have gathered to conspire with Zedekiah against Nebuchadnezzar (27:1–3), several of them will turn on Judah and join the Babylonians. So "serving" implies joining in the invasion, both for the nations and probably in a figurative way for the wild animals (as in 12:9).

28:15 *you have persuaded this nation to trust in lies.* The Hebrew puts a strong stress on "you." A rough literal rendering reads, "But you, you have caused this people to trust in a lie."

28:16 *I am about to remove you.* The word translated as "remove" most commonly means "send." It is the same word used in 28:15. The wordplay running through these two verses is something like this: since Hananiah preached without being "sent" by God (28:15), God will now indeed "send" him from the face of the earth (28:16).

28:17 *In the seventh month of that same year.* The events at the beginning of the chapter take place in the fifth month. Hananiah dies in the seventh month, two months later. Hananiah had prophesied (falsely) in the name of God that the exiles and the looted temple materials would return within two years (28:3). With ironic poetic justice, God strikes him dead after two months.

Theological Insights

Throughout the Bible there does not seem to be one universal and consistent way that God deals with those who seek to counter his message with lies in his name. Certainly in this chapter Hananiah is killed by God (and note the gruesome fate of the false prophets in 29:20–23). Note also that within a few short years of this event just about everyone who has been opposing Jeremiah is either killed or exiled. Yet on the other hand, Jeremiah had to endure this opposition for most of his life. Only at the end of the story is Jeremiah proved right and his enemies silenced. That is, God did not immediately strike dead all the false prophets who opposed Jeremiah and proclaimed lies in the name of God, but it does appear that all of them eventually did experience the consequences of their opposition to God and his messenger. Thus the biblical evidence indicates that God does judge "false prophets" and those who persecute his messengers, but he does so according to his timing, which he does not reveal to us.

The New Testament similarly has numerous warnings about "false prophets" and false teachers who opposed the true teachings of Jesus and the early church (e.g., Matt. 7:15–23; 24:11–12, 23–24; 1 Tim. 1:18–20; 2 Tim. 4:14–15; 2 Pet. 1:14–2:22; 1 John 4:1–3; Rev. 2:14–15, 20–24).[3] Like Jeremiah 28, many of these texts are warnings to God's people about these false teachers, but several of them also contain strong declarations of coming judgment on the false teachers. As in the Old Testament, sometimes the judgment comes immediately and sometimes the judgment lies in the eschatological future. The judgment varies in its form and timing, but it will always come.

Teaching the Text

Several lessons are to be drawn from this passage. First, note that Hananiah's message sounded true. He couched his message in the typical terminology of true prophets, sounding very much like Jeremiah in claiming that his message was from God. His main image of breaking the yoke echoed that found in Isaiah. His message was very much audience-oriented, a message of hope and deliverance that all his listeners would love to hear. Yet his message was completely wrong and at loggerheads with the true message God was delivering to the people via Jeremiah. Hananiah said nothing of sin and disobedience. He issued no call to repentance. He skipped over any reference to judgment and only focused on immediate restoration. Likewise today, Christians should be cautious and discerning about those who look like Christians and sound like Christians but who preach a message that omits anything that might be offensive to their listening audiences, crucial matters such as sin, judgment, repentance, and atonement. There is nothing wrong with focusing on the "good news" salvation aspects of the gospel, but we must keep in mind that there is no salvation without the cross.

Second, it is possible that even Jeremiah was taken in by this message for a short period. For those of us who lead God's people and preach the word of God regularly, it is imperative that we be very discerning about what we hear (and read), continually evaluating writers and speakers by the word of God. No matter how popular the message is, and no matter how much we would like for it to be true, if it contradicts the word of God and leads people away from the truth of Christ, then we must reject it and point out the error of it to our people.

Third, God is deadly serious about false teaching in his name, especially when that teaching persuades people to turn away from the truth of the gospel. This is not an offense that he takes lightly. Whether we are writing, preaching, leading a Bible study, or teaching Sunday school, we need to study hard and pray diligently that we proclaim the word of God accurately. To baptize one's own personal views or soapbox understandings with "thus saith the Lord" is extremely dangerous. This displeases God. No, actually it angers God. We should always handle God's word with a certain degree of "fear and trembling," always striving to present his message accurately.

Yet today we should exert caution in trying to predict the timing of God's judgment on specific false teachers. The grace of God is immense, and we should first respond with a call to repentance. But certainly God is angry when lies are proclaimed continuously in his name, and the general truth that people who do this will fall under his terrible judgment either now or in the future is a valid message today, as it was in Jeremiah's day.

Illustrating the Text

It is often hard to distinguish false prophets from real ones.

Everyday Life: Many millions of Americans are the victims of identity theft each year. The odds are pretty good that you or someone you know has been victimized by this crime. On average, a crime of this kind takes place every three seconds, and, worse, the criminals are getting more and more sophisticated. Internet fraud, credit card theft, and e-reader and phone scams are happening with alarming regularity. PINs and passwords need to be guarded with ever-increasing diligence.[4]

But as bad as it is when people steal someone else's identity, it is even worse when false prophets claim to be speaking for God because then the loss is not simply goods and services but eternal security.

News Stories: Every few years there seems to be another case of a television evangelist who gets caught in some kind of financial or moral impropriety. Each time it happens, the news media revel in reporting the details of the cover-up, the cars, the money, the houses, the vacations, the extravagant lifestyle, and, in many cases, evidence that the perpetrator was running a religious scam and not a Christ-honoring ministry. Without turning it into an incrimination of a specific person or ministry, talk about how offensive it is to God when people run financial scams and claim to be doing the will of God.

Other examples of modern-day false prophets are those whose cultic practices have ended in gun violence, death, abuse, and destruction of property when they are challenged by outside authorities. Charles Manson, David Koresh, and Warren Jeffs are recent examples, but perhaps the most famous is Jim Jones. He was an American religious leader who led a large group of misguided followers to a commune in Guyana. Under allegations of abuse, his Peoples Temple Agricultural Project, commonly known as Jonestown, came under national scrutiny that ended in tragedy. In November 1978, US congressman Leo Ryan of California led a group of reporters and concerned family members to personally investigate the Jonestown community. When Ryan and his party attempted to leave with some disgruntled members of the cult, violence erupted, and five members of the party, including Ryan, were killed. Ultimately, over nine hundred members of the Jonestown community committed mass suicide.[5]

False prophets are not confined to the ancient world. Every generation seems to produce a new crop. We need to be discerning and identify those who claim to be speaking in the name of God but instead are misleading people.

God's Plans for His Exiled People

Big Idea

Be content where you are and trust in God's long-range plans.

Key Themes

- God tells the exiles to settle down and find blessings even in their exile.
- Those in exile should not trust in lies promising a quick restoration.
- Those in exile should trust in the knowledge that God has a good plan of *shalom* for them.
- Those who prophesy lies about the future in God's name will be judged.

Understanding the Text

The Text in Context

In 597 BC the young king Jehoiachin surrendered Jerusalem to the Babylonian king Nebuchadnezzar. Much of the entire "nobility" class, along with many of the artisans and military officers, were exiled to Babylon. The three chapters of Jeremiah 27–29 are connected in that all three deal with the fate of these exiles in relation to the domination of Judah by the Babylonians. In Jeremiah 28 the false prophet Hananiah declares that the exiles will return within two years. God strikes him dead for preaching such a misleading lie in his name. In Jeremiah 29, in contrast, Jeremiah tells these exiles that it will be seventy years before they return, so they might as well settle down and experience the blessings of God in Babylon.

The larger unit (Jer. 11–29) is united by the theme of Jeremiah in conflict with the leaders of Judah. The latter half of this unit (Jer. 21–29) adds a focus on the consequent judgment that God brings upon those leaders who oppose Jeremiah with hostility and mislead the people to trust in their lies, all in the name of God. In Jeremiah 28 Jeremiah is opposed face-to-face by the false prophet Hananiah, who dies at the end of the chapter. In Jeremiah 29 Jeremiah is opposed via letter correspondence by Shemaiah, a leader of the exiles in Babylon. Thus most of the chapter consists of Jeremiah's letter to the exiles in Babylon (29:4–23) and Shemaiah's written response back to the leaders in Jerusalem (29:24–28). The text suggests that God's judgment on Shemaiah (29:30–32) was also put into a third letter and sent back to the exiles in Babylon. Jeremiah 29 concludes with a scathing judgment upon Shemaiah and his descendants, thus paralleling the ending of Jeremiah 28 and also drawing Jeremiah 11–29 to a conclusion with a clear prophecy of judgment on those who oppose the word of God and his messenger Jeremiah.

Also note that the promise of *shalom* and restoration in Jeremiah 29 leads directly into the "Book of Restoration" in Jeremiah 30–33. That is, deliverance and restoration promised in Jeremiah 29 are defined much more fully in Jeremiah 30–33. At the heart of this deliverance and restoration are the coming messianic king and the new covenant, fulfilled in Jesus Christ.

Historical and Cultural Background

A fascinating discovery among the Dead Sea Scrolls was a small fragment (called 4Q339, dating probably to the late first century BC), written in Aramaic, whose opening line reads, "false prophets who have arisen in Israel." This brief introduction is followed by a list of eight false prophets. Four of these prophets are from Jeremiah 28–29: Ahab and Zedekiah (29:21–22), Shemaiah (29:24–32), and Hananiah (28:1–17).[1] This indicates that probably during the intertestamental period the false prophets in Jeremiah 28–29 and their fates were well remembered and used as paradigms of false prophecy.

Interpretive Insights

29:1 *the text of the letter.* This probably refers to text written on a papyrus scroll.

29:7 *seek the peace and prosperity.* The imperative verb translated "seek" is plural. The English phrase "peace and prosperity" is a good attempt at translating the word *shalom*, although "restful and complete well-being" might be a better phrase to use for *shalom* than "prosperity," which in English can have negative connotations.

because if it prospers, you too will prosper. Literally, the Hebrew reads, "for in her *shalom* is your [plural] *shalom*." God is telling them not to be rebellious or hostile against Babylon. Neither should they live as malcontents, hoping the situation to be but temporary. God is telling them to accept the situation in which he has placed them and even to find blessing in the midst of their exile in Babylon.

29:10 *seventy years.* Jeremiah first mentions the seventy-year period in 25:11–12 (see the unit on 25:1–14, especially the sidebar "Which Seventy Years?"). Although the number "seventy" certainly carries a symbolic connotation of completeness, here in Jeremiah 29 it also represents a lifetime. That is, very few of the current exiles will actually live to see the return.

29:11 *For I know the plans I have for you.* Grammatically, there is a strong emphasis on the independent first-person pronoun ("I"), which is emphasized in both phrases. The word for "plan" also occurs twice, first as a noun and then as a participle. A rough reading is "*I* know the plans *I* am planning for you [plural]." The emphasized "I" stands in contrast to the false prophets in 29:8–9, and God's plans are in contrast to the "dreams" and "lies" of those false prophets.

declares the LORD. Literally, this phrase translates as "oracle of the LORD." It is used to stress the origin and authenticity of the message.

plans to prosper you and not to harm you. The word for "plans" used twice earlier in the verse is repeated here, as is the word *shalom*. The pronoun "you" likewise continues to be plural. Jeremiah contrasts two of his favorite terms: "plans to give you *shalom* and not *ra'ah* [bad stuff; disaster]." These "plans of *shalom*" are spelled out in the following verses (29:12–14).

29:12 *you will call . . . come . . . pray . . . and I will listen.* What is described is a renewed communication with God. Recall the results of the broken covenant expressed with the same words back in 11:14: "Do not *pray* for this people . . . because I will not *listen* when they *call* to me." When the covenant was shattered, God ceased to "listen" to the people of Judah. But now, as part of God's good plan for the restoration, they will once again be able to come to him and pray to him, confident that he will listen and act.

29:13 *You will . . . find me when you seek me with all your heart.* The Hebrew particle translated as "when" can mean "when" (temporal or conditional) or "for" (causal). The causal idea is that they will find God because they will be seeking him with all their heart. The Hebrew word for "heart" refers to the seat of volition; that is, the heart is particularly the place where one decides to obey or disobey. Seeking God with all one's heart means coming to him with the willingness to listen and to obey him completely. One can hear echoes of Deuteronomy 4:29 in this verse.

29:21 *Ahab . . . and Zedekiah.* These are two false prophets who are active among the Judahite exiles in Babylon. This Ahab is not the King Ahab of Israel who opposed Elijah in 1–2 Kings. Likewise, this Zedekiah is not King Zedekiah of Judah, who is back in Jerusalem contending with Jeremiah.

29:22 *whom the king of Babylon burned in the fire.* The word translated as "burned" is more specifically "roasted." It is normally used of roasting/ toasting grain. Here it is the graphic (and grim) fate of those who prophesy lies in the name of God (29:21).

29:31 *has persuaded you to trust in lies.* The verb form used here connotes a causation involving the object in an action: "he has caused you to trust in a lie." Shamaiah has not just spoken lies; he has effectively convinced many of the people to believe and trust in the lies, and thus God will judge him severely.

Theological Insights

Since the destruction of Jerusalem by the Babylonians came as a result of Israel's extensive idolatry and continued social injustice within the context of a shattered covenant, it seems theologically appropriate to parallel this with the fate of unbelievers who hear and know about Christ but who never actually trust in him or commit to following him. Those who go into the exile of 597 BC, however, seem to be in a different theological category. As we see in Jeremiah 29, those in the exile of 597 BC are treated (at least symbolically) as being in an "already but not yet" kind of category. They are still God's people, exhorted to trust in him in the exile as they await the future restoration. The New Testament picks up the "living in exile" theme as an image of those trusting in Christ while living as exiles waiting for him to return. The letter of 1 Peter in particular develops this theme, often drawing directly from Jeremiah 29.[2] Christians today experience the kingdom of God and the glorious restoration in a similar "already but not yet" manner. There is a sense in which we as Christians are already in the kingdom, but there is also a sense of the kingdom that awaits the future and ultimate fulfillment when Christ returns. While we wait for that fulfillment, we are like exiles living in a foreign land.

Teaching the Text

Jeremiah 29:11 may be the best-known verse in Jeremiah; indeed, it is certainly a favorite for many Christians. Certainly 29:11 encapsulates much of this passage, but we must understand it from within the context of the rest of the chapter and realize that it is not a context-free promise made directly to us but rather a specific word of encouragement from God embedded within a letter written directly to the Judahite exiles in Babylon.

Most of us live in a world that promotes instant gratification while usually downplaying virtues such as patience. When we turn to God in prayer (claiming verses such as Jer. 29:11), we not only desire him to act on our behalf but also desire that he do so *now*, or at least in the very near future. Thus there is much we can learn from this passage.

First of all, note that God has a plan for his people in exile, both for the short term and for the long term. He describes the plan as *shalom*, a contented state of well-being, a true inner peace. Yet note that God tells them of an immediate plan for day-to-day *shalom* while in exile and then a long-range plan for ultimate *shalom* (seventy years later, after most of them have died). Likewise for us, many of our prayers and pleas (heal this cancer, end this pain, correct this injustice) will be totally and completely answered only in the ultimate restoration, when Christ returns and establishes his kingdom. In the meantime, just as God told the exiles to settle down and to find *shalom* while in Babylon, he exhorts us to make the most of our situation now. We should seek *shalom* now, even though in a sense we remain exiles in this world. Yes, we do long for the ultimate deliverance and restoration, but in the meantime we pray for *shalom* and seek it from God on a day-to-day basis. This is the plan that God has for our lives in the "already but not yet."

It is interesting to note that what these exiles probably want most is to return to Jerusalem. However, that would put them right at the center of the coming terrible destruction and devastation of Jerusalem. Unknown to them, at the present time it is much safer to remain in Babylonia. Likewise for us, often the plan that we think would be wonderful is in fact a disastrous plan, and God says no just to protect us.

Also, God tells us that we will find *shalom* when we seek him with our whole heart. That is, we will not experience God's *shalom* if we only commit to follow and obey halfheartedly.

Likewise, God's people are exhorted to avoid listening to people who do not know God or his plan, those who do not truly speak for him. There are always those who distort God's message of *shalom*. Peace and restoration do not come to those who arrogantly oppose God and refuse to acknowledge their sin and repent. Those today who promise *shalom* apart from the cross of Christ are "persuading people to trust in a lie." Jeremiah 29 tells us to ignore these people and to trust God and his sovereign plan instead, for he alone can bring *shalom*, both now on a day-to-day basis and ultimately in the final restoration when Jesus Christ establishes complete *shalom* in his kingdom.

God also has an ultimate long-term plan for his people. We should not lose the connection between the promise of *shalom* in Jeremiah 29 and the detailed description of the coming messianic era and the new covenant in Jeremiah 30–33. The return of the exiles under Ezra and Nehemiah did not actually bring about the "restoration." They were still much like exiles (the point of view taken by the New Testament). The actual restoration and great salvation truly got under way with the advent of Jesus Christ, especially as the new covenant was inaugurated. Knowing salvation through Jesus Christ and walking with him in the new covenant relationship are a huge part of the "plans I have for you" promise that God made to the exiles in Babylon in Jeremiah's day.

On a final note, it is perhaps significant to observe that all the "you" pronouns and second-person verbs in 29:11–14 are plural. This passage implies a community-oriented application. The stress is that God has a plan of *shalom* for *us*, not just for *me*. This passage has more direct relevance for a church congregation than for an individual.

Illustrating the Text

God calls us to trust in his plan, not to understand it.

Popular Culture: We live in a world of instant gratification. When our phone pings, it is hard to resist the urge to stop what we are doing and look at the message immediately, even when we are driving or in the middle of a conversation. In this high-tech society, this is who we are. Waiting is a thing of the past. Technology has intensified our expectation of an immediate response. Realizing this, retailers have jumped at the chance to satisfy our every whim instantly.

There are drive-through restaurants, dry cleaners, and pharmacies. It seems that nowadays we are too busy to get out of the car for anything. We have put a huge premium on not having to wait. We have the express check-in at the airport, self-checkout at the grocery store, the express pass at Disney World, and instant access to our money at the ATM.

And if we would rather not go out to shop, we can do so from home via the internet, find anything we want, and have it shipped overnight (or even the same day) right to our front door. And we no longer have any tolerance for slow DSL. We want our information and we want it fast—so fast, in fact, that we no longer even take the time to spell out words in our messages. It seems that whether it is the latest model on the showroom floor, or immediate financing for a new home, or speed dating our way to eternal love, if we want something, we want it now.

The problem is this: God does not always work on our timetable.

The Promise of Restoration

Big Idea

God's presence and his messianic ruler will overcome the impossible and restore his broken people.

Key Themes

- God's powerful presence will deliver his people and calms their fears.
- God can restore even when restoration seems impossible.
- God's great deliverance will lead to joyful worship.
- The coming messianic restoration will be the fulfillment of the Davidic and Abrahamic covenants.
- The messianic leader of the restoration will have a special connection to God's presence.

Understanding the Text

The Text in Context

Jeremiah 30–33 typically is called the "Book of Consolation." It is perhaps better to call it the "Book of Restoration." The major point of this unit is not necessarily to console (although consolation is present) but rather to create faith in God and hope in the great, glorious future restoration brought about by the coming messianic king and the new covenant. One of the major features of the Book of Restoration is that it picks up most of the negative judgment imagery of Jeremiah 1–29 (destroyed city, diminished population, exile, sickness, end of joy, broken covenant, Israel like a harlot, foreign domination, etc.) and reverses it into imagery of restoration (rebuilt city, increased population, regathering, healing, etc.).[1]

Jeremiah 30–33 opens and closes (30:3; 33:26) with the same phrase, which is usually translated as either "I will bring . . . back from captivity" (e.g., NIV) or "I will restore the fortunes" (e.g., ESV, HCSB, NRSV). This promise of restoration is a central theme of Jeremiah 30–33, and in various forms this phrase occurs numerous times (30:3, 18; 31:23; 33:7, 11, 26).

The two chapters of Jeremiah 30–31 flow together, indicated by the introductory words in 30:1–2 compared with 32:1, which clearly starts a new unit. Characteristics of the restoration presented in Jeremiah 30–31 include the following: (1) there is no mention of rebuilding the temple; (2) there are frequent allusions to the Davidic and Abrahamic covenants, which serve to provide the theological basis for the restoration; (3) there are no historical dates provided, perhaps pointing to the timelessness of the promised restoration; and (4) unlike Jeremiah 27–28, the restoration described in Jeremiah 30–31 is not tied to the downfall of Babylon; it seems to be "bigger" than the end of Babylon.

After several chapters consisting almost entirely of prose (Jer. 26–29), in Jeremiah 30–31 the text is composed primarily of poetry. Jeremiah 30:1–3, however, the introduction to Jeremiah 30–31, is in prose. The promise of restoration in 30:1–3 serves as a summary for the following two chapters. Jeremiah 30:4–11 is in poetry. It opens with a lament, describing the same kind of judgment imagery that we have seen throughout the first twenty-nine chapters of Jeremiah but then transitioning to deliverance and restoration. The next subsection, 30:12–17, is likewise written in poetry, starting with judgment but concluding with restoration. It centers on the sickness/healing motif. Jeremiah 30:18–22 continues in poetry but contains no judgment, only joyful restoration. The concluding subsection, 30:23–24, also in poetry, describes the wrath of God. The time of deliverance and restoration for God's people will simultaneously bring his wrath upon his enemies. These final two verses in Jeremiah 30 are identical to 23:19–20, where the recipients of God's wrath are identified as the false prophets.

Interpretive Insights

30:2 *Write in a book all the words I have spoken to you.* The implication is that this refers to Jeremiah 30–31 (the new introductory words in 32:1 indicate a new section). The word translated as "book" refers here to a scroll.

30:3 *I will bring my people . . . back from captivity.* The word *shub* ("to turn, return, repent") has been used frequently throughout Jeremiah in numerous wordplays. God has called upon Judah to *shub* (repent) from its sins and to *shub* (turn) back to God so that he can *shub* (turn) from his wrath. In this thematically central expression in 30:3, God promises to *shub* (return) his people from their captivity. The Hebrew word for "captivity" is *shebut*, a soundalike wordplay with *shub*. God will *shub* the *shebut* of his people.

and restore them to the land. The word translated as "restore" is *shub* again, but the grammatical form stresses the causal aspect. "I will cause them to return to the land." That is, God is the one who will bring about their return.

I gave their ancestors. This refers to the promise of the land that God gave to Abraham and then to Isaac and Jacob in the book of Genesis.

30:8 *in that day.* References to "that day" (30:7, 8) or to "days are coming" (30:3) allude to the "great day of the LORD." This "day" is referred to frequently throughout the prophets. It is a time (or the times) when God crashes into history to bring about his great plan. It includes both deliverance for God's people and judgment on his enemies.[2]

I will break the yoke off their necks. In Jeremiah 27–28 the "yoke" (the harness assembly for oxen) was one of the central thematic images. In those chapters the people of Judah were to bow their neck to the yoke of Babylon as part of their punishment. Here in 30:8 the yoke continues to be a symbol of foreign domination. God declares that he will break this yoke as part of his great deliverance and restoration for his people.

30:9 *David their king.* This alludes to the fulfillment of the Davidic covenant (2 Sam. 7:10–17).

30:10 *Jacob.* Remember that back in Genesis the twelve tribes of Israel (thirteen, including Levi; recall that Jacob's son Joseph produces two tribes, Ephraim and Manasseh) come from the twelve sons of Jacob, who is later renamed "Israel." Thus the name "Jacob" represents Israel as a unified entity, before the split into the northern kingdom, Israel, and the southern kingdom, Judah. The name "Jacob" occurs five times in Jeremiah 30–31 (30:7, 10, 18; 31:7, 11), suggesting an emphasis in these two chapters on the restoration of a unified Israel.

30:11 *I am with you and will save you.* The Hebrew grammar suggests a causal rather than a sequential relationship between the two main clauses: "I am with you to save you." It is the powerful presence of God that delivers his people.

declares the Lord. This phrase (lit., "revelation of the Lord" or "oracle of the Lord") stresses the certainty that this is the specific prophetic word of God. Here in 30:11 it is actually inserted into the middle of the sentence. That is, the text literally reads, "I am with you—revelation of the Lord—to save you."

30:12 *Your wound is incurable.* The sin and rebellion of Judah have been so great that God uses an analogy of a mortal wound or fatal sickness to represent it. This theme continues throughout 30:12–15. The theme of an incurable wound/sickness has been used by God repeatedly throughout Jeremiah to represent Judah's sin and the consequences of that sin (e.g., 6:7; 8:11, 22; 10:19; 14:17). In their current situation, with the Mosaic covenant shattered and the people so entrenched, rebellious, and obstinate in their sin, humanly speaking there is no possibility of healing (their sin being forgiven and their relationship being restored). God enumerates several reasons for this in the following verses (30:13–15). This certainty and the dire situation underscore the radical, gracious, and spectacular reversal of their plight that God declares in 30:17, where he promises healing and restoration to health.

30:17 *But I will restore you to health.* The image portrayed by the Hebrew words suggests that of flesh growing over a wound. This is in stark contrast to the hopeless, incurable situation described in 30:12–15.

30:19 *I will add to their numbers.* This is a clear allusion to the Abrahamic covenant (Gen. 12:1–3; 15:5; 22:17). At the time when the Mosaic covenant is shattered, the book of Jeremiah reaches back to the unilateral covenant promises made to Abraham and ties the restoration to the fulfillment of those promises.

30:22 *my people . . . your God.* The formula "I will be your God; you will be my people" is the most basic covenant formula in the Bible, used in both the Abrahamic and the Mosaic covenants. This is the climactic verse of Jeremiah 30. The very essence of the restoration will come out of a new covenant relationship that nonetheless centers on the continuation of the most central feature of the earlier covenants (God's relationship with his people).

Theological Insights

Several of the Old Testament prophets, and Jeremiah in particular, provide a helpful theological bridge between the Old Testament and the New Testament in the way they connect to the biblical covenants. Allusions to the Abrahamic covenant (Gen. 12:1–3; 15:4–21; 17:1–8) and the Davidic covenant (2 Sam. 7:4–16) are common whenever Jeremiah is prophesying about the coming messianic age and the restoration. The importance of these two covenants is that their fulfillment is based on God's grace, not on human obedience. Jeremiah also refers to the Mosaic covenant (especially as encapsulated in the book of Deuteronomy) frequently, especially throughout Jeremiah 1–29. The focus of the references to the Mosaic covenant is judgment due to failure to keep the law. Israel and Judah have broken the Mosaic covenant (law) and thus are deserving of judgment. But beyond the judgment there is hope for a future restoration based on the Abrahamic and Davidic covenants, because fulfillment of these covenants is driven by God's grace. The contrast between law and grace in the context of the Mosaic and Abrahamic covenants is likewise continued and explained more fully in the New Testament by Paul in Romans 3–4 and Galatians 3.

Yet it is important to keep in mind the complexity of these prophecies about the future restoration. One challenge is what can be called the "near view, far view" phenomenon. Often the prophets will paint a two-dimensional picture of the future where events that will happen soon ("near view") are blurred with events that will happen much later ("far view"). Thus when Jeremiah paints his picture of future restoration, he includes some elements that find fulfillment in the return of the exiles under Ezra and Nehemiah, some that find fulfillment at the first advent of Christ, and some that still await the return of Christ for ultimate fulfillment. The problem is that these images are blurred together in the prophet's vision without any clear indication of the time distance between them. We only see the time difference clearly as we are able to look backward.

Teaching the Text

After twenty-nine chapters focusing on judgment, we finally come to four chapters (Jer. 30–33) that focus on hope, salvation, and restoration. This glorious restoration era, however, finds its ultimate fulfillment not in the return of the exiles under Ezra and Nehemiah but in the first and second advents of Jesus Christ.

One of the most critical and foundational driving forces for deliverance and restoration is the presence of God. Because God is with us, we should not fear. His presence is powerful, and it is his presence that not only comforts us but also acts to deliver us. For New Testament believers, the powerful presence of God is manifested in the indwelling of the Holy Spirit.

Like a serious injury or fatal sickness, the sin and rebellion against God that run rife throughout our world result in a grim and dismal prognosis: death, no hope of a cure. But the good news is that God works miracles and is in the business of saving those who cannot be saved and restoring those who have given up hope of restoration. This is one of the central characteristics of the messianic era.

It is fascinating to note that in Jeremiah the image of an incurable sickness/wound is used of sin, and that in the glorious restoration the image of healing is used to symbolize restoration of life and relationship with God. The healing actions of Jesus should be placed in this context. As he brings about the new-covenant time of restoration prophesied by Jeremiah, Jesus will heal people both literally (physically) and symbolically (spiritually). The Greek word *sōzō*, which can mean either "to heal" or "to save," captures this double meaning. For example, in Mark 5:34 Jesus says, "Your faith has healed/saved [*sōzō*] you."

The appropriate response from those who were once shattered and plagued by sin but are now delivered and restored is joyful worship and thanksgiving. As God moves to fulfill his great covenant promises to Abraham and David through Christ, he pours out such blessing upon us that our response should be joyful adoration and praise.

At the center of these wonderful promises of God is the special ruler, the coming righteous king, who has a special relationship with God. This is, of course, Jesus Christ. All these future promises made by God through Jeremiah find their climactic culmination in the first and second comings of Christ. And ultimately we will be restored to that wonderful relationship with God, wherein he will be our God and we will be his people.

Finally, note that there is never any universalistic salvation proclaimed in Jeremiah. On the contrary, even here in a chapter focusing on deliverance and salvation, God reminds everyone that his great act of delivering and saving his people also brings about at the same time a judgment on those who oppose him and his plan.

Illustrating the Text

God can and does do the impossible.

Personal Testimony: This is a great opportunity to use a personal testimony either by the speaker or by members of the congregation. If possible, videotape the testimony in advance so that you know what will be said and how long it will take. Also, if possible, use more than one testimony.

These witnesses perhaps can talk about a time when they saw a dramatic or miraculous healing of some kind, or about how their life was restored in some way, or about how with God's help their marriage was redeemed.

Visual: An effective way of having people share a short version of how they were restored by God is to do what is called a "cardboard testimony." Several participants write their struggles on one side of a piece of cardboard, and how God restored their lives on the other side. Then they walk across the first half of the stage showing the "struggle" side of the cardboard, and then turn it around and reveal what God has done to change their lives. There are many examples on YouTube.

The comforting presence of God

Personal Testimony: Take a page of your personal memories to illustrate this point. I remember, from when I was a teenager, the comfort of knowing that my father was in the house. My father, an Air Force officer, was stationed in Southeast Asia for a full year, most of my junior year of high school. Even though I was seventeen years old, I remember how scary the house was at night and how unsettled my mom and I could be when we were alone in the house at night. I remember lying in bed after dad returned and thinking how comforting and reassuring it was to have him in the house. I slept much better after he came home. Perhaps tell a similar story of a time when the knowledge that a parent was present brought comfort.

Love, Redemption, and Joy

Big Idea

God's people should respond to God's great love and redeeming restoration with joyful worship.

Key Themes

- God loves his people and promises to restore them.
- People restored by God respond with joyful worship.
- God redeems lost people and turns their sorrow into joy.
- God's great redemption and restoration include all people, especially the weak and vulnerable.

Understanding the Text

The Text in Context

Jeremiah 30–33, the Book of Restoration, presents God's great promise of redemption, deliverance, and restoration of his shattered people. Jeremiah 30 opened this unit by emphasizing God's presence, the coming messianic leader, and the fulfillment of the Abrahamic and Davidic covenants. The central imagery used was that of the incurable sickness replaced with healing. Jeremiah 31 continues describing the coming restoration but shifts focus to God's love, his redemption of his people, and the wide range of people included in this redemption. The central imagery is that of a "new exodus," people coming back into the land, wiping away their tears, and celebrating joyfully as they come. The joyful response of the people to God's redemption and restoration, especially joyful worship, is a common theme in Jeremiah 30–31, connecting the two chapters. The special nuance of this theme in 31:1–26 is that this joy will replace weeping. As in Jeremiah 30 and throughout Jeremiah 30–33, the subsection 31:1–26 continues to take the judgment images of Jeremiah 1–29 and reverse them into blessings.

Interpretive Insights

31:1 *At that time.* This refers to 30:3 ("the days are coming") and 30:8 ("in that day"). It refers to the great coming day of the Lord, a time when God will bring about his great salvation and restoration of his people.

I will be their God . . . and they will be my people. This is the most basic covenant relationship formula of the Old Testament. It indicates that the time of the "broken covenant" is over and that God is reestablishing a covenant relationship with his people.

all the families of Israel. The description of the future restoration described in Jeremiah 30–33 expands dramatically beyond just a return of the Judahite exiles carried off to Babylon (as recorded in Ezra-Nehemiah). The word translated as "families" refers to a clan-sized group, smaller than a tribe but still much larger than what the word "family" suggests to most Westerners. Sometimes it is translated as "peoples." There may also be an allusion here to Genesis 12:3: "In you all of the families of the earth will be blessed."

31:3 *loved you with an everlasting love.* Both the verb and the noun for "love" here are from the Hebrew root *'hb*. This is a common Hebrew word for "love" with a semantic range similar to our English word "love."

I have drawn you with unfailing kindness. This phrase is connected to the phrase before it by a Hebrew term meaning "therefore." The word translated as "drawn" can mean "to drag, pull," but it can also mean "to continue," as it probably does here (cf. Neh. 9:30; Pss. 36:10; 85:5; 109:12). The word translated as "unfailing kindness" is *hesed*, which refers to loyal, ongoing covenant love. These two phrases are similar and doubly stress the eternal nature of God's love. Because God loves (*'aheb*) them with an everlasting love, he will continue *hesed*, which by its definition will always continue.

31:4 *Virgin Israel.* Recall that frequently in the judgment passages of Jeremiah 1–29 (and especially in Jer. 1–10) God referred to Israel and Judah as a promiscuous and unfaithful wife who had become a harlot. In the reversal of imagery used for the restoration, the harlot has been restored as an innocent virgin. Furthermore, the terminology used here suggests that God is reclaiming Israel as his wife.

31:5–6 *Samaria . . . Ephraim.* Samaria was the capital city of the northern kingdom, Israel, and its name was used to refer to the region around it. Ephraim (31:6, 9, 18) was one of the largest of the ten tribes that composed the northern kingdom. Yet recall that Samaria and Ephraim were completely destroyed by the Assyrians in 722 BC. The population was decimated and scattered. For all practical purposes, the northern kingdom, Israel, ceased to exist in 722 BC. So here in 31:5–6 God is promising to restore not only exiled Judah but also Israel (which actually was no longer in existence). This implies that the promised restoration was much broader in scope than just the return of those recently exiled by the Babylonians.

31:8 *from the land of the north . . . from the ends of the earth.* These two descriptions are used several times elsewhere in Jeremiah to describe the areas from which God brings the invading Babylonians to judge Judah (6:22;

25:32; 50:41). Now God reverses the image, and from these far-flung regions he now brings back his scattered people.

a great throng. The Hebrew implies a great or even "powerful" assembly of people. Sometimes this even refers to an "army" of people. But note the irony. This "great assembly" or "great army" is composed of the weakest and most vulnerable people—the blind, the lame, pregnant women about to give birth.

31:10 *like a shepherd.* The shepherd motif is reflected in several of the terms and phrases used in 31:8–10.

31:11 *will deliver Jacob and redeem them.* Verb tenses are often difficult to translate in Hebrew poetry, but these two verbs probably should be understood in the past or past perfect tense (e.g., NASB, NRSV, ESV, KJV) rather than future tense (NIV). The two Hebrew verbs (*padah, ga'al*) are similar in meaning and here are in poetic parallelism. Both verbs have to do with paying a price to buy something, often buying something back again. The first word (*padah*) is more general and is often used in the Pentateuch for redeeming a firstborn animal (e.g., Num. 18:15–16). It is also used frequently of God "redeeming" or "buying back" Israel from slavery in Egypt (Deut. 9:26; 15:15; 21:8). The second word (*ga'al*) is specifically tied to family law. It is used of

Matthew's Use of Jeremiah 31:15

Jeremiah 31:15 is cited in Matthew 2:18. Jeremiah 31:15 states, "A voice heard in Ramah . . . Rachel weeping for her children." Rachel, one of the matriarchs of Israel, was the wife of Jacob. Note that repeatedly throughout Jeremiah 30–31 Jacob is used as a metaphor for all Israel. The mother of Benjamin and Joseph, Rachel was also the grandmother of Ephraim, who likewise is used to represent all of Israel. So in a figurative sense Rachel is the mother of all Israel. Jeremiah 40:1 explains that Ramah, a village just north of Jerusalem, was the staging area where the defeated Israelites were organized for the long trip into exile in Babylon. Thus in a graphic but figurative description, Jeremiah paints a picture of Rachel, the mother of Israel, weeping for her children who have either died or are taken away.

A common tradition in the first century AD was that the tomb of Rachel was near Bethlehem. Thus when King Herod executed all the infants in Bethlehem, Matthew connected this event to the prophecy of Jeremiah 31:15. However, it is the full context of Jeremiah 31 that Matthew is alluding to, and not just this one isolated verse. Note that immediately after 31:15 the Lord goes on to proclaim, "Restrain your voice from weeping. . . . There is hope for your descendants. . . . Your children will return to their own land." Following Jeremiah 31, Matthew is implying that beyond this present horrific time of tragedy (as Herod kills the infants) there is the expectation of something new and glorious, a spectacular restoration that includes the new covenant.[a]

[a] Hays, *Message of the Prophets*, 179; Knowles, *Jeremiah in Matthew's Gospel*, 33–52.

people within a family buying back family land, houses, or other family members (Lev. 25:25; Ruth 4:1–6).[1]

31:12 *they will rejoice in the bounty of the* L ORD. The word translated as "rejoice" means "to shine, be radiant." It implies that their faces are glowing in joy. The word translated as "bounty" is the very common word that basically means "good." Here it refers to all the good things that God has done and provided for them.

31:13 *I will give them comfort and joy instead of sorrow.* The grammar implies not that God is giving them "comfort and joy" instead of sorrow but rather that God is comforting them and then (as part of that comfort) replacing their sorrow with joy. There is a stressed contrast between joy and sorrow.

31:20 *my heart yearns for him.* The word translated as "heart" actually refers to the entire internal organ area of the body. This phrase describes that internal "deep-down-in-your-gut" love and longing that parents feel for their children.

I have great compassion for him. The Hebrew grammar is not so much stressing the extent of the compassion (i.e., "great") as the certainty of it. "I most certainly, most assuredly, have compassion on him."

31:22 *the woman will return to the man.* A more literal translation reads, "A woman will surround (i.e., protect) the strong warrior." In the topsy-turvy "strength out of weakness" reversals of the restoration, the metaphoric image here is probably that the woman (Virgin Israel, Daughter Israel) is now powerful enough (or perhaps the times are peaceful enough) to reverse roles and provide protection rather than the warriors.[2]

31:25 *refresh the weary and satisfy the faint.* The words used here connote an image of people who have been languishing for a long time in the hot desert without any water and now drink their fill of water.

31:26 *At this I awoke.* This verse implies that 31:1–25 is part of a vision given to Jeremiah as he slept.

Theological Insights

Redemption is an important aspect of salvation. In both the Old Testament and the New Testament, the word "redemption" is used in regard to paying a price to release a person, an animal, or property from bondage. The basic principle was presented in the Pentateuch, as Israelites were required to "redeem" their firstborn animals. In the exodus story God becomes the great "redeemer" by freeing the Israelite slaves. God's redeeming role in the exodus is celebrated by the Old Testament frequently calling him "redeemer" (e.g., Pss. 19:14; 78:35; Isa. 49:26; 63:16). Conceptually, redemption is needed because of the weakness of the ones in bondage, who cannot redeem themselves. The theme of redemption culminates in Christ, who redeems us from slavery to sin and frees us to be slaves of God. Just as God redeemed Israel from Egypt to be his people and to serve him, so Christ redeems us from sin to be his people and to serve him. Throughout both Testaments joy is a closely related subtheme.[3]

Teaching the Text

At the heart of this passage is the stress on how wonderful God is and how incredibly fantastic is his redemption of us. His love for us is continuous and everlasting. Not only has his love for us provided for our salvation through Christ, but also, whenever we stray from him, it is his constant love that continually works to restore us to him.

God has redeemed us. The New Testament explains the full meaning of redemption to us as God pays the ultimate price of his Son to purchase us, to buy us back, so that we can be restored into the family.

Whether redeeming the lost or restoring the wayward, God takes broken, shattered, sorrowing, and despairing people and infuses joy, hope, and wonderment into their lives. The contrast is startling. Those who once were lethargically despairing and sorrowing now feel like dancing joyfully like giddy adolescents.

This joy we feel as a result of our redemption and/or our restoration should carry over into our worship of God. As we praise and worship God, we should be ecstatic with joy over the salvation and the blessings that he has given us.

And the good news is that this wonderful redemption or restoration is for everyone. No one is too outcast or too sinful or too weak or too weary to be saved or restored by God. Indeed, God especially enjoys saving the weak and weary.

Illustrating the Text

We are redeemed by the love of God in Christ Jesus.

Bible: Ephesians 1:7 says, "In him we have redemption through his blood, the forgiveness of sins, in accordance with the riches of God's grace." Romans 5:8 says, "But God demonstrates his own love for us in this: While we were still sinners, Christ died for us." Here the apostle Paul reminds us that we are unable to redeem ourselves, but Christ loves us even in our sinful state.

Christian Music: **"My Redeemer Lives," by Nicole C. Mullen.** The chorus of this song repeats the line "I know my redeemer lives." If possible, have someone sing the song live; Mullen's video version can be found on YouTube.[4] She has also made available a Spanish version.

The joy of being rescued

News Story: In 2010 a mine in Chile collapsed, trapping thirty-three miners deep in the earth. On the surface, rescuers worked frantically to locate any survivors and then drilled a deep shaft through the rock down to the trapped miners. Sixty-nine days after the cave-in the first miner, Florencio Avalos, was brought up through the rescue shaft and was joyfully greeted by his anxious wife and son. People around the world watched this dramatic deliverance. If possible, show the YouTube video of Avalos being rescued and hugged by his family.

The Glorious
New Covenant

Big Idea

Through the new covenant God forgives his people and empowers them to know him.

Key Themes

- The new covenant is superior to the old covenant.
- The new covenant enables us to know God.
- The new covenant is characterized by forgiveness.
- The new covenant is as certain as the sunrise.

Understanding the Text

The Text in Context

Each major subsection of this passage opens with "'The days are coming,' declares the LORD" (31:27, 31, 38), the identical phrase that opened the Book of Restoration back in 30:3. Likewise, similar references such as "in that day" (30:8), "at that time" (31:1), and "in those days" (31:29) serve to remind the reader that all of Jeremiah 30–31 is basically describing one great coming event, which the other prophets call "the day of the LORD."

At the heart of this great coming event ("the day of the LORD") is the new covenant. The redemption and restoration promised in 31:1–26 are based on the new covenant promises of 31:27–37.

The opening subsection (31:27–30) and the closing subsection (31:38–40) are in prose, while the middle two subsections (31:31–34, 35–37) are in poetry.

Interpretive Insights

31:27 *I will plant . . . with the offspring of people.* The Hebrew uses the word for "seed" twice in this verse. Literally, "I will seed . . . with the seed of people." This is a clear allusion to God's promise to Abraham in regard to "seed" (descendants), as in Genesis 13:14–17; 17:7. Also note Paul's interpretation of Abraham's "seed" in Romans 4 and Galatians 3 as the people of faith.

31:28 *to uproot and to tear down . . . to build and to plant.* This verse alludes to 1:10, where God used these same terms to define the task to which he was calling Jeremiah.

31:29 *The parents have eaten . . . the children's teeth are set on edge.* This apparently was a popular proverb at the time of Judah's exile to Babylon (cf. Lam. 5:7; Ezek. 18:2). It states that when parents eat bad grapes, their children's teeth hurt, implying that the children will suffer for the sins of the parents.

31:30 *whoever eats . . . their own teeth will be set on edge.* In contrast to the proverb, in the coming days of the great restoration (and the new covenant) the descendants of those sent into exile will not be forced to experience judgment due to their parents' sin. The new covenant (described in the next few verses) will replace the old proverb with a new proverb that stresses personal generational accountability instead of corporate inclusion in the punishment for the sins of one's parents.

31:31 *I will make a new covenant.* The word translated as "make" normally means "to cut." To "cut a covenant" probably implied cutting an animal in half to seal the covenant (cf. Gen. 15:9–19; Jer. 34:8–20, esp. 34:18). "Covenant" was the term used for the foundational "contractual/legal" relationship between God and his people. Thus God is declaring that he will establish a new kind of contractual relationship with his people. This is not a mere renewal of the old covenant. The old (Mosaic) covenant has been shattered and will be replaced with this new covenant.

with the people of Israel and with the people of Judah. In both cases "people" translates the Hebrew word for "house" (i.e., the "house of Israel"). Israel as a country separate from Judah was destroyed by the Assyrians more than one hundred years before Jeremiah and had ceased to exist. Thus to include its people in this promise implies that the coming new covenant will be with an entity that is conceptually much bigger than just the remnant of Judah.

31:32 *not like the covenant I made with their ancestors.* This refers to the Mosaic covenant, which God made with Israel when he delivered it from Egypt. This old covenant is the one described in Exodus–Deuteronomy.

because they broke my covenant. The grammar stresses the independent pronoun "they." The word translated as "broke" is *parar.* Although not all scholars agree on the matter, *parar* does not seem to mean "broke" in terms of violating the covenant (as in "I broke the law"); rather, it appears to mean "broke" in the sense of shattering and/or annulling (see 11:10; 14:21).[1] A new covenant was needed because the old one was no longer in effect.

though I was a husband to them. In contrast to the fact that "they" broke the covenant, God points out that "I" had continued to be a faithful husband to them (Israel). As the word "they" was stressed in the preceding phrase, so "I" is stressed in this phrase. The word for "husband" is actually a verb: literally, "I husbanded." Note that in introducing the new covenant, God continues to use the marriage metaphor.

31:33 *This is the covenant.* In Hebrew this verse has an opening connecting conjunction, *kiy* ("for"): "For this is the covenant." This beginning phrase suggests a contrast between "this" new covenant and the old one made with their ancestors (the Mosaic covenant).

I will put my law in their minds. The word translated as "law" is *torah*, which has a broader nuance of "teaching" rather than narrowly "law." The word translated as "minds" (*qereb*) refers to the inside or inward area of someone, often translated as "midst." To the ancient Hebrews, this was the seat of one's thoughts, emotions, and will.

write it on their hearts. "It" refers back to *torah* (teachings about God and his will). "Heart" in Hebrew includes the place of emotion, but it primarily stresses the place within a person where decisions are made. The phrases "put my law in their minds" and "write it on their hearts" are very similar in meaning. This kind of synonymous parallelism is common in Hebrew poetry. The imagery of writing the *torah* on the hearts of people is graphic and stands in strong contrast to the old covenant, where God wrote the *torah* (represented by the Ten Commandments) on stone. The old covenant *torah* was external, but the new covenant *torah* will be internal. Ezekiel makes similar statements but also includes God's Spirit (Ezek. 11:19; 36:26–27).

their God . . . my people. Throughout the Old Testament the basic covenant relationship between God and his people is expressed by "I will be their God; they will be my people; I will dwell in their midst." In this sense, "midst" meant dwelling among the people in the tabernacle or later in the temple. The new covenant likewise reestablishes this basic relationship. The twist here in 31:33, and a slight wordplay on the word "midst" (*qereb*), is that God repeats the basic formula but states that he will put his *torah* in their midst as well. Here "midst" refers neither to the tabernacle nor the temple but rather to one's "heart."

31:34 *Know the Lord.* The word translated as "know" indicates having not only cognitive knowledge but also experiential or relational knowledge. In the Old Testament to "know the Lord" meant having a relationship with him through proper worship and obedience to his *torah*. The phrase "to know the Lord" usually also involved experiencing firsthand his powerful acts of deliverance. This verse is not saying that there will be no need at all for theological teaching or Bible study; rather, it is saying that under the new covenant there will be a new, internalized connection between God and his people that will facilitate their ability to know (worship and obey) him.

from the least . . . to the greatest. Neither age, gender, nor sociopolitical status will determine who knows God and who does not. All those in the new covenant will know God. Note that earlier in Jeremiah this phrase was used to show the widespread totality of the people's sin (6:13; 8:10).

For I will forgive their wickedness. The conjunction "for" communicates that the realities of 31:33–34 (internalized *torah*, knowing God) are based on forgiveness. The word translated as "forgive" is used in the Old Testament only of God. It includes the cancellation of any merited punishment and the reestablishment of a close relationship.

will remember their sins no more. The lines "forgive their wickedness" and "remember their sins no more" poetically are in synonymous parallel. This text does not imply that God can no longer even recall acts of sin. The word translated as "remember" can mean "to mention, commemorate, reflect upon for the purpose of reacting to." Here it indicates that God will no longer (or ever) recall or even mention that act of sin against someone for the purpose of punishment. It stresses the permanence of the forgiveness expressed in the first line.

31:36 *Only if these decrees vanish.* The phrase "these decrees" refers to 31:35: God is the one who established and continues to control the regularity of the sunlight, moonlight, and waves of the sea. The coming of the new covenant is as certain as the rising of the sun and the roaring of the ocean waves.

Theological Insights

At the Last Supper Jesus states clearly that his death inaugurates the new covenant (Matt. 26:28; Mark 14:24; Luke 22:20; 1 Cor. 11:23–26). The book of Hebrews goes even further, making two direct citations of Jeremiah's new covenant promise (Heb. 8:8–12; 10:16–17). Then, whereas Jeremiah 31 briefly mentions the superiority of the new covenant over the old covenant, Hebrews 8–10 expands upon this comparison in detail. What Hebrews 8–10 explains is that the fulfillment of God's new covenant promises in Jeremiah 31 is foundational to the essence of Christianity, especially in regard to the theology of salvation (soteriology) and to our understanding of the past and present work of Christ (Christology). Also, Hebrews 8:13 echoes Jeremiah 11 in declaring that the old covenant is "obsolete"; it has been replaced by the new covenant.

There is wide disagreement among evangelical scholars over the significance of the fact that God promises to make the new covenant with Israel and Judah. Some argue that God does make the covenant specifically only with Israel/Judah, and that the church, though not the recipient, enjoys the benefits of the covenant. In contrast, others argue that the church has become the "new Israel" and thus has replaced Israel as the recipient of the covenant. Still others point to the tree analogy in Romans 11:11–24, arguing that although the covenant was made specifically with Israel, now gentile believers have been grafted onto the tree as people of God and thus come under the new covenant.

Teaching the Text

The new covenant is one of those key events that connect the New Testament tightly to the Old Testament. Although the old (Mosaic) covenant, characterized by the laws of Exodus, Leviticus, Numbers, and Deuteronomy, was a gracious provision by God that would enable Israel to live a blessed life in the promised land, Israel was unable to keep that covenant. Jeremiah 1–29 chronicles the failure of Israel to keep that covenant. In fact, the Israelites rebelled against it, going so far as to shatter and annul their covenant relationship with God. Only judgment remained. But God, in his grace and due to his great love, promised a new covenant for his people—a "better" covenant based on his grace.

This is the story not just of Israel but of all people. We are unable to keep God's law and to live righteously by our own power. Under the old covenant (law) we deserve judgment, but under the new covenant (grace) God offers us forgiveness, imputed righteousness, and spiritual empowerment.

Under the old covenant God dwelled in the tabernacle and then the temple, and his law, represented by the Ten Commandments, was written on stone. In the New Testament fulfillment of the new covenant, the Holy Spirit of God dwells right inside each believer, and his teaching (*torah*) is written right on the believer's heart. The presence of God for believers under the new covenant is enhanced in every regard. God does not dwell in the tabernacle or in the temple, separated from us by fences, veils, and priests; rather, he dwells within us. Thus we are able to "know" God in a much more intimate and powerful way. Knowing God includes knowing and obeying his will and thus living in worshipful daily relationship to him. Our ability to do this is likewise enhanced by the indwelling Holy Spirit. This does not obviate the need to study the Bible. Knowing God through the indwelling Spirit drives us to study and listen to his word so that we might know and obey him even better in order to live in an increasingly closer relationship with him.

Likewise, because the sacrifice of Christ for the new covenant was so far superior to the sacrifice of animals under the old covenant (only a foreshadowing of Christ's coming sacrifice), those under the new covenant can experience a rich and complete forgiveness.

Finally, God underscores that this new covenant promise is as certain as the sunrise. God reminds us that he is the one who has established the most reliable and regular features in the natural world (sun, moon, waves). We do not question whether the sun will come up tomorrow. We do not worry about this. So too we should neither question God's promises nor worry about how he will fulfill them. The all-powerful Creator of the universe will fulfill all his new covenant promises. This is as certain as the sunrise.

Illustrating the Text

The new covenant is characterized by forgiveness.

News Story: The world was shocked in October 2006, when a lone gunman, Charles Roberts, walked into a one-room Amish schoolhouse and shot ten young girls, killing five of them, and then turned the gun on himself.

The one thing that has stood out in the tragedy is the way the Amish community expressed forgiveness to the killer and his family. Some of the Amish went to the funeral of the killer of their children and hugged his widow at the graveside. It was reported that many of the Amish even donated money to the killer's widow and her three children.

If you want to explore in more depth how their faith helped them forgive the unforgivable, consider reading the book *Amish Grace: How Forgiveness Transcended Tragedy*.[2]

The promises of God are as sure as the sunrise.

Everyday Life: Someone who is ten years old has experienced 3,650 sunrises; twenty years old, 7,300 sunrises; thirty years old, 10,950 sunrises; and so forth. By the age of eighty, a person has experiences 29,200 sunrises. Ask those eighty years old or older to raise their hands. Ask them, based on their experience, if they think that the sun will rise tomorrow morning.

The new covenant is superior to the old.

Contrasting Concept: In the 1920s Alfred P. Sloan, president of General Motors, decided to identify cars according to the year they were manufactured. Although at the time he did not realize what he had done, his decision to use the model-year identification was the first time the auto industry built in a planned obsolescence for its inventory.

Naturally, if there were two identical automobiles on a dealer's lot, and one had a model-year designation newer than the other, the newer one was more desirable to the buying public. This was the beginning of our fascination with having a new car. Soon the auto manufacturers started to capitalize on this by changing the appearance of their products to coincide with the model-year change. This was particularly true with American manufacturers, and the trend reached its peak in the 1950s and 1960s, when almost every model got a makeover every year.

Because advertising eventually became such a big part in showcasing the model-year change, the increased Nielsen ratings of the fall television lineup pushed manufacturers to change their new model year not with the calendar but with the television fall lineup.

We live in a world that is fascinated with and drawn to that which is new. This can sometimes give way to artificial manipulation, as advertisers encourage us to want something just because it's the new thing. But many times (such as can be the case in cars, where there are often improvements in safety, performance, and design, or in the case of medicine, where today's treatments far exceed those available a century ago) newer is better. God's new covenant in Jesus Christ is superior to the covenant of the Old Testament.

Hope and the Purchase of a Field

Big Idea
As judgment approaches, God encourages Jeremiah to maintain hope in the joyful future restoration.

Key Themes
- Jeremiah's purchase of land symbolizes hope for the future restoration.
- God reassures Jeremiah: nothing is too difficult for me.
- The new covenant will be everlasting.
- God rejoices in bringing good things to his people.

Understanding the Text

The Text in Context

Within the Book of Restoration (Jer. 30–33), the first two chapters (Jer. 30–31) are primarily in poetry and without specified historical setting, while the last two chapters (Jer. 32–33) are in prose and given a very specific historical context. The "tenth year of Zedekiah" (32:1) is 587 BC, the final year of the last king. The city of Jerusalem is under siege by the Babylonians. Jeremiah is in prison. The end is near for Zedekiah and for Jerusalem and all its inhabitants.

The central theme running through Jeremiah 30–33 is the restoration and establishment of the new covenant. God restates his commitment to the restoration and the new covenant in Jeremiah 31. In Jeremiah 32 he uses an acted-out symbol (buying land during the Babylonian siege) to teach the certainty of the restoration.

This chapter flows very much like a story. The first section (32:1–5) gives the setting (Jeremiah is in prison). In the next section (32:6–25) Jeremiah recounts how and why he has purchased a field. Embedded within this section is a prayer in which Jeremiah seems to question the wisdom of buying the field at this particular time (32:17–25). The final section (32:26–44) is God's explanatory response to Jeremiah.

Historical and Cultural Background

Jeremiah 32:7–8 alludes to the right of a relative to purchase land. The background for this practice is evident in Leviticus 25:25–31. According to that text, it was not permissible to sell land outside the family (although few people in Judah at this time seemed concerned with obeying the laws of Leviticus). If a severe financial situation forced someone to sell land, the seller was required first to offer the sale to the nearest relative. If that relative declined, the seller approached the next nearest relative, and so on. Since the Babylonians now controlled the countryside, a Judahite deed to a parcel of land was a questionable asset. To purchase land at this time would be foolish. During a siege cash would be worth much more than property. Probably numerous other relatives closer than Jeremiah had already declined.

Interpretive Insights

32:1 *the tenth year of Zedekiah . . . the eighteenth year of Nebuchadnezzar.* Using a dual method of dating (both Judahite king and foreign king) is ominous. Soon dates will be determined only by the foreign kings.

32:7 *your uncle . . . at Anathoth . . . as nearest relative.* Anathoth is Jeremiah's hometown (1:1). There is irony in the current land offer to Jeremiah. In 11:21–23 the people of Anathoth (Jeremiah's relatives) were plotting to kill him and were trying to persuade him to cease prophesying in the name of God.

Buy my field. Variations of this phrase using the two words "buy" and "field" occur seven times in this chapter (32:7, 8, 9, 15, 25, 43, 44). Although Jeremiah does not realize it yet, the purchase of this field is a symbolic act. The symbolism of this will be explained as the story unfolds.

32:25 *you, Sovereign Lord, say to me, "Buy the field."* In 32:15 Jeremiah had publicly declared that God had instructed him to purchase this land because "houses, fields and vineyards will again be bought in this land." But here in 32:25, in his address to God, Jeremiah seems to doubt the wisdom of this action. That is, he seems to believe in the fulfillment of his prophecies regarding the Babylonian invasion and the destruction of Jerusalem, yet he seems to doubt the promises of restoration beyond the destruction.

32:27 *Is anything too hard for me?* God quotes back to Jeremiah one of his earlier statements of praise (32:17). The word translated as "too hard" can mean "wonderful, marvelous, extraordinary, something beyond one's power to do." In the Old Testament it is often used (as Jeremiah does in 32:17) in praising God for the "wonderful" deeds that he did in delivering Israel in the exodus. Ironically, here God is using the term to describe two things, both of which are "amazing" or "extraordinary": (1) the destruction of Jerusalem and the removal of its people (cf. Lam. 1:9); and (2) the establishment of an everlasting covenant and the restoration of the city, symbolized by the promise of future land transactions.

32:31 *From the day it was built.* God probably is referring not to the ancient Jebusite occupation of Jerusalem but rather to the spectacular expansion of the city under Israelite occupation, primarily that carried out by Solomon, who built the temple and the palace complex but who also constructed pagan temples and high places to other gods (1 Kings 11:5–8).

I must remove it from my sight. The word translated by the NIV as "sight" is "my face," and it is used regularly and consistently to represent God's presence. "It" in this verse refers to Jerusalem, and God is declaring that the city's sin is so great that it must be separated from God's presence. This phrase is used several times in 2 Kings in reference to sending away both Israel and Judah from the presence of God (2 Kings 17:18, 23; 23:27; 24:3).

32:33 *They turned their backs to me.* Turning one's back toward a king was a sign of serious and intentional disrespect.

32:35 *to sacrifice their sons and daughters.* The sacrifice of children to the gods Molek or Chemosh in the Valley of Ben Hinnom (right outside Jerusalem's gates) was one of the sins that most disgusted and infuriated God (Jer. 2:23; 7:31–32; 19:2–6).

32:37 *my furious anger and great wrath.* The Hebrew here actually uses three nearly synonymous words: "in my anger and in my rage and in my great wrath."

32:38 *They will be my people, and I will be their God.* This formula statement is the most basic covenant formulation in the Old Testament. What God is saying here is that a new covenant relationship will be established (cf. 31:33). Note the strong contrast with 32:37: from wrathful banishment to reestablishment as "my people."

32:39 *I will give them singleness of heart and action.* Literally, this reads, "I will give them one heart and one way/road." Recall that in the Old Testament the heart is the place where one makes decisions. Duplicity (worshiping idols while trying to maintain a relationship with God) had been a serious shortcoming of the Israelites. Under the new covenant God will give them an obedient heart and the one right path to follow.

fear me. The word translated as "fear" means "to revere, respect, worship."

go well. The word *tob* ("good, the good life, the blessed life") is used here as well as in 32:40 ("doing good to them") and 32:41 ("doing them good"). It is the opposite of *ra'ah* ("disaster, bad stuff, evil"), used in 32:23 ("disaster") and 32:30–32 ("evil").

32:40 *an everlasting covenant.* The word translated as "everlasting" can stress continuation, constancy, a long time, or for all time. In 31:31 God called the new relationship a "new covenant," placing it in contrast to the old covenant. Here he calls it an "everlasting" or eternal covenant, placing it in contrast to the temporariness of the old covenant, which came to an end due to Israel's great sin and rebellion. This new covenant, God is promising, will outlast the old one.

I will never stop doing good to them. This statement is connected to the previous reference to the everlasting covenant by a Hebrew particle that means "which, by which, or according to which." Literally, it reads, "an everlasting covenant by which I will not turn [*shub*] from after them to cause good [*tob*] for them."

I will inspire them to fear me. Literally, this reads, "I will put the fear (reverence, respect) of me in their hearts." Recall that in Hebrew the "heart" is the seat of volition, where one makes decisions. Notice the continued theme in the new covenant of how God will change hearts.

32:41 *with all my heart and soul.* These are identical to the first two terms used in Deuteronomy 6:5. As we have noted often, in the Old Testament the heart is the seat of volition, where one makes decisions. "Heart" has been used of the people twice already in this context (32:39, 40 [cf. NRSV]). The word translated as "soul" is *nepesh*, and it refers to one's complete person or being. Even though Israel had sinned terribly against God, infuriating him (32:30–37), he has no lingering reluctance in restoring it to covenant relationship. He will restore Israel joyfully, with all his essence and being.

Theological Insights

Throughout the Bible God's people are taught to balance the obedient life in the here and now with the life of faith and hope for the future. Christians today live in the "already but not yet" reality of Christ's new covenant kingdom. There is a sense in which the kingdom, with its new covenant promises, is already here with its forgiveness, internalized presence of God, new way of knowing God, and so on. But there is also a sense in which complete fulfillment of the kingdom is still in the future. Christ is coming back to restore all things. As in the time of Jeremiah, God wants his people to live in the present with a faith that reflects hope in the future promises as well.

From a human point of view, the command of God to buy the field looks foolish. Yet God stresses that nothing is too hard for him, implying that he has control of the future. He asks Jeremiah to trust him for the future, which later would shed new light on the wisdom of this immediate action. God in his wisdom and sovereignty often asks his people to trust him and to act now based on his promises for the future, not on what they can see for certain right now.

Teaching the Text

With the Babylonians at the gates, Jeremiah is able to see the fulfillment of his prophecies of judgment unfolding. No doubt he has rock-solid faith in these prophecies, which will be fulfilled in a rather short time. When God tells him to buy a field, however, Jeremiah complies but seems to doubt the wisdom of it. That is, although he appears to accept the "near view" fulfillment of the promise (judgment), he seems to struggle with grasping the full implications of the "far view" fulfillment of the promise (restoration). It is important to God, however, that Jeremiah not only proclaim the coming restoration but also believe in it and act accordingly, looking beyond the imminent events of his day.

For us who live under the new covenant, it is easy to forget that our life and times are not the ultimate consummation of the coming kingdom or the final form of the new covenant blessings. So it is important that we keep this in mind as we make day-to-day decisions. We live in the here and now, so there is a need to be practical and contemporary in our actions and decisions, but we also live with hope and expectation for a coming glorious restoration, so our actions should likewise reflect this reality. We also live for the future and all eternity. This affects our priorities.

In this context God's message to us regarding the future restoration is similar to the arguments that he gave to Jeremiah in this chapter. First, God reassures us, as he did Jeremiah, that nothing is too difficult (or too awesome or too spectacular) for him. Likewise, when we embrace a pessimistic view of the future driven by a doubt that God could ever fix things here, we are much like Jeremiah in his doubt, and God reminds us that the future coming kingdom of Christ is not too difficult (or too awesome or too spectacular) for him. He can do it.

Another reason for hope in the future is that the new covenant, this wonderful relationship we now have with God through Jesus Christ, is everlasting. There will never be a time when it will fail or be replaced.

Finally, God reminds us that since the new covenant brings such wonderful blessings on his people, he is quite joyful about it. He rejoices over providing us with spectacular blessings under the new covenant that we enjoy even now (his forgiveness, presence, etc.), but he will also rejoice when he brings the new covenant to its consummation. God consummates this great story not begrudgingly but joyfully and wholeheartedly. Thus we too should look forward to this consummation of the kingdom with joyful expectation.

Illustrating the Text

Nothing is too difficult or too awesome or too spectacular for God.

Science: Imagine going back in time fifty years and telling people that you would have a telephone that fits in your pocket, is not connected to a cord, and identifies any caller before you answer it. Suppose you told them that television screens would be flat, receive signals from satellites, and have instant access to hundreds of channels. Or imagine trying to explain the internet, or laptop computers, or 3D printers, or genetic engineering to cure disease, or a host of other things that we now take for granted. Their response probably would be, "That sounds impossible, too good to be true."

Sometimes, like Jeremiah, we have difficulty believing in the awesome promises that God has made about what waits for us in the future, but the prophet reminds us that we have the word of the one who never breaks his promise.

Christian Music: **"I Know Who Holds Tomorrow," by Ira Stanphill.** The chorus of this classic gospel song speaks directly to trusting God when we cannot see the future. While there is much uncertainty and many things beyond understanding, Stanphill writes, "I know who holds tomorrow."

Jeremiah's purchase of land was a symbol of hope and a good investment.

Analogy: On October 1, 1970, an obscure company in Arkansas, named "Walmart," went public with an initial stock price of $16.50 per share. If you had purchased one hundred shares of Walmart stock then, spending $1,650, and held the stock, along with the additional stock you received in 2-for-1 splits, your $1,650 investment would be worth $31 million today.

Cleansing, Forgiveness, and the Coming Davidic King

Big Idea

The new covenant brings forgiveness, joy, and a righteous priestly king.

Key Themes

- The wonderful promise of the future restoration comes to Jeremiah while he is in prison.
- The coming new covenant will be characterized by cleansing, forgiveness, joy, and worship.
- The new covenant is connected to the ultimate fulfillment of the Abrahamic and Davidic covenants.
- Since God is the Creator of the world, his promise of a coming Davidic king is absolutely certain.
- The fulfillment of the Davidic covenant will merge royal and priestly aspects.

Understanding the Text

The Text in Context

Jeremiah 33 is connected directly to Jeremiah 32 by the introductory verse, "While Jeremiah was still confined . . . , the word of the LORD came to him a second time" (33:1). The implied "first time" would be in Jeremiah 32, when God told him to buy the field from his uncle.

The final phrase in Jeremiah 33 ("I will restore their fortunes") closes out the larger unit of Jeremiah 30–33 (the Book of Restoration) with an inclusio. That is, it repeats the same phrase (in Hebrew) that opened the unit in 30:3. It is important to keep the entire unit of Jeremiah 30–33 as the context. The many details of the restoration provided in Jeremiah 33 are simply expansions on the coming new covenant described in Jeremiah 31.

As throughout Jeremiah 30–33, here most of the restoration images (healing, building, planting, joy, flocks, etc.) are exact reversals of the judgment images used in Jeremiah 1–29.

Jeremiah 33 contains direct allusions to the fulfillment of the Davidic covenant (33:14–22; cf. 2 Sam. 7) and the Abrahamic covenant (33:22, 26; cf. Gen. 12; 15; 17). The Davidic promises cited in 33:15–16 are very similar to 23:5–6.

Jeremiah 33 proclaims a simultaneous fulfillment of royal aspects from the Davidic covenant and priestly aspects from a less-known covenant with the Levites (cf. Num. 25:13). Yet it is important to note that David himself was a priest-king (2 Sam. 6:13–19), and the citation of a popular verse from Psalms in Jeremiah 33:11 perhaps serves to remind us of that. The implication (made clear in the book of Hebrews) is that the one coming as the ultimate Davidic king will also be the ultimate priest.

Interpretive Insights

33:2 *made . . . formed . . . established.* Three different words are used to stress the fact that God is the great Creator of the world. This has implications for the rest of the chapter. Since God is the one who actually created the whole earth, he has the authority and power to forgive, purify, and restore Israel and Judah, in spite of their terrible sin.

33:3 *Call to me.* The word translated as "call" is a common word that basically means "to draw attention to oneself by the audible use of one's voice in order to establish contact with someone." It is used in the Bible over eighty times specifically in regard to calling on/to God, and in this usage it includes calling for help as well as calling out in thanksgiving, praise, and prayer (cf. 29:12).[1]

unsearchable things. The word translated as "unsearchable" refers to something made inaccessible, a word usually used in regard to fortifying a city to make it inaccessible or impregnable. Undoubtedly, this is a bit of an ironic wordplay on the fortification of Jerusalem described in 33:4. The "great and unsearchable things" probably refer to the events described in the following verses, especially the description of the promised restoration in 33:6–26.

33:5 *I will hide my face from this city.* The word translated as "face" regularly refers to the presence of God, and it should be understood in that sense here. The loss of God's powerful and protective presence has left them vulnerable to powerful destructive forces.

33:6 *abundant peace and security.* The word translated as "security" carries a range of possible meanings: "truth, faithfulness, reliability, firm, stable." The combination "peace and security" probably connotes "lasting peace" or "reliable, faithful peace" (cf. 2 Kings 20:19; Jer. 14:13).

33:8 *I will cleanse.* The Hebrew word here can mean "to wash clean, make clean, purify." It is used frequently in regard to the cleansing and/or purification of the temple, tabernacle, and associated furniture and utensils, so it would logically refer to making the people acceptable for sacred use and as having access to the presence of God.

will forgive all their sins of rebellion against me. This verse uses all three primary Hebrew words for "sin." A literal rendering is "I will forgive all their iniquities [*'awon*] which they have sinned [*hata'*] against me and which they have rebelled [*pasha'*] against me." This promise of cleansing and forgiveness of sin echoes the promise associated with the new covenant in 31:34.

33:9 *This city will bring me renown, joy.* The reference to "this city" (i.e., Jerusalem) is implied from the feminine verb used. The word translated as "renown" literally means "name." The concept of renown is conveyed in Hebrew by the idea of making a name or having a name. There is probably a subtle contrast here with Genesis 11, where those building the tower of Babel were trying to make a name for themselves by constructing sacred space (the ziggurat) instead of using that sacred space to make a name for God. Also "name" and "joy" in 33:9 are connected in the Hebrew grammar (lit., "a name of joy," as in the NASB, NRSV, HCSB, ESV). It will be the joyful name that produces the praise and honor that follow.

honor. The word translated as "honor" has a basic root meaning of "beauty, splendor." From this basic meaning come related meanings such as "glory, honor." But even when it means "honor" or "glory," as it does here, it implies that this honor comes because of some aspect of "beauty" or "splendor." The incredible reversal from wickedness, punishment, death, and destruction to cleansing, forgiveness, joy, praise, peace, and good is the spectacular splendor or beauty that will bring honor and glory to God.

at the abundant prosperity and peace I provide. There is a stress on the first-person pronoun "I." The word translated as "provide" is the same word that elsewhere means "to make, do." The verb form implies an ongoing action. "Peace" translates the word *shalom*, which refers to total well-being, including the absence of war, but not limited to that. *Tob* ("good") is the word translated as "abundant prosperity." It is used twice in this verse, being translated earlier in the verse as "good things." It is used regularly in the Old Testament and in Jeremiah as the opposite of *ra'ah* ("bad stuff, calamity, disaster, evil"). Jeremiah 33:4–5 states that God removed his presence from Jerusalem because of the city's *ra'ah* (translated as "wickedness"), and this resulted in warfare and a terrible siege filled with death. In the restoration, by stark contrast, God will respond with the exact opposite, making good (*tob*) and peace/well-being (*shalom*) for Jerusalem.

33:11 *his love endures forever.* The word translated as "love" is *hesed*, the word used to describe God's loyal and faithful covenant love. This entire praise declaration, with slight variations, occurs frequently in the psalms (Pss. 100:5; 106:1; 107:1; 136:1).

33:15 *a righteous Branch.* On this term, see comments at 23:5. The reference is to the coming royal Messiah, ultimately fulfilled in the New Testament by the coming of Christ.

he will do what is just and right. One of the central criticisms of the kings in Judah throughout Jeremiah 1–29 is the lack of justice and righteousness in the way the kings ruled. Under the new covenant, however, the coming Davidic king will rule with justice and righteousness.

33:16 *the name by which it will be called.* The reference "it" is a feminine pronoun that clearly refers back to Jerusalem. In 23:6 it is the coming Davidic king, who is called "The LORD Our Righteous Savior," but here it is the restored city of Jerusalem that is given that name. This connects back to 33:9.

Theological Insights

The biblical covenants play an important role in this passage. Throughout Jeremiah 1–29 the prophet has proclaimed how Israel/Judah has violated Deuteronomy, leading to the end of the old covenant. In Jeremiah 31 the prophet proclaims that a coming new covenant will be inaugurated to replace the old covenant.[2] In Jeremiah 33 (and elsewhere) the prophet makes it clear that the new covenant is also a fulfillment of the Abrahamic covenant and the Davidic covenant. The New Testament (especially Paul's writings) will associate this distinction and change in covenants with the contrast between law and grace. Israel was unable to keep the old covenant (law); thus it experienced judgment. However, Jeremiah (and other prophets) reaches back to the two covenants characterized by grace (the Abrahamic and Davidic covenants) and uses those as the basis for the proclamation of the new covenant, which pulls together the Abrahamic and the Davidic covenants into a wonderful future time of new covenant restoration that is fulfilled through Jesus Christ.

Teaching the Text

Stated in both Jeremiah 32 and 33 is the fact that these conversations between God and Jeremiah take place while he is in prison. The immediate suffering of God's prophet stands in strong contrast to the wonderful blessings God promises in the restoration. That is, God expects Jeremiah to find hope and encouragement in the promise of the future new covenant while continuing to suffer persecution for proclaiming this message in the meantime. Likewise today, God wants us to find hope and encouragement in the wonderful promise of the return of Christ and the consummation of his kingdom (the great restoration) even while we might be suffering as his servants here in the meantime.

The New Testament clarifies without doubt that Jesus Christ came as the fulfillment of the new covenant (Heb. 8–10). Furthermore, at the Last Supper Christ also appears to "inaugurate" the new covenant (Matt. 26:28; Mark 14:24; Luke 22:20; 1 Cor. 11:23–26). Likewise, it is in Jesus Christ that the Abrahamic and Davidic covenants come to fulfillment and completion. Thus all that Jeremiah is proclaiming regarding the wonderful future restoration in Jeremiah 33 finds fulfillment in Jesus Christ, some of it in the "already" aspects of his first coming and some of it awaiting the "not yet, not completely" aspects of his second coming.[3] Thus Jesus Christ pulls together and fulfills all the promises of the Old Testament. This was no accident but rather part of God's great salvation plan, the unfolding and fulfillment of which was as certain as the rising of the sun. God is, after all, the Creator of the world, and he has the power to bring about this second "new creation" and wonderful restoration that parallel the spectacular wonder of the first creation.

As people of God under the new covenant, we experience firsthand the wonderful sequence of relation-restoring transformations described in Jeremiah 33: cleansing, forgiveness, joyful celebration, and worship. The atoning death of Jesus Christ provides cleansing from sin and forgiveness, thus restoring us to relationship with God. This restored relationship brings all kinds of wonderful blessings (the goodness of God) to which we should respond with overflowing joy. This leads immediately to a joyful worship in which we thank God profusely for his goodness and his everlasting *hesed*.

In his fulfillment of Jeremiah 33, we see that Jesus Christ is not only the totally righteous and just king (emphasized throughout the Gospels) but also the totally perfect high priest, which is emphasized at length in Hebrews 4–10. One of the reasons that Israel failed to keep the old covenant, as explained in Jeremiah 1–29, was that it had weak, corrupt, and selfish kings and priests. Under the new covenant, God fixes that problem by giving us Jesus as our king and high priest.

Illustrating the Text

The new covenant is characterized by cleansing.

Everyday Life: In most households the coming of spring provides the opportunity to give the house a thorough cleaning. Windows are washed and opened, screens are cleaned and installed, rugs are shaken out, bedding is changed, blankets are put away, furniture is rearranged, and floors are swept and vacuumed.

In the new covenant Christ cleanses those who believe in him, washing away all sin and making all things new. It is like "spring cleaning" on a massive scale.

God's promises are absolutely certain.

Statistics: According to a 2012 report in the *Journal of the American Medical Association*, patients are misdiagnosed 10 to 20 percent of the time. Often something is missed, or delayed, or misinterpreted. Most of these errors are inconsequential and often are caught in later diagnostic work. However, such errors still result in 40,000 to 80,000 deaths per year in the United States, and the number of patients injured is even higher.[4]

Ask your listeners what they think the acceptable failure rate is for doctors, for weather forecasters, for parents, for government, for pastors. God is the only one who never breaks a promise. What do you call the medical student who graduated last in the class? Doctor! What do you call a god who does not keep promises? False!

Food: Most of us hope that our food is 100 percent contaminant-free, but according to the United States Food and Drug Administration (FDA) Center for Safety and Applied Nutrition, certain levels of things such as maggots, insect fragments, mold, and rodent hairs are acceptable. For example, according to the FDA, the acceptable level of insect fragments per 100 grams of peanut butter is 30. (It does not say whether the peanut butter is crunchy or smooth.) The acceptable level of insect fragments per 100 grams of wheat flour jumps to 100. If you like cinnamon on your toast, it is okay to find 800 insect fragments per 100 grams with that, and if you are thinking about just sticking to fresh fruits and vegetables, you might want to think again. The FDA's acceptable level of insect parts for carrots is 8,000 per 100 grams. Bon appétit.[5] To some this may seem like a broken promise. With God, his word is sure and genuine, and his promises will come true and exceed our expectations.

Contrasting Covenants and Faithfulness

Big Idea

God is faithful to his promises, and he expects his people to be faithful to their promises.

Key Themes

- God expects his people to keep their commitments.
- Those whom God has freed from slavery should not put others into bondage.
- Hypocritical, superficial promises made in the name of God profane his name.
- God is faithful to his promises, though we often are not.

Understanding the Text

The Text in Context

Jeremiah 34 is connected to the surrounding chapters by the theme of covenant faithfulness. Jeremiah 30–33 presents the coming new covenant and the faithful fulfillment by God of his covenants with Abraham, David, and the Levites in spite of Israel and Judah's unfaithfulness. Jeremiah 35 stresses the faithful obedience of the Rekabites to the traditions of their ancestors. Jeremiah 34, in strong contrast, emphasizes how King Zedekiah and the officials in Jerusalem betrayed the covenant that they had made with the Hebrew slaves in Jerusalem.

Another connection is the similarity between the judgment on Zedekiah that opens Jeremiah 32 (vv. 1–4) and the judgment on Zedekiah that opens Jeremiah 34 (vv. 1–7). Cementing this connection is the repeated (and stressed) reference in both chapters to the "hands of the Babylonians/Nebuchadnezzar" (32:3, 4, 24, 25, 28, 36, 43; 34:2, 3, 20, 21).

Historical and Cultural Background

The events in Jeremiah 34 take place during the Babylonian siege of Jerusalem (588–586 BC). According to 37:5, during the siege an Egyptian army marches up out of Egypt to attack the Babylonians and relieve Jerusalem. The Babylonian army thus withdraws from Jerusalem to deal with the Egyptians (cf. 34:21), whom they quickly send scampering back to Egypt in defeat.

The episode recounted in 34:8–22 takes place in this context. With the strong Babylonian army and its allies besieging Jerusalem, King Zedekiah needs all the support and manpower that he can muster for the defense of Jerusalem. Thus he makes a covenant (a formal, legal agreement) that provides freedom for all Hebrew slaves in Jerusalem, ostensibly so that they would help to defend the city. Yet when the Egyptian army enters into the conflict, causing the Babylonians to temporarily withdraw from the siege of Jerusalem, Zedekiah apparently gets his hopes up for a victory and thus has second thoughts about the freedom that he has just given the Hebrew slaves in Jerusalem. Since he thinks that he will no longer need them as loyal soldiers, he breaks his covenant with them in a dishonest double cross and puts them back into slavery.

Jeremiah 34:7 mentions that the only two Judahite cities still holding out against the Babylonians were Lachish and Azekah (two fortress cities about ten miles apart, both to the southwest of Jerusalem). While excavating Lachish, archaeologists discovered several brief letters (or copies of letters) written on pieces of pottery (called "ostraca") that record the communication between the commander of the fortress at Lachish and the king in Jerusalem during the Babylonian siege described in Jeremiah. One of the letters (Lachish Ostracon IV) grimly notes that from Lachish they can no longer see the signal fires from Azekah.[1] This meant, of course, that Azekah had fallen and only Lachish and Jerusalem remained.

Interpretive Insights

34:1 *all his army and all the kingdoms and peoples.* Numerous other nations in the region have submitted to the Babylonians and joined them in the siege of Jerusalem. This stresses the overwhelming forces arrayed against the Judahites in Jerusalem.

in the empire he ruled. The Hebrew reads literally, "kingdoms of the land ruled by his hand." "Ruled by his hand" is an idiomatic expression connoting the power of King Nebuchadnezzar over those kingdoms. As noted above, the theme of "the hands of the Babylonians" is central and ominous.

34:2 *this city . . . he will burn it down.* The declaration that the king of Babylon will burn down Jerusalem opens (34:2) and closes (34:22) this episode, forming an inclusio.

34:3 *you will see the king of Babylon with your own eyes, and he will speak with you.* The fall of Jerusalem and the capture of Zedekiah are recorded in Jeremiah 39 and 2 Kings 25. Nebuchadnezzar does indeed speak to Zedekiah, but this conversation is a grisly pronouncement of judgment regarding Zedekiah and his eyes: all of Zedekiah's sons and nobles are killed "before his eyes," and then Zedekiah's own eyes are gouged out (39:5–7).

34:5 *they will make a fire in your honor.* On the surface, this refers to an honorable funeral. But in light of the opening and closing verses regarding the burning of Jerusalem (34:2, 22), one wonders if God is not ironically saying that the conflagration of Jerusalem will be Zedekiah's honorary funeral fire.

34:8 *freedom.* The word translated as "freedom" is used specifically in the Old Testament to refer to the release or manumission of slaves or the return of property to its original owners. This word is used four times in this passage (34:8, 15, 17 [2x]). The release of slaves in times of crisis appears to be a fairly common practice in the ancient Near East. In a letter from Mari (ca. 1765 BC), King Hammurabi is said to have decreed the freedom of slaves in Babylon to help reinforce his army while under attack.[2]

34:13 *out of the land of slavery.* Literally, this phrase says "from the house of slaves." God is reminding the people in Judah that their ancestors were slaves in Egypt when he delivered them in the exodus. Thus, as they enslave their fellow Hebrews, they are following in the pattern of Pharaoh and the Egyptians.

34:14 *you must free any fellow Hebrews.* A Hebrew who was in financial difficulties could voluntarily go into slavery or be forced into slavery in order to pay a debt. However, the Sabbatical law decreed that after six years of service such slaves must be released and then even provided for (Deut. 15:12–18). As in Jeremiah 34:13, the release of slaves in Deuteronomy 15 is placed in the context of remembering their own redemption from slavery in Egypt (15:15).

34:15 *made a covenant before me in the house that bears my Name.* The covenant ceremony described in 34:18 had been carried out right in the temple. "Before me" and "bears my Name" emphasize the very presence of God. Thus this legal agreement to free their slaves had been intentionally transacted right in front of God, the point being to convince the Hebrew slaves that the king and his nobles were serious about upholding this covenant. They were, in essence, swearing fidelity to this covenant of release in the name of God and with God as their primary witness. The presence of God at this covenant ceremony is stressed again in 34:18 ("before me"). God is driving home the point that the location of this ceremony in the temple in his presence underscores the seriously binding nature of the agreement.

34:16 *you have turned around.* This phrase translates the word *shub* ("to turn, turn back, repent"), a word used repeatedly by Jeremiah.

profaned my name. The word translated as "profaned" can mean "to defile, pollute, desecrate." At its essence it refers to treating as ordinary or unclean something that is in reality holy and pure. Zedekiah and his nobles had sworn a covenant oath in the presence of God in the temple that carried his name.

Thus when they break their oath and go back on their covenant agreement, they are treating the witness and presence of God as if he were insignificant or impotent. This is what "profaning" means in this context.

has taken back. This translates the word *shub* ("to turn, return, repent"), which occurs twice in this verse.

34:17 *You have not obeyed me.* The Hebrew stresses the plural pronoun "you." Thus it includes not only Zedekiah but also all those who went back on their promise to free their slaves. The groups are specified in 34:19.

you have not proclaimed freedom. In Hebrew this statement is an infinitive that continues the thought from the previous phrase, "you have not obeyed me to proclaim freedom." The word translated as "freedom" is the same as in 34:8, 15.

to your own people. The Hebrew word for "brother" (translated as "own people") is used idiomatically in this construct and can refer to a wide relationship such as a "people," but it nonetheless also carries connotations of the closer and more emotional familial relationship. This same word ("brother") is also used in 34:9, 14.

34:18 *Those who have violated my covenant.* A wordplay occurs in 34:18. The word translated as "violated" often connotes "to cross over" or "to pass through." It can be used figuratively to mean "transgressed" (as it does here). Later in the verse this same word is translated as "walked between" in reference to Zedekiah and his nobles "passing between" the two halves of the calf. This same word occurs again in 34:19, translated as "who walked between."

the covenant they made . . . the calf they cut. The wordplay continues. These two phrases are in parallel, and both use the same word, *karat*, which can mean "to cut something in half" but is also used idiomatically for making a covenant.

I will treat like the calf they cut in two. The Hebrew grammar of 34:18–20 is complicated and difficult to explain because all three verses are closely connected. The NIV translation captures the gist of these verses. Those who have "crossed over" (violated) God's covenant he will make like the dead calf that they cut in two and "crossed over."

Zedekiah and his nobles had ratified the covenant that released the Hebrew slaves by cutting a calf in two and then walking between the cut pieces, as if pledging, "May this happen to me if I fail to honor my obligation to this legal agreement." This was a recognized method of transacting an important treaty or legal agreement.[3] Earlier in Scripture Abraham and God carried out a similar ceremony in the formal establishment of God's covenant with Abraham (Gen. 15:9–18).

34:20 *Their dead bodies will become food for the birds and the wild animals.* Those who went back on the covenant made by cutting a calf in two will become like the calf—a corpse ravaged by scavenger birds and wild animals.

Theological Insights

In the Old Testament, to profane the name of God meant to treat him or to act as if he were insignificant, as if he were not really there or could not actually do anything. It was, in essence, a denial of the power and holiness that surrounded the presence of God, particularly in the temple/tabernacle, a power and holiness that demanded proper awe and respect. And the Old Testament is quite clear on this: he is angered when his name is profaned.

Throughout the Old Testament profaning the name of God is identified with a wide range of sinful actions: sacrificing children to idols (Lev. 18:21); treating the offerings at the tabernacle/temple disrespectfully (Lev. 22:2); using "magic" in false prophecy (Ezek. 13:19); worshiping idols (Ezek. 20:39; 36:21–22); and practicing cultic sexual immorality (Amos 2:7). Thus it is unclean or sinful actions that profane the name of God.

The importance of revering God's name and treating it as holy is emphasized by Jesus in the Lord's Prayer (Matt. 6:9–13).

Teaching the Text

Just as God is faithful to his commitments, he expects his people to be faithful to theirs. When we make promises, God wants us to keep our promises. This is true for casual promises to our friends, but even more so in formal promises such as business transactions. Perhaps the most obvious application of needed covenant fidelity is in marriage. Right in the presence of God, each couple that gets married pledges to remain faithful. Infidelity in marriage is a violation of the covenant made between spouses in the presence of God, and it thus amounts to treating the primary witness of marriage vows, God himself, as trivial or as carrying little weight in regard to our behavior. This is, in essence, profaning his name.

Likewise, any time we make superficial or hypocritical promises in God's name, we are profaning his name. If a company advertises itself as a Christian business, it must be sure to act as such, and not like a secular business that is just trying to attract Christian customers.

Today if we treat God as absent or insignificant or less than holy, we are profaning his name. To use his name (and this includes the name of Jesus Christ) in swearing is certainly profaning his name. But to preach falsehood or personal agendas in the name of God ("thus saith the Lord") is also to profane his name. In the first case we would be treating God's name as if it were powerless, while in the second instance we would be recognizing the power but exploiting it for our benefit. Both instances profane the name of God. Any time we talk about God without the cognizance of his omnipotence and his powerful holiness, we are, in essence, belittling him and thus profaning his name.

God had saved Israel from slavery in Egypt, and he wanted the Israelites to always remember that and to treat one another accordingly. In similar fashion, God wants us to treat one another with the love and compassion that he has shown toward us. He has saved us by grace, not because of anything we have done. And now he wants us to act accordingly, treating others with grace and not trying to put them into slavery to the law or to other traditions that we were freed from.

Finally, this passage teaches us that God is not like us. He is faithful to his promises, while we often are not. People lie to each other and betray or trick one another. God does not. He is faithful to all his covenant promises.

Illustrating the Text

Faithfulness

Literature: *The Fellowship of the Ring*, by J. R. R. Tolkien. Frodo says, "But it does not seem that I can trust anyone." Merry replies,

> You can trust us to stick to you through thick and thin—to the bitter end. And you can trust us to keep any secret of yours—closer than you yourself keep it. But you cannot trust us to let you face trouble alone, and go off without a word. We are your friends, Frodo. Anyway: there it is. We know most of what Gandalf has told you. We know a good deal about the Ring. We are horribly afraid—but we are coming with you; or following you like hounds.[4]

Children's Book: *Horton Hatches the Egg*, by Dr. Seuss. In this classic story Horton the elephant commits to protecting and taking care of a nest full of eggs. He stays faithful to his word despite the long wait and freezing cold because "an elephant's faithful, one hundred per cent!"[5]

Bible: In Hebrews 11 we are told about the virtues of faithfulness. For example, Abel faithfully made an acceptable offering to God. Noah faithfully built an ark, though the rest of the world called it a folly. And Abraham faithfully left his family and his country behind and followed God's call to go to the promised land. The writer continues to talk about Enoch, Moses, Sarah, Isaac, Jacob, Joseph, and Rahab, and tells us that they too were faithful. All of them are scriptural examples of faithfulness, and their stories challenge us to be faithful in our lives.

Personal Testimony: Have church members share a story (live or on video) of how God has been faithful in their lives even when they have not fully trusted or followed his will. Have them talk about how God's faithfulness and consistent commitment to his promises have taught them to grow in their desire to live for Jesus. Also, have them share how their commitment to be faithful to God is growing as they experience God's faithfulness in their lives.

A Lesson in Faithfulness and Obedience

Big Idea

If family traditions can be maintained, then faithfulness to God can be maintained.

Key Themes

- The Rekabites provide a lesson in faithfulness and obedience.
- The faithfulness of the Rekabites underscores the inexcusable lack of faithfulness in Jerusalem.
- The fate of Jerusalem is contrasted with the fate of the Rekabites.
- The Rekabites foreshadow the future inclusion of the gentiles.

Understanding the Text

The Text in Context

While Jeremiah 34 takes place during the reign of Zedekiah during the Babylonian siege of 588–586 BC, the story in Jeremiah 35 occurs earlier, during a previous Babylonian invasion of Judah during the reign of Jehoiakim (either around 605 BC or around 597 BC). Thus the connection between Jeremiah 34 and Jeremiah 35 is not chronological but thematic. The connecting theme is faithful obedience. The faithlessness of Zedekiah is placed in strong contrast to the faithfulness of the Rekabites.

Jeremiah 35 is in prose, as are the surrounding chapters. Jeremiah 35 opens and closes with a word from Jeremiah to the Rekabites (35:2, 18–19).

Historical and Cultural Background

The central players in the story of Jeremiah 35 are the Rekabites (spelled "Rekabites" in the NIV 2011; "Recabites" in the NIV 1984; "Rechabites" in the NASB, ESV, NRSV, KJV, HCSB). The Rekabites were a nomadic group descended from the Kenites, a non-Israelite people who had nonetheless joined Israel in the promised land very early in Israel's history (Judg. 1:16; 1 Chron.

2:55). While maintaining a good relationship with Israel (2 Kings 10:15–28), they had kept their tribal identity and had not been absorbed into the Israelite tribes.[1] They lived as nomads in tents, holding to their strict tribal prohibitions against living in houses and cities, planting crops or vineyards, and drinking wine. The Bible is silent regarding the origin of these traditions.[2] Jeremiah neither praises nor condemns their lifestyle. Likewise, whether they were faithful to God is not the issue. The point they make in Jeremiah 35 is that they were faithful to their ancestors while those in Judah and Jerusalem were not faithful to God. It is also interesting to note that a descendant of the Rekabites is mentioned as one of those who returned after the exile and helped Nehemiah rebuild the wall of Jerusalem (Neh. 3:14).[3]

Interpretive Insights

35:11 *to escape the Babylonian and Aramean armies.* Normally, when a foreign army invaded a land, the people of the land fled to their fortified cities for protection. The Rekabites, a nomadic people, have no fortified cities to run to when the Babylonians appear, so they flee to Jerusalem for protection. It is significant that they are still siding with and identifying with the Israelites and not turning against them. "Aramean" refers to the people who lived in the region just to the north of Israel (now called Syria), who were under Babylonian control at this time. In 2 Kings 24:2 we are told that the invading army during Jehoiakim's reign (probably the invasion of 599–598 BC) was composed of Babylonian, Aramean, Moabite, and Ammonite soldiers.

35:13 *The LORD Almighty, the God of Israel.* This long formal title for God is used at the beginning of each of the three pronouncements that God makes in this passage (35:13–16, 17, 18–19). The word translated as "Almighty" has military connotations. It pictures God at the head of a great army. The repeated stress on the God of Israel is ironic, for it is the Rekabites, a non-Israelite people, who find deliverance in this passage.

Will you not learn a lesson and obey my words? The word translated as "lesson" refers elsewhere to "correction, discipline, chastening." It involves the instilling of moral values and standards of conduct. The word translated as "obey" is *shamaʿ*. This is the same verb that often means "to hear," but it is also used idiomatically, as here, with "voice" or "words" to mean "obey." It occurs frequently throughout Jeremiah (186x) and occurs eight times in Jeremiah 35 (vv. 8, 10, 13, 14, 15, 16, 17, 18).

35:14 *But I have spoken.* There is a strong stress in the Hebrew grammar on "I." It stresses the contrast between "their forefather," who was listened to (obeyed), and "I" (God), who was not listened to (obeyed).

35:15 *turn from your wicked ways.* These terms are likewise used frequently throughout Jeremiah. The word translated as "turn" is *shub*, which means "to turn, return, repent." "Wicked" is a translation of *ra'ah*, which can mean "evil, disaster" or just "bad stuff" in general.

reform your actions. In Hebrew the contrasting opposite of *ra'ah* ("evil, disaster, bad stuff") is *tob* ("good"). The word translated as "reform" is a verbal form of *tob*, carrying the nuance of "to make good" or "cause to be good."

35:17 *I am going to bring . . . every disaster.* The word translated as "disaster" is *ra'ah*, the same word used in 35:15. This is a frequent wordplay in Jeremiah. The failure of Israel to repent and turn from its *ra'ah* ("wickedness, bad stuff") will bring *ra'ah* ("disaster, calamity, bad stuff") upon it.

I spoke to them . . . I called to them. There are two parallel sentences here: "I spoke to them, but they did not listen [*shama'*]; I called to them, but they did not answer." However, the second line deepens the offense. God had taken the initiative to speak to them repeatedly, and they did not even show enough respect to answer him or acknowledge him.

35:18 *to the family of the Rekabites.* This phrase uses the Hebrew term usually rendered as "house" ("to the house of the Rekabites"). The Hebrew word can mean "descendants" or "family," as it does here. Yet there is a wordplay taking place as well. This same Hebrew word for "house" was used to refer to a residential living place in 35:7 ("you must never build houses"). God makes a promise to the "house of the Rekabites" because they were faithful in not building any houses.

35:19 *a descendant to serve me.* The Hebrew reads, "one serving in my presence all the days." In strong contrast to the coming destruction of the Israelite inhabitants of Jerusalem, God promises not only survival to the Rekabites but also a continuing role in serving the presence of God. Although the text is somewhat ambiguous, this promise probably should be understood in the context of the coming destruction of the temple, when the presence of God will be lost to Israel. At the precise time that Israel loses the temple and the presence of God, God promises to the Rekabites (a gentile group) a certain presence and opportunity to serve him.

Theological Insights

The Rekabites in Jeremiah 35 and Ebed-Melek in Jeremiah 38–39 play an important theological role in the story because they both foreshadow and symbolize the inclusion of the gentiles among the people of God through their faith/faithfulness. Just as judgment falls on the inhabitants of Jerusalem, something new emerges as God proclaims deliverance for certain faithful gentiles. The promise that a Rekabite will always serve in the presence of God is very significant, for when the temple is destroyed, Israel will lose the wonderful blessings associated with the presence of God. These gentiles, on the other hand, are promised that they will always have a descendant enjoying the wonderful benefits of serving in God's presence. It is perhaps best to view the Rekabites as representative of the gentiles as a whole, and thus the fulfillment of this promise is seen in the New Testament book of Acts as the gospel spreads throughout the gentile world and gentiles experience the presence of God and the opportunity to serve God through the indwelling of the Spirit. The people of God are being redefined as those who are faithful to God.

Teaching the Text

This passage is about faithfulness and, by extension, remaining faithful to God by listening to and obeying him. In this sense, the ancient Rekabites become a model of faithfulness for us as well as for ancient Israel. During difficult times and in countercultural ways, they were able to keep their family traditions and stay faithful to their ancestors, even if that meant being very different from all those around them in the society.

If groups such as the Rekabites can continue to listen to their ancestors and stay faithful to their traditions generation after generation, then we ought to be able to listen to our Father, God himself, and stay faithful to him generation after generation, even if this obedience conflicts with the accepted behavior of our surrounding culture. There is also a suggestion in this passage that family tradition itself can play a strong role in keeping God's people faithful to him generation by generation. The importance of continually listening to and obeying the word of God generation by generation cannot be overstressed. Each new generation needs to hear God's word in all its richness and authority and be called to obedience to that word. Family tradition and family identity are very strong influences on people, their beliefs, and their behavior. What a great thing it is when children identify themselves as part of a Christian family that honors the word of God and follows Jesus Christ wholeheartedly instead of the fads that blow across our culture. This identity and family tradition will serve them well as they grow up and come to grips with "who they are" as adults. Family traditions of prayer, Bible study, church-community participation, Christmas, Easter, and lived-out faith in general provide great strength and support as each new generation leaves home and finds its way in the world. When faithfulness to God and faithfulness to the beliefs and traditions of one's family coincide, there is a powerful force that strengthens and encourages us to continue in this faithfulness.

There is also a "wake-up call" in this passage for those who grew up in Christian homes but later in adulthood drifted away from Christ and the church for one reason or another. Perhaps it was their parents or perhaps a grandparent who first influenced them to believe in Christ. It is time to reconsider that connection, that family tradition of faith. It is also time for those who have drifted away to think about what traditions of faith they want their children to have. Children are not likely to grow up as strong Christians if their parents barely attend church and barely reflect Christ in their lives.

Likewise, as we have seen throughout Jeremiah, there are disastrous consequences for those who rebelliously ignore the voice of God and choose instead to pursue a life defined by their own poor, ungodly standards. As in the days of Jeremiah, God continues to call out to these people, sending his "prophets" constantly to proclaim the call to repentance and faith in Christ. But those who refuse to listen, repent, and turn to Christ will experience severe consequences.

This passage also teaches that the future new people of God will be defined not by their ethnic identity with Israel but by their faith. We see this story, foreshadowed in Jeremiah, played out in full clarity in the book of Acts as the gospel moves away from recalcitrant Israel to believing gentiles. Like a constant drumbeat throughout the Bible come stories of very unusual people continually being grafted onto the people of God by their faith. The gospel, by its very nature, calls the "outsiders" to become "insiders," part of the people of God.

Illustrating the Text

Faith is passed down from one generation to another.

Culture: Brand loyalty is often passed down from parent to child. You even hear people say, "My parents drove a Ford, my grandparents drove a Ford, and as long as I can, I'll be driving a Ford." From tractors to toothpaste, from purses to perfume, from shoes to shaving cream, we often use products because we saw our parents using them.

Take a few minutes and ask the congregation to respond to a list of products by answering the question, "Do you use the brand your parents used?" A short list of products to ask about could include things such as toothpaste, automobiles, breakfast cereal, power tools, blue jeans, toilet paper, and soda.

Sports: The word "fan" is shorthand for the word "fanatic." Sports fans usually are dedicated to and passionate about their favorite teams. This loyalty often is passed down from one generation to the next. Parents who love their alma mater or their professional sports team will often buy their children clothing with the team logo on it. You can even get Detroit Tigers or Dallas Cowboys diapers! Here is a good opportunity to share a personal story about someone who is a fanatic about a particular sports team, and then challenge the congregation to be that fanatical about their faith.

Everyday Life: The influence of parents on their children diminishes as the children get older. When children are in their preschool years, parents have almost exclusive influence and control over their children. As children age and mature, that influence, while remaining essential and formative, steadily decreases, as teachers, peers, media, and other influences hold increasing sway. While it is healthy for a child's development that they differentiate themselves from their parents as they mature, it also shows the importance of making the most of the opportunities parents are given. The point is simply that, as Proverbs 22:6 says, the time to influence our children is when they are young. The problem is that parents' time can be eaten up by other things, such as career advancement, recreational activities, marital conflict, and continuing education. This only increases the need to be diligent in our faith walk and set the example of our priorities while our children are still young.

Can the Word of God Be Destroyed?

Big Idea

The powerful word of God cannot be destroyed or stymied.

Key Themes

- The written word of God presents his message in a special and powerful way.
- Those who disregard the word of God repeatedly are without excuse.
- At the heart of rebellion is the rejection of God's word.
- Trying to destroy God's word rather than obeying it results in serious judgment.
- Because leaders have strong influence over people, they carry special responsibility to obey the truth.

Understanding the Text

The Text in Context

Although the book of Jeremiah often reads something like an anthology, there is a certain flow of themes presented. Jeremiah 11–29 presents God's prophet Jeremiah in conflict, especially with the leaders in Jerusalem. The second half of this unit, Jeremiah 21–29, focuses on the ensuing judgment that is coming to Jerusalem because of the hostility of the leaders in Jerusalem to God's word through the prophet. King Jehoiakim plays a major role in this theme (note especially the similarities between Jer. 26 and Jer. 36). The interruption in the theme created by Jeremiah 30–33 underscores the stark contrast between God, who is faithful to his covenant promises, and the kings in Judah, who are not, the point stressed in Jeremiah 34–35. In Jeremiah 36 King Jehoiakim appears again, playing his final narrative role in the book. His actions in this chapter function as the climax of royal hostility to the word of God and clearly demonstrate the culpability of the leadership in Jerusalem in bringing the judgment and destruction upon them that is presented in the following chapters. So just as Jeremiah 36 caps off the hostility theme reaching back all the way to Jeremiah 11, it also serves to introduce Jeremiah 37–44, which is a chronological account of the end of Jerusalem and Judah.

Jeremiah 36 is also connected with the surrounding chapters by the theme of fire. Jeremiah 34 opens and closes (an inclusio) with the prophetic promise that Jerusalem will be destroyed by fire (34.2, 22). Jeremiah 36 reveals the poetic justice behind this judgment, for in this chapter the king foolishly tries to thwart the fulfillment of the word of God by burning the word of God in the fire. But it is Jerusalem, including the temple and the royal palace, that will be burned in the fire. This is stressed several times in the chapters that follow (37:8, 10; 38:23; 39:8; see also the summary in 52:13), underscoring the irony of Jehoiakim's attempt to thwart this prophecy by burning the prophetic word in a fire.

Historical and Cultural Background

Baruch son of Neriah is mentioned in 36:4. The name "Baruch" means "blessed" and is a shortened form of "Berechiah" ("Yahweh [the LORD] blesses"). Baruch was a scribe who worked with Jeremiah and was responsible for writing down much of the book of Jeremiah (at least Jer. 1–25, and probably the rest of it too). He helps Jeremiah document his deed in 32:12, and God protects him along with Jeremiah when the Babylonians overrun Jerusalem (43:3, 6; 45:1–2).

Interpretive Insights

36:2 *Take a scroll.* There are two Hebrew words for "scroll" used in this passage, and both are used together here and in 36:4. The word *mᵉgillah* refers to the shape of the document, meaning a document that is rolled up—a scroll. The other word is *seper*, which stresses the writing aspect; this was a scroll with writing on it. Thus the passage will use both words to refer to the document as the written scroll (36:2, 4) and then use each of the separate words throughout the passage: the scroll (*mᵉgillah* [36:6, 14, 21, 23, 25, 27, 28, 29, 32]) or the writing (*seper* [36:2, 4, 8, 10, 11, 13, 18]). The word *soper*, a form of *seper*, is also used to describe the occupation of "secretary" or "scribe" (36:10, 12, 20, 21, 23, 26, 32). The material used to make the scroll was probably either papyrus or parchment (animal hide).

all the words I have spoken to you. Probably this includes most, if not all, of Jeremiah 1:1–25:13.

36:3 *Perhaps.* The Hebrew word used here means pretty much the same as the English word "perhaps." It can connote uncertainty but also possibility. God says "perhaps" in 36:3 as he gives instructions to Jeremiah. As Jeremiah passes the instructions on to Baruch, he likewise says "perhaps" (36:7).

hear . . . disaster . . . wickedness. The three Hebrew words used in this verse with "perhaps" in hopefulness of repentance are used again in reverse order in 36:31 in finality of judgment. The similarities of the two verses are illustrated thus:

> 36:3: *"Perhaps* when the people . . . hear [*shama'*] about every disaster [*ra'ah*] I plan to inflict on them, they will turn . . . I will forgive their wickedness [*'awon*]."

> 36:31: "I will punish him . . . and his attendants for their wickedness [*'awon*]; I will bring on them . . . every disaster [*ra'ah*] . . . because they have not listened [*shama'*]."

they will each turn from their wicked ways. Familiar Hebrew words are used here. "Turn" translates *shub* ("to turn, return, repent"), and "wicked" translates *ra'ah* ("evil, wicked, disaster, bad stuff"). The same phrase is used in 36:7.

36:6 *read to the people.* A more literal rendering of the Hebrew is "proclaim in the ears of the people." The Hebrew word for "ears" is repeatedly used in this idiomatic expression in this chapter (36:6, 10, 13, 14, 15, 20, 21).

36:7 *Perhaps they will bring their petition before the LORD.* The word translated as "petition" refers to making a request or supplication for a favor, mercy, or pardon. This word is the subject of the sentence. Also, the word translated as "bring" most frequently means "to fall." Thus a literal reading is "Perhaps their petition/request for mercy will fall into the presence of the LORD."

36:10 *Baruch read to all the people at the LORD's temple.* This is the first reading of the scroll. "Read" could perhaps be better translated as "called out" or "proclaimed."

36:15 *So Baruch read it to them.* This is the second reading of the scroll. This time the audience ("them") is the numerous "officials" in the secretary's room in the royal palace (36:12). The word *sar*, translated as "official" and sometimes as "prince," implies a high-ranking official or someone of noble birth. Several of these specific "officials" are named in 36:12.

36:16 *they looked at each other in fear.* The Hebrew verb used here (*pahad*) means "to tremble with fear, terror, dread." The text does not identify specifically what frightens the officials. Perhaps they are frightened by the visions in the scroll of God's terrible judgment on Jerusalem and its inhabitants. Or perhaps they are terrified at the thought of how King Jehoiakim might react against anyone associated with reading this scroll. He might consider them as subversive and critical of his rule.

36:21 *Jehudi . . . read it to the king and all the officials standing beside him.* This is the third reading of the scroll. These "officials" (*sar*) likewise are probably those nobles who served in the royal court.

36:24 *The king and all his attendants.* The word translated as "attendants" is *'ebed*, which basically means "servant" or "slave" but is also used of officials who "serve" the king. The use of the term here is setting up a contrasting wordplay with the story of Ebed-Melek ("servant of the king") in Jeremiah 38.

showed no fear. The word translated as "fear" is *pahad*, the same word used above in 36:16. Thus in Hebrew a direct contrast is being made. Those officials who listen to the scroll being read in 36:16 tremble in fear when they hear it, but those around the king foolishly respond with no fear at all. They probably are following the king's lead in treating the scroll as powerless and something that can be destroyed.

36:26 *the LORD had hidden them.* In 36:19 the officials who hear Baruch read the scroll warn him to take Jeremiah and go hide. The same Hebrew word for "hide" is used here, but now the text makes clear that this is not just a mere suggestion by some officials. God himself is behind this. The passage implies that Jeremiah and Baruch are very well hidden, not because of their own fear but by the will of God.

36:32 *And many similar words were added to them.* The earlier scroll may have contained major portions of Jeremiah 1–25 but not the totality, and now Jeremiah and Baruch fill it out most likely to what we have in those chapters in the canon now. Or this editorial comment may refer to later prophecies of Jeremiah (i.e., during the reign of Zedekiah) that were added to this scroll.

Theological Insights

There are a few Old Testament texts that refer to prophetic messages being written down in some form (Jer. 29:1; 30:2; 51:60; Isa. 8:1, 16; 30:8; Hab. 2:2), but Jeremiah 36 is the only account that clearly describes a prophetic message written down for the express purpose of being read to the people and leaders.[1] Yet the written form of Jeremiah's message that plays such a huge role in this chapter seems to carry a special authoritative significance, and when Jehoiakim destroys it rather than venerating and honoring it, he seems to have committed an acutely serious transgression. Thus we learn that the written word of God is very special and carries the authority of God with it. To reject the written word of God is to reject God himself.

Teaching the Text

The written word of God carries a special spiritual (and somewhat awe-inspiring) authoritative power. There is nothing like it in any other literature. Thus it is foolish (and dangerous) to choose to ignore it or to deny its authoritative power. Even more foolish is to think one can destroy it or render its prophetic decrees ineffective. Whether in the ancient court of Jehoiakim or in the halls of governments and in factories and on farms today, nations, families, and individuals stand or fall based on how they respond to the word of God. It contains the good news of salvation with blessings for those who listen and terrible warnings of God's judgment on those who fail to listen. Both realities will come true. This cannot be stopped by human defiance.

The point of reading Jeremiah's scroll three times in Jerusalem is to stress that the leaders and inhabitants of the city were completely without excuse for their defiant rebellion and failure to heed God's warnings. It underscores how fully they had been warned. Likewise, there are many today who grow up in the church hearing the word of God repeatedly throughout their younger years but who later choose to ignore it and to follow their own way through life rather than God's. This defiance is both foolish and dangerous, for these people are without excuse.

Today, how one understands and interacts with God's word is foundational to one's relationship with God, and the decision to obey or to ignore his word will impact one's life profoundly. This is one of the most critical decisions that one makes in life. Those who say that they are followers of Jesus but who deny the authority of the Bible over their lives are not really his followers, for at the very heart of sin and rebellion is the rejection of the authority of God's word over our lives.

Finally, it is interesting to note that the second group of listeners in this story responds to God's word with fear (and concern for Jeremiah's and Baruch's safety). Yet the third group, the king and his powerful inner circle, override them and lead the entire nation down a foolish and rebellious path. Because leaders do sway people who trust them or who are under their authority, they carry a special responsibility to lead their people into truth according to God's word. To lead people in rebellion against God's word is extremely offensive to God, and it produces very serious consequences.

Illustrating the Text

The power of the word of God

Theological Book: *Translating the Message: The Missionary Impact on Culture*, by Lamin Sanneh. In this book Yale University missiologist Lamin Sanneh underscores the direct connection between the explosive expansion of Christianity in the global south during the twentieth century and the translation of Scripture into the vernacular languages of these regions.[2]

History: In 1525, against the strict orders of the Roman Catholic Church, William Tyndale completed his translation of the New Testament from Greek into English, something that had never been done before on that scale. Although prohibited by powerful bishops in England, copies of this small English New Testament were printed in Germany and the Netherlands and smuggled into England at great risk, both to the smugglers and to the purchasers. Several of these powerful bishops either confiscated or purchased most of these English New Testaments as fast as they could, and thus the vast majority of Tyndale's English New Testaments were intercepted and burned. These bishops likewise continued their hunt for Tyndale, who was now in Antwerp working on translating the Old Testament into English. Betrayed by an acquaintance, Tyndale was captured in 1535. His office was raided, and all his papers and books confiscated. Tyndale was tried as a heretic and then strangled and burned in 1536, never knowing if his translation work would survive or continue. John Rogers, however, one of Tyndale's friends, apparently had been able to hide most of what Tyndale had translated of the Old Testament. Rogers quickly translated the rest of the Old Testament, added it to Tyndale's New Testament, and within months of Tyndale's execution Rogers defiantly printed fifteen hundred copies of the complete Bible in English (the Matthew Bible). Politically and theologically, things were also now changing rapidly back in England. Those who had opposed and hunted Tyndale soon lost their power. In 1539 another revision of Tyndale's English Bible was published (known as the Great Bible), and soon it was accepted and then even authorized for use by the new Church of England. English Bibles flooded into England. During the reign of Elizabeth (1558–1603), English Bibles (still using most of Tyndale's original translation) were printed in England and Scotland and sold openly and freely throughout the British Isles. Tyndale paid a high price for his translation work, but the translation and proliferation of the Bible in English in the British Isles during the sixteenth century was powerful and unstoppable.[3]

Testimony: Have several people read one short passage of Scripture that has impacted their life. After the person reads the passage, he or she will declare something like, "This powerful passage of Scripture has changed my life because . . ."

Bible: Read Matthew 4:1–11 and hold up Jesus as an example of quoting the written word of God in a time when he was tempted by the enemy. Three times he declared, "It is written."

The Prophet in Prison

Big Idea

Persecution cannot stop the power and authority of God's word.

Key Themes

- Those who oppose God's word with hostility are foolish to expect a last-minute deliverance by God.
- Persecution against Jeremiah adds to the list of covenant violations warranting the destruction of Jerusalem.
- As Jeremiah's prophecies start to come true, he encounters increased hostility and persecution.
- Even in prison Jeremiah speaks with the power and authority of God.

Understanding the Text

The Text in Context

Jeremiah 37 opens a long prose section (Jer. 37–44) that is in chronological order. This unit describes the prophesied fall and destruction of Jerusalem as well as the immediate aftermath. All the judgments on the leaders and people of Judah and Jerusalem that Jeremiah has been prophesying for years finally arrive. Jeremiah 37:2 serves as an explanatory summation that introduces the "fall of Jerusalem" narrative that follows.

Jeremiah 37 and 38 are closely related in that they describe the trials and persecution that Jeremiah endures during these final days. In Jeremiah 36 an attempt is made to destroy the message; in Jeremiah 37–38 an attempt is made to destroy the messenger. Both are examples of rebellion and hostility toward the word of God; both thus also point to the culpability of Jerusalem's leaders in regard to the destruction of Jerusalem.

Historical and Cultural Background

The historical context of Jeremiah 37 takes us into the final days of Jerusalem. King Zedekiah and the nobles of Judah rebelled against the Babylonian king Nebuchadnezzar, who responded angrily with an invading army. In 588 BC he began the siege of Jerusalem, and in 586 BC the city finally fell to the Babylonian army. The events in Jeremiah 37 take place early in this siege. Probably sometime during 588 BC, the Egyptians sent an army north to challenge the Babylonians and to try to relieve the Judahites under siege in Jerusalem. The Babylonians briefly withdrew from their siege to deal with the Egyptians, but they soon sent the Egyptians back to Egypt in retreat and then returned to their siege of Jerusalem. The events of Jeremiah 37 (as well as the events in Jer. 34) take place during this interlude.

Interpretive Insights

37:2 *his attendants.* As in 36:24, the word translated as "attendants" is *'ebed*, which is the word for "servant" or "slave" but is also used of officials who "serve" the king. The use of the term here and in 37:18 adds to the usage in 36:24 in providing a contrasting wordplay on the term *'ebed* in the story of Ebed-Melek ("servant of the king") coming next in Jeremiah 38.

paid any attention. Throughout Jeremiah (see especially 36:31), judgment has been pronounced because the king, his leaders, and the people do not listen (*shama'*) to the word of God through Jeremiah. The word translated as "paid any attention" is once again *shama'*. This word carries strong nuances of "obey." The point here is that they did not obey any of the words spoken by God through Jeremiah.

37:3 *please pray on our behalf.* The word translated as "pray" carries a more specific connotation of "to intervene, intercede" or even "to arbitrate on behalf of." This is the same word used in several other places (7:16; 11:14; 14:11) where God explicitly prohibits Jeremiah from praying for the people of Jerusalem in any kind of intercessory role. The irony is rich in light of 37:2, which points out that the people making the request for this intercessory prayer have never listened to Jeremiah when he proclaimed the word of God to them.

37:8 *and burn it down.* A more literal translation is "and burn it with fire" (NRSV). The reference, of course, is to the fate of Jerusalem. The same phrase occurs in 37:10. The specific reference to fire suggests a strong connection back to 36:23, where the king cut up the word of God and burned it in the fire. It is Jerusalem, not the word of God, that will be destroyed in the fire. Likewise, the same phrase is used in 34:2, 22.

37:12 *to get his share of the property there.* We must keep in mind that much of the book of Jeremiah is not in chronological order. In Jeremiah 32 the prophet purchases a field from a relative in his hometown of Anathoth, which was in the region of Benjamin. That event, however, happens at a later stage in the siege of Jerusalem. The earlier event described here in 37:12 probably is the background for the episode in Jeremiah 32. The word translated as "to get his share of the property" implies obtaining one's share of an inheritance.

Probably a relative had died, and Jeremiah was going to see about his claim to the land.

37:14 *he arrested Jeremiah.* The word translated as "arrested" means "to seize" or "to grab firmly" and implies a rough physical action. This was not a quiet, urbane arrest. The same word is used in 37:13.

37:15 *They were angry.* The word translated as "angry" is a strong word for anger, implying something like "flew into a rage" or "became furious."

had him beaten. The Hebrew word used here can connote a very serious beating, for often this word is used to convey the killing of someone.

imprisoned in the house . . . which they had made into a prison. In Jerusalem, as in much of the ancient world, the king did not maintain regularly operating prisons. Long-term confinement was not a normal penal option. Short times of confinement usually were followed by a trial or just a decree of punishment that could be carried out immediately. Yet here in Jeremiah 37 the king and other officials appear reluctant either to kill Jeremiah or to release him. What they desire is to silence him. Thus they convert the house of one of the king's top officials into a special-purpose prison.

37:16 *a vaulted cell in a dungeon.* The word translated as "vaulted cell" describes an underground room with an arched or vaulted ceiling. The English word "dungeon" is misleading because it implies a permanent structure constructed to be a prison. The Hebrew word used here refers to an underground cistern normally used to collect and store rainwater. This is the same word used repeatedly in Jeremiah 38 (vv. 6–13). This facility would have been wet and completely dark.

37:17 *he asked him privately.* The word translated as "asked" can also mean "to inquire," sometimes specifically in regard to oracles from deities. It can also mean "to request" or even "to beg for." The interesting thing is that the king is "asking" or "requesting" something from his prisoner. The word translated as "privately" means "secret" or "hidden." It is not an adverb but rather a noun with a preposition and definite article ("in the hidden/secret place"). The irony in this usage is drawn from Jeremiah 36, where the verbal form of this same word is used when God has "hidden" Jeremiah (36:26). In 36:26 Jeremiah is hidden from the king. Here in 37:17 it is the king who "hides" him. Zedekiah, who apparently does not even trust his own officials, now meets with Jeremiah in secret.

Is there any word from the LORD? This has to be one of the dumbest questions ever asked by anyone in the Bible. Jeremiah has been prophesying very clearly for years that if there is no repentance, Jerusalem will be captured and destroyed by the Babylonians. With the Babylonians at the gates, for Zedekiah to think that Jeremiah would have a positive word from God is rather ludicrous. Yet in spite of all this, Zedekiah probably is hoping that Jeremiah will give him a new and fresh oracle from God about their deliverance.

37:19 *Where are your prophets . . . ?* In sarcastic exasperation Jeremiah points out to Zedekiah that his court prophets had been frequently countering Jeremiah with prophecies that Babylonian power would soon end, and that the Babylonians would never besiege Jerusalem (14:13; 23:16–22; 27:14–16; 28:1–17). Jeremiah wants to know why he is the one prophet put into prison, now that the Babylonians have come according to his predictions, proving that he is the true prophet who has been prophesying the truth while the others have been prophesying lies. Jeremiah had been arrested on the treasonous charge of collaborating with the Babylonians. His plea to Zedekiah shifts the focus from treason to that of true and false prophecy.

37:20 *Do not send me back . . . or I will die.* Jeremiah probably is not exaggerating here. His life does seem to be hanging in the balance.

37:21 *King Zedekiah then gave orders.* Zedekiah apparently agrees with some of Jeremiah's argument. He moves the prophet to a healthier and safer, yet still confined, area. What Zedekiah does not do is actually listen to Jeremiah and repent.

for Jeremiah to be placed in the courtyard of the guard. The "courtyard of the guard" is the same facility to which Jeremiah is confined in 32:2; 33:1; 38:6. It appears to be where the royal guard was housed, and thus it was in or adjacent to the king's palace.

Theological Insights

There is a certain "theology of persecution" taught in the book of Jeremiah. The persecution that he endures is a central part of the biographical material in the book, and it appears to be part of the purpose of the book. Those who take up the mantle of proclaiming God's word, especially about sin and judgment, can expect serious "pushback" from the culture. Within the biblical texts, of all the Old Testament prophets, Jeremiah is the most persecuted. He is the one who experiences trials, beatings, and imprisonment, ironically from his own people, whom he was trying to save. At the time of the New Testament, Jeremiah was well known as the prototypical "persecuted prophet." Thus when Jesus experiences persecution (trials, beatings, execution) in the Gospels and when the apostles experience persecution (trials, beating, execution) in the early chapters of Acts, there are numerous parallels and allusions to Jeremiah. In like manner, just as Jeremiah's persecution led to the destruction of Jerusalem in 586 BC, so the persecution of Jesus and the apostles seems to foreshadow the similar judgment that came on Jerusalem in AD 70 when the Romans destroyed the city.

Teaching the Text

Zedekiah's actions in these final days of Jerusalem are inconsistent and uncertain. He never repents and turns to God, and he stays rather hostile toward the true word of God; but as he begins to see the truth of Jeremiah's prophecy unfold, his esteem and respect for Jeremiah seem to grow. But this will not save him. Likewise today, occasionally there are unbelievers in the world who do show some respect to those proclaiming God's word to them. They may even inquire about spiritual things, but then they continue to defy the call to believe in the Lord, and they refuse to repent. Their interest and respect will not save them. Obviously, God is gracious, and through Christ people can be saved at the very last minute, but only as they accept God's word and repentantly believe in his message.

The destruction of Jerusalem in 586 BC was horrific. A similar fate fell on the city in AD 70, after the Jewish leadership rejected Jesus. Both in Jeremiah and in the New Testament, evidence that warrants this terrible judgment is presented in abundance, clearly establishing that the judgment on Jerusalem came only because of repeated covenant violations and the hostile rejection of numerous calls to repentance. The persecution against God's messengers is a culminating act of rebellion in which harm is done to those very ones who have come to save.

From Jeremiah's perspective, these events at the end seem very illogical. His years of preaching are clearly vindicated by the Babylonian siege. Yet for him, the persecution grows even stronger as his message comes true. In today's world our ability to point out direct cause-and-effect phenomena based on biblical principles or in fulfillment of biblical prophecies should lead to thankfulness and a softening among unbelievers who are opposed to us. But it rarely does. Often clear and logical biblical truth is met only with increased hostility and persecution. Note the statement by Jesus that even if someone came back from the dead, there are still some people who would not believe (Luke 16:31).

Obviously, the power with which Jeremiah speaks does not diminish with his negative circumstances. Even in prison he speaks with the power and authority of God. Likewise, for believers today, the power and authority of the word of God continue in spite of all opposition and hostility. His word controls history, and his plan will be accomplished. His written word can be thrown into the fire and his spoken word can be imprisoned, but the power of his word breaks out in spectacular and awesome control of history. It cannot be stopped.

Illustrating the Text

Persecution will not stop the power and authority of God's word.

Testimony: In the mid-1980s the Marxist government in Ethiopia attempted to crush the vibrant, indigenous evangelical churches in southern Ethiopia (called the Kale Heywet Church). This included the closing and sealing of hundreds of church buildings, the confiscation of church property, and the arrest and imprisonment of dozens of key church leaders. Woldegiorgis Hirbaye, the director of the Bible school in the town of Dilla, was one of those arrested. He and eleven other Ethiopian church leaders were taken to the government prison in Awasa. As they entered the prison compound, Woldegiorgis noticed that the prisoners were housed in six different buildings. He asked his colleagues to pray that they would be split up so that they could provide a Christian witness in each building. They were then taken to the prison warden, who told them that in order to keep them (the Christians) from congregating together, he was going to split them up and place two of them in each of the six buildings. Encouraged by this answer to prayer, these Christian men went to work evangelizing the thousand-plus men in this prison, and over the next year they led many men to the Lord. As Woldegiorgis told this story, he smiled and said, "They couldn't go anywhere, and we had all day long to talk to them. What better evangelistic opportunity could you hope for?"[1]

Those who oppose God's word will eventually regret it.

History: Early in the American Revolution, the infamous traitor Benedict Arnold was a commander in the American army, but as the war continued, he abandoned his compatriots and joined forces with the British. Legend has it that on his deathbed his heart was filled with regret, and he is reported to have said, "Let me die in this old uniform in which I fought my battles. May God forgive me for ever having put on another."[2]

As Jeremiah's persecutors would discover, there will come a time when God will hold us all accountable for our words and actions.

Ebed-Melek Saves Jeremiah's Life

Big Idea

In times of hostility and negative public opinion, faithfulness to God requires courage.

Key Themes

- Convicted of treason, Jeremiah faces imminent death.
- Ebed-Melek, an African foreigner, acts courageously to rescue Jeremiah.
- The hostile actions of the Hebrew officials in Jerusalem are contrasted with the saving action of Ebed-Melek the Cushite.
- The weak king Zedekiah foolishly follows public opinion rather than the word of God.

Understanding the Text

The Text in Context

Jeremiah 37–44 is in chronological order. Thus the events in Jeremiah 38 take place near the end of the long Babylonian siege of Jerusalem (588–586 BC) and provide additional theological context for understanding the capture and destruction of Jerusalem in Jeremiah 39. Thus the major theme connecting the two chapters is "Who will live, and who will die?" Likewise, another central theme running through these two chapters is the contrast in "officials/officers" (the Judahite officials/officers, the Babylonian officials/officers, and the Cushite official/officer). This theme connects the two sections in Jeremiah 38 (38:1–13, 14–28) and continues into Jeremiah 39.

Historical and Cultural Background

Cush was an African kingdom that straddled the Nile River south of Egypt, in the territory that is now the country of Sudan. Ebed-Melek's Cushite ethnicity is stressed in this story, for he is identified as a Cushite four times (38:7, 10, 12; 39:16). The Cushites were distinctively African in their appearance (note 13:23), and they were famous in the ancient world as skilled mercenary soldiers.[1]

King Zedekiah seems very uncertain and even fearful of his own officials in this passage. This may reflect his memory of what happened the last time the Babylonians advanced against Jerusalem (597 BC). As the Babylonians drew near, the king of Judah (Jehoiakim) died, probably murdered by officials in his court. Thus Zedekiah seems to be as frightened by his own officials as he is by the Babylonians.

Interpretive Insights

38:2 *Whoever stays in this city will die.* The Hebrew word for "die" (*mut*) occurs nine times in this chapter (38:2, 4, 9, 10, 15, 16, 24, 25, 26), indicating the central role that dying/living plays in it.

38:3 *sword, famine or plague.* Jeremiah has used this triad several times. It normally stresses that the Babylonians will kill numerous inhabitants with the sword as they capture Jerusalem, but that a great many will also die in the aftermath of the invasion as famine sets in and plagues break out. In the context of Jeremiah 38, however, as the inhabitants of Jerusalem suffer through a two-year siege, no doubt many in the city have already died from these three scourges, and everyone now faces the real possibility of this kind of death.

38:4 *the soldiers who are left.* Ironic statements such as this occur throughout the passage as a subtle testimony from the lips of Jeremiah's accusers that the siege is not going well for Jerusalem. The word translated as "who are left" implies that numerous soldiers have already either died or defected to the Babylonians.

This man. The officials avoid referring to Jeremiah as "the prophet."

is not seeking the good of these people but their ruin. The word translated as "good" is *shalom*. The word translated as "ruin" is *ra'ah* ("evil, disaster, bad stuff"). This word occurs throughout Jeremiah ironically to refer both to the sin (evil) that the people have done and the consequences (disaster, calamity) that God will bring on them. The officials have it backward; only by listening to Jeremiah can *ra'ah* be avoided.

38:6 *put him into the cistern.* "Cistern" translates one of the same Hebrew words used in 37:16. It probably is referring to an underground water-storage structure.

Malkijah, the king's son. This reference to the king's son implicates the royal family in this plot to kill Jeremiah. Note that all the king's sons will be slaughtered by the Babylonians (39:6).

by ropes. This suggests that the cistern was quite deep.

no water . . . only mud, and Jeremiah sank down into the mud. The fact that this cistern is empty of water suggests that the siege is not going well for those in Jerusalem. The text is not clear about the significance of sinking down into the mud. Perhaps the mud is extremely deep (this same Hebrew word for "sank down," but in a different stem, is translated by the NIV as "drowned" in Exod. 15:4). Or perhaps the mud is a knee-deep, humiliating annoyance (the same word for "sank down" is used in 38:22 of Zedekiah's feet being "sunk" in the mud). At any rate, no one is going to feed him down there, and this is definitely a life-threatening situation (38:9).

38:7 *Ebed-Melek.* The name "Ebed-Melek" literally translates as "servant of the king." During the sixth and seventh centuries BC, this term was often used as a title for fairly high-ranking officials. Earlier commentators often argued that he was a slave, but everything in the context and in the normal semantic use of the term suggests that he was a high-ranking official and probably a military officer.[2] The word *'ebed* is used in Jeremiah 36–37 to refer to "attendants" (NIV) who give advice to the king (36:24, 31; 37:2, 18). Thus an implied ironic wordplay probably is taking place, contrasting this servant/attendant/officer (*'ebed*) of the king who listens to the word of God through Jeremiah and those servants/attendants/officers (*'ebed*) of the king who do not. Note especially the summary statement in 37:2.

an official. The Hebrew word used here (*saris*) can refer specifically to a eunuch or more generally to an official. In Jeremiah it is used regularly of a high-ranking official in a military context ("chief officer" [39:3, 13]; "the officer in charge of the fighting men" [52:25]). Ebed-Melek is most likely a military officer of some kind, perhaps a liaison between Judah and its Egyptian allies.[3]

sitting in the Benjamin Gate. In ancient Israel court was held at city gates. The terminology "sitting at a gate" meant that one was holding court. Thus Ebed-Melek approaches the king in public. This underscores the courage of Ebed-Melek as well as a certain amount of political or military clout as he confronts the king in public.

38:9 *these men have acted wickedly.* The word translated as "wickedly" is *ra'ah*, the same word used to accuse Jeremiah in 38:4. The courage of Ebed-Melek is seen as he publicly accuses the powerful officials of *ra'ah*. Ebed-Melek does not seem to fear them the way that Zedekiah does.

the prophet. In 38:4 the officials refer to Jeremiah as "this man" instead of "the prophet"; here in 38:9 Ebed-Melek refers to them as "these men" and refers correctly to Jeremiah as "the prophet."

38:16 *King Zedekiah swore this oath secretly.* The story in Jeremiah 34 has already established that Zedekiah's word cannot be trusted. This oath is quite the farce in light of 38:24, where Zedekiah quickly threatens to kill Jeremiah. "Secretly" implies that none of the officials hear this, but certainly both Jeremiah and God hear it.

as surely as the LORD *lives.* Literally, this translates as "by the life of the LORD." This is an extremely ironic oath to take in light of the life/death theme of the passage.

who has given us breath. The word translated as "breath" is *nepesh*, which connotes one's total being or life in general. Probably without realizing it, the king has declared one of the central truths of this episode. God is the one who gives (and takes away) *nepesh*.

to those who want to kill you. This phrase can be translated as "these men who seek your *nepesh*," thus ironically connecting back to the use of *nepesh* in the king's oath.

38:17 *the officers of the king of Babylon.* The word translated as "officers" is the same word used for the "officials" in Jerusalem (38:4, 25, 27).

your life will be spared. This phrase ("your *nepesh* will live") connects back to the same two words ("life" and *nepesh*) used in 38:16. This same Hebrew phrase occurs again in 38:20 (NIV: "your life will be spared").

38:22 *All the women left in the palace . . . will be brought out to the officials of the king of Babylon.* The women mentioned here probably are concubines in the royal harem. Jeremiah paints a picture of these women ridiculing Zedekiah for his poor judgment as they are being handed over to the Babylonians. Zedekiah's decision seems to be driven by his concern for his own safety. In this verse Jeremiah reminds him of the severe consequences for the women in his family if he continues to disobey God.

sunk in the mud. The Hebrew words used here poetically in regard to the king are the same as those used of Jeremiah in 38:6.

38:24 *Do not let anyone know about this.* Zedekiah foolishly remains more concerned about the threat from his own officials than he is about the Babylonians.

or you may die. The English word "may" is misleading. The Hebrew simply says "or you will die." This warning underscores the farcical nature of Zedekiah's oath to Jeremiah in 38:16. Jeremiah is between the proverbial rock and hard place: Zedekiah will kill him if he reveals this conversation, and the officials will kill him if he does not.

Theological Insights

Ebed-Melek plays an important theological role in Old Testament theology. His role as an "outsider" or gentile is important, indicated by the repeated stress on his identity as a Cushite in Jeremiah (38:7, 10, 12; 39:16). As national judgment falls on the people of Judah, Ebed-Melek represents those individuals who because of faith in Yahweh side with the prophet and his message and are thus delivered from the judgment. In this sense, within the narrative Ebed-Melek represents the "remnant of faith." Significant for Old Testament theology is the fact that this individual who symbolizes the remnant of faith is not an Israelite but a foreigner, a Cushite.

Teaching the Text

Ironically, the persecution against Jeremiah seems to crescendo to a climax just as his prophecies are proven irrefutably to be true. For Christians today, it is often just as the gospel starts to take hold in an area that hostility grows rapidly. God protects and delivers Jeremiah just as he promised in Jeremiah 1, but from Jeremiah's point of view, God certainly cuts it very close. Proclaiming God's word truthfully can be a dangerous occupation.

At the heart of this passage is the role of Ebed-Melek. He is not even an Israelite; he is a black African from Cush. As such, he serves as the paradigmatic gentile who believes Jeremiah at the exact time when nearly everyone in Jerusalem has rejected God's prophet and his message. This is an important text for ethnic relations in the church. A black African is presented as one of the biggest heroes in the prophetic literature of the Old Testament and as a central symbolic foreshadowing representative of the inclusion of the gentiles as God's people. Here, as throughout the rest of the Bible, God's true people are multiethnic.

There is also a lesson here about courageously trusting in God in spite of the circumstances. What was happening to Jeremiah was actually none of Ebed-Melek's business. He could have easily accepted the decision of the powerful officials, condoned by the king. But he knows that Jeremiah is a true prophet who proclaims God's word, so he risks his life to confront all the powerful leaders in Jerusalem publicly in order to save Jeremiah. Christians today can be tempted to simply sit back and quietly accept the actions and moral decisions of leaders. But God calls us to stand up for justice and to defend the truth of the word of God publicly, even when it is risky. Indeed, faithfulness to God and his word often requires courage in the public arena. A courageous trust in God is needed to confront injustices and to stand up for God's word against prevailing public opinion.

Finally, the weak and vacillating King Zedekiah, who fails to listen to Jeremiah and refuses to trust in God, presents us with a powerful negative model. As the end approaches, God continues to give him chance after chance to listen to Jeremiah and be delivered. Yet he continues foolishly to worry more about public opinion and his standing among the nobles and officials of Jerusalem than about God's word and God's upcoming judgment. Many today are in a similar situation. They hear the gospel of Jesus Christ with its promise of salvation, but they also feel the pressure of their peers and public opinion to reject Christ and to continue to live in rebellion against him. Will they accept Christ and receive salvation, or will they cave in to public opinion, defy God, and perish?

Illustrating the Text

Sometimes those who appear to be on the outside are actually on the inside.

Television: In an episode of "Monsterpiece Theatre" called "Inside/Outside Story," from the children's series *Sesame Street*, two lovers are unable to get together because she is inside the building and he is outside the building. It is a classic Romeo and Juliet–type of parody (specifically patterned after *West Side Story*), showing how we often divide the world into insiders and outsiders. In the end, the two lovers switch places, the outsider becoming the insider and vice versa, demonstrating that we are not so different after all.

The irony of Jeremiah 38 is that Ebed-Melek, who appears to be an outsider because of his ethnicity, is actually on the inside with God and his prophet. Showing this clip from *Sesame Street*, available on YouTube,[4] will allow you to talk about who is really in and out in Jeremiah's story and in life today.

The truly courageous ignore public opinion and follow God.

True Story: During World War II conscientious objectors were considered cowards. Their unwillingness to take another person's life because of their Christian beliefs flew in the face of the patriotic fervor that had seized most of the country. Desmond Doss had been ridiculed because of his unwillingness to carry a weapon, but he proved his bravery when, as a US Army medic on Okinawa, he risked his life to rescue seventy-five of his comrades by carrying them to safety one at a time while under enemy fire. For Doss's act of astonishing bravery and heroism, President Harry S. Truman later awarded him the Medal of Honor.[5] Like Ebed-Melek, Doss did what was right in spite of the harm that might have come to him.

Film: *Schindler's List*. During World War II, Oskar Schindler, an ethnic German industrialist and Nazi, was moved to action when he witnessed the despicable things that his government was doing to the Jewish people in Poland. Schindler, a wealthy industrialist who had profited greatly from the war, was running a textile plant in Krakow when he realized that the Jewish workers who were loaded on trains and sent to concentration camps were being systematically executed.

He spent his fortune bribing officials to allow his Jewish workers to remain in his employ, thus saving their lives. Some twelve hundred Jews were saved from certain death by Schindler's heroic and sacrificial act of courage, which left him penniless at the end of the war.

Showing a clip from this powerful film will allow you to talk about the need for Christians to do what is right even when it flies in the face of public opinion. Schindler's story also underscores the point that you cannot judge a book by its cover. Those who appear to be outside of God's camp, in this case a German Nazi, are sometimes on the inside doing the work that is close to God's heart.

The King and the Cushite: Who Will Be Saved?

Big Idea

Those who trust in God find deliverance, while those who defy and rebel against God experience judgment.

Key Themes

- As Jeremiah had predicted, Jerusalem is captured and burned by the Babylonians.
- The deliverance of Ebed-Melek and Jeremiah is contrasted with the punishment of those leaders who opposed Jeremiah.
- Ebed-Melek, a foreigner from Africa, is delivered because he trusted in God.

Understanding the Text

The Text in Context

Jeremiah 37–44 is in chronological order. Jeremiah 39, chronicling the fall of Jerusalem and the fate of those within it, is the climactic or focus chapter of this unit. After a two-year siege, in 586 BC the Babylonians breach the walls of Jerusalem and destroy the city. All the horrific things that Jeremiah has been prophesying about Jerusalem and Judah throughout Jeremiah 1–29 now actually happen. Also after chronicling the continued hostility and opposition to Jeremiah in Jeremiah 11–29, now the text describes how those who have opposed and persecuted God's prophet are either killed or taken to Babylonia in exile.

The description of the fall of Jerusalem in 39:1–10 is very similar to the parallel descriptions in 52:4–16 and 2 Kings 25:1–12. Surprisingly, the actual fall of the city is described in very brief fashion (39:1–3). The focus of Jeremiah 39 is on the contrasting fates of those who were living in Jerusalem: Zedekiah and the nobles (39:4–7), the people (39:8–10), Jeremiah (39:11–14), and Ebed-Melek (39:15–18).

Saris and Sarim: An "Official" Wordplay

An extended contrasting wordplay on *saris* and *sarim* runs through Jeremiah 37–39, uniting these three chapters around this subtheme. Both words refer to officials / army officers and are used of Judahite officials, Babylonian officials, and Ebed-Melek, a Cushite official. In Jeremiah 37 the Judahite *sarim* beat Jeremiah severely and imprison him in a cistern, where he would have soon died if Zedekiah had not intervened. In Jeremiah 38 these Judahite *sarim* arrest him again and throw him again into a cistern to die (38:4). The Cushite *saris* Ebed-Melek (38:7) rescues Jeremiah (at least temporarily), allowing Jeremiah to survive and stay in the court of the guard during the Babylonian siege. Zedekiah fears his own Judahite *sarim* (38:25, 27), even though Jeremiah warns him sternly that he should be more concerned with the Babylonian *sarim* who are besieging the city, because if he does not surrender to them, they will capture him and burn down the city (38:17–18, 22). Sure enough, in Jeremiah 39 the Babylonian *sarim* and *saris* capture Zedekiah and destroy Jerusalem, while also freeing Jeremiah (39:3, 13–14).[a] This wordplay further emphasizes the role of the Judahite leaders in their national rebellion against God, underscoring that the fate that awaited them was directly connected to how they treated God's prophet, Jeremiah.

[a] For further detail on this extended wordplay, see Hays, *From Every People*, 134–35.

Interpretive Insights

39:2 *the city wall was broken through.* The Hebrew text only has the word "city," but the walls are obviously implied. The word translated as "broken through" means "to split open, break open, rip apart" ("the city was split open").

39:3 *all the officials of the king of Babylon.* These victorious Babylonian officials (both *saris* and *sarim*) are contrasted with the officials of Jerusalem (see the sidebar). Note the list of Babylonian names and offices, paralleling the names and offices of those numerous Judahite officials cited in Jeremiah 36–38. *Saris* can refer to a eunuch or, as throughout Jeremiah, to a high-ranking official or military officer. *Sarim* (plural of *sar*) is a broad term normally used for those high-ranking officials, princes, and military officers who were just below the king in power.

took seats in the Middle Gate. To "sit at the gate" was a metaphor for holding court. These Babylonian officials, having captured Jerusalem, now sit as judges at a gate in Jerusalem, indicating that they, rather than the king and officials of Judah, now rule in Jerusalem. This had been predicted by Jeremiah (1:15). They probably are deciding who lives and who dies, as well as who goes into exile and who stays.

39:4 *they left the city.* The word translated as "left" (*yatsa'*) is the same word used in 38:17–18, where it is translated as "surrender." Note the ironic wordplay taking place. In 38:17–18 Jeremiah tells Zedekiah that if he "goes out" (*yatsa'*; NIV: "surrender") to the officers of the Babylonians, he will live and the city will not be burned. In 39:3 the Babylonian officers enter the city, at which point Zedekiah now "goes out" (*yatsa'*: NIV: "left"), not to surrender, but to flee (39:4), and the Babylonians do indeed burn the city (39:8).

39:5 *in the plains of Jericho.* The mention of Jericho is significant because it brings the story of the Israelite conquest and life in the promised land to a complete circle ("Jericho to Jericho"). In the book of Joshua the Israelites move into the land, conquering the city of Jericho as the sign of their future success in conquering the rest of the land. Here things are in reverse, as it is the Israelites whose city (Jerusalem) is conquered, and they are then exiled out of the land.

where he pronounced sentence on him. The word translated as "sentence" is the plural form of *mishpat*, which means "justices" or "judgments." These pronouncements probably include the executions of the royal family members and other nobles, the blinding of Zedekiah, and perhaps also the exile of the people (39:9) and the redistribution of the land to the poor people (39:10).

39:6 *the king of Babylon slaughtered the sons of Zedekiah.* The word translated as "slaughter" is normally used to refer to the killing of animal sacrifices (36x in Leviticus). Here the word is used in a grim figurative sense as the sons of Zedekiah are slaughtered like helpless sacrificial animals. Malkijah, one of the king's sons, was the owner of the cistern in which Jeremiah was imprisoned in 38:6.

39:7 *Then he put out Zedekiah's eyes.* The word "eyes" is emphasized by the Hebrew word order. The last thing that Zedekiah sees before he is blinded is the death of his sons and the nobles, no doubt many of them relatives of his. In 32:4 and 34:3 Jeremiah has predicted that Zedekiah would actually see Nebuchadnezzar with his own eyes. This is certainly fulfilled, but just briefly, as Zedekiah goes in captivity to Babylon blinded.

39:10 *some of the poor people, who owned nothing.* The word translated as "poor" also carries connotations of being "weak" or "lowly" in a socio-economic sense.

at that time. This phrase literally translates as "on that day." Throughout Jeremiah (and the other prophets) "that day," along with "those days" or "the day," usually refers to the coming "day of the LORD," a time of both judgment and deliverance/blessing (4:9; 25:33; 39:16; 48:41; 49:22, 26; 50:30).[1] In 39:10 both judgment and blessing are described. The leaders are executed, and many of the people are exiled, but the poorest of the land are given farms and vineyards, obviously a blessing. This same phrase, "that day," is used again in 39:16.

39:12 *look after him; don't harm him but do for him whatever he asks.* In Hebrew all three of these imperatives imply strong contrasting reversals of how the Israelite leaders in Jerusalem have been treating Jeremiah. "Look after him" (lit., "put your eyes on him") contrasts with the attempts to hide Jeremiah away underground in the cisterns (Jer. 37–38) and perhaps ironically alludes back to the removal of Zedekiah's eyes in 39:7. The word translated as "harm" is related to *ra'ah*, the word used by Ebed-Melek in accusing the officials in 38:9 ("these men have acted *wickedly* . . . to Jeremiah"). Likewise, the word translated as "asks" is the basic Hebrew word used to refer to speaking. Literally, it translates as "do whatever he says." What Jeremiah "says" is exactly what Zedekiah and his officials did not "do."

39:16 *tell Ebed-Melek the Cushite.* The repeated addition of his ethnic origin ("the Cushite") stresses that he is not a Hebrew from Jerusalem but a gentile from black Africa.

the LORD *Almighty, the God of Israel.* God formalizes this prophecy of deliverance for Ebed-Melek with the complete citation of his name. Recall that the term translated as "Almighty" has military associations, picturing God at the head of his armies.

39:17 *But I will rescue you.* "But" points to the stark contrast. God is still going to bring terrible judgment on Jerusalem, as he repeats clearly in 39:16. In contrast, he will "rescue" Ebed-Melek. The word translated as "rescue" can mean "to rescue, deliver, snatch away," but often it is used to refer to a rescue in an urgent or crisis situation. In several Old Testament passages it is used of the urgent, last-minute "snatching away" of a helpless animal from the mouth of a lion (1 Sam. 17:35; Amos 3:12; see also Ezek. 34:10).

declares the LORD. This literally translates as "oracle of Yahweh [the LORD]" and serves as a strong declaration formula of certainty. For Ebed-Melek's short prophecy of deliverance, God uses this formula statement twice (39:17, 18), underscoring the importance and certainty of this proclamation.

39:18 *I will save you.* The word translated as "save" means to "escape from one's enemies" or to "get away from a dangerous situation." It is a fitting word to use in regard to "escaping" from a city falling to its attackers. The Hebrew grammar stresses the certainty of this action, implying something like, "I will most certainly ensure that you escape." This stands in strong contrast to Jeremiah's words to Zedekiah in previous chapters, where he tells Zedekiah that he will not escape the Babylonians (32:4; 34:3; 38:18, 23).

will escape with your life. The word translated as "life" is *nepesh*, which refers to one's total being. In 38:17 Jeremiah tells Zedekiah that only if he surrendered to the Babylonians would his *nepesh* live. The NIV's "will escape" does not quite capture the gist of the Hebrew words used here. Literally, God tells Ebed-Melek that "your *nepesh* will be to you as a prize of war" (cf. NRSV). In the context of a siege and the fall of Jerusalem, when the victorious army will be carrying off the "spoil" and "plunder" of war, God uses a similar term for Ebed-Melek and his life. The imagery is that of Ebed-Melek walking out of the city with his "spoil" or "plunder" of war being his own life.

because you trust in me. The word translated as "trust" is *batah*, a central word for "trust" used in the Old Testament and frequently in Jeremiah. Often Jeremiah criticizes those in Judah and Jerusalem for trusting in false gods or trusting in "the lie" about false gods (7:4, 8; 13:25; 28:15; 29:31). In 17:5–7 Jeremiah presents the contrast between those who trust in human beings and thus are cursed, and those who trust in God and thus are blessed. Ebed-Melek serves as a prime illustration from 17:5–7 of one who trusts in God.

Theological Insights

Although the book of Jeremiah does not speak directly to our modern theological concept of "universalism," passages like this one do provide some theological insight into the issue. Jeremiah presents clearly the biblical-theological truth that only by listening to and obeying God's word, including repenting from sin and turning back to worship God alone, will the people of Judah be delivered from the coming judgment. Those who reject the message and defy God, even if they are priests, prophets, or the king of Judah, will experience his wrath and be destroyed. There is no ambiguity about this in Jeremiah. Thus the theology seen in Jeremiah clearly contradicts any notion that all people will somehow be delivered in the end from any judgment regardless of what they do or believe. Those who come to God in faith will be delivered; those who refuse to repent and come to God will perish.

Teaching the Text

The word of God is always certain. Just as Jeremiah had been warning, the Babylonians came and destroyed Jerusalem. Many of the people in Jerusalem thought that this could never happen. Their leaders who opposed Jeremiah had reassured them that this would never happen. Nonetheless, it did. Today sometimes there is a tendency among Christians to downplay the wrath of God and judgment on those who refuse to listen to and obey him, as if this would discourage people from believing. But this wrath is coming on them nonetheless. We do not do anyone any good service by ignoring this truth or by "sweeping it under the rug" as if it were not going to happen.

Many in Jerusalem thought that this city was so special that it was inviolable. But God is not concerned with cities; he is concerned with people and how they relate to him. The judgment will come. Those who trust in God, as Jeremiah and Ebed-Melek did, will be saved. Those who oppose God's word (now revealed through Jesus Christ) and who defy him will not be saved. The contrast is stark and is the most critical contrast in human existence.

The role of Ebed-Melek in Jeremiah is huge. He represents the inclusion of the gentiles among the people of God. He exemplifies salvation by faith. At the exact time when nearly all the Israelites in Jerusalem have rejected God, Ebed-Melek, a black African, believes and becomes the foreshadowing, paradigmatic, believing gentile.

This paradigm is repeated in a very similar fashion in Acts 7–8. The leaders and many of the people of Jerusalem reject God's word, persecute God's messengers (the apostles), and even execute one of God's messengers (Stephen). At this precise time, it is an African gentile (the Ethiopian eunuch) who believes and is saved (interestingly, biblical Ethiopia and Cush are the same place). Jerusalem is then likewise destroyed in AD 70, roughly forty years after Acts 7–8.

Illustrating the Text

The multiethnic look of global Christianity

Statistics: Ebed-Melek reminds us of the multiethnic look of God's people who compose the global church today and helps us not to envision Christianity as primarily a Western institution. Indeed, in *The Next Christendom*, Philip Jenkins notes that in 1900 only 10 million Christians lived in Africa and that by 2000 there were 360 million Christians in Africa, 100 million more than in North America. Likewise, based on current growth patterns, the overall number of Christians in North America is predicted to stay rather flat, while by 2025 the numbers of Christians in the global south will swell to 633 million in Africa, 640 million in South America, and 460 million in Asia.[2]

Those who trust in God find deliverance.

Parable: A little girl and her father were crossing a bridge. Her father was rather scared, so he said to his little daughter, "Sweetheart, please hold my hand so that you don't fall into the river."

The little girl said, "No, Dad. You hold my hand."

"What's the difference?" asked the puzzled father.

"There's a big difference," replied the little girl. "If I hold your hand and something happens to me, chances are that I may let your hand go. But if you hold my hand, I know for sure that no matter what happens, you will never let my hand go."[3]

After telling the story, remind the congregation that, as he did with Jeremiah, God has promised to never let go of our hand.

Christian Music: **"You Never Let Go," by Matt Redman.** Many people know this worship song, but few people know the backstory. Redman says that he wrote the song with his wife, Beth, the week after she had a miscarriage. The inspiration for the song came from Psalm 23, and it was written to give hope and remind people that despite our circumstances, "there's a God who never lets go." His words remind us that trust is always a choice.[4]

Some people trust in God; some trust in themselves.

Contrasting Concepts: Jeremiah 39 shows the contrast between Jeremiah and Ebed-Melek, who trusted in God, and King Zedekiah and the nobles, who trusted in themselves. This would be a good time to compare the fate of those in Scripture who trusted in God, and those who trusted in themselves (e.g., Joseph versus his brothers, Abraham versus Lot, Moses versus Pharaoh, David versus Absalom).

Television: In the series *24*, the show's star, agent Jack Bauer, always seems to be able to somehow overcome impossible odds and save the world. Compare this savior with the true Savior of the world. In *24* the yellow clock is always ticking, reminding us that time is running out. The same thing can be said about real life.

Rejecting a Second Chance

Big Idea

It is foolish to reject God and his offer of deliverance; it is even more foolish to do so twice.

Key Themes

- God offers an undeserved second chance to those who remain in Judah.
- Obedience must be on God's terms, not on people's terms.
- God's offer of grace is repeatedly rejected.
- Once again God's word through the prophet Jeremiah is ignored.
- The chance to be part of God's future restoration is squandered through disobedience.

Understanding the Text

The Text in Context

Jeremiah 40–44 is a postscript of sorts, narrating the events that take place in Judah in the aftermath of the Babylonian invasion. The point of Jeremiah 40–44, however, is to explain how those who remained in Judah rejected God's offer of blessing and restoration and thus removed themselves and their descendants as candidates to participate in the great restoration promised in Jeremiah 30–33. Jeremiah 40–44 comprises a unified story, but there are two major episodes in this narrative: events in Judah (40:1–43:7) and events in Egypt (43:8–44:30).

Jeremiah 40–44 is framed with two accounts of individual salvation. Ebed-Melek is promised deliverance in 39:15–18, and Jeremiah's scribe Baruch is similarly promised deliverance in Jeremiah 45 (both have the phrase "you will escape with your life"). In between these two episodes of individual deliverance is the contrasting story of how the remnant in Judah rejects God's offer of deliverance.

Historical and Cultural Background

Climaxing all that Jeremiah has been proclaiming throughout the book, in Jeremiah 39 Nebuchadnezzar and his Babylonian army finally arrived to crush rebellious Judah. In 586 BC the Babylonians completely destroyed Jerusalem, executed many of the leaders, and then took most of the inhabitants, along with the blinded and defeated Zedekiah, back to Babylon in exile. In Zedekiah's place Nebuchadnezzar appointed a governor, Gedaliah, to rule over Judah on behalf of the Babylonians. The events in this story seem to occur immediately after the fall of Jerusalem. If so, Gedaliah ruled for but a few months, and all the events in Jeremiah 40–42 transpire within a year of Jerusalem's fall.[1]

Interpretive Insights

40:1 *at Ramah.* Ramah was a town north of Jerusalem where the Babylonians gathered the Judahites before starting the trek to Babylon. Apparently, sometime after the Babylonians had released Jeremiah from the courtyard of the guard in Jerusalem (39:11–14), he had been mistakenly swept up with other Judahites who were being taken to Babylon.

40:2 *decreed this disaster.* Ironically, in 40:2–3 the Babylonian commander gives an accurate assessment of what happened using the same terminology that Jeremiah has been using throughout the book. For example, the word translated as "disaster" here is *ra'ah* ("disaster, bad stuff, calamity, evil"), a word used repeatedly by Jeremiah.

40:5 *Gedaliah . . . whom the king of Babylon has appointed.* The fact that Gedaliah was "appointed" by the king of Babylon is stressed repeatedly throughout this story (40:5, 7, 11; 41:2, 10, 18).

40:6 *at Mizpah.* With Jerusalem in ruins, the Babylonians set up a provincial capital at the town of Mizpah, north of Jerusalem. This was the town from which Samuel ruled (1 Sam. 15–16).

40:7 *all the army officers and their men who were still in the open country.* As Jerusalem and the other fortified cities of Judah fell to the Babylonians, apparently quite a number of officers and soldiers escaped from the cities and into the hills.

40:10 *you are to harvest the wine, summer fruit and olive oil, and put them in your storage jars.* Gedaliah is giving them authority to harvest the abandoned crops throughout the land. Conspicuously missing is any reference to taxes to be paid to the Babylonians out of this harvest. The implication is that those who remained behind were not under a brutal, oppressive rule, as might be expected, but were doing quite well.

40:12 *harvested an abundance of wine and summer fruit.* The harvest was of grapes and probably figs. Abundant harvests were to be understood as a direct blessing from God (Deut. 11:14) and thus were a surprising, even shocking feature in the aftermath of the judgment on Jerusalem and Judah (Deut. 28:39, 51).

40:14 *Don't you know . . . ?* The Hebrew grammar can stress the certainty of the knowledge ("Don't you know for certain?") or, perhaps more likely, incredulity ("Really? Don't you know?").

Baalis king of the Ammonites. Ammon was a bordering kingdom to the northeast of Judah. This is the only text in the Bible where Baalis is mentioned, but his name occurs on a seal impression discovered in modern Jordan (ancient Ammon). An envoy of Baalis probably was present at the conspiracy gathering mentioned in 27:3. Here he may be supporting an attempt to reestablish a Davidic king on the throne in Jerusalem under Ammonite control, or more likely, he was simply seeking to destabilize Judah to enhance his own influence in the region.[2] Jeremiah will proclaim judgment on the Ammonites in 49:1–6.

41:1 *Ishmael . . . who was of royal blood and had been one of the king's officers.* "Royal blood" translates a phrase that means "seed of the kingship" or "seed of royalty." The word translated as "officers" (*rab*) implies someone higher than a mere officer, more like "commander." Several of the Babylonian commanders mentioned in Jeremiah 39 have this word in their title (39:3, 9, 10, 11, 13). So Ishmael is probably the highest-ranking Judahite remaining in the region. Perhaps he has aspirations for the throne of Judah and hopes that the Ammonites will help him.

41:2 *struck down Gedaliah . . . killing the one whom the king of Babylon had appointed.* The redundant phrase "whom the king of Babylon had appointed" stresses the seriousness of this action. Whether due to blind patriotism or sheer stupidity, this action no doubt will bring a swift response from the Babylonians.

41:3 *as well as the Babylonian soldiers who were there.* King Nebuchadnezzar apparently had left a small contingent of soldiers with Gedaliah to help him project Babylonian authority and keep an eye on things. The murder of Gedaliah and the Babylonian soldiers is a direct challenge to Nebuchadnezzar.

41:5 *eighty men . . . from Shechem, Shiloh and Samaria.* All three of these cities are in Israel, not Judah. Israel and Judah have not been united since the death of Solomon in 922 BC. God's promise of restoration in Jeremiah 30–33 includes the regathering of both Israel and Judah. The coming of these eighty men from Israel to worship in Judah is significant, suggesting perhaps the possibility that Jeremiah's promised restoration (as a regathering of Israel and Judah together) could be starting to be fulfilled. To murder these eighty

Israelites who came to worship in Judah shatters that possibility, at least for the near future.

41:9 *the cistern where he threw the bodies . . . King Asa . . . Baasha king of Israel.* These eighty men who came in peace from Israel to worship in Judah (perhaps symbolizing the reunification of the two kingdoms) are murdered and then thrown into a cistern, ironically constructed in former years by King Asa of Judah as a defense measure during a war with Israel.

42:1 *from the least to the greatest.* This phrase stresses that all segments of the society were represented, both the very poor and the very rich and powerful. Jeremiah uses this phrase in judgment passages to show the culpability of the entire nation (6:13; 8:10), but in 31:34 it is used to show the wide extent of blessings in the new covenant. It is used again in judgment in 44:12.

42:6 *Whether it is favorable or unfavorable.* The two Hebrew words used here are *tob* ("good") and *ra'* ("bad stuff, disaster, calamity, evil").

we will obey the LORD our God. On the surface, this is a very encouraging statement, and it is repeated twice in this verse. They reaffirm that the Lord is their God, thus implying that they have ceased worshiping other gods. Likewise, they promise to "listen to the voice" (i.e., "obey"), the precise thing that the people failed at so miserably prior to the Babylonian invasion.

42:10 *if you stay in this land, I will build you up . . . I will plant you.* Since Jeremiah's call in 1:10, the images of building and planting have been favorite metaphors for God's blessing and the promised restoration.

for I have relented concerning the disaster. The word translated as "relented" is *niham*, which means "to change one's mind" or "to change plans." "Disaster" translates the Hebrew word *ra'ah* ("disaster, bad stuff, calamity, evil"), one of the central words that God has used throughout the book of Jeremiah to refer to judgment. Here God is promising to end the current ongoing judgment that is occurring in Judah. In 42:11 he explains clearly what he means: no longer will the king of Babylon be empowered by God to judge Judah.

42:11 *for I am with you and will save you.* The syntactical structure indicates that God's presence with them is specifically focused on his determination to deliver them. This same wording occurs in 30:11 to describe the future restoration.

42:17 *the sword, famine and plague.* These are the same words used throughout the book of Jeremiah to describe the means of death that the Babylonians will bring in judgment (27:8, 13; 29:17–18; 32:24, 36; 34:17; 38:2). God warns those remaining in Judah that if they disobey him again and go to Egypt, he will bring on them the same severe judgment that just fell on Jerusalem in the recent Babylonian invasion.

42:19 *Be sure of this.* The Hebrew text uses the word *yada'* ("to know") in a grammatical construction that stresses certainty or gives strong emphasis,

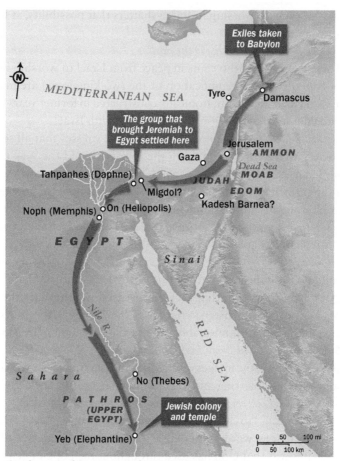

The aftermath of the conquest of Jerusalem by the Babylonians

such as "You will most certainly know!" There is no ambiguity about the consequences of this disobedience.

43:2 *You are lying!* The Hebrew construction stresses the word "lie" (*sheqer*). Recall that *sheqer* is used repeatedly in Jeremiah (37x), but most of the time Jeremiah or God is using the term to refer to the lies that the leaders and false prophets were proclaiming to the people. Ironically, here they are accusing Jeremiah of the same thing. They dislike what they hear back from God, so they decide that this word must not be from God.

43:4 *Johanan . . . all the army officers and all the people disobeyed the LORD's command.* "Disobeyed the LORD" translates the Hebrew phrase "they did not listen to the voice of the LORD." However, the Hebrew text separates the words for emphasis, placing the phrase "they did not listen" right at the beginning of the verse. The earlier disastrous pattern of king, officials, and all the people is paralleled here and once again leads to very bad decisions.

43:7 *in disobedience.* This translates "they did not listen to the voice of the LORD," underscoring their failure to keep their promise of 42:6.

as far as Tahpanhes. Tahpanhes was an Egyptian fortress city in the Sinai guarding the Egyptian border. Arrival here meant that they were now in Egypt. Jeremiah mentions this city back in 2:16 as he warned about the dangers of any political entanglement with Egypt. Likewise, in 46:14 the prophet includes this city in his proclamation of judgment on Egypt. A first-century AD document of nonbiblical Jewish folklore narrates that Jeremiah was stoned to death by his own people in Tahpanhes (*Lives of the Prophets* 2.1).

Theological Insights

After the destruction of Jerusalem and the exile of many of the inhabitants, God seems to once again offer a chance for obedience and blessing. This is not an indication of a capricious or inconsistent character in God but rather a reflection of his love and grace. This second chance is hardly deserved. The people have done nothing to deserve it. But God is a God of second chances—up to a point.

There are numerous parallels regarding the second chance between the events in the book of Jeremiah and those in Luke-Acts. Here in Jeremiah 40–42, as in Acts 2–3, God gives those in the land yet another chance to accept his blessing and to participate in the restoration. As in Acts 2–3, here in Jeremiah 40–42 that offer is rejected. This second chance offer reflects the gracious, patient, and loving character of God. Yet this additional offer of salvation does not go on forever. When rejected repeatedly, God eventually withdraws his gracious offer and replaces it with judgment.

Teaching the Text

Miraculously, undeservedly, and totally by the grace of God, those who were left behind by the Babylonians in Judah are offered a second chance. Not everyone received a second chance; many were killed by the Babylonians. But this particular group was offered a chance to live peacefully and rather comfortably in the promised land in good fellowship with God. Truly, our God is one who often gives second chances to people even though they clearly do not deserve them. Frequently there are people who have had ample opportunity throughout their lives to repent and accept Christ but who instead reject that opportunity. Then sometimes God in his grace gives them yet another chance, even though they do not deserve it. The message from this chapter to them is, "Don't be stupid like the people in Jeremiah's day! Repent and accept God's offer of forgiveness and salvation!"

Another important lesson can be drawn from the attitude toward prayer that these people displayed. Using Jeremiah as the intermediary, they went to God in prayer, promising to listen to his answer and obey him, whatever his answer might be. But in reality they were being dishonest, for they already had an agenda of acceptable answers, and when God's answer to their "prayer" was relayed to them through Jeremiah, they rejected it because they disliked it. Sometimes today we come to God in prayer, but we will accept only certain answers. Our obedience to him is conditioned on his giving answers that we like or preapprove. Yet God emphatically stresses that he speaks to us not according to what we want to hear but rather according to his will. We cannot approach God with our conditions, nor can we promise conditional obedience. When we pray, we must be willing to obey God's answer, whatever it is. And this obedience must be demonstrated through our action, not glib verbal affirmation.

Illustrating the Text

God offers an undeserved second chance.

Contrasting Concepts: It used to be that pawnshops were located in the more questionable neighborhoods and were frequented by an unsavory clientele, persons who sometimes tried to pawn stolen merchandise. However, as the popularity of television shows such *Pawn Stars*, *Cajun Pawn Stars*, and *Hardcore Pawn* demonstrates, pawnshops have gone mainstream. Housewives and college students are pawning their jewelry and electronics for a fast cash advance. But despite the recent change in public perception, the pawn business is all about the bottom line.

The pawnbroker's stock-in-trade is making secured loans to people who bring in something of value that acts as collateral. The interest rate is high, generally 10 percent a month or more, and the strict terms for redemption are set when the loan is made. If the person fails to claim the pawned item and pay the interest in full by the due date, the item becomes the property of the pawnbroker. With pawnbrokers, unlike God, there is no second chance.

Drama: Gather some players from your congregation and present the following short drama during the worship service. A person comes into a pawnshop looking for a loan, and when the pawnbroker asks for collateral, the borrower responds, "Well, I guess I could put up my soul." "That will do," says the pawnbroker, and the loan is made. The same scene is then repeated with a second customer.

Later both borrowers come back wanting to redeem the pawned items, but neither of them is able to repay the loan or the exorbitant interest. The borrowers argue and plead for a second chance hoping to be able to bargain with the pawnbroker, but the pawnbroker will not budge.

Then at the last minute a total stranger walks into the shop, and the borrowers begin to beg the stranger for help. The stranger offers to pay the debt in full if the borrowers will give him what they have lost.

The first borrower says, "No, I want to keep it." But the second borrower agrees. The stranger pays the pawn, and the two of them leave the store together.

The play ends as the pawnbroker turns and snaps at the first borrower saying, "Come on. It's time to go. You're coming with me." As the two of them walk off stage, the pawnbroker says, "That Jesus is killing my business."

When the play is concluded, remind the congregation that we cannot redeem ourselves from our sins. The only one able to pay the price is Jesus Christ.

The Foolishness of Rejecting God's Gracious Second Chance

Big Idea

When God offers someone a second chance, it is foolish and irrational to reject it.

Key Themes

- Disobedience to God often is based on irrational thinking.
- Ignoring God's word and worshiping other gods have disastrous consequences.
- Faithfulness to God is a family issue.
- Trust in anything other than God is misplaced trust.
- In the midst of national judgment an individual finds life.

Understanding the Text

The Text in Context

Jeremiah 40–44 is a story about what happens to those Judahites who were left behind in the land of Judah by the Babylonians after the destruction of Jerusalem and the exile of most of the population in 586 BC. The first half of the story (40:1–43:7) takes place in Judah, and the second half (43:8–44:30) in Egypt. This large unit (Jer. 40–44) is bracketed by "deliverance oracles" given to Ebed-Melek (39:15–18) and to Baruch (45:1–5). Both of these "deliverance oracles" have the phrase "your *nepesh* will be to you as a prize of war" (cf. NRSV; NIV: "you will escape with your life"), serving as an opening/closing inclusio and in stark contrast to the story in between.

Likewise, the section that deals with the Judahites in Egypt (43:8–44:30) opens (43:8–13) and closes (44:29–30) with a prophecy of judgment on Egypt. In between are the ominous words of judgment against the Judahites who have come into Egypt for protection. First, God reminds them of what just happened in Jerusalem because of idolatry (44:1–6). Then God asks those Judahites in Egypt why they would want to follow the same path and be destroyed (44:7–10). Finally, God tells them bluntly that he is going to destroy them (44:11–14). In a clear, almost boastful confession of guilt, the Judahites defiantly respond to Jeremiah that they would rather trust and worship another god (44:15–19). Jeremiah then restates that terrible judgment is coming upon them (44:24–28).

The judgment pronounced in Jeremiah 44 on these Judahites who fled to Egypt is in strong contrast to the *shalom* promised to those exiled in Babylon in 597 BC in Jeremiah 29 and to the new covenant promises of restoration in Jeremiah 30–33.

Jeremiah 45:1–5, the "deliverance oracle" concerning Baruch, is located chronologically in earlier years, during the fourth year of Jehoiakim (605 BC). It is placed here for literary and theological purposes, providing a contrasting and closing inclusio, as mentioned above.

Note also that Jeremiah 46 begins the Judgment on the Nations section of Jeremiah, but that the first nation listed is Egypt, continuing one of the themes in Jeremiah 44.

Historical and Cultural Background

Migdol and Tahpanhes (44:1) were fortress cities near Egypt's northeastern border in the Sinai. They would be among the first cities that travelers from Judah would encounter. Memphis (44:1) was on the Nile River, in the very heart of Egypt. The word translated as "Upper Egypt" refers to southern Egypt, which was upstream on the Nile. The mention of these four locations implies that the Judahites had settled all across Egypt. Perhaps time had elapsed since the arrival of the Judahites at Tahpanhes in 43:7, allowing them to continue to migrate throughout the country, or perhaps these are Judahites who had moved into Egypt earlier.

The goddess referred to as the Queen of Heaven (44:17) is probably a syncretistic adaptation of the Mesopotamian astral deity Ishtar, known through the region surrounding Israel and Judah as the goddess Asherah, consort of Baal. Underscoring the popularity of Asherah among the Judahites, archaeologists have uncovered over eight hundred figurine statues of this goddess from sites in Judah, more than half of which were found in Jerusalem.[1]

Interpretive Insights

43:13 *temple of the sun . . . sacred pillars.* Literally, this reads, "house of the sun." It probably refers to Heliopolis, an Egyptian city dedicated to the worship of the sun-god Re. The "sacred pillars" reference describes obelisks—tall, slender, four-sided shafts of rock that often adorned the entrances of Egyptian temples and for which Egypt was famous.

44:2 *You saw the great disaster I brought on Jerusalem.* The Hebrew grammar puts an emphasis on "you," implying something like "you yourselves saw." The phrase translated as "the great disaster" is literally "all the *ra'ah* [disaster, bad stuff, calamity, evil]." *Ra'ah* is a central theme of this unit, occurring fifteen times. The same *ra'ah* that they had seen fall upon Jerusalem (44:2, 3, 5) will now fall upon them (44:7, 9 [5x], 11, 17, 23, 27, 29; 45:5) if they persist in their disobedience and idolatry.

44:5 *burning incense to other gods.* Burning incense to gods was a common religious practice throughout the ancient Near East. While the actual sacrifice of animals (both the slaughter and burning) usually was done by priests, incense burning could be done by private citizens, even at home. In Jeremiah 44 the burning of incense to other gods is stressed as the representative act of idolatry that God objects to so angrily. Incense burning becomes the central issue in Jeremiah 44, occurring ten times (44:3, 5, 8, 15, 17, 18, 19, 21, 23, 25).

44:9 *Have you forgotten the wickedness committed by . . . kings . . . queens . . . you . . . your wives . . . ?* This verse repeats *ra'ah* ("disaster, bad stuff, calamity, evil") five times and mentions the wives twice. Literally, the verse reads, "Have you forgotten the *ra'ah* of your fathers and the *ra'ah* of the kings of Judah and the *ra'ah* of their wives and your *ra'ah* and the *ra'ah* of your wives?" Apparently, the women of Judah had played a major role in the burning of incense to other gods, probably a "family-oriented" worship at their houses instead of temple worship (see 19:13).

44:11 *I am determined to bring disaster on you.* Literally, this reads, "Behold I am setting my face against you for *ra'ah*." "To set one's face" is a Hebrew idiom for being very determined. The Hebrew word for "face," however, is also often used to represent God's special presence, so probably there are connotations of that here. The presence of God can bring great blessing or, as here, terrible judgment.[2] There is also a wordplay with 44:12, where in Hebrew the phrase "set their face" is used of the Judahites. Thus God "sets his face" to do *ra'ah* to those Judahites who "set their face" to go to Egypt in violation of his word.

to destroy all Judah. The word translated as "destroy" means "to cut off, remove, eradicate." This same word is used in 44:7 (translated as "cutting off") and 44:8 (translated as "destroy"). In the context of Jeremiah 44 it carries connotations of ending all family lineage continuation. Ironically, it is also the same word used to make ("cut") a covenant (31:31), and the dual nuance probably is not accidental. For these doubly disobedient people, God will not "cut" them a new covenant but will indeed "cut" them off from having any future at all.

44:15 *all the men who knew that their wives were burning incense to other gods.* The implication here is that the wives took the lead in burning incense to other gods, identified in the next verse as an astral deity, the Queen of Heaven. The point is not to exonerate the men but to demonstrate the family-wide acceptance of the idolatry.

all the men who knew . . . the women who were present—a large assembly . . . and all the people. This grouping implicates all the Judahites, but the added emphatic inclusion of the women is different from the inclusive groupings normally used elsewhere in Jeremiah. That is, earlier in the story it was the leaders of Judah who often were listed as groups in order to underline the culpability of the entire nation; here the women are included.

44:19 *did not our husbands know that we were making cakes impressed with her image . . . ?* There is no Hebrew word for "know" used in this verse ("Was it without our husbands that we made sacrificial cakes for her in her image?"), and it is ambiguous regarding whether the husbands merely know about what the women are doing or are actually participating (cf. 7:16–19, where entire families are involved). Archaeologists have discovered several molds with the images of goddesses in sites associated with baking.[3]

44:27 *For I am watching over them for harm, not for good.* The word translated as "watching" implies "to be vigilant" or "to watch carefully in order to accomplish something." It is the same word used in the wordplay on the almond branch in 1:12. "Harm" translates Hebrew *ra'ah* ("disaster, bad stuff, calamity, evil"), the word used repeatedly throughout Jeremiah to describe both the people's sin and God's judgment. This verse is a summary of the coming judgment on those in Egypt and proclaims the exact opposite of what was promised to the exiles in Babylon in 29:11.

Theological Insights

In the midst of national judgment on Israel/Judah, God always seems to have a remnant that finds salvation. This concept works at several levels in Jeremiah. As God destroys Jerusalem and Judah in 586 BC, he nonetheless promises a future for a remnant, those people who were exiled earlier in 597 BC (Jer. 29). Jeremiah 40–45 is demonstrating that those who remained in Judah after 586 BC and then fled to Egypt rejected their second chance and thus do not belong to the true remnant. The true remnant out of this group is represented by the stories of deliverance that form bookends for this section: Ebed-Melek (39:15–18) and Baruch (45:1–5).

Teaching the Text

The shocking thing in this story is that these Jews in Egypt could make such foolish choices in the face of such overwhelming rational evidence to the contrary. With the ruins of Jerusalem still smoldering, how could they ignore Jeremiah's words of warning? How could they possibly think that safety and peace for them would come from worshiping the Queen of Heaven and trusting in Egypt? Yet the tragic truth is, now as in the time of Jeremiah, people often have very short and selective memories; and it is amazing how irrational people can be when it comes to obeying the word of God. In like fashion, the shocking thing in the New Testament is that people encountered Jesus himself in person, even witnessing the miracles he performed, yet still rejected him. Sometimes today we evangelize under the illusion that if we make the message clear and logical enough, people will automatically accept the Lord because it is the rational or logical thing to do. Rational presentations of the gospel certainly are valuable and necessary, but the causes of true faith are complex and cannot be reduced to mere rational presentation. The New Testament teaches that the power of the Spirit plays an important role in guiding people, irrational as we are, to have faith in Christ, the only really rational thing to do.

As we have seen throughout Jeremiah, there are very serious consequences for those who reject God's clear word to them. God presented very strong evidence of his power and how his word always comes true. He even gave them a second chance, but to no avail. Many people today have heard the word of God proclaimed to them. They may have even seen his promises fulfilled in the lives of people they know. God is gracious and patient, often giving second (and third, fourth, and more) chances. But eventually he says that enough is enough, and the day of judgment comes.

This passage seems to imply that the Judahite women were leading the way as these families worshiped the Queen of Heaven. One lesson to be learned from this is that the power and influence of mothers and wives on the beliefs and worship practices of families should not be underestimated. Women today continue to be major influences on whether families are faithful to God. On the flip side, the men in this passage seem to cave in and go along meekly with the idolatrous practices of their wives. The men are, of course, held equally guilty. The lesson for men in the church today is to stand up and be leaders in their families in true faith and in the true worship of God.

The disobedient people in this story trusted in Egypt and in the Queen of Heaven to provide safety and well-being for them. What do people today trust in for their safety and well-being? Is their trust in God and his word? Or is it perhaps in things such as jobs, bank accounts, or stock markets?

As Ebed-Melek and Baruch demonstrate, even in the midst of terrible times and national judgment individuals continue to find God and be delivered. This holds true today as well. No matter how hostile and disbelieving a group of people can seem to be, there will always be those few individuals among them who see the truth and believe.

Illustrating the Text

Faithfulness to God is learned through family and community.

Bible: Proverbs 22:6 teaches, "Train children in the right way" (NRSV). Part of the Shema, the centerpiece of Jewish prayer, charges us to "impress" the words of the Lord on our children and to talk about God's commandments constantly from sunrise to sunset (see Deut. 6:4–9).

Ask for a show of hands regarding the question "Who taught you how to pray, read the Bible, and trust in God?" There are sure to be a diversity of responses, but many will likely respond, "My parents." Next, ask for a second show of hands regarding the question, "Where did you first make a commitment to the Lord?" Again, there are sure to be numerous different ways that God has reached out to people, but many will likely respond, "At camp" or "In church."[4]

Hymn: **"A Christian Home," by Barbara Hart.** In this hymn, set to Jean Sibelius's well-known tune "Finlandia," we find a beautiful prayer in which "ev'ry child is taught His love and favor." The verses build on this prayer, and the final verse proclaims, "Our homes are Thine forever!"—a declaration of consecration, offering our homes (and those in them) to God. This hymn can be used in congregational singing, in a ministry of music, or simply as a prayer used in a sermon or lesson. Since faithfulness to God is truly a family issue, praying for our homes and family members is essential.

Testimony: If you have the capacity to do so, create and show a short video. Assemble a series of people in your congregation looking at the camera and saying something like, "I thank God for my [mother, father, parents, grandparents] and how they have raised me to love and follow Jesus." Nothing fancy is needed, only heartfelt thanks expressed as a declaration to those who have taken family faith seriously.

Trust in anything other than God is misplaced trust.

Culture: According to a 2013 Nielsen report, the "holy grail" of a successful advertising campaign is consumer trust.[5] But our ability to trust has been undermined by many events over the last half century. Many of today's senior citizens were once the rebellious teenagers of the 1960s. They witnessed the assassinations of John F. Kennedy and Martin Luther King Jr. They watched the horror of the Vietnam War unfold each night on their television screens, and they endured the lies, cover-ups, and underhanded politics of the Watergate scandal and President Nixon's resignation. Add to that the number of fallen televangelists, President Clinton's liaison with Monica Lewinski, the 9/11 attacks, the Enron collapse, Bernie Madoff's Ponzi scheme, and more, and it is easy to understand why so many in the United States today are plagued with skepticism.

Judgment and Salvation

Big Idea

God in his sovereignty will bring judgment on prideful nations, but he will provide salvation for the remnant that truly believes.

Key Themes

- The prideful power of Egypt will crumble before God.
- God promises judgment on Egypt and on those who trust in Egypt.
- Yet God provides a brief and vague promise of a future for Egypt.
- God comforts a remnant of Israel with his presence and promise of restoration.

Understanding the Text

The Text in Context

Jeremiah 46–51 is appropriately referred to as the Judgment on the Nations. In 1:10 God appoints Jeremiah to be "over nations and kingdoms to uproot and tear down." The prophet fulfills this role in Jeremiah 46–51 as he prophesies judgment on the surrounding nations. The nations included in this list are arranged roughly in geographical order, moving from southwest to northeast: Egypt, Philistia, Moab, Ammon, Edom, Damascus, Kedar and Hazor, Elam, and Babylonia. Starting with Egypt (46:1–26) provides continuity with Jeremiah 43–44, which likewise includes judgment on Egypt. Ending with Babylonia is appropriate because Babylonia is the most powerful nation in the region, the one that brings the judgment on the other nations, including Judah, and the nation whose future most affects that of the remnant of Israel.

In the Septuagint, the early Greek translation of the Old Testament, the Judgment on the Nations unit (Jer. 46–51 in English Bibles) is placed right after 25:13.

After several chapters in chronological order, Jeremiah 46 (like Jeremiah 45) harkens back to an earlier time. Jeremiah 46:2 is tied to the Battle of Carchemish (605 BC), one of the most significant battles of the Old Testament era, in which Babylon, the new power in the region, defeated an alliance of Assyria and Egypt, the older powers in the region, dramatically altering the geopolitical landscape of the entire region. This battle marked the end of Egypt's position as an "international superpower," a status it had held for nearly two thousand years.

The brief positive prophecy of salvation for a remnant of Israel (46:27–28) at the end of Jeremiah 46 parallels earlier prophecies in which long judgment passages were concluded with short salvation oracles for those who symbolized the remnant. For example, Jeremiah 39 is about the judgment on the people living in Jerusalem, yet it concludes with deliverance for Ebed-Melek (39:15–18). Jeremiah 43:8–44:30 is about the coming judgment on Egypt and the Judahites living there, yet it concludes with salvation for Baruch. Jeremiah 46 follows this pattern. God will judge Egypt, but he will save a remnant of Israel (like Baruch) from among the nations.

Jeremiah 30:10–11, an oracle of deliverance that introduces the Book of Restoration (Jer. 30–33), is nearly identical to 46:27–28, which similarly and ironically seems to introduce the Judgment on the Nations unit.

After fourteen chapters of prose (Jer. 33–45), the text now returns to poetry for the Judgment on the Nations, with but a few introductory or summary verses in prose.

Historical and Cultural Background

Important for understanding Jeremiah 46 is the fact that as part of his involvement in the alliance with Assyria to confront Babylon, Pharaoh Necho of Egypt (reigned 610–595 BC) subdued Judah, defeating it in battle and killing King Josiah, the last good king of Judah (609 BC). Necho replaced him with Jehoiakim, the corrupt king who opposed Jeremiah and led Judah back into full-fledged idolatry.

Jeremiah 46:13 refers to another invasion of Egypt by the Babylonian king Nebuchadnezzar, but scholars are uncertain about which invasion this was. Suggested dates vary (601–600 BC, 582 BC, 568 BC).[1]

Interpretive Insights

46:2 *son of Josiah king of Judah*. A not-so-subtle mention of Josiah is a reminder that Pharaoh Necho had been the one to kill Josiah and to install Jehoiakim as king.

46:5 *terror on every side*. This phrase has been used several times in Jeremiah to describe confusion and terrifying situations (6:25; 20:3, 10; 49:29). Many of the terms of judgment on Judah used earlier in Jeremiah are employed in Jeremiah 46 in regard to Egypt.

46:9 *Cush . . . Put . . . Lydia*. These three nations are used as personifications of mercenary units in the Egyptian army. The mercenaries are mentioned as a group in 46:21. Cush (to the south of Egypt) and Put (probably modern Libya, to the west of Egypt) were under Egyptian control and regularly provided mercenaries for Egypt. The location of "Lydia" in this passage is uncertain.[2]

46:11 *Gilead . . . balm . . . Virgin Daughter . . . no healing.* Jeremiah employs much of the same imagery that he used of Judah in Jeremiah 1–29. The double reference to Egypt as God's "daughter" (46:11, 24) is surprising but reminds us that all people are God's children.[3]

46:18 *declares the King, whose name is the* LORD *Almighty.* Occurring frequently throughout Jeremiah is the phrase "oracle of the LORD," usually translated as "declares the LORD." In 46:18 the phrase is modified to "oracle of the King," which connects back in contrast to the mention of Pharaoh as king of Egypt (46:17), serving to clarify who "the King" really is: Yahweh ("the LORD") Almighty. As elsewhere throughout Jeremiah, the word translated as "Almighty" means "the armies" and carries military connotations. It is not just the king of Babylon (46:13) whom the king of Egypt has to worry about. Yahweh ("the LORD"), the real King and commander of a great heavenly army, is the one who is marching against him.

46:25 *Amon god of Thebes.* Amon, one of the most important gods of Egypt, was often merged with Ra, the sun-god, and called "Amon-Ra." He was known as the "king of the gods" in the Egyptian pantheon. Worship of Amon originated in and was centered in the Egyptian temple city of Thebes.[4]

on those who rely on Pharaoh. The word translated as "rely" is the same word translated as "trust" when used of Ebed-Melek's trust in God (39:18). The Hebrew reads, "on Pharaoh and on those who are trusting in him." "Those who trust in Pharaoh" would also include those Judahites in Jeremiah 44 who had fled to Egypt for protection.

46:26 *Egypt will be inhabited as in times past.* Although somewhat vague, this text does offer hope that Egypt will not be totally destroyed without any continuation of life. God does not describe it here in any detail, but he does declare that there will be a future for Egypt.

46:27 *Do not be afraid.* In Hebrew the second-person pronoun at the front of the verse connotes a very strong conjunctive contrast, "But you, do not be afraid, my servant Jacob." This same imperative, including the contrasting conjunction ("but you") at the front, occurs again in 46:28. The contrast is between the Egyptians, who should be afraid of the coming judgment (46:2–26), and the remnant of Israel, who should not be afraid, since God is with it and will save it.

Jacob, my servant . . . Israel. Jacob, the patriarchal father of the twelve tribes, was renamed "Israel" in Genesis 35:10. The two names used in synonymous parallel here harken back to the time before Israel split into two separate and hostile nations. Throughout the book of Jeremiah, God has referred to the prophets as his servants (e.g., 25:4; 26:5), to David as his servant (33:21–26), and even to Nebuchadnezzar as his servant (25:9; 27:6; 43:10), but only here in 46:27–28 and in the parallel passage 30:10–11 does he call Jacob/Israel his "servant." In the future, restored and regathered Israel will once again be the servant of God.

I will surely save you. The Hebrew verb used here is a participle, which normally describes an ongoing state of affairs rather than a specific event ("Behold, I am saving you," or "Behold, I am the one who is saving you").

your descendants. The word translated as "descendants" is literally "seed," no doubt an allusion to the fulfillment of the Abrahamic covenant, where God uses this word repeatedly in his promises to the patriarchs.

Jacob will again have peace. The first Hebrew verb used here is *shub*, which can mean "to turn to, turn away from, return, repent." As noted frequently, this word is used repeatedly throughout Jeremiah, often in wordplays. Here it could mean "Jacob will repent and have peace," or perhaps "Jacob will return [i.e., to the land] and have peace." In light of the frequent wordplays on *shub* throughout Jeremiah, it is possible that both nuances are suggested.

46:28 *"I am with you," declares the* LORD. It is the powerful presence of God that dispels all fear. This statement of God's presence also implies a covenant relationship between God and this remnant of Jacob. The phrase translated as "declares the LORD" is, more literally, "oracle of the LORD." It stresses the source of the statement (from "the LORD") and the certainty of the statement. In Hebrew it comes not at the end of the sentence but in the middle, after the imperative "Do not be afraid, Jacob my servant," and before the promise of God's presence, "I am with you." The startling thing is that God makes this promise in the context of the broken covenant and the departure of his presence from the temple, which is completely destroyed by the Babylonians.

I will not completely destroy you. The pronoun "you" is placed at the front of the sentence for contrast and stress, reading literally, "But you, I will not bring to an end." Once again the perpetuation by God of a remnant of Israel is implied. As Jeremiah 44 made clear, there were many Judahites in Egypt who were going to be destroyed and "cut off" from any participation in the coming restoration. Here, however, God clarifies that some Judahites who are now living among the nations will be delivered.

but only in due measure. The word translated as "measure" here is *mishpat* ("justice, judgment"). God says that he will discipline them justly. That is, God is not vengeful but acts according to justice.

Theological Insights

One of the central tensions at the heart of God's character as presented in the Old Testament is the tension between his righteous demand for justice and his desire to save people because he loves them. In 46:27–28 the text presents the tension between God's statement that he will save them (46:27) and the requirement that he enact justice against them because he cannot acquit them of their wrongdoing (46:28). In this chapter the tension is increased but not resolved. The question of how God will do this is left unanswered until the New Testament, when the atoning death of Jesus provides the means for God to save people while still enacting justice and due punishment for sin.

Teaching the Text

God in his sovereignty works both in our individual lives and in the great events of world history. God's gracious love and righteous judgment are demonstrated both at the personal level and at the international, even cosmic, level. So far in Jeremiah God has focused on the people of Judah in regard to judgment and salvation. Now, starting in Jeremiah 46, he explains that he is the sovereign King over all the earth, and that he will bring justice on all the earth, demonstrated by his judgment on those nations of the world that have lived by violence, especially violence against his people.

It is not the nations of the world with powerful armies that control world history but rather the sovereign Lord. Especially as nations turn away from God and embrace violence and injustice, it becomes critical for God's people to put their trust in him and not in the power of nations and empires.

In the midst of these strong passages of judgment on the nations, we find brief glimpses of hope. There is a future, God seems to suggest, even for Egypt. Although fairly faint in this passage, this is an allusion to the future gentile inclusion among the people of God, earlier implied by the deliverance of Ebed-Melek.

In the midst of war and exile, God comforts his people and tells them not to be afraid. Through it all his powerful presence sustains them and protects them. Likewise for us, living as exiles in this world, God's powerful presence brings assurance, comfort, and protection. Even as God's justice and judgment fall on sinful nations, God will save his people.

The tension between God saving his people and judging them with justice has been resolved for us in Jesus Christ. Judgment will fall on the sinful nations of the world, a judgment that we also deserve, but God in his grace saves us through the atonement of Christ, thus also allowing judgment and justice to prevail.

Illustrating the Text

The sovereign Lord, not the powerful nations, controls the world.

Scripture: In 2 Kings Elisha's servant awakens one morning and sees the powerful army of Aram coming for his master. Terrified, he runs to Elisha to warn him of the impending danger. Elisha calmly tells him not to worry, and then he prays, "Open his eyes, LORD, so that he may see" (2 Kings 6:17). Then the servant looks up and sees that the hillside is filled with horses and chariots of fire.

What the servant did not know, and what we often fail to realize, is that the powers of this world pale in comparison to the power of the Lord. Whenever we feel vulnerable and under attack spiritually, emotionally, physically, or financially, our natural reaction is to worry. However, we need to remember that we are not alone. The Lord is able to protect us in ways we cannot even imagine.

Testimony: On May 28, 1968, during the Vietnam War, Col. Roger Ingvalson ejected from a fighter jet. Moments later he landed with a thud in a dried-out rice paddy behind enemy lines. Seeing the enemy running toward him, and knowing that he would most likely be killed or captured, Roger asked Christ to "take over his life." For almost five years Ingvalson endured torture, starvation, disease, and isolation. In spite of his ordeal, he managed to survive. He later reflected on his time of solitary confinement. His captors thought he was really suffering by being alone. "Actually," he remembers, "I kept from going crazy by knowing that God was with me. I had a cellmate named Jesus Christ."[5]

After his release, Ingvalson said, "The Lord sustained me through 1,742 days of tragedy; nevertheless, I count my blessings. I was set free by the North Vietnamese Communists but had already been fully liberated by Jesus Christ."[6]

The Library of Congress Veterans History Project has video of an interview with Ingvalson. Part 2 contains Ingvalson's testimony of his conversion and capture.[7]

Jeremiah 46:1–28

Judgment on the Nations

Big Idea

God is at work throughout the world, judging and restoring.

Key Themes

- God is the powerful and sovereign King over all nations.
- God judges the nations especially for their arrogance.
- God is consistent and just in his judgments.
- Some gentiles will participate in the future restoration.

Understanding the Text

The Text in Context

The Judgment on the Nations unit (Jer. 41–51) opens with Egypt (the past power, in the southwest) and closes with Babylon (the current power, in the northeast). In between are seven oracles of judgment against smaller kingdoms (Philistia, Moab, Ammon, Edom, Damascus, Kedar and Hazor, and Elam). This list of neighboring nations is not all-inclusive; among others, conspicuously missing is the powerful city of Tyre (barely mentioned [47:4]). In contrast, Ezekiel, a contemporary of Jeremiah, spends three chapters on Tyre in his Judgment on the Nations unit (Ezek. 26–28). So these seven nations probably are functioning symbolically to represent "the rest of the world." The introductory verses for the first nation, Philistia (47:1), and the last nation, Elam (49:34), are quite similar, likewise suggesting that these seven judgment oracles form a literary unit.

Although judgment is the dominant theme, at the end of three of these oracles God promises restoration, to Moab (48:49), Ammon (49:6), and Elam (49:39). In contrast, he specifically states that Edom and Hazor will remain uninhabited (49:17–18, 33). The end of Philistia is implied in 47:4, while the final fate of Damascus (Syria) is left ambiguous.

Although some of the oracles in Jeremiah 47–49 probably were composed before the fall of Jerusalem, their placement here, between the narrative of the fall of Jerusalem (Jer. 37–44) and the postscript summary of that fall (Jer. 52), implies that they should be understood in that context. That is, after

Jerusalem and the temple were destroyed by the Babylonians, it was important to underscore the fact that God was still sovereign over all nations.

Historical and Cultural Background

Chemosh (48:7, 13, 46), the most important god in the Moabite pantheon, is one of the few foreign gods mentioned in Jeremiah 46–51. Chemosh was known as a war-god but also was closely associated with child sacrifice, for which this god acquired the biblical appellation "the detestable/vile god of the Moabites" (1 Kings 11:7; 2 Kings 23:13). Solomon introduced the worship of Chemosh into the life of Israel (1 Kings 11:7), and the child sacrifice so abhorred by God in Jeremiah probably was connected with the worship of Chemosh as well as Baal (Jer. 7:31; 19:4–5). Perhaps it is due to this connection that Chemosh is mentioned several times. Also note that the city of Carchemish (46:2) was the site of the decisive battle that crippled the Egyptians and brought Babylon to power. The meaning of "Carchemish" is "city of Chemosh."

Three of the seven oracles have introductions that tie the oracle to a specific historical setting. The first oracle (Philistia) dates to around 609 BC, the sixth oracle (Kedar/Hazor) to around 599–598 BC, and the final oracle (Elam) to around 597–595 BC. The other four are not dated, but the chronological order of these three suggests that the others fall in this range as well.

Interpretive Insights

48:13 *as Israel was ashamed when they trusted in Bethel.* After the northern kingdom, Israel, split from the southern kingdom, Judah, Jeroboam I installed calf idols at Bethel to replace the worship of God at Jerusalem.[1] Trust in this calf idol was hardly able to stop the invading Assyrians, who destroyed the northern kingdom in 722 BC.

48:15 *declares the King, whose name is the LORD Almighty.* Throughout Jeremiah the phrase "oracle of the LORD" (usually translated as "declares the LORD") is inserted frequently (173x), often in the middle of sentences, to add certainty and profundity to God's prophetic statements. On three occasions in the Judgment on the Nations (Egypt [46:18], Moab [48:15], Babylon [51:57]) this formula is differently worded, reading "oracle of the King" followed by a description of who the King is: Yahweh ("the LORD") Almighty. The certainty and profundity of the prophecy are emphasized by the fact that Yahweh is the true King of all. "Almighty" translates a word that means "armies." The entire phrase serves to present Yahweh as the sovereign King riding at the head of his great heavenly army.

48:26 *she has defied the LORD.* The word translated as "defied" basically means to "make great." A literal translation of this phrase is "she [Moab] has made herself great against the LORD." The phrase implied that Moab was attempting to exalt herself above God himself. This same phrase is repeated in 48:42, underscoring that pride and arrogance are among the central indictments against Moab.

48:29 *We have heard of Moab's pride . . . arrogance . . . insolence . . . conceit . . . haughtiness.* All five Hebrew words used here (and "pride" is used twice) connote arrogance and pride. Several of the words have the connotation of exalting oneself to be up high above all others in regard to status and power. The arrogance of Moab is stressed repeatedly throughout this chapter (48:26, 29, 30, 42).

48:36 *So my heart laments for Moab like the music of a pipe.* The word translated as "laments" actually refers to making a low-pitched sound. A literal rendering is "my heart makes a low-pitched sound like a flute for Moab." This is a colorful, poetic way for God to describe the fact that he is grieving over the judgment falling on Moab. A similar statement is made in Isaiah 16:11, but referring to a harp instead of a flute.

48:47 *I will restore the fortunes.* This phrase is a complex wordplay on the word *shub* ("to turn, return, cause to turn, repent"), forms of which occur twice in this phrase. It can mean "restore the fortunes" or "bring back / cause to return from captivity." The NIV uses both translations, depending on the context. God uses this same phrase in his promise of restoration to the Judahite exiles in Babylon (29:14), and then it is repeated numerous times in the Book of Restoration (30:3, 18; 31:23; 32:44; 33:7, 11, 26). In the context of the Judahites, "to bring back from captivity" fits, but in regard to the Moabites, "restore the fortunes" probably is better. The meaning for the Moabites is that they will not always know God's judgment, for in the future there will be a time of restoration. The nature of this restoration is ambiguous, yet to use the same words in promising restoration to the Moabites as used to promise restoration to the Judahites is obviously not accidental. It is indeed rather startling, strongly suggesting some similarity in participation in the future time of restoration. This identical phrase is also used of the Ammonites (49:6) and the Elamites (49:39).

49:16 *you who live in the clefts of the rocks.* The Edomites occupied the mountainous region to the southeast of Judah. This area is characterized by steep rock cliffs and high mountain crags, excellent for military defensive positions. Although constructed by the later Nabateans, the rock-cliff city Petra in modern Jordan lies in the heart of ancient Edom and illustrates the rocky, mountainous nature of the Edomite kingdom.

49:18 *As Sodom and Gomorrah . . . their neighboring towns.* The destruction of Sodom and Gomorrah, along with the other associated cities of the plain described in Genesis 19:1–29, was the Old Testament paradigmatic picture of God's wrath destroying sinful cities. In Jeremiah 23:14 God compares the people of Jerusalem to those at Sodom and Gomorrah. Jeremiah 49:18 is repeated in 50:40 in reference to the Babylonians. This analogy was especially pertinent for judgment on Edom because the region occupied by Sodom, Gomorrah, and the cities of the plain during the time of Abraham was controlled by the Edomites at the time of Jeremiah.

no one will live there; no people will dwell in it. The word translated as "dwell" connotes sojourning or temporarily living somewhere as a foreigner. This verse is saying that Edom will no longer have any permanent residents, nor even any temporary foreign residents. The phrase translated as "people" is *ben-'adam* (lit., "son of adam"). In this context *'adam* does refer to "people," but the name "Edom" (*'edom*) sounds very similar to *'adam*, so there is a certain ironic wordplay here as well.

Theological Insights

Much of the book of Jeremiah deals with the coming judgment on Judah and Jerusalem, followed by a future grace-driven restoration. One of the theological truths, however, emerging out of this Judgment on the Nations unit is that God is consistent in how he deals with people, whether they are from Israel or from the foreign nations.[2] God's justice is revealed in judgment for sin, both on Judah and on the nations, and his grace is revealed through his deliverance and restoration, again both for Judah and for the nations.

Teaching the Text

The destruction of Jerusalem and the temple by the Babylonians might have led some to question God's power in regard to the nations of the world. This section in Jeremiah reminds those exiles and their descendants that God is still in complete control over history and is sovereign over all nations. It is a reminder to us today that God is the Lord of history. While things happening in the world may confuse us or terrify us, the book of Jeremiah reminds us that God is sovereign over all the earth and over all peoples and nations.

Of all the sins of these nations that could have been cited and stressed, it is interesting to observe that "arrogance" was the one that God zeroed in on. A quick perusal of the rest of the Bible reveals that this is not unusual. God is very consistent in his disdain of prideful and arrogant human behavior, a theme running from Genesis to Revelation. In Jeremiah 47–49 we see that God is particularly angry at nations that elevate themselves above him. This is quite disturbing in light of the strong movement today within the United States public forum to marginalize the word of God completely and then arrogantly put forth alternative formulations of morality and truth that are in conflict with God's biblical revelation. Will God respond negatively to such arrogance?

Likewise, as individuals, it is important for us to grasp how much God dislikes prideful people. This passage in Jeremiah should encourage us to imitate the humility that Jesus demonstrates in the Gospels and to be humble before God and people.

Another aspect of God's character that we see in this passage is that he is consistent and just in his judgment. The same standard of justice that he applied to Israel he applied also to the rest of the world. But this is also true of his grace. It is because of grace that there will be a future restoration for a remnant of Israel; this same grace will be poured out on the gentile nations as well.

The theme of gentile inclusion among the people of God runs throughout the Old Testament as an important but secondary theme; then it moves to center stage in the book of Acts and in the Pauline Epistles. In the midst of these long judgment passages in Jeremiah 47–49, God sprinkles in promises of restoration. While these are ambiguous in Jeremiah, with few details, we see the definite beginning of that fulfillment in the book of Acts, as the gospel shifts to the gentiles and they become the main story line in the narrative of the people of God. That story continues today, as we strive to carry the gospel to all peoples across the entire world.

Illustrating the Text

God will one day judge the proud and arrogant.

Quote: In *Mere Christianity*, C. S. Lewis writes, "The essential vice, the utmost evil, is Pride. Unchastity, anger, greed, drunkenness, and all that, are mere flea bites in comparison: it was through Pride that the devil became the devil: Pride leads to every other vice: it is the complete anti-God state of mind."[3]

We can always trust in God's promise of restoration.

Hymn: "God Moves in a Mysterious Way," by William Cowper. This hymn, reportedly the last one that Cowper (1731–1800) wrote, charges us to trust God to bring about his sovereign will: "Judge not the Lord by feeble sense, but trust Him for His grace."

Christian Life: All of us have had times when it felt as if life was put on hold. Maybe we applied to college, or interviewed for a job, or reached a place of uncertainty in a relationship with someone who really mattered to us. At such times we are often forced to simply wait.

At first most of us wait with a certain amount of anticipation and hope for what might be, but as time passes, our hopes begin to fade into worries.

The longer we wait, the less we allow ourselves to believe that things will turn out in our favor, and mentally we begin to fear the worst.

The stories of Scripture were written for just such occasions. Again and again we read about people such as Joseph, Abraham, Hannah, Moses, David, and Paul, and what we discover is that at some point in their lives all of them were forced to wait on the Lord. Those who have invested their lives in the reading of Scripture know full well that God's timing is rarely in line with ours, but his promises are true.

As the great British preacher Charles Spurgeon once said, "A Bible that's falling apart usually belongs to someone who isn't." People who invest their time reading God's word know that his sovereign will is at work in the world even when we do not see it.

God is actively working out his will behind the scenes of life.

Scripture: In Judges 7:9–15 Gideon is about to go into battle against the Midianite forces. He knows that he is outnumbered, and fear begins to play with his thoughts. On the night before the battle, God brings Gideon to the edge of the enemy camp and allows him to overhear the fears of the opposing forces. As Gideon eavesdrops on their conversation, he realizes that God is already waging a war in their minds. The story serves as a reminder that God is working to bring about his will in the world in ways we may not see or anticipate.

The End of Babylon and the Future of Israel

Big Idea

The end of Babylon is contrasted with the everlasting restoration of God's people.

Key Themes

- God is extolled for his power and justice.
- God will destroy Babylon for what it did to Jerusalem.
- The fate of Babylon is contrasted with the restoration of Israel.
- The future restoration will be characterized by forgiveness of sins.

Understanding the Text

The Text in Context

The oracle against Babylon (Jer. 50–51) brings the Judgment on the Nations section (Jer. 46–51) to a climactic close. Babylon was the reigning power that had been the instrument of judgment against the other nations, including Judah. Although God had used the Babylonians to bring about his judgment, God still holds the Babylonians accountable for their violence and atrocities, along with their pride and imperialistic expansion. As the climax of the Judgment on the Nations section, Jeremiah 50–51 is by far the longest and most graphic of the judgments on the surrounding nations.

The oracle against Babylon has a short prose opening (50:1) and closing (51:59–64). The rest of the unit is in poetry typical of the poetic judgment language against Judah in Jeremiah 1–29. Jeremiah 50–51 is a loosely organized collection of short oracles of judgment on Babylon, with several contrasting passages of restoration and/or vindication for united Israel and Judah sprinkled in (50:4–5, 20, 33–34; 51:5, 10).

Historical and Cultural Background

Jeremiah 51:59 provides the historical setting for Jeremiah's oracle of judgment against Babylon. In 593 BC, four years after the exile of 597 BC, King

Zedekiah, the Judahite puppet king appointed by the Babylonians, makes a visit to his masters in Babylon. Accompanying him on this trip is an official, Seraiah, who probably is the brother of Jeremiah's scribe, Baruch. Jeremiah writes what is now Jeremiah 50–51 and then sends this document with Seraiah to those exiles in Babylon.

What did become of ancient Babylon after Jeremiah's prophecy? The Persian king Cyrus, along with the Medes who were now under his control, humbled Babylon by capturing it without a fight in 539 BC. This was the beginning of the end of Babylon, for never again was it even an independent entity, much less a world power. Over the next three hundred years, Babylon continued to slowly decline, dismantled in stages by the Persians, Alexander the Great, the Seleucids, and the Parthians. By the second century BC, Babylon was nothing but a desolate ruin, just as foretold in Jeremiah 50–51. Thus Babylon went from being the most prestigious and spectacular city in the world to being an insignificant pile of rubble.[1]

Interpretive Insights

50:1 *through Jeremiah the prophet.* The Hebrew reads, "by the hand of Jeremiah the prophet." Of the many verses that refer to the Lord speaking through or to Jeremiah, this is the only time that "by the hand of Jeremiah" is used. Perhaps this draws a contrast to the numerous other places in Jeremiah where "the hand of Nebuchadnezzar" or "the hand of the Babylonians" is used to refer to their power in conquering and/or subduing people in judgment (e.g., 27:6; 32:4; 34:3; 38:3; 46:26). Thus the final word on judgment comes by the hand of Jeremiah, not the hand of Nebuchadnezzar.

50:2 *Bel . . . Marduk.* "Bel" is a title that essentially means "lord," similar to the name "Baal" in the Canaanite pantheon. In earlier periods the name "Bel" was associated with numerous Mesopotamian deities, especially the Sumerian storm-god Enlil. By the time of Jeremiah, in Babylonia the term was associated with Marduk, the primary god of the Babylonians, who was then referred to as "Bel Marduk." Thus "Bel" and "Marduk" are not the names of two different gods but rather two different names for the same god.[2]

50:4 *the people of Israel and the people of Judah together.* Israel and Judah had been separate nations and hostile enemies since the civil war that followed Solomon's reign (931/930 BC). Israel as a political entity disappeared in 722 BC when the Assyrians destroyed the country. Yet now the images of restoration in Jeremiah show the two nations back together in unity.

will go in tears to seek the LORD their God. The Hebrew text has two parallel clauses reading, "Weeping they will come, and the LORD their God they will seek." Weeping implies coming to God in repentance. The word translated as "seek" is the same word used in 29:13. With God as the object, it implies worship, striving to move into his presence, seeking favor rather than seeking an oracle.

50:5 *bind themselves to the LORD in an everlasting covenant.* The word translated as "bind" refers to joining someone or to becoming part of a group. Here the implication is that they will be seeking to approach God and to become part of his people again in a special eternal covenant relationship. The "everlasting covenant" refers to the "new covenant" of 31:31–34.

50:13 *because of the LORD's anger she will not be inhabited.* The word translated as "anger" implies a strong wrath or rage. In 21:5 and 32:37 it is used of God's rage against Judah and its inhabitants. Jeremiah 10:10 declares that "the nations cannot endure his wrath." Babylon will be totally desolate, with no inhabitants, precisely because of God's great wrath against it.

50:20 *Israel's guilt, but there will be none . . . the sins of Judah . . . none will be found.* In Hebrew the phrases "guilt of Israel" and "sins of Judah" are in poetic parallel. That is, the text says the same basic thing twice. No one will be able to find the sins or iniquities of God's restored people. This is an amazing and startling statement, for Jeremiah has listed their numerous sins at length throughout the book.

for I will forgive the remnant I spare. The context introduced by 50:18 suggests a portrayal of God in these verses as a conquering King issuing verdicts of judgment or of blessing, but the word *salah* ("to forgive, pardon") carries relational connotations. Compare this with 50:34, where God plays the role of family member advocate (kinsman-redeemer). "The remnant I spare" refers to those who survive the Babylonian destruction and who will be present and repentant when God inaugurates his future restoration. Remember that this oracle (Jer. 50–51) was sent to those in Babylon who had been exiled in 597 BC and who serve, at least representatively, as the remnant (see Jer. 29).

50:29 *she has defied the LORD, the Holy One of Israel.* The word translated as "defied" indicates acting with insolence or arrogance toward someone, especially in a proud or even rebellious way. Babylon's actions against God are not only defiant but also insulting. Often in judgment texts like these the power or reign of God is stressed, but here it is his holiness. Remember that the Babylonians destroyed the temple in Jerusalem and carried off all the sacred utensils and other items used in the worship of God, an insolent action against his holiness.

50:31 *declares the Lord, the LORD Almighty.* The phrase "oracle of the LORD" ("declares the LORD") occurs frequently in Jeremiah (173x), often in the middle of sentences, to add certainty to God's prophetic statements. Here that formulaic phrase is noticeably different, reading "oracle of the Lord." The word translated as "Lord" is *'adonay* ("lord, master"). It is a title used to address someone of higher standing, like the king. The Lord (*'adonay*) is then identified clearly as "the LORD ["Yahweh," God's covenant name] Almighty," connoting that he is the leader of a great heavenly army. These three aspects of God's name ("Lord," "LORD," "Almighty") are used to underscore the ridiculous and insulting arrogance of Babylon.

50:34 *their Redeemer is strong.* "Their" refers to the people of Israel and Judah (50:33). "Redeemer" (*go'el*) refers to one who rescues a family member from a difficult legal situation. That is, God takes this personally. The family connotations of this word are strong, and thus some translations opt for "Kinsman-Redeemer." This is a startling concept: the Lord Almighty acts like a close relative to Israel and seeks to intervene on its behalf to deliver it from a difficult legal situation.

He will vigorously defend their cause. The legal terminology used here continues the legal setting implied by the term *go'el* ("Redeemer") used above, and the Hebrew legal term *rib* is used three times. The noun form refers to a legal case (NIV: "cause"). The verb form refers to trying the case or contending with someone in court. The grammatical form of the verbs stresses the certainty or full extent of the verb (NIV: "vigorously defend"). God, the "close relative" of Israel, will most certainly and powerfully present his case, thus delivering Israel and bringing turmoil to Babylon.

Theological Insights

This passage points to a future time when Israel and Judah's relationship with God will be restored and a time when he will forgive them for their sin. It is rather incredible that God would take them back, given the terrible indictments against them that Jeremiah proclaimed so eloquently in Jeremiah 1–29. Yet this text underscores God's deep capacity for complete forgiveness and thus a complete and permanent renewal of the relationship (50:4–5, 20). When in the future his people will return and repent, God will respond with complete forgiveness.

Teaching the Text

As Jerusalem falls and the tattered remnant of Judah trudges off into exile, God reminds his people that he is the all-powerful God, and that he will act to bring about ultimate justice. In our world today, no matter how chaotic or confusing world events may seem, it is critical to remember that God sits on his throne and rules over the entire world, including all the nations. He will ultimately bring complete justice to the world through the inauguration of his kingdom. Thus we should never panic or despair.

In these two chapters, at one of the lowest and most humanly discouraging points in Israel's history, God reminds his people that there are two interrelated sides of his ultimate plan. He will graciously restore his repentant people as he also judges all who arrogantly defy him and refuse to recognize his sovereignty. The contrast in these two consequences cannot be overstressed, whether in Jeremiah's day or today. God offers forgiveness and total pardon to those who come to him through faith in Jesus Christ. Those who arrogantly reject this offer, however, will be like the Babylonians and will experience God's wrath and judgment.

In this passage we see several wonderful aspects of the character of God. As a close relative, he defends our case in court. Then as the judge, he is convinced by that defense and pardons all our sin. His pardon/forgiveness is so complete that our sins can no longer even be found. The means to this reality is not explained in Jeremiah; it awaits the revelation of Jesus Christ in the New Testament. But in these texts that promise the new covenant and the

The Prophecy about Babylon

Because Babylon was not destroyed through a major battle and siege as portrayed in the poetry of Jeremiah 50–51, some "prophecy writers" in the 1990s concluded that Babylon must be rebuilt and made into a major world capital again so that it could be destroyed literally as Jeremiah predicted.[a] This view, however, suffers from a misunderstanding of how Old Testament prophecy works. First of all, recall that these prophecies in Jeremiah 50–51 are poetic, filled with colorful figures of speech. The central thrust of the prophecy—Babylon will go from being the most powerful city to a desolate ruin—did indeed come true. But the imagery of soldiers with swords and arrows that Jeremiah described does not demand a literal fulfillment of actual soldiers with swords and arrows.

Also it is important to recall the conditional aspects of prophecy that God describes in Jeremiah 18, where he teaches that the enactment of God's prophecies of judgment is conditioned on the response of the people who are being warned. It is

significant to note that when Jerusalem surrendered to the Babylonians in 597 BC, the people dodged the destruction that Jeremiah had been warning them about. Yet later, when Jerusalem failed to surrender to the Babylonians in 587–586 BC, the city was utterly destroyed, as Jeremiah had foretold. In like fashion, when the armies of Cyrus approached Babylon in 539 BC, the people assassinated their king and surrendered to Cyrus, even welcoming him. Perhaps this is a parallel to the situation in Jerusalem, and the city of Babylon delayed its total demise (physically) until later.

Also, because Babylon had destroyed Jerusalem, Babylon became the paradigmatic enemy of God's people in later biblical references (Zech. 5:5–11; 1 Pet. 5:13; Rev. 17–18), as well as in nonbiblical Jewish literature (*Sibylline Oracles* 5.155–70), a theme that started in Genesis 11 with the tower of Babel. This does not point to a reconstructed Babylon in our times but rather represents a figurative use of "Babylon" as the symbol of opposition to God.[b]

[a] See, for example, Dyer, *Rise of Babylon*; Chambers, *Palace for the Antichrist*.
[b] Pate and Hays, *Iraq*, 90–92, 100–112.

wonderful restoration that will accompany it, the essence of New Testament grace and justification is foreshadowed for us quite clearly.

Illustrating the Text

God promises both restoration and judgment.

Object Lesson: (This lesson would be particularly effective during a children's time at worship.) Show a coin, and explain that it has two sides, heads and tails. Then toss it into the air, and have someone call it. Then explain that the Bible, like the coin, has two sides. It contains both warnings and promises. Judgment and restoration are the currency of God, and each one of us has to make the call to put trust in him and follow his word or to ignore his warning.

History: Historically, civilizations go through cycles. They rise and they fall. They wax and wane with a predictable regularity. The greatness that once was Assyria, Babylon, Egypt, Rome, the Mayans, the Ming Dynasty, and the Vikings are now reduced to relics displayed in the corners of museums. And the constant, the one thing that all of them have in common, is that at their height they had a sense of arrogance and invincibility as well as a serious moral decline. And inevitably, at some point, there arose a prophet like Jeremiah who issued a warning of repentance, and just as inevitably the warning was ignored.

Like those who heard Jeremiah's warning, many in the United States today want to believe that what is will always be. History and Scripture, however, tell us otherwise. We too are destined to go the way of all flesh. The question is not "Will it happen?" but "*When* will it happen?" Knowing that, Christians must put their trust not in the things of this world but in its Creator and his word.

Only God can completely restore our lives.

Visual: A number of manufacturers have recently started selling a new 100-percent acrylic resurfacing product. It promises to restore old, cracked, and splintered wood and concrete decks and patios. The coating rolls on like paint but fills in cracks up to one-quarter inch thick with a barefoot-friendly, multicolor, durable surface that will resist fading and mildew. A sample of the product can be purchased at most home improvement stores if you want to use it as an illustration. First show an old surface and then a freshly resurfaced one. Explain that God promises to restore us like new and to forgive us in Jesus Christ, not just cover up our old sins.

Christian Music: The worship song "Create in Me a Clean Heart," based on Psalm 51:10–12, speaks to our need for restoration.

The End of Jerusalem, Yet Hope for the Future

Big Idea

Even in the context of imminent and well-deserved judgment, God offers hope.

Key Themes

- God's anger banishes sinful Judah from his presence.
- The punishment on Jerusalem is most severe on its leaders.
- The furnishings of the temple, which had been used in Judah's hypocritical worship, are also taken to Babylon.
- Even as Jerusalem falls, hope is given to the exiles in Babylon.

Understanding the Text

The Text in Context

Jeremiah 51:64 ("The words of Jeremiah end here") indicates that the prophecies and narratives of Jeremiah conclude at the end of Jeremiah 51. Jeremiah 52, therefore, seems to have been added by someone else as a historical summary, recapping what happened to Jerusalem and the exiles, once again adding emphasis to the significance of the destruction of Jerusalem and the exile. This basic story is told in similar fashion four times in Scripture (2 Kings 24:18–25:21; 2 Chron. 36:11–21; Jer. 39:1–10; 52:1–27). The account in Jeremiah 52 is very similar to the account in 2 Kings 24:18–25:21, and the closing verses about Jehoiachin (Jer. 52:31–34) are nearly identical to 2 Kings 25:27–30, the text that closes out the story of Israel that runs from Genesis 12 to 2 Kings.

Jeremiah 52 has several features that are characteristic of 1–2 Kings and 2 Chronicles. The naming of the king's mother (52:1), for example, is common in those books, occurring twenty-six times. Likewise, the phrase "he did evil in the eyes of the LORD" (52:2) is the most frequent negative assessment of the bad kings in 1–2 Kings and 2 Chronicles, occurring twenty-nine times. Also, the story of Jerusalem's fall in Jeremiah 39–44 features Jeremiah as one of the central characters, but he is not even mentioned in Jeremiah 52 or in 2 Kings.

Jeremiah 52 breaks down into six parts: the negative fate of Zedekiah and his court (52:1–11); the destruction of Jerusalem (52:12–16); a description of the items taken from the temple by the Babylonians (52:17–23); the execution of priests and other leaders (52:24–27); a list of the exiles (52:28–30); and the positive fate of Jehoiachin (52:31–34). The opening account of Zedekiah's negative fate and the closing account of Jehoiachin's positive fate form strong contrasting bookends for the chapter. Zedekiah is blinded, shackled, and put into prison "till the day of his death" (52:11), while Jehoiachin is released from prison, treated kindly, and given a seat of honor "till the day of his death" (52:31–34).

Historical and Cultural Background

Most of the chapter focuses on recounting the fall of Jerusalem to the Babylonians in 586 BC. The earlier exile of 597 BC is mentioned in 52:28. A third exile, in 582 BC, is also mentioned in 52:30. This exile, not mentioned anywhere else in the Bible, probably was related to the murder of Gedaliah and the other rebellious acts of the remaining Judahites in the land in the aftermath of the destruction of Jerusalem (Jer. 40–41).

An ancient tablet discovered in the excavations of Babylon contains an accounting list of food rations from the king's palace that were allocated to various people. Jehoiachin is one of those mentioned on the list.[1]

In 562 BC Nebuchadnezzar died, and his son Amel-marduk (biblical name "Awel-Marduk") succeeded him on the throne of Babylon and released Jehoiachin. In the biblical world at this time, for a new king to release some distinguished captives or prisoners from the earlier administration was not unusual.[2]

Interpretive Insights

52:2 *he did evil in the eyes of the* LORD. This is a summary statement of Zedekiah's reign. The word translated as "evil" is *ra'ah*, one of the most frequently used terms in Jeremiah. When used of people, it refers to "bad stuff" in general, often translated by the NIV as "evil."

52:3 *because of the* LORD's *anger . . . he thrust them from his presence.* The Hebrew implies that the Lord's anger grew to the extent that he finally had to drive the people from his presence (NRSV: "so angered the LORD that he expelled them from his presence"). The tragedy is not only the destruction of Jerusalem and the exile to Babylon; the sin of Judah and Jerusalem has resulted in the loss of God's presence, which encapsulates his power, his blessings, his holiness, and his covenant relationship. This recalls Genesis 3, where God's presence was lost as Adam and Eve were expelled from the garden. Indeed, the theme of God's presence as the essence of the relationship between God and his people is a central biblical theme, stretching from Genesis to Revelation.

52:6 *the famine in the city.* Throughout the book Jeremiah repeatedly warns about famine as a consequence of the coming Babylonian invasion and siege (e.g., 18:21; 21:7–9; 38:2).

the people. The Hebrew reads "people of the land." In Jeremiah the phrase "people of the land" refers to those in Jerusalem and Judah who were not part of the royal court. It makes sense that those outside the royal court with its princes and officials would run out of food first.

52:8 *Jericho.* As discussed in 39:5, the mention of Jericho is significant, especially in the closing episode of Israel's story of living in the promised land. The Israelites' life in the land started with Joshua's capture of the city of Jericho. Now it is Jerusalem that is falling, and Israel's leader is captured near Jericho as he tries to flee the promised land.

52:9 *Riblah in the land of Hamath.* The region of Hamath and the city of Riblah are located in Syria, to the northwest of Damascus. Nebuchadnezzar established a central camp here, where he could also keep an eye on some enemies to the north, while his commander Nebuzaradan actually supervised the siege of Jerusalem in person.

52:10 *the king . . . killed the sons . . . also killed all the officials.* The word translated as "killed" normally is used of slaughtering an animal in sacrificial worship. This word probably is used to paint the graphic image of these men being executed in the same helpless fashion as sacrificial animals are sacrificed. These are the men who had been persecuting Jeremiah and trying to kill him.

52:11 *where he put him in prison.* Just as Zedekiah allowed Jeremiah to be put into prison (38:5), so now Zedekiah goes into prison, blinded and alone.

52:17 *the bronze pillars, the moveable stands and the bronze Sea.* The bronze pillars were the two huge freestanding pillars named "Jachin" and "Boaz" that stood at the temple entrance (1 Kings 7:15–22). The moveable stands were freestanding bronze bases that held lavers (1 Kings 7:38) used for washing and cleansing after burnt offerings. The bronze Sea was a large round tank, approximately seven feet high and fifteen feet in diameter, with a capacity of ten thousand gallons of water, also used for priestly washings.[3] Jeremiah 52:17–23 gives an extensive and detailed description of the furnishings and utensils plundered from the temple. This and the mention of King Solomon (52:20) perhaps serve to remind the Judahites of how far they have fallen. It is also possible that the citation of this extensive list is a mocking reminder of those days when these items were being made and put into the temple as a symbol of pride and blessing (1 Kings 7).

52:28–30 *the number of the people Nebuchadnezzar carried into exile . . . 3,023 . . . 832 . . . 745.* The first number (3,023) represents those exiled in 597 BC, and the second number (832) represents the second exile of 587 BC. The third number (745) is dated to 582 BC and probably corresponds to the reprisal for the murder of Gedaliah (41:1–3). The numbers here probably include only the adult men, and perhaps only the leaders. Note the descending number of people carried into exile and the probable rhetorical significance. These probably should be viewed as the survivors, the remnant that God protected in order that there might be a future for Israel. The larger number (3,023) came in 597 BC when Jehoiachin surrendered to Nebuchadnezzar without a fight, thus implicitly bowing to the will of God, since God had raised up the Babylonians to judge Jerusalem. The rebellions and refusal to submit resulted in fewer survivors carried into exile.

52:31 *Jehoiachin.* Jehoiachin serves as the representative or perhaps the symbol of those exiled in 597 BC. These were the people to whom Jeremiah's letter, now Jeremiah 29, is addressed, telling them to settle down and find *shalom* in Babylon. The positive account of what happened to Jehoiachin in 52:31–34 illustrates the short-term fulfillment of Jeremiah 29.

king of Judah. Jehoiachin served as king in Judah for less than one year, in 598–597 BC. Now, after thirty-six years in exile in Babylon (582 BC), he is still called "king of Judah." This probably is a reminder of Jeremiah's prophecies regarding the future Davidic king (e.g., 23:5; 30:9; 33:17–26). Even though Jerusalem is destroyed and most of Zedekiah's family is executed, the lineage of David survives through Jehoiachin.

Awel-Marduk. Marduk was one of the central Babylonian gods. The son of Nebuchadnezzar who becomes the new king is Amel-Marduk, whose name means "man of Marduk." Jeremiah 52:31, however, calls him "Awel-Marduk" (ESV, NRSV: "Evil-merodach"), which in Hebrew means "foolish Marduk," probably an intentional insulting wordplay on the new Babylonian king. Amel-Marduk reigned for just two years (562–560 BC) and then was assassinated.

Theological Insights

The brevity and ambiguity of the snapshot of hope presented at the very end of Jeremiah is instructive. We like our prophecies and biblical teachings to be crystal clear, with modern precision. Here, however, God gives the exiles (and us) only a brief concluding episode in the life of a man we barely know. But this moderate "restoration" of Jehoiachin is like the faint light of the sunrise, a signal that the dawn of God's great restoration is indeed coming. Several of the promises in Jeremiah 29 are fulfilled in Jehoiachin, implying that the rest of the promises, as well as the spectacular new covenant, cannot be far behind. The final verses about Jehoiachin are the first streaks of light at dawn, and Jesus Christ will be the sunrise that brings the new day.

Teaching the Text

Living in God's presence is perhaps the single most important factor in finding meaning and blessing in this life, both for these ancient Judahites and for us. The tragedy of this story is not just that they lost the promised land but that they were removed from the very presence of God. Those today who do not know Christ are separated by sin from the presence of God. They cannot know him in any effective way or worship him meaningfully or enjoy the wonderful blessings of his presence. Only through Christ can their sin be forgiven and can they then come into the presence of God.

For Christians, there is a warning here as well. Our sins are forgiven in Christ, but repeated and unrepentant sin negatively impacts our relationship with God and the blessings that his close presence brings. It threatens our "nearness" to him and hinders the fellowship we have with God through the Holy Spirit. It steals our joy in life and cripples our ability to worship him meaningfully.

In this passage we also see yet another example of how angry God becomes with the leaders of Judah because of their opposition to him and their disastrously negative influence on the people. He holds them accountable, and when the judgment comes, it is particularly terrible for them. This text is a warning to leaders who oppose God and his message. Likewise, it is a sober reminder to all of us who play a role in leading God's people that godly and obedient leadership is critically important in the life of God's people.

Not only are the rebellious leaders killed and the disobedient people sent into exile, but also the utensils from the temple—those items that played a critical role in the rituals of the temple—are "sent" into exile away from God's presence. The book of Jeremiah describes how the people had assumed that maintaining the basic rituals of the temple would ensure their protection and well-being even if they worshiped other gods (e.g., Jer. 7). The mention of these "sacred utensils" being carried away as the temple is dismantled is a final reminder in the book of Jeremiah that ritualistic religious practice, devoid of any real relationship with God or any obedience to his call for justice, is worthless, and such ritualism certainly will not cover over our sin or provide a means of deliverance from judgment.

Yet in spite of all the judgment prophesied and realized in the book of Jeremiah, the final brief episode is one of hope for the exiles in Babylon. A descendant of David finds blessing in Babylon. Some of the promises of Jeremiah 29 are realized. Hope is dawning. Often in our lives God may not provide us with the ultimate rescue or total deliverance. He may give us but a brief glimpse of the future restoration and then ask us to persevere as we trust in that hope. We have been shown a brief glimpse of the kingdom of Christ. Yet as we long for the ultimate realization of that kingdom, like these exiles, we embrace the promise of the future with faith, leading our lives in obedience to God, even if still in exile.

Illustrating the Text

Even in the worst of times God continues to offer hope.

Film: *The Lord of the Rings: The Two Towers.* In many of the best stories, no matter how bleak things become, there is a promise of hope. Evil will be defeated. Right will ultimately get the upper hand. Darkness will turn to dawn. They give us a glimpse into a world of nobler and truer values that in their own way reflect the kingdom of God.

Likewise, in the 2002 film adaptation of J. R. R. Tolkien's epic novel *The Two Towers*, Sam gives a speech that inspires hope. "It's like in the great stories, Mr. Frodo," he says, "the ones that really mattered. Full of darkness and danger they were. And sometimes you didn't want to know the end, because how could the end be happy? How could the world go back to the way it was when so much bad had happened? But in the end it's only a passing thing, this shadow. Even darkness must pass."

Like the faint glow of an early morning sunrise, the restoration of Jehoiachin is God's candle of hope in a dark situation.

It is often darkest just before the dawn.

History: A thirty-five-year-old American lawyer, Francis Scott Key, was a reluctant witness to the shelling of Fort McHenry in the harbor of Baltimore by the British navy during the War of 1812. He was under arrest by the British on a vessel in the harbor, and he watched the intensive shelling under the darkness of night. The bombardment was so intense that he was sure his compatriots had been defeated. But as the sun broke over the eastern horizon, he caught a glimpse of the flag fluttering gloriously over the fort. With pen in hand, he scratched out the words to the now famous "Star-Spangled Banner."

Point out that, like Key, we sometimes sit in the darkness and see little hope of victory, but one day soon the light of the Prince of Glory will break across the sky, and we will know we did not hope in vain.

Quote: In his book *A Long Obedience in the Same Direction*, Eugene Peterson gives a definition of hope:

> Hoping does not mean doing nothing. . . . It is the opposite of desperate and panicky manipulations, of scurrying and worrying. And hoping is not dreaming. It is not spinning an illusion or fantasy to protect us from our boredom or our pain. It means a confident, alert expectation that God will do what he said he will do. It is imagination put in the harness of faith. It is a willingness to let God do it his way and in his time.[4]

Introduction to Lamentations

Title and Genre

In Hebrew the title of this book is *'eykah* ("how"), which is the first word in the Hebrew text of Lamentations 1:1. The Septuagint (LXX), the early Greek translation of the Old Testament, gave it the descriptive title *Threni*, which means "lamentations." This was followed by the Latin Vulgate translation, which titled it *Lamenta*, also meaning "lamentations." Thus modern English translations have followed the Greek and Latin tradition in calling this book "Lamentations."

"Lamentations" is an apt title, for the book consists of five laments or lamentations. A lament is a sad, agony-filled cry of mourning, usually in poetic form. There are numerous laments in the book of Psalms, where either an individual or the community cries out to God in pain and suffering. In Psalms, however, the laments almost always end with a strong affirmation that God will indeed provide deliverance or with a vow of praise to God because of his great deliverance. The book of Lamentations, by contrast, has statements of hope, but these are somewhat tentative and faint. In the lament psalms the affirmations of faith in God's deliverance are central, while in the laments of Lamentations the cry of pain and suffering is central.

Similar literature has been discovered in other cultures of the ancient Near East. Some of these ancient cultures produced corporate "city laments" that bemoaned the destruction of prominent cities.[1] The closest genre to lament in our culture today probably is American blues music or the "funeral dirge" of the last century.

Location in the Canon and Authorship

In the Hebrew editions of the Bible, Lamentations is anonymous. It is not located right after Jeremiah but rather in the third section of the canon called the "Writings." Following Ecclesiastes and preceding Esther in the Hebrew Bible, the book of Lamentations is part of a five-book section called the *Megillot* ("Scrolls"), which is read in Jewish tradition on major annual festivals. Lamentations is read on the ninth of Ab, a date that commemorates major disasters in Jewish history (especially the fall of Jerusalem). Lamentations is followed by Esther and then Daniel, books that deal with the trials and difficulties of the exile.[2]

In the Septuagint, Lamentations is placed near Jeremiah, often immediately after the book of Jeremiah. In the fourth-century AD Greek Bible called "Codex Sinaiticus," Lamentations starts on the same page on which Jeremiah ends, without even a page break. Furthermore, in the Septuagint there is an additional introductory verse, missing in the Hebrew text, which reads, "And it happened, after Israel was taken captive and Jerusalem was laid waste, Jeremiah sat weeping and gave this lament over Jerusalem and said."[3] Since this introductory verse is not in the Hebrew text, most modern translators conclude that it is not part of the original text, and thus they omit it. On the other hand, practically all modern English translations follow the order of the Septuagint in placing Lamentations directly after Jeremiah.

Because the Hebrew text is anonymous, many scholars are cautious about attributing Lamentations to Jeremiah. Others, especially those who place a higher emphasis on the Septuagint and early church tradition, often accept the tradition that ascribes Lamentations to Jeremiah. Some scholars conclude that there is insufficient evidence to make a firm and final decision.[4] The view of this commentary is that since the Hebrew text is anonymous, the issue of authorship must not have been critically important when the text was written. Thus, although certainly Jeremiah might have authored it, faith in the inspiration of Scripture does not demand it.

On the other hand, this commentary places a high interpretive value on the canonical location of Lamentations in the Septuagint and in our English Bibles (right after Jeremiah). Lamentations contains numerous allusions and connections to the book of Jeremiah that are important for understanding Lamentations. Thus Lamentations is best interpreted and understood as a "sequel" or "postscript" to Jeremiah. Here, therefore, the book of Jeremiah will be viewed as the context for understanding, preaching, and teaching Lamentations.

Historical Setting

Scholars disagree over the specific authorship of Lamentations, but there is nearly a consensus about its historical setting. Practically all scholars concur that Lamentations was produced within a few years of the fall of Jerusalem in 587 BC and within that context.[5]

Central Message and Purpose

Lamentations is a cry of agony and suffering, but this cry is also a confession that this terrible suffering is very much deserved, a result of repeated and unabated disobedience and defiance of God and rejection of his word. Lamentations is a graphically horrific first-person testimony to the real consequences of sin.[6]

The faithfulness and love of God are affirmed in Lamentations, so hope is present in the midst of suffering. Yet the book is reluctant to move too quickly to a glib "everything will be all right" theology. The judgment on sin and disrespectful defiance of God cannot be passed over too quickly, for it is a serious matter that deserves plenty of contemplation. There is a tension in Lamentations between the belief that God in his faithful love will take his people back and their recent experience with the terrible wrath of God, which has completely destroyed Jerusalem and devastated them. This is a tension that is not resolved until the substitutionary death of Christ in the New Testament.

Lamentations is also a sad, solemn acknowledgment that Jeremiah had been right all along about the coming judgment on Jerusalem and Judah and about how horrific it would be. He warned repeatedly for years that if the people in Jerusalem and Judah did not repent and turn back to God, then the Babylonians would invade and God would use that terrible invasion to bring judgment upon them. Jeremiah, however, was not only ignored by the leaders in Jerusalem, but he was also persecuted. Thus the horror in Lamentations is a vindicating affirmation that Jeremiah's words about the coming judgment were indeed true. It does also suggest, however, that if his words about judgment are true, then his words about the future restoration and new covenant are also true, leaving the readers with hope.

Literary Features

The book of Lamentations is composed of five separate poems corresponding to the five chapters. The first four poems (Lam. 1–4) are alphabetic acrostics.[7] That is, each poem plays off the Hebrew alphabet by starting the first word in sequential verses with sequential letters of the Hebrew alphabet. This will be explained in more detail in the "Text in Context" section of each chapter.

Also, the Hebrew alphabet has twenty-two letters, and Lamentations 1, 2, 4, and 5 have twenty-two verses each. Lamentations 3, which allots three verses to each letter of the Hebrew alphabet, has sixty-six verses.

The point of using these acrostics, however, is not clear. Perhaps they serve as aids in memorization. Many scholars suggest that the acrostic may imply an "A to Z" idea of completeness—that is, a "cry of woe from A to Z." Others note that Lamentations 5 is not in acrostic form, perhaps signifying a loss of all structure and order in the life of the survivors.

The entire book of Lamentations is poetic and throughout employs terseness, figures of speech (especially personification), parallelism, wordplays, hyperbole, and vivid imagery.

No Comfort for the Grieving Widow Jerusalem

Big Idea

Rebellion and sin against God result in sorrow, tragedy, and pain.

Key Themes

- Sustained rebellion and sin against God have terrible, tragic consequences.
- Like a widow left all alone, personified Jerusalem weeps over her tragic fate.
- Jerusalem finds no comfort for her pain, isolation, and humiliation.
- The acknowledgment of sin and guilt opens the way for a possible repentance and restoration.

Understanding the Text

The Text in Context

As mentioned in the introduction, the Septuagint (an early Greek translation of the Old Testament used by the early church) contains an additional, introductory verse prior to 1:1, which reads: "And it happened, after Israel was taken captive and Jerusalem was laid waste, Jeremiah sat weeping and gave this lament over Jerusalem and said."[1] Thus the Septuagint places the opening of Lamentations squarely in the context of the fall of Jerusalem as described at the end of Jeremiah.

Lamentations 1 is a highly structured acrostic Hebrew poem. In Hebrew the first letter of the first word of each verse moves consecutively through the Hebrew alphabet. That is, verse 1 starts with *alef*, the first letter in the alphabet; verse 2 starts with *bet*, the second letter in the Hebrew alphabet; and so forth through the alphabet. Also, in Hebrew each verse has three lines, and each line has two major clauses or statements. Most English translations, like the NIV, format this as six lines in each verse.

There are two "voices" or speakers in Lamentations 1. In 1:1–11 the narrator speaks, using third-person feminine ("she") references for Jerusalem, whom he personifies as a former royal princess who is now a devastated, grieving widow. The other speaker is the personified Jerusalem, the grieving widow herself, who uses first-person pronouns ("I," "my") to cry out in despair. She interrupts the narrator twice, at the end of 1:9 and 1:11. Then she gives two impassioned speeches (1:12–16, 18–22). In between these two speeches is a brief summary or interruption by the narrator (1:17). Even as the speakers change and the pronouns change, the poetic form and style remain constant, and the acrostic alphabetic sequence continues. The analogy of Jerusalem as a grieving, weeping widow likewise runs throughout the chapter. Further uniting the chapter is the phrase "there is no one to comfort her/me," which is repeated five times (1:2, 9, 16, 17, 21).

In Lamentations 1 there are several fairly direct allusions to Jeremiah, especially Jeremiah 52. Thus the leaders of Jerusalem flee before the enemy (Jer. 52:7; Lam. 1:6), the people suffer from a famine (Jer. 52:6; Lam. 1:11), and the treasures of the temple are taken (Jer. 52:17–23; Lam. 1:7, 10). Likewise, the image of Jerusalem's sin (lit., "rebellions") being shaped into a yoke and placed on her neck (Lam. 1:14) seems to be an obvious and rather ironic allusion to the yoke episode in Jeremiah 27–28, where the same word for "yoke" is used repeatedly (Jer. 27:8, 11, 12; 28:2, 4, 11, 14). The cry of "no comfort" throughout Lamentations 1 echoes Jeremiah 16:7; 31:15, and the trampling of grapes in Lamentations 1:15 continues the judgment image of trampling grapes introduced in Jeremiah 25:30.

Interpretive Insights

1:1 *How deserted lies the city.* The Hebrew reads, "How she sits alone." In the aftermath of the destruction of Jerusalem, the city is portrayed as a lonely widow sitting in its ruins, weeping over her isolated, tragic situation and all that has been lost.

How like a widow is she. Since Jeremiah had frequently personified Jerusalem as a woman, especially as God's unfaithful wife, it follows that after the city's destruction Jerusalem is personified as a widow. Jeremiah had already used the widow analogy in his prophetic warning of judgment (Jer. 15:5–9). The Hebrew poetry in this verse follows an A B B′ A′ parallel pattern called "chiasm": A (she is a widow), B (the one who was great among the nations), B′ (the one who was a princess among the provinces), A′ (she is a slave).

1:2 *Among all her lovers.* Jeremiah uses the term "lovers" several times to refer to Jerusalem's foreign allies. That is the surface meaning here as well. The same word is translated as "allies" in 1:19. All the surrounding nations that had conspired with Judah as allies had quickly turned against her. Yet in Jeremiah Jerusalem is frequently figuratively portrayed as God's unfaithful wife, so signifying her foreign allies as "lovers" carries connotations of unfaithfulness to God as well. Jerusalem had trusted in her foreign allies, her "lovers," instead of in God, her true husband.

there is no one to comfort her. The word translated as "comfort" means "to console" or "to show compassion to someone in distress." The irony is that one's "lovers" should be the very ones who give consolation and comfort. But Jerusalem's "lovers" have turned against her.

All her friends. "Friends" is in parallel with "lovers" and refers to the same foreign allies. Not only did Jerusalem's foreign allies fail to help her, but also they had changed allegiance and gone over to the Babylonians.

1:4 *The roads to Zion mourn.* "Zion" is a reference to the hilltop on which the temple was built. It is used synonymously with "Jerusalem." To use it in this context after the destruction of the temple is ironic. This verse personifies the roads that lead up to the temple. In the past these roads "rejoiced" as they would be filled with joyful worshipers streaming to the temple to worship at the times of the appointed feasts—Passover, Pentecost, Tabernacles (Ps. 122).[2] Now, however, they mourn over its desolation.

1:5 *Her foes have become her master.* The word translated as "foes" opens and closes this verse. The word translated as "master" means "head, chief."

because of her many sins. The word translated as "sins" (*pesha'*) carries a more specific nuance of "rebellion." The stress is not on Jerusalem's shortcomings but on her repeated willful and defiant rebellion against God. This same word is used in 1:14, 22. Thus both voices in this chapter acknowledge the sin and rebellion of Jerusalem, perhaps suggesting a move toward repentance.

1:6 *Daughter Zion.* Just as Jeremiah had used the images of the unfaithful wife and of the beloved daughter for Jerusalem, so both images are used in Lamentations. The intimate term "daughter" connotes the relationship that she once had with God, underscoring how far she has fallen. In the midst of Jerusalem's pain, however, the use of the term "daughter" suggests an ongoing love from God and hints at his pain as well. Note that in 1:15 she is referred to as "Virgin Daughter Judah," an ironic reference that seems wistfully to refer to Judah as she was in the past—young and innocent—before she was defiled by all her "lovers" (through worship of other gods).

1:8 *Jerusalem has sinned greatly.* The Hebrew grammatical construction clearly stresses the sin of Jerusalem, but the exact nuance is not as clear. This construction can imply that Jerusalem has sinned repeatedly or perhaps grievously (NIV: "greatly"). Or it may stress the unquestionable certainty of the sin ("Jerusalem has most certainly sinned").

1:12 *Is it nothing to you, all you who pass by?* The image is of the grieving, weeping widow (Jerusalem) looking up and addressing those who walk by.

1:14 *My sins have been bound into a yoke.* At the material level, a yoke is the piece of wood, along with the attachments, that connects an ox to a plow or a wagon. Yoke imagery often was used in the biblical world to symbolize being forced into submission by a conquering king (cf. Jer. 27–28). Here the yoke imagery refers to the humiliating submission of Jerusalem to the Babylonians. The new twist, however, is the modification in the image, for God declares that the yoke that put the Judahites into this submission is made up of their rebellion against him, who should be their proper ruler.

Theological Insights

In the Old Testament we see God as both the judge and the comforter. Away from his presence and in his judgment, there is no comfort at all, as the grieving widow in Lamentations so sorrowfully expresses. Yet it is significant to note the central theological role that comfort plays in biblical texts about the great restoration. It is no accident that as the prophet Isaiah begins his great prophecy regarding the coming Messiah, he begins his message to the future exiles with "Comfort, comfort my people" (Isa. 40:1). For those in exile who turn to God and embrace the messianic hope, there is comfort indeed. Likewise the point of Ezekiel 37 is that the Spirit of God can resurrect people and nations, no matter how hopeless things might seem. Then in the New Testament the apostle Paul expounds at length on the theme of comfort, anchoring it firmly in our life in Christ (2 Cor. 1:3–7).

Teaching the Text

The central point running throughout Lamentations is the sad and sorrowful reflection on the terrible consequences of sin and rebellion against God. The fall and the destruction of Jerusalem were horrific and devastating beyond description. In essence, Lamentations presents a time of looking back and reflecting on how right Jeremiah had been in his warnings and how tragically wrong and foolish those in Judah and Jerusalem had been in their hostility toward Jeremiah and their refusal to repent and to obey God. The haunting reality floating throughout Lamentations is "This did not have to be; if only they had listened and repented." While it is proper for us today to proclaim the positive side of the gospel—those wonderful benefits of following Jesus Christ—Lamentations is a strong reminder that there is an equally true negative reality for those who reject the gospel. The consequences of rejecting Christ today are just as tragic, devastating, and sorrowful as the fall of Jerusalem was to those who rejected the word of God through Jeremiah. The message today to those without Christ is "Do not be like these people."

The theme of comfort/consolation powerfully illustrates the difference between facing adversity with God there to comfort and support and facing adversity completely away from God. For those who are apart from God and who fall under the judgment of God, there is no comfort and consoling hope for the future. That is, indeed, part of the judgment. Yet for those who have turned to God and who trust in God, wonderful consoling and comforting hope is given to sustain them, even in the midst of terrible and trying adversity.

Many today in the midst of suffering and agony are in a very different context from that in Jeremiah and Lamentations. That is, often people are suffering from events and consequences that they themselves did not cause. In these cases the suffering and the anguish are not a part of God's judgment or a result of their sin but rather are part of the conditions of living in a fallen world (cancer, car wrecks, abuse, etc.). Nonetheless, these people often feel exactly like the devastated widow Jerusalem: their lives are shattered, and there is no comfort for them. While Lamentations 1 probably captures how they feel and may resonate with them, the cry of hopelessness from the widow Jerusalem is not a good parallel for them. The reality is that for God's people there is always hope; one can always turn to God and find comfort.

Illustrating the Text

Rebellion has consequences.

Prop: Lamentations is an acrostic Hebrew poem. This means that the first letter of the first word of each verse moves consecutively through the Hebrew alphabet. In one sense, it really is the ABC's of consequence, the most basic explanation of what happens when we rebel. If we talk back to our parents, we will be disciplined; if we fail to study our lessons in school, we will fail the class; and if we rebel against God, there will be consequences.

As a visual illustration of this, place on the stage large cardboard boxes, painted to look like children's wooden alphabet blocks, with the letters "A," "B," and "C" on them.

Rebellion and sin result in sorrow and pain.

Theological Book: *Peculiar Treasures*, by Frederick Buechner. In this book Buechner does what he does best. He shares his unique perspective on some of the Bible's most genuinely human characters. His fresh and witty prose sometimes rides the razor's edge of sacrilege, but in doing so, he captures the essence of who we are when only God is looking.

One of the best illustrations of that is his portrayal of Gomer and Hosea. He sees Gomer as a fallen woman who was "a little heavy with the lipstick maybe, a little less than choosy about men and booze."[3] He captures the spirit of how Lamentations describes Jerusalem as a woman who went whoring after other gods. Reading all or part of Buechner's story will help people resonate with the first chapter of Lamentations.

There is nothing sadder than the absence of God's presence.

Popular Music: "The Thrill Is Gone," by B. B. King. Perhaps the closest thing we have to the genre of Lamentations is blues music. In this classic blues hit, B. B. King captures something of how God must have felt about Judah's rebellion when he sings, "You know you done me wrong, baby, and you'll be sorry someday."

Bible: In 1 Thessalonians 4:13 the apostle Paul writes, "Do not grieve like the rest of mankind, who have no hope." One of the saddest things about Lamentations is the utter desolation of Jerusalem, because she faces this tragedy without God's comfort. Any pastor can tell you that when you visit someone from church who is grieving the loss of a loved one, there is great pain in the room, but for those who have put their hope in Christ, there is also a very real sense of God's presence and comfort. Many times such persons will say, "I don't know how people do this if they don't have any faith."

The Anger of God

Big Idea
Even as the anger of God brings judgment, he still listens for the cry of repentance.

Key Themes
- God's anger has destroyed Jerusalem, her religious rituals, and her rulers.
- Jerusalem's enemies triumph over her because God has become her primary enemy.
- Devastated Jerusalem is personified as God's daughter.
- The survivors are exhorted to call out to God in their pain and suffering.

Understanding the Text

The Text in Context

In regard to form and structure, Lamentations 1 and Lamentations 2 are similar. Both start with the exact same Hebrew word (translated as "how"). Both are identical in their poetic, acrostic form, wherein the first letter of each consecutive verse moves through the Hebrew alphabet. In both chapters each verse has three lines (in Hebrew), and each line has two cola. The NIV translation presents this as six lines of poetry. Lamentations 2:19 is an exception, probably for stress. In Hebrew it has four lines, with two cola each for eight lines in English.

Lamentations 2 reflects the same two voices of Lamentations 1, that of the narrator (2:1–19) and that of personified Jerusalem (2:20–22). But thematically there are differences. While Lamentations 1 stresses the despair and sorrow of devastated Jerusalem, Lamentations 2 focuses on the cause for that devastation: the anger of God. The Hebrew word for "anger" occurs in the opening and closing verses (2:1, 22), thus forming thematic bookends for the chapter. Also, even though Lamentations 1 refers to Jerusalem as a "daughter," the central analogy is that of a grieving widow. In Lamentations 2 the central analogy is that of Jerusalem/Judah as a daughter (of God, presumably). The Hebrew word for "daughter" occurs twelve times in Lamentations 2, connected to five different words: "Daughter Zion" (2:1, 4, 8, 10, 13, 18), "Daughter Judah" (2:2, 5), "daughter of my people" (2:11), "Daughter Jerusalem" (2:13, 15), and "daughter of your eyes" (2:18; NIV translates just as "your eyes"). As in Lamentations 1, the use of "daughter" has strong emotional connotations. Jerusalem is not just some distant and detached city that God destroys; it is his "daughter." Jeremiah uses similar terminology, frequently referring to "Daughter Zion" (3x) and "daughter of my people" (9x).

Interpretive Insights

2:1 *The Lord.* The word translated as "Lord" is *'adonay,* which stresses the authority of God.[1]

covered daughter Zion with the cloud of his anger! The Hebrew verb translated as "covered" means "to envelop something like a cloud or like smoke." Some scholars suggest that in this verse the word paints a picture of God's dark storm cloud completely covering Jerusalem. Yet the point being stressed probably is the totality of the anger. God's anger engulfed or enveloped Jerusalem like a thick fog or like a dense cloud.

the splendor of Israel. "Splendor" is a figure of speech referring to the temple, underscoring how spectacular and beautiful the temple was.

his footstool. Literally, "the footstool of his feet." The footstool was the resting place for the feet of the king as he sat on his throne. It was a symbol of his presence and his power. In Psalms 99:5 and 132:7 the temple (or perhaps the ark within the temple) in Jerusalem is referred to as God's footstool, portraying God as sitting on his throne in heaven with his feet in the temple (i.e., the lower part of his throne).

in the day of his anger. Not only does the entire chapter open and close with "anger," but also the opening verse (2:1) has the Hebrew word for "anger" near the beginning and at the end.

2:2 *swallowed.* The Hebrew verb used here means "to devour completely by eating, to gulp down." It occurs here, twice in 2:5, in 2:8 (NIV: "destroying"), and in 2:16.

the dwellings of Jacob. The word translated as "dwellings" means "pastures for livestock." This term can be used figuratively of a nice place to live, especially when the king is compared to a shepherd. The image of a pasture connotes peace, protection, and plenty to eat. This verse no doubt alludes to Jeremiah 25:37, which uses the same word.

2:6 *he has destroyed his place of meeting . . . forget her appointed festivals.* "Place of meeting" and "appointed festivals" are translations of the same Hebrew word (*mo'ed*). Occurring over 150 times in Exodus, Leviticus, Numbers, and Deuteronomy, this word can refer to an "appointed time" (a religious festival) or "an appointed place" (the tabernacle/temple). Whether referring to the place or to the time, the stress is on "meeting" with God. The temple is where God's people "met" with him (appointed place), and the festivals of Israel were the means and the times for meeting with God (appointed times). This word occurs twice in this verse and again in 2:7 ("appointed festival") and 2:22. The destruction by God of the *mo'ed* (either place or activity) signals a serious rupture in the covenant relationship between God and the people of Judah/Jerusalem.

2:8 *The Lord determined to tear down the wall.* The word translated as "determined" means "to plan, to calculate." It is the same word used in Jeremiah 29:11, but in contrast here in Lamentations 2:8, the plan of God is to destroy the walls of Jerusalem. This judgment for those in the 587–586 BC destruction of Jerusalem is in stark contrast to God's good plans for those in the exile of 598–597 BC (Jer. 29:11).

He stretched out a measuring line. Usually measuring lines (i.e., similar to long tape measures) are used to design and lay out the construction of new walls. Here, in an ironic reversal, God is metaphorically using a measuring line in his planning of the destruction of Jerusalem's walls. It is possible that this reference is to the measurements taken by a conquering army to determine which sections of the walls were to be pulled down as part of the destruction of the city.[2] At any rate, the destruction of Jerusalem was neither random nor haphazard; God planned it meticulously.

He made ramparts and walls lament. The word translated as "wall" refers to the primary stone wall that encircled the city. At this time in Jerusalem the wall was twenty-two feet thick. The word translated as "ramparts" refers to compacted dirt, sometimes covered with stone, which was placed at the bottom of the wall to protect it from battering rams.[3] The word translated as "lament" means "to mourn." Thus in this personified figure of speech, God causes the fortifications of Jerusalem to mourn their demise. Note that in 2:18–19 the walls of Jerusalem will be called upon to cry out in repentance.

2:18 *The hearts of the people cry out to the Lord.* The NIV's addition of "the people" is inferred but not clear ("their hearts cry out to the Lord"). The nearest subject is the "walls of Daughter Zion," which probably is figurative for the entire city. The word translated as "cry out" (*tsa'aq*) can connote a cry of pain or a cry for help. In some cases, and perhaps here, these two nuances overlap. It is not just a wail of suffering but rather a lamenting appeal for help that has the potential to provide a real change in the circumstance.[4] Thus it implies that there is hope.

let your tears flow like a river day and night. In Jeremiah 14:17 similar language is used, but there it is God who is crying day and night. In Lamentations 2:18 the imperative verb used is a call for repentance. Note that in 2:18–19 seven Hebrew imperatives are used to call the people (lit., "the walls of Daughter Zion") to repentance: "Let your tears flow . . . give yourself no relief, [give] your eyes no rest. Arise, cry out . . . pour out your heart. . . . Lift up your hands."

your eyes no rest. This idiomatic expression reads literally, "do not be silent, daughter of your eyes," with "daughter of your eyes" paralleling "Daughter Zion" in the opening line of this verse. "Daughter of your eyes" probably is a figure of speech referring to tears.

2:19 *pour out your heart like water.* This water metaphor continues the image from 2:18 of tears flowing like a river day and night. In Hebrew the heart is often the place where one makes choices and decisions. Thus it is precisely the place where true repentance takes place. A heart that pours out tears is the opposite of a hard, stony heart, the image often used of stubbornness and rebellion in Jeremiah (e.g., Jer. 5:23; 17:1).

in the presence of the Lord. God has abandoned his temple, which has been destroyed (2:6–7), along with Jerusalem's walls (2:7–8). Thus it is significant that the walls are called upon to repent and pour out their heart "in the presence of God." This implies that God is still there to hear the cry of repentance, and though he may have abandoned and rejected his altar and sanctuary (2:6–7), he is still there to hear the cry of his people.

2:20 *Should women eat their offspring . . . ?* This reflects the fulfillment of the terrible but crystal-clear warnings that God gave to Israel in Deuteronomy 28:53–57 and repeated in Jeremiah 19:9.

Theological Insights

A very sobering theological insight emerging from Lamentations 2 is that God became the enemy of the rebellious ones in Jerusalem. He did not just remove the protection and blessing that accompanied his presence; he became their hostile enemy who actually fought against them. Some may argue that this representation of God is merely an anthropomorphic figure of speech; that is, the judgment was so bad that "it seemed" that God was their enemy. The portrayal of God as a warrior, however, is fairly frequent in the Old Testament, particularly in the prophets. In the Old Testament God often fights as a protecting warrior to defend and deliver his people, but when they rebel against him and turn to worship other idols, then he is often portrayed as an enemy fighting against them. Although this image of warrior may seem unethical to some modern readers, the Old Testament stresses that God the divine warrior is righteous and uses warfare to bring about justice. Thus in Jeremiah and Lamentations God becomes Jerusalem's enemy and fights against the city to bring about his justice. This theme is present in the New Testament, especially in Revelation as the Lamb of God is portrayed as the conquering warrior who "treads the winepress of the fury of the wrath of God Almighty" (Rev. 17:14; 19:11–16). The image of God as warrior is both a warning to those who rebelliously defy him and a source of hope for deliverance to those who are being oppressed.[5]

Teaching the Text

Along with the rest of the Old Testament, the book of Jeremiah attests to the long-suffering patience of God, who definitely is slow to anger. But eventually, after continual rebellion and disrespectful rejection of God and his word by the people in Jerusalem, he finally unleashes his anger against the city. It is not a pretty sight. His anger and wrath are terrible and devastating. As we noted in Jeremiah, this is a biblical universal truth that is still true today but not regularly recognized. God continues to be loving, patient, and long-suffering today, but his patience has limits, and those who continue to defy him disrespectfully and spurn his offer of grace with scorn run the risk of experiencing his terrible wrath and anger.

Yet there is also a strong tension between God's anger, stressed repeatedly in the chapter, and the use of the relational word "daughter" to describe the people whom he has just destroyed. The just wrath of God against sin and his continued love and compassion for the sinner create a tension in the biblical story that is not resolved until Jesus provides justification and reconciliation through his atonement.

It is remarkable that in the midst of a chapter describing how God's anger has totally destroyed Jerusalem and the temple comes an optimistic exhortation to cry out for deliverance with a repentant heart. Likewise today, there is always hope. No matter how serious our sin has been or how angry God is at our sin, his heart is always open to hearing our cry of repentance and to rescuing us from his wrath.

Also, note that God not only became angry and removed his presence and blessing from Jerusalem but also became its enemy. Likewise today, the continual hostile and disrespectful actions of sinful humankind can make God into an enemy, which is a terrible thing, as Jerusalem learned. The New Testament continues this very theme in Romans 5, which also portrays God as the enemy of sinful humankind (Rom. 5:10). The good news for us today, of course, is that through faith in Christ we can be reconciled with God and change from being his enemies to being his friends (Rom. 5:9–11). This reconciliation saves us from his wrath and provides us with eternal life.

Illustrating the Text

God's heart is always open to our cries of repentance.

Bible: The story of the prodigal son, in Luke 15:11–32, beautifully demonstrates God's willingness to welcome the repentant home. "Quick!" the son's father says. "Bring the best robe and put it on him. Put a ring on his finger and sandals on his feet. Bring the fattened calf and kill it. Let's have a feast and celebrate. For this son of mine was dead and is alive again; he was lost and is found." And then the celebration begins. The story is told to remind us that no matter what we have done, no matter how far we might have strayed from our Father in heaven and his plan for our lives, God is always open to our cries of repentance. The 2014 film *Wayward: The Prodigal Son* provides a modern retelling of this story of rebellion, mercy, and forgiveness, and helps a modern audience connect with the story.

Pain is the prerequisite to comfort.

Theological Book: *Mere Christianity*, by C. S. Lewis. Lewis talks about God and his goodness in the sense that God is not soft or indulgent or sympathetic to sin. "There is nothing indulgent about the Moral Law," he says. "It is hard as nails. It tells you to do the straight thing and it does not seem to care how painful, or dangerous, or difficult it is to do."[6] He then implies that God is similar in the sense that he expects and demands absolute obedience. And will he forgive us when we fall short of that? Of course he will, but not at the expense of the pain that accompanies the sin. Lewis explains it this way: "The Christian religion is, in the long run, a thing of unspeakable comfort. But it does not begin in comfort; it begins in the dismay I have been describing, and it is no use at all trying to go on to the comfort without first going through that dismay."[7]

Given the choice, many would choose to have a God who would allow us to live any way we want and would still welcome us through the doors of heaven. But that is not the God of the Bible. As Lewis also says, "God is the only comfort, He is also the supreme terror: the thing we most need and the thing we most want to hide from."[8] In other words, comfort is ours only when we are willing to accept who we really are, sinful by nature, and who God really is, totally holy and repulsed by sin. Because this is so uncomfortable to do, we often avoid it. We deny or dismiss our sin so that we do not have to stand with our heads bowed in the presence of a holy God, but going through the uncomfortable process of repentance leads us to the comfort of forgiveness.

The Faithfulness of God in the Midst of Judgment

Big Idea

Because of God's faithful, loyal love, there is always hope.

Key Themes

- The personified soldier of Jerusalem bemoans his defeat at the hands of God.
- Because of God's loyal love, there is hope beyond the judgment.
- God has tremendous love and compassion; thus he judges reluctantly.
- The proper response to judgment is repentance.

Understanding the Text

The Text in Context

Lamentations 3 continues the cry of lament over fallen and devastated Jerusalem that was proclaimed in Lamentations 1–2, but from a slightly different perspective. In Lamentations 1–2 two voices spoke, that of a narrator and that of personified Jerusalem, a grieving widow. Thus the dominating perspective, especially in Lamentations 1, was that of a bereft woman. The first-person voice ("I," "me," "my") speaking in Lamentations 3 is masculine and presents a man's perspective on the devastation of Jerusalem and the exile. Although there is some disagreement about the identity of this man, it probably is best to see him as a literary representative or symbol of all the men of Jerusalem who survived, rather than the words of one specific individual like Jeremiah.[1] Lamentations 1 is the languishing cry of a woman as she bemoans her slaughtered or exiled children. Lamentations 3 is the anguished cry of a defeated Hebrew soldier who was unable to defend his city and his people, as he reflects on the terrible destruction and his own disgrace.

Lamentations 3 is also an acrostic poem, but the acrostic style is different from that in Lamentations 1–2. In Lamentations 3 each letter of the Hebrew alphabet appears in the first letter of the first word in three consecutive verses. That is, *alef*, the first letter of the Hebrew alphabet, is the first letter of the first word in verses 3:1, 2, 3; then *bet*, the second letter, appears at the beginning of 3:4, 5, 6; and so on. Thus Lamentations 1 and Lamentations 2 each has twenty-two verses (matching the Hebrew alphabet), but Lamentations 3 has sixty-six verses (three verses for each letter). However, since the verses in Lamentations 1 and Lamentations 2 are approximately three times as long as the verses are in Lamentations 3, the overall length of the chapters is similar.

There is some thematic movement in the chapter. Lamentations 3:1–24 reflects the suffering, despair, and hope of the soldier. Lamentations 3:25–39 reflects general advice from the soldier on how to deal with the tragedy. In Lamentations 3:40–51 the soldier calls on Israel to repent, and in Lamentations 3:52–66 he calls on God to deliver him from those who continue to persecute him.[2]

Interpretive Insights

3:1 *I am the man.* The word translated as "man" (*geber*) connotes specifically a "strong man of military age," used especially in distinction from the women, children, and elderly whom he is to defend. In the context of sieges, battles, and weapons, this word draws attention to this individual as a soldier, not necessarily as a professional, but as a citizen-soldier fighting man nonetheless. This word occurs four times in Lamentations, all in this chapter (3:1, 27, 35, 39).

the rod of the LORD's wrath. The word translated as "rod" refers to the shepherd's staff (Ps. 23:4). Lamentations 3:1–11 has several allusions to God in a shepherd's role, but ironically and tragically, he is a shepherd who is attacking the sheep and not defending them.[3] The word translated as "wrath" is a strong word, often connoting fury or rage: "By the wrath of the LORD Almighty the land will be scorched and the people will be fuel for the fire" (Isa. 9:19); "the scepter of the rulers, which in anger struck down peoples with unceasing blows" (Isa. 14:5–6).[4]

3:18 *My splendor is gone and all that I had hoped from the LORD.* The word translated as "splendor" can mean "glory, luster, beauty," but it can also refer to something that is lasting or perpetual. Here it is used in parallel with "hope," so the "lasting, perpetual" meaning probably is to be preferred (ESV: "endurance"; NASB: "strength"). "Gone" translates a Hebrew word that means "to be destroyed, perish" or "to be lost." The nuance of this verse is that their hope and their endurance (which comes from that hope) have been destroyed. This loss of hope will be counteracted by 3:21.

3:21 *Yet this I call to mind and therefore I have hope.* "This" refers to the following verses (3:22–25). A literal translation of the Hebrew behind "I call to mind" is "I caused to return [*shub*] to my heart." The verb translated as "I have hope" (*yahal*) connotes "to hope," but it especially implies "expectant hope with endurance." The lost hope of 3:18 (where the same word is used) is now restored to his heart.

3:22 *Because of the* LORD's *great love.* The word *hesed*, stressing God's faithful and loyal covenant/relational love, stands at the front of the verse and is plural. The NIV's "great" is implied. This plural construction of *hesed* is fairly rare, occurring only five times in the Old Testament. In some of these texts it refers to actions or deeds resulting from this covenant love: "I will tell of the kindnesses of the LORD, the deeds for which he is to be praised" (Isa. 63:7); "do not blot out what I have so faithfully done" (Neh. 13:14). If this is the nuance, then it is God's faithful loving actions (plural) and his compassions (plural) that are new (plural) every morning (3:23).

we are not consumed, for his compassions never fail. The words translated as "consumed" (*tamam*) and "fail" (*kalah*) are practically synonyms, both meaning "to come to an end" or "to be completely finished." The NIV translation correctly understands the subject of *tamam* as "we," although several other translations understand the subject to be God's *hesed*.[5] The nuance is "We have not come to an end because his compassions have not come to an end." The word translated as "compassions" conveys warm, emotional, tender care like that of a mother for her newborn. The term probably refers to what God does ("acts of compassion") and not just what he feels. The stressed aspect of God's tender, compassionate acts is their continuity; they never cease or stop. This is what gives hope in the midst of an otherwise hopeless situation. The term "new" refers to a fresh renewal of God's acts of faithful love and compassion.

3:23 *great is your faithfulness.* The word translated as "faithfulness" connotes firmness, reliability, steadfastness, or fidelity. This line is a summary of the three lines above. God is incredibly trustworthy, as is seen through his repeated and renewed acts of faithful love and compassion.

3:24 *The* LORD *is my portion.* The word translated as "portion" is used of the portions created when either splitting up captured spoils of war or splitting up land for inheritance purposes. Although both meanings fit the context (spoils of Jerusalem carried off by Babylonians; all land inheritance lost), the reference probably is to the lost land inheritance. Having lost his land inheritance, the speaker turns to God as his inheritance—an inheritance that cannot be lost.

therefore I will wait for him. The word translated as "wait" (*yahal*) is the same word translated as "hope" in 3:21 and "wait" in 3:26. The noun form of this word occurs in 3:18, translated as "hoped." This word implies an enduring expectant hope.

3:33 *For he does not willingly bring affliction.* The word translated as "affliction" is from the same root as the word used in the opening statement of

3:1, where it serves as a summary of the following verses. "Willingly" is an attempt to translate the Hebrew "from the heart." In Hebrew the heart is the center of both emotions and volitional decision making. This verse conveys reluctance on God's part to bring affliction; he does not want to, but he must.

3:40 *Let us examine our ways and test them.* The previous verses (3:1–39) reflect the lament of "the soldier" and thus are in first-person singular ("I," "me"). He switches to first-person plural ("we," "us") here in 3:40 as he begins to call for repentance from corporate Israel, those in Judah who have survived the Babylonian destruction. Both verbs have similar meaning, "to search out, examine closely." This self-examination is the first step to repentance.

let us return to the LORD. This is a strong and clear call for repentance using the word *shub* ("to turn, return, repent"), the central term used throughout Jeremiah in his call for Judah to repent and turn back to God.

3:53 *They tried to end my life in a pit.* Jeremiah's experiences in the pit (Jer. 37:16; 38:6–13) provide an ironic background for this statement (the same word, *bor*, is used). As Jeremiah was placed in a pit where he nearly died, so this personified soldier of Jerusalem describes his plight at the hands of his enemies using similar language, thus revealing a certain poetic justice in the fate of this personification of Jerusalem.

Theological Insights

Without doubt Lamentations 3 contains the strongest declarations of hope found in the entire book. It is interesting, however, that this affirmation of hope lies at the middle of the chapter and at the middle of the book, perhaps leaving open whether shattered Israel will rally around that hope. The lament psalms provide an interesting contrast. Most of them generally follow a common thematic pattern: address to God, complaint, confession of trust, petition, words of assurance, and a vow to praise God for his deliverance.[6] Lamentations contains the complaint, the confession of trust (3:21–33), and even the petition (5:21), but Lamentations never quite gets to the words of assurance or the final confident vow to praise God. This structural contrast underscores the contrasting purposes. The main point of the lament psalms is to show that God delivers his people out of their distress when they call on him; the main point of Lamentations is that the consequences of sin and rebellion are terrible.

Teaching the Text

As throughout Lamentations, this chapter reiterates the horrible consequences of defying God and thus falling under his judgment. The personified soldier who cries out and describes all the terrible things that have happened to him and his city is basically telling the audience not to do what he has done (i.e., rebel against God).

This chapter also gives us insight into the character of God. In the midst of terrible judgment, the speaker underscores God's continuous faithful love and compassion. This neither negates God's anger and wrath nor eliminates the reality of the judgment, but God does not judge and destroy with pleasure. He is not capricious or vindictive. He is completely righteous and always "right" in his justice, from which he never wavers. But he judges reluctantly; it seems as if he *must* judge this terrible sin of Jerusalem's. He would much rather show his love and compassion, which for God never end or run out. Indeed, even in the midst of the judgment he stands ready to respond to repentance with forgiveness and restoration. Love and justice are equal aspects of God's character, and we see both of them in this chapter.

For people today, God himself has already paid the painful price for sin through the death of his Son, Jesus, so that we do not have to experience the necessary judgment for our sin. We have the opportunity to accept God's great love and compassion demonstrated in the death of Christ and thus have our sin covered. God does not want to pour out his anger and wrath on us today, and he is still reluctant to judge, but he definitely will pass judgment if we reject Christ and spurn God's love and compassion.

Regardless of our past sins or our past history of rejecting God and his word, he continues to call us to repentance. We need only to turn to him, confess our sins, and trust in Christ. This hope is always there. It is constant because God's love and compassion are constant. His great love and compassion are renewed each and every morning. They never cease and never end.

Illustrating the Text

Those who continue to defy God's warning will fall under his judgment.

Everyday Life: We live in a world of warning lights. If there is road construction, workers set up brightly colored barrels with flashing lights to alert us to the danger ahead. If the battery on our laptop computer is low, a battery warning light will appear, alerting us to plug it in or shut it down. If we shut the electric stove off but the burner is still hot, a warning light will advise us to be cautious.

But the epitome of the display of warning lights may be the modern automobile. Vehicle dashboards are equipped with colored warning lights that will instantly alert the driver when the onboard computer detects that something is wrong. The display may show an icon of an engine, an oilcan, a lightbulb, a deflated tire, a dead battery, or a thermometer. No matter which light comes on, the driver should pay attention. Ignoring the warning would be foolish and could lead to system failure of some kind that likely would result in major repair costs. (This illustration could be extended by relating a personal story of what happened when a dashboard warning light was ignored.)

Several passages in Proverbs underscore the foolishness of ignoring clear warning signs. For example, Proverbs 22:3 reads, "The prudent see danger and take refuge, but the simple keep going and pay the penalty." Likewise, Proverbs 1:7 declares, "The fear of the LORD is the beginning of knowledge, but fools despise wisdom and instruction." In the same way, Jeremiah and Lamentations serve as flashing warning lights alerting us to the horrible consequences of defying God and thus falling under his judgment.

Because of God's faithful, loyal love, there is always hope.

Bible: In 1 Corinthians 13:1–8 the apostle Paul describes love's ideal. Surely he is talking about the absolute faithfulness of God's love when he says, "It always protects, always trusts, always hopes, always perseveres. Love never fails."

True Story: Most of us have seen how faithful dogs can be. They greet us with joy when we walk in the door, they follow us around wherever we go, and they perform tricks or acts of service simply because we ask. But the faithfulness of "man's best friend" was taken to new heights by a dog named "Capitan."

After his owner died in 2006, Capitan, a German shepherd, ran away from home. A week later he was found sitting guard over his master's grave in Villa Carlos Paz, in central Argentina. For six years after his owner's death Capitan has returned each night to the gravesite to sleep by his master's side.[7]

Hymn: "Great Is Thy Faithfulness," by Thomas Chisholm. The words for this beloved hymn come from Lamentations 3:22–26.

Sin and Its Tragic Consequences for Children

Big Idea

The sin of adults can lead to terrible and tragic consequences for children.

Key Themes

- Jerusalem's rebellion against God had terrible consequences for the city's children.
- The sin of Jerusalem's leaders was a central cause of God's judgment.
- Yet God will restore his people and judge the nations.

Understanding the Text

The Text in Context

The central theme of Lamentations is that the consequences of continued sin and rebellion against God are terrible, with horrific aftershocks. Lamentations 4 continues this theme.

Lamentations 4 starts off with the same Hebrew word that begins Lamentations 1 and Lamentations 2, translated as "how." Lamentations 4 is also an alphabetic acrostic poem similar in structure to Lamentations 1 and Lamentations 2, except that in Hebrew Lamentations 4 has only two lines of text per verse, each with two statements or cola, while verses in Lamentations 1 and Lamentations 2 have three lines of text, likewise each with two cola. So in most English translations Lamentations 1 and Lamentations 2 have twenty-two verses each (matching the Hebrew alphabet), each with six lines, while Lamentations 4 has twenty-two verses, each with four lines.

In Lamentations 1 the focus is on Jerusalem as the grieving widow. In Lamentations 2 the emphasis shifts to Jerusalem as a daughter. In Lamentations 3 the central perspective is that of the defeated male soldier. In the beginning of Lamentations 4 the focus is on the children. As many as six different Hebrew terms for "children" are used in 4:1–10. Likewise, the references to "they" and "those" in 4:8–9 probably refer to the children.

The narrator, speaking of Jerusalem and the people in the third person, bemoans the fate of the children in 4:1–10. Then in 4:11–16 he lays the blame for this on the priests and prophets of Jerusalem. A first-person-plural voice representing all the survivors speaks in 4:17–20, reliving how their enemies hunted them down while their allies did nothing. This leads into the closing judgment oracle on Edom (4:21–22), probably the voice of the narrator again.

Historical and Cultural Background

Lamentations 4 ends with a proclamation of judgment on Edom, Judah's neighbor to the southeast. Although apparently allied with Judah in the initial rebellion against Babylon (Jer. 27:3), Edom switched sides at some point and participated in plundering Judah, an event alluded to frequently in the Old Testament (Ps. 137:7; Ezek. 35:15; Obad. 7–8). Edom is one of the nations included in Jeremiah's Judgment on the Nations unit (Jer. 49:7–22). Yet along with Babylon, Edom is sometimes singled out to play a more representative role as the prototypical enemy of Judah (Ps. 137:7–8; Ezek. 35:1–14; Obad. 1–21). Uz (Lam. 4:21) probably was a region within Edom, although little is known about it.[1]

Interpretive Insights

4:1 *the gold has lost its luster . . . The sacred gems are scattered.* At first glance, this appears to be a reference to the gold and valuable gems that were in the temple. But certainly the Babylonians did not leave gold and gems scattered in the streets. Rather, the gold and the gems are metaphors for the children of Jerusalem, as 4:2 clarifies.

at every street corner. Streets are mentioned four times in this chapter (4:1, 5, 8, 14). With the houses of Jerusalem in ruins, people live in the streets.

4:2 *the precious children of Zion.* Literally, this is "the precious sons of Zion." This probably includes all the children, with the word "precious" connecting back to the metaphor of gold and gems in 4:1.

as pots of clay. It is the shattered and/or abandoned common clay pots that lie scattered in the streets throughout the ruins of Jerusalem (4:1). The children who survived the destruction of Jerusalem now are seen all over the streets, like the broken and abandoned clay pots.

4:3 *jackals . . . nurse their young.* Jackals were common canine scavengers in the ancient world. Because they normally showed up after disastrous battles or sieges, they are commonly associated with judgment or misfortune. The word translated as "young" refers specifically to the young of animals, like our English word "cub." The irony is that the Hebrew children roaming the desolate streets after the fall of Jerusalem were left to fend for themselves, in contrast to the cubs of the jackals that probably also were roaming the streets.

heartless like ostriches. The word translated as "heartless" carries connotations of "cruel." There was a common perception that ostriches abandoned their eggs (Job 39:14–16). The aftermath of the destruction of Jerusalem is so bad that the adults have cruelly, heartlessly abandoned the children to pick through the rubble and garbage for food.

4:4 *the infant's tongue.* The word translated as "infant" refers to a nursing baby. The implication is that this nursing baby is receiving no milk, again providing a contrast with the jackals in 4:3, which did nurse their young.

4:5 *who once ate delicacies . . . brought up in royal purple.* These too probably are references to children. Even those children from royal families have been turned out into the streets.

now lie on ash heaps. The Hebrew verb used here means "to embrace." The noun translated as "ash heaps" probably is a reference to piles of garbage or refuse thrown outside the city. This depicts an image of children digging through the garbage looking for food.

4:6 *The punishment of my people is greater than that of Sodom.* Sodom, of course, was the prototypical sinful city of the Old Testament that was destroyed by God. The Hebrew of this verse specifies that "the *'awon* of the daughter of my people is greater than the *hatta't* of Sodom." Although *'awon* normally means "iniquity" and *hatta't* normally means "sin," both words can also refer to punishment, the meaning that the NIV has decided upon due to the context. Yet it is quite possible that both meanings are present. The iniquity and the punishment of Jerusalem were greater than the sin and the punishment of Sodom.[2] These same two words occur in 4:13, where they clearly mean "sin," and again in 4:22, where they seem to be used in a wordplay with both meanings.

4:8 *they are blacker than soot.* The word translated as "blacker" refers not to the specific color "black" but rather to darkness. It is often used for contrasting things against "light," and it generally carries negative connotations. Note that several earlier verses contained references to color—"gold" (4:1), "royal purple" (4:5), "whiter than milk" (4:7), "more ruddy than rubies" (4:7), "like lapis lazuli" (4:7)—all of which set up the stark contrast with the image of famine in 4:8, dark and shriveled (gray).[3]

4:9 *killed by the sword . . . die of famine.* The same Hebrew verb is used twice here, in a colorful but grim wordplay. The verb means "to be pierced" or, more specifically, "to be killed by being pierced." It is an appropriate verb to use when speaking of swords. It is repeated metaphorically in regard to the famine. Thus a literal reading is "It is better for those who were pierced by the sword than for those who were pierced by the famine."

4:10 *women have cooked their own children.* This is the ultimate horror of famine and starvation, driving home the point being made in 4:9: it would have been better to have been killed by the Babylonians.

4:13 *sins of her prophets . . . iniquities of her priests . . . blood of the righteous.* The central theme in Jeremiah 11–29 is the hostility he faced from the leaders in Jerusalem (prophets, priests, and king). The "blood of the righteous" probably is synonymous with Jeremiah's phrase "blood of the innocent" (Jer. 2:34; 7:6; 19:4; 22:3, 17), which he uses to refer to the execution of defenseless poor people and, especially, the practice of child sacrifice (Jer. 19:4; 32:32–35).[4]

4:16 *The Lord himself has scattered them.* The Hebrew text refers specifically to the face or presence of the Lord as scattering or dividing them. Often in the Old Testament the presence of God is closely associated with power, holiness, and glory. Thus it seems fitting to refer to his presence as the entity that executes his righteous judgment. "Them" refers especially to the priests and prophets (4:13) as well as the elders (4:16). Ironically, it was the priests who were intended to minister before the face of Yahweh (i.e., in his presence).

4:22 *your punishment . . . Daughter Zion . . . your sin, Daughter Edom.* See comments at 4:6 on *'awon.* In a colorful wordplay it is used twice here. The *'awon* ("punishment") of Daughter Zion will come to an end, but the *'awon* ("iniquity") of Daughter Edom will be punished.

he will not prolong your exile . . . he will . . . expose your wickedness. Another colorful wordplay that uses the same word in two very different senses occurs here. The word *galah* can mean "to send into exile" or "to uncover, expose." It occurs twice here, translated correctly as "exile" in the first instance (regarding Zion), but "expose" in the second (regarding Edom).

Theological Insights

In Deuteronomy 28, as the Israelites are entering the promised land, God states very clearly the blessings that they will receive if they obey him and the terrible tragedies that will befall them in judgment if they reject him and turn to idols. One of these horrific consequences described is a siege that produces a famine so severe that parents will eat their children (Deut. 28:53–57; see also Lev. 26:29). Jeremiah warns of this terrible consequence of judgment in Jeremiah 19:9. Likewise, several other times Jeremiah pointedly tells the people of Jerusalem and Judah that their sin will have huge repercussions for their children (Jer. 6:11; 18:21; 32:18). Ironically, one of their sins that most angered God was the idolatrous practice of child sacrifice. Truly, the Old Testament is consistent in proclaiming that parents who defy and disobey God repeatedly bring very negative repercussions upon their children. Sin brings tragic consequences, not only on the ones who sin but also often on their children.

It is important to realize that God is not the reason that these terrible things happen. Sin has its tragic consequences, and the moral responsibility for those consequences belongs to those who have sinned. Likewise, the terrible consequences of God's judgment that are portrayed in Lamentations (and elsewhere in the Old Testament) are not in conflict with the character of God in the New Testament. God is seen as loving in both Testaments; likewise his righteous justice and the penalty for sin are consistent across the canon.

Teaching the Text

In the Western world, and particularly in the United States, people tend to think very individualistically, especially regarding their relationship with God and the consequences, either salvation or judgment. The truth is, however, that parents play a huge role in whether their children accept the Lord and experience salvation or reject the Lord and experience judgment. Obviously, parents are not the only factor in whether a child believes in Christ, but they are a very important one. There are many people who reject Christ because they were taught to be suspicious of Christianity by their parents, who had rejected it themselves. These parents share in the culpability of the judgment coming on their children.

On a positive note, Christian parents should do everything they can to see that their children (as well as the children of others) inherit their faith and continue to follow Christ. This passes along blessings to their children and not judgment. It is the greatest inheritance that can be passed down to the next generation.

Also, as we saw repeatedly in Jeremiah, religious leaders play a very influential role in shaping the beliefs and behavior of people who follow them. Those contemporary "false prophets" who today lead people away from Christ are held accountable for the consequences of their actions. Likewise, this reality should send a certain shiver down the spines of all of us who lead and teach God's people. Like Jeremiah, we should always work to proclaim the word of God accurately, drawing people to Christ.

Finally, in Lamentations 4, as in several other chapters, there is a reminder that the destruction of Jerusalem is not the last event in God's plan. He has a future planned for the exiles. He will bring about a glorious time of restoration for his people while at the same time bringing judgment on his enemies. There will be a future consummation of God's kingdom, a time when all suffering and pain will end, and the Lord will rule with absolute love and justice.

Lamentations 4:1–22

Illustrating the Text

Remembering our past sins helps us avoid them in the future.

Television: The Discovery channel program *Fast N' Loud* shows car restoration projects done by the Gas Monkey Garage in Dallas, Texas. They typically buy old cars and trucks, restore them mechanically and cosmetically, and then resell them for some fast cash. In a 2013 episode titled "Dodge Hodge Podge," they mechanically restore a 1964 Dodge Sweptline pickup truck, replace its interior, and put on new wheels and tires, but in this case they clear-coat over the truck's rusty exterior to preserve its authentic heritage. This technique is becoming more and more common in the restoration business because it reminds people of what the vehicle has been through. They even have a name for this category of restoration: the "preservation" class.

Lamentations preserves the tragic consequences of Israel's past sins so that we might learn from its mistakes.

Children often suffer the consequences of their parents' bad decisions.

Statistics: The Centers for Disease Control and Prevention present the following data:[5]

In 2011 more than 650 children twelve years and younger died as occupants in motor vehicle crashes; more than 148,000 were injured. Of the children who died, 33 percent were not buckled up.

From 2001 to 2010, 20 percent of child-passenger deaths involved drunk driving; 65 percent of the time it was the child's own driver who had been drinking.

Restraint use among young children often depends upon the driver's seatbelt use. Almost 40 percent of children riding with unbelted drivers were themselves unrestrained.

Popular Culture: There are many proverbial sayings that demonstrate the close connection between generations: like father, like son; the acorn doesn't fall far from the tree; a chip off the old block. It is common in our experience that children will be shaped by their parents and reflect their values, characteristics, and skills. But even as this is often a good thing, a fundamental part of growing up, the influence can extend to sins and failures as well. Not only do children suffer consequences for parents' decisions; they often emulate those actions themselves.

Woe to Us, for We Have Sinned

Big Idea

God is always on his throne; thus we should confess our sins and trust him for deliverance.

Key Themes

- The judgment for sin is devastating and terrible.
- The voice of the survivors confesses their sin and the sin of their fathers.
- Even with Jerusalem in ruins, God sits upon his throne and rules.
- Because of the seriousness of their sin, the survivors are tentative in their prayer for restoration.

Understanding the Text

The Text in Context

Unlike the first four chapters, Lamentations 5 is not an alphabetic acrostic, although it is still highly structured poetry and does have twenty-two verses, matching the Hebrew alphabet as in Lamentations 1; 2; and 4. Unlike the other chapters, there is only one voice in Lamentations 5, a first-person plural ("we," "us") voice that probably represents the entire community that survived the destruction of Jerusalem. It is also possible that the identification of the speakers as "orphans" in 5:3 (NRSV) alludes to the tattered street kids in 4:1–10 and implies that they are the ones who call out for restoration in Lamentations 5, figuratively representing the entire devastated community.

Lamentations 5 opens and closes with imperative cries to God: "Remember, LORD" in 5:1 and "Restore us to yourself, LORD" in 5:21. The middle section (5:2–18) continues the main theme of Lamentations, recounting the terrible aftermath of the Babylonian destruction of Jerusalem. This chapter bears some similarities to the community laments in the psalms (e.g., Pss. 44; 60; 74; 79; 80; 83), but whereas lament psalms typically conclude with a strong word of assurance and/or a vow to praise God for his deliverance, Lamentations 5 (and the book as a whole) ends with but a qualified and tentative affirmation of cautious hope (5:19–22).

Interpretive Insights

5:1 *Remember, LORD.* The word translated as "remember" connotes "to look on with favor and act accordingly." Remembering is not a function of the mind, but rather it pertains to actions taken on one's behalf. In 5:20 the speakers bemoan that God seems to have forgotten them perpetually. The opening cry, then, is a plea for God to reverse this and to look on them (with favor).

5:2 *Our inheritance.* The word translated as "inheritance" occurs frequently in both Jeremiah and Deuteronomy in reference to the physical land that God gave to Israel.

5:3 *We have become fatherless.* Many of the men in Jerusalem had fled, been killed in battle, executed by the Babylonians, or taken into exile. Lamentations 4:1–10 paints a tragic picture of children alone in the streets of Jerusalem. Yet this text may also carry a figurative sense in which the survivors mourn over having lost their king (mentioned in 4:20) or even in which they have lost God himself as their Father. The image of God as Israel's Father is common in the Old Testament (e.g., Isa. 64:8; Jer. 31:9; Hosea 11:1–4). If these figurative senses are present, then the image is one of being totally and completely fatherless, without human father, king, or God to care for them.[1]

our mothers are widows. The word "widow" is a reminder of 1:1, where Jerusalem is portrayed as a grieving widow.

5:4 *we must buy the water we drink.* It is possible that the Babylonians or their representatives were actually controlling the limited water supplies and charging the survivors for their own water. In a figurative sense, these are children who now have to pay for things that used to be supplied freely to them by their fathers.

5:5 *at our heels.* Literally, this reads, "upon our necks" (cf. NRSV). Many scholars take this as an idiom, similar to "hot on our heels" or "breathing down our necks." Yet the Hebrew word for "neck" is used eight times in Jeremiah 27–28 in the context of foreign domination, and a similar phrase ("upon your neck") occurs in Jeremiah 27:2.

5:7 *Our ancestors sinned . . . we bear their punishment.* "Ancestors" translates the word for "fathers." In light of the "orphan" imagery in 5:3, the term "fathers" probably should be retained.

5:8 *Slaves rule over us.* The word translated as "slaves" probably is better rendered as "servants," and it refers figuratively and ironically to those governors and other officials ("servants") whom the Babylonians installed to govern Judah (Jer. 39–40). It might also include some of the neighboring countries like Edom, which once were ruled by Judah but now, under Babylonian rule, govern parts of Judah.

5:11 *violated.* The Hebrew word here means "to be bowed down, afflicted, humiliated, humbled." It is sometimes used figuratively to refer to rape.

5:14 *the elders are gone from the city gate.* Local government typically was carried out through courts held at city gates, with elders of the city hearing and deciding cases. Most of these elders have now either been killed or taken to Babylon in captivity. At any rate, the new rulers probably do not allow this kind of local government to continue. There is also probably a wordplay here. The word translated as "gone" is *shabat.* As a verb, it means "to rest, cease, stop." As a noun, it refers to the Sabbath day. In Jeremiah 17:19–27 the prophet preached at some length about violations of the Sabbath day at the gates of Jerusalem. The usages of *shabat* in Lamentations 5:14–15 probably are echoing with ironic wordplay the judgment predicted back in Jeremiah 17:19–27.

5:15 *Joy is gone from our hearts.* As in 5:14, here the word translated as "gone" is *shabat.* The language used here is very similar to Jeremiah 7:34, and it probably also echoes Jeremiah 17:19–27.

5:16 *Woe to us, for we have sinned!* "Woe" translates a word that can simply be a cry of despair and/or pain, but it can also be a warning cry of coming judgment. It occurs eight times in Jeremiah, used in both senses (e.g., Jer. 10:19; 13:27). Note, however, that in 5:7 the blame is on their fathers (maintaining the orphan imagery). Here the representatives of the entire surviving community are confessing that they are all guilty of the sin that brought such terrible judgment.

5:19 *You, Lord, reign forever, your throne endures.* The word translated as "reign" (*yashab*) basically means "to sit, dwell, remain." When used in the context of "throne," it implies "reigning," as in the NIV. But this verse, and especially the opening "you," stands in strong contrast with 5:18, where jackals (wild canine scavengers) dwell in Zion, in essence saying, "Jackals may roam in Zion, but you, God, will still sit forever on your throne."

from generation to generation. This phrase is an idiom meaning "for a long time" or "forever." In light of the fathers/orphans theme (5:3, 7), however, it is very appropriate in a literal sense as well. Generations will change, but God still sits on his throne for each generation.

5:21 *Restore us to yourself, Lord, that we may return.* The word *shub* is used twice in this verse ("restore," "return"). This word basically means "to turn" or "to return." It is the most central term for repentance and restoration in the book of Jeremiah, occurring 115 times. The verb form of *shub* that is translated as "restore" is a causative verb form, literally, "cause us to return" or even "cause us to repent." These words imply that this verse is a call for covenant renewal, as described in Jeremiah 31.

5:22 *unless.* The two small Hebrew words that begin this verse are difficult to translate with certainty.[2] Probably to be preferred over the NIV's "unless" is that idea of "even though, although." The call for restoration in 5:21 is not conditioned on whether God has rejected them (5:22). He very definitely has rejected them. The call for restoration, then, is a call in spite of the fact ("even though," "although") that God has rejected them.[3]

you have utterly rejected us. The Hebrew grammatical construction can stress the certainty or the extent of the main verb, "reject," either of which makes sense and fits the context. The stress could very well be the certainty of this past event, "you have most certainly rejected us" or "you have obviously rejected us." The point would be that even though God has clearly rejected them (evidenced by the destruction of Jerusalem), they now call on him to restore them. If the grammar stresses the extent, however, the focus probably is not on the depth of God's rejection ("utterly rejected") but rather on the extent of "us" ("rejected utterly all of us"). Jeremiah 31:37 and 33:24–26, which employ the same word for "reject," lend support to this understanding. God has rejected Judah and Jerusalem, but not all of them forever. There will always be a remnant from which God will restore his people.

Theological Insights

God is neither flippant nor capricious, either in his judgment or in his gracious restoration. God, in his gracious love, will forgive and restore those who confess their sin and repent, but this is not an "easy" action. There is no "cheap grace" involved.[4] Those who cry out in Lamentations 5 seem to recognize that. Their sin was so bad and the judgment they experienced so terrible that it seems difficult for them to accept the concept of an easy restoration, even though they try to affirm those attributes of God that would give them hope. Will he take them back? How can he? As we noted in Jeremiah, this tension between God's righteous judgment on sin and his gracious, forgiving love for his people is not resolved until the New Testament, when Christ dies as atonement for sin, allowing God to judge sin with righteousness and yet still forgive and restore people in grace and love. Lamentations drives home how tenuous the idea of restoration would be if not for the sacrificial death of Christ.

Teaching the Text

Like the steady, sad beat of a drum in a funeral dirge, the book of Lamentations continues through all five chapters to cry out painfully how terrible and devastating is the judgment of God on sin. The final chapter does not back off this message. Like the people in Jerusalem who ignored Jeremiah's message, many people today shrug at the possibility of God's wrath and go about their business as if it does not exist. Yet the message in this chapter is crystal clear: those who defy and reject God will experience his terrible wrath. Reading through Lamentations, one wonders how the people of Jerusalem could have been so foolish on such a big issue. The same can be asked today.

The speakers in Lamentations 5 confess their sin and hope that God will restore them. The realization of the seriousness of their sin and the massive scale of the judgment that God has poured out on them cause them to be tentative about whether God will ever actually take them back. Yet in the New Testament, as one of the thieves dying next to Jesus discovered, there is nothing "tentative" about the forgiveness and salvation offered through Christ (Luke 23:39–43). Anyone at any time who confesses and comes to Christ requesting salvation is welcomed with open arms. Lamentations says, "Perhaps God will take us back if we repent." Jesus answers, "Most certainly I will." Yet this is not "cheap grace," for the horror of sin and judgment described in Lamentations does not disappear; it is dealt with by the sacrificial death of Christ.

Finally, Lamentations 5 teaches us to recognize and reaffirm that God does indeed still sit on the throne and will rule forever. There is no tragedy or disaster from which he cannot deliver us. There is no breach in our relationship that he cannot restore. He is always there on his throne, ruling over the world with love and justice.

Illustrating the Text

The judgment for sin is destruction and ruin.

Art: *The People Mourning over the Ruins of Jerusalem*, by Gustave Doré. This 1866 engraving cites Lamentations as the source of inspiration and provides a graphic illustration to help capture the devastating consequences of sin.

If we confess our sins, we can trust in God for our deliverance.

Bible: The parable of the prodigal son, in Luke 15:11–32, provides a powerful illustration of God's gracious character and eagerness to see his children repent. A contemporary retelling, such as Philip Yancey's tale of a wayward daughter, can make this familiar story fresh.[5] In Yancey's version, a young woman leaves behind what she sees as her overly restrictive parents to explore freedom. But eventually she realizes the depravity and emptiness of her new life, and she resolves to return home. When she exits the bus in her hometown, an unexpected scene awaits her.

> She walks into the terminal not knowing what to expect, and not one of the thousand scenes that have played out in her mind prepare her for what she

sees. There, in the concrete-walls-and-plastic-chairs bus terminal in Traverse City, Michigan, stands a group of forty brothers and sisters and great-aunts and uncles and cousins and a grandmother and great-grandmother to boot. They're all wearing ridiculous-looking party hats and blowing noise-makers, and taped across the entire wall of the terminal is a computer-generated banner that reads "Welcome home!"

Out of the crowd of well-wishers breaks her dad. She stares out through the tears quivering in her eyes like hot mercury and begins the memorized speech, "Dad, I'm sorry. I know . . ."

He interrupts her. "Hush, child. We've got no time for that. No time for apologies. You'll be late for the party."[6]

Bible: John 11:1–44 describes the mourning and sadness that Lazarus's family and friends experienced at his death. At funerals there is always a sense of sadness and loss, but if the deceased was a Christian, then there is also a strong message of hope. As Martha said of Lazarus, "I know he will rise again in the resurrection," to which Jesus replied, "I am the resurrection and the life." We serve a God who graciously offered his own Son as a sacrifice for our sin, but those who reject his offer of forgiveness will have to pay the penalty for sin themselves.

None of us knows exactly what has gone on in another person's inner conversations with God, so we try to leave the door open slightly for the hope of restoration; but like the citizens of ancient Jerusalem, we know that apart from God there is no hope.

Notes

Introduction to Jeremiah

1. Clements, *Old Testament Prophecy*, 115.
2. Another good suggestion for Jeremiah's title is the "Dirty Harry" of the Old Testament. In a series of movies starring Clint Eastwood, the character of the detective Harry Callahan was always assigned the most difficult, sometimes impossible, tasks of his police department and thus was given the nickname "Dirty Harry." In similar fashion, Jeremiah is assigned the very difficult, indeed impossible, task of calling Jerusalem to repentance. See Hays, *Message of the Prophets*, 147.
3. Ibid., 146–47.
4. See the discussion of this issue in Hays, "Inerrancy," 133–49.

Jeremiah 1:1–19

1. Lundbom, *Jeremiah 1–20*, 227.
2. Ibid.
3. Hill and Walton, *Survey of the Old Testament*, 535.
4. *ZIBBCOT* 4:237.

Jeremiah 2:1–37

1. *BIBD* 154.
2. *ZIBBCOT* 4:241–42.

Jeremiah 3:1–4:4

1. For a discussion on the numerous theories regarding the fate of the ark, see Hays, *Message of the Prophets*, 152–53.
2. See the extensive development of this theme in Fretheim, *Suffering of God*.

Jeremiah 4:5–31

1. *GBPET* 479–80.
2. *ZIBBCOT* 4:245–46; Lundbom, *Jeremiah 1–20*, 336.
3. *DBI* 514–15.

Jeremiah 5:1–31

1. *Sheqer* ("lies, falsehood") occurs in the following verses of Jeremiah: 3:10, 23; 5:2, 31; 6:13; 7:4, 8, 9; 8:8, 10; 9:2, 4; 10:14; 13:25; 14:14; 16:19; 20:6; 23:14, 25, 26, 32; 27:10, 14, 15, 16; 28:15; 29:9, 21, 23, 31; 37:14; 40:16; 43:2; 51:17.
2. http://www.covenanteyes.com/.

Jeremiah 6:1–30

1. Fiona MacRae and Richard Spillett, "Pinocchio Would Have Only Been Able to Tell 13 Lies," *Daily Mail*, May 5, 2014, http://www.dailymail.co.uk/news/article-2620446/Pinocchio-able-tell-13-lies-research-shows.html.
2. "'Pinocchio Effect' Confirmed: When You Lie, Your Nose Temperature Rises," *Science Daily*, December 3, 2012, http://www.sciencedaily.com/releases/2012/12/121203081834.htm.

Jeremiah 7:1–8:3

1. *ZIBBCOT* 3:254–55; *BIBD* 127–28.
2. Lundbom, *Jeremiah 1–20*, 483.

Jeremiah 8:4–9:11

1. Wikipedia, "Superior Orders," http://en.wikipedia.org/wiki/Superior_orders.

2. Barna Group, "The Bible in America, 2014," April 8, 2014, https://www.barna.org/barna%20.%20.%20.%20/664-the-state-of-the-bibl.

Jeremiah 9:12–26

1. Recall that in Exodus, for example, since Pharaoh saw fit to drown God's innocent infant children in the Nile River, God responded by killing all the Egyptian firstborn and then drowning all of Pharaoh's army in the Red Sea.

2. Aaron Krause, "Stolen Stop Signs Found in Pickup of Norwalk Teen Killed in Wreck," *Norwalk Reflector*, September 24, 2012, http://www.norwalkreflector.com/article/1483091.

Jeremiah 10:1–25

1. Walton, *Ancient Near Eastern Thought*, 114–18.

2. Tanya Basu, "Feeling Lucky? How Lotto Odds Compare to Shark Attacks and Lightning Strikes," *National Geographic News*, December 19, 2013, http://news.nationalgeographic.com/news/2013/12/131219-lottery-odds-winning-mega-million-lotto/.

Jeremiah 11:1–17

1. *ZIBBCOT* 1:444.

2. Rata, "Covenant."

3. W. Becket Soule, *Preserving the Sanctity of Marriage: The Catholic Teaching on Annulment* (New Haven: Catholic Information Service, Knights of Columbus Supreme Council, 2009), 5.

4. http://www.staffordloan.com/.

Jeremiah 11:18–12:6

1. This story was told to me by SIM relief workers in Ethiopia.

Jeremiah 12:7–17

1. Lundbom, *Jeremiah 1–20*, 653–54.

2. Van Groningen, "שׁוּב," 880.

3. Lundbom, *Jeremiah 1–20*, 659.

Jeremiah 13:1–27

1. Lundbom, *Jeremiah 1–20*, 668–69; *ZIBBCOT* 4:267.

2. Stephen Macmillan, "Lance Armstrong's Doping Denials—in Quotes," *Guardian*, January 18, 2013, http://www.theguardian.com/sport/2013/jan/18/lance-armstrong-doping-denials-quotes.

3. Armstrong's interview with Oprah Winfrey can be viewed on YouTube at https://www.youtube.com/watch?v=N_0PSZ59Aws.

Jeremiah 14:1–16

1. *GBPET* 150–51, 353–54.

Jeremiah 14:17–15:9

1. Note that while 2 Kings 21 stresses how terrible are the sin and idolatrous worship instituted by Manasseh, 2 Chronicles 33 describes him as one who repents. See the discussion in Tiemeyer, "Manasseh."

2. http://www.wikihow.com/Tell-if-an-Egg-is-Bad.

Jeremiah 15:10–21

1. Longman, *Jeremiah, Lamentations*, 125. Lundbom (*Jeremiah 1–20*, 735), however, argues that both "iron" and "bronze" refer to Jeremiah.

2. Wikipedia, "Press-on-Regardless Rally," http://en.wikipedia.org/wiki/Press-on-Regardless_Rally.

Jeremiah 16:1–21

1. Rob Bell, *Love Wins: A Book about Heaven, Hell, and the Fate of Every Person Who Ever Lived* (New York: HarperOne, 2011).

2. https://www.youtube.com/watch?v=BjAdRJZib3Q.

3. Francis Chan and Preston Sprinkle, *Erasing Hell: What God Said about Eternity and the Things We Made Up* (Colorado Springs: David C. Cook, 2011).

4. "U.S. Officials Return Painting Stolen by Nazis during World War II to Poland," *CBS New York*, February 6, 2014, http://newyork.cbslocal.com/2014/02/06/u-s-officials-return-painting-stolen-by-nazis-during-world-war-ii-to-poland/.

Jeremiah 17:1–27

1. *BIBD* 127–28.

2. Kenneth W. Osbeck, *Amazing Grace: 366 Inspiring Hymn Stories for Daily Devotions* (Grand Rapids: Kregel, 1990), 287.

3. "Insanity—The Ride," Stratosphere Hotel, http://www.stratospherehotel.com/Activities/Thrill-Rides/Insanity.

Jeremiah 18:1–23

1. Barna Group, "What Americans Believe about Universalism and Pluralism," April 18, 2011, https://www.barna.org/barna-update/faith-spirituality/484-what-americans-believe-about-universalism-and-pluralism.

2. Dietrich Bonhoeffer, *The Cost of Discipleship* (New York: Touchstone, 1995), 44–45.

Jeremiah 19:1–15

1. Lundbom, *Jeremiah 1–20*, 495.

2. *ZIBBCOT* 4:278–79.

3. http://www.abort73.com/abortion_facts/us_abortion_statistics/.

4. https://www.childhelp.org/child-abuse-statistics/.

Jeremiah 20:1–18

1. David Daniell, *William Tyndale: A Biography* (New Haven: Yale University Press, 2001).
2. Elisabeth Elliot, *Through Gates of Splendor* (New York: Harper, 1957).
3. Bryan M. Litfin, *Early Christian Martyr Stories: An Evangelical Introduction with New Translations* (Grand Rapids: Baker Academic, 2014), 53–64.
4. Eugene H. Peterson, *God's Message for Each Day: Wisdom from the Word of God* (Nashville: Thomas Nelson, 2006), 317.

Jeremiah 21:1–14

1. See Eric Metaxas, *Bonhoeffer: Pastor, Martyr, Prophet, Spy* (Nashville: Thomas Nelson, 2010).
2. C. S. Lewis, *The Lion, the Witch and the Wardrobe* (New York: HarperCollins, 2005), 80–81 (adapted).
3. An early printing of the letter in the *Christian Century* can be viewed on the King Center's website, http://www.thekingcenter.org/archive/document/letter-birmingham-jail.
4. Quoted in Kenji Sugimoto, *Albert Einstein: A Photographic Biography* (New York: Schocken, 1989), 166.

Jeremiah 22:1–12

1. Ken Wytsma, *Pursuing Justice: The Call to Live and Die for Bigger Things* (Nashville: Thomas Nelson, 2013).
2. Nicholas D. Kristof and Sheryl WuDunn, *Half the Sky: Turning Oppression into Opportunity for Women Worldwide* (New York: Knopf, 2009).

Jeremiah 22:13–30

1. Jehoiachin does show up (called "Jeconiah") in Matthew's genealogy of Jesus (Matt. 1:11–12). But note that Matthew is tracking the genealogy of Joseph, and Matthew is very clear that the virgin birth of Jesus implies that Joseph was not the father. Thus while Joseph was a descendant of Jehoiachin, Jesus Christ was not.
2. Zerubbabel (Hag. 2:20–23) was a descendant of Jehoiachin who served as the governor in Judah during the postexilic time of Haggai. But Judah was under Persian rule (stressed in the opening verses of Haggai), and Zerubbabel was appointed as governor by the Persians; Judah was not being ruled by a Davidic king.
3. John R. W. Stott, *Issues Facing Christians Today* (Grand Rapids: Zondervan, 2006), 181–82.
4. "The Fall of Enron," *Business Week*, December 16, 2001, http://www.bloomberg.com/bw/stories/2001-12-16/the-fall-of-enron/.
5. Craig L. Blomberg, *Christians in an Age of Wealth: A Biblical Theology of Stewardship*, ed. Jonathan Lunde (Grand Rapids: Zondervan, 2013), 243.

Jeremiah 23:1–8

1. *GBPET* 107–9.
2. Lundbom, *Jeremiah 21–36*, 173.
3. W. Phillip Keller, *A Shepherd Looks at Psalm 23* (Grand Rapids: Zondervan, 1970).

Jeremiah 23:9–40

1. Federal Trade Commission, "Gut Check: A Reference Guide for Media on Spotting False Weight Loss Claims," http://www.ftc.gov/tips-advice/business-center/guidance/gut-check-reference-guide-media-spotting-false-weight-loss#claims.

Jeremiah 24:1–10

1. Lundbom, *Jeremiah 21–36*, 223.
2. *DBI* 283–84.
3. For a list of these terms, their distribution in Jeremiah, and a discussion of each, see Lundbom, *Jeremiah 21–36*, 234–35.

Jeremiah 25:1–14

1. Lundbom, *Jeremiah 21–36*, 241.
2. *ZIBBCOT* 4:290.

Jeremiah 25:15–38

1. Longman, *Jeremiah, Lamentations*, 176.
2. Varughese (*Jeremiah 1–25*, 318) suggests that God's judgment falls on these nations because of "their claim of autonomy and freedom from God's sovereignty over the world."
3. Rose Eveleth, "Lions and Tigers Bear Vocal Cords for Roars," *Scientific American*, November 2, 2011, http://www.scientificamerican.com/podcast/episode/lions-and-tigers-bear-vocal-cords-f-11-11-02/.

Jeremiah 26:1–24

1. Lundbom, *Jeremiah 21–36*, 297–98.
2. For a good discussion on the use of "perhaps" (*'ulay*) in divine speech see Fretheim, *Suffering of God*, 45–47. From another perspective, on the use of *'ulay* in this verse Calvin writes, "God indeed has perfect knowledge of all events, nor had he any doubt respecting what would take place . . . but what is pointed out here . . . is the obstinacy of the people; . . . that it was indeed difficult to heal those who had grown putrid in their evils, yet he would try to do so. And thus God manifests his unspeakable goodness, that he does not wholly cast away men who are almost past remedy, and whose diseases seem to be unhealable." Calvin, *Isaiah 59–Jeremiah 32:20*, 3812.
3. Samaritan's Purse, "Pastor Saeed's Letter to His Daughter Rebekka," September 26, 2014, http://samaritanspurse.org/article/pastor-saeeds-letter-to-his-daughter-rebekka/.

Jeremiah 27:1-22

1. Lundbom, *Jeremiah 21–36*, 304.
2. Longman, *Jeremiah, Lamentations*, 187–88.
3. Sermon illustration provided by W. A. Criswell in a chapel message delivered to students at Dallas Theological Seminary in 1977.

Jeremiah 28:1-17

1. Lundbom, *Jeremiah 21–36*, 332.
2. Ibid., 334.
3. See the discussion in Aune, *Prophecy in Early Christianity*, 218–19, 222–25.
4. Kate Rogers, "One New Identity Theft Victim Every 3 Seconds in 2012," FOXBusiness.com, February 20, 2013, http://www.foxbusiness.com/personal -finance/2013/02/20/one-new-identity-theft-victim -every-3-seconds-in-2012/.
5. Wikipedia, "Jonestown," http://en.wikipedia .org/wiki/Jonestown.

Jeremiah 29:1-32

1. Wise, Abegg, and Cook, *Dead Sea Scrolls*, 323–24.
2. Richards, "General Epistles and Hebrews," 240–43.

Jeremiah 30:1-24

1. Hays, *Message of the Prophets*, 175.
2. *GBPET* 109–10.

Jeremiah 31:1-26

1. For a thorough discussion of these two Hebrew words, see *NIDOTTE* 3:578–82; 1:789–94.
2. This verse is notoriously difficult to interpret, and there is no consensus among scholars. For good discussions, see Lundbom, *Jeremiah 21–36*, 451–52; Thompson, *Jeremiah*, 575–76.
3. Alexander and Rosner, *New Dictionary of Biblical Theology*, 716–20.
4. https://www.youtube.com/watch?v=6QvX4 CwSmwY.

Jeremiah 31:27-40

1. Those sources indicating that the old, Mosaic covenant was broken in the sense that it was annulled or rendered ineffective include Clements, *Jeremiah*, 190–91; Lundbom, *Jeremiah 21–36*, 467; Williams, "*prr*," *NIDOTTE* 3:696–97; and McKane, *Jeremiah*, 2:818–19. Arguing in favor of continuity between the covenants, and thus not seeing the Mosaic covenant totally annulled, would be Longman, *Jeremiah, Lamentations*, 12.
2. Donald B. Kraybill, Steven M. Nolt, and David L. Weaver-Zercher, *Amish Grace: How Forgiveness Transcended Tragedy* (San Francisco: Jossey-Bass, 2007).

Jeremiah 33:1-26

1. *NIDOTTE* 3:971–72.
2. Some scholars are more comfortable with seeing the old, Mosaic covenant as continuing in some modified fashion and not being totally abrogated. Thus they see the new covenant as moving the old covenant to a new phase or a new level, thus maintaining the continuity.
3. Note also that certain elements of the promise of restoration were fulfilled or began to be fulfilled in the return of the exiles during the postexilic period. Thus a certain element of "already" began then. This is part of the "near view, far view" phenomenon, discussed in the "Theological Insights" section in the unit on Jeremiah 30:1–24.
4. Mark L. Graber, Robert M. Wachter, and Christine K. Cassel, "Bringing Diagnosis into the Quality and Safety Equations," *Journal of the American Medical Association* 308, no. 12 (September 26, 2012): 1211–12.
5. Wikipedia, "The Food Defect Action Levels," http://en.wikipedia.org/wiki/The_Food_Defect _Action_Levels.

Jeremiah 34:1-22

1. *ANET* 322. For a summary of possibly different contexts for interpreting this letter (Lachish Ostracon IV), see the discussion in Lundbom, *Jeremiah 21–36*, 552–53. It is also quite interesting to note that Lachish Ostracon III mentions an unknown individual called "the prophet." Although it is impossible to speak with any certainty, since this ostracon was written during the time when Jeremiah was prophesying in Jerusalem, it is at least possible that "the prophet" is a reference to Jeremiah.
2. *ZIBBCOT* 4:312.
3. For discussion of the historical background for this ceremony, see Lundbom, *Jeremiah 21–36*, 565–66.
4. J. R. R. Tolkien, *The Fellowship of the Ring* (New York: Houghton Mifflin, 2004), 103.
5. Dr. Seuss, *Horton Hatches the Egg* (New York: Random House, 1940).

Jeremiah 35:1-19

1. The Druze in modern Israel have a similar relationship to the Israelis.
2. For more discussion on the Rekabites and on their possible motives for nomadism, see Lundbom, *Jeremiah 21–36*, 572–74.
3. Although, as Martens (*Jeremiah*, 218), points out, the Rekabite in Nehemiah 3:14 does not appear to be following the Rekabite traditions any longer.

Jeremiah 36:1-32

1. Lundbom, *Jeremiah 21–36*, 585.

2. Lamin Sanneh, *Translating the Message: The Mission Impact on Culture*, rev. ed. (Maryknoll, NY: Orbis Books, 2009).

3. David Daniell, *The Bible in English* (New Haven: Yale University Press, 2003), 133–57.

Jeremiah 37:1–21

1. As told to the author by Woldegiorgis Hirbaye in Dilla, Ethiopia, after he was released.

2. Wikiquote, "Benedict Arnold," http://en.wikiquote.org/wiki/Benedict_Arnold.

Jeremiah 38:1–28

1. Hays, "Land of the Bow."

2. Hays, *From Every People*, 130–34.

3. Ibid., 136.

4. https://www.youtube.com/watch?v=4q8kWZRmgPo.

5. "The Conscientious Objector," http://www.desmonddoss.com/.

Jeremiah 39:1–18

1. Lundbom, *Jeremiah 37–52*, 91.

2. Philip Jenkins, *The Next Christendom: The Coming of Global Christianity* (Oxford: Oxford University Press, 2002), 2–6.

3. http://www.citehr.com/89599-trust-small-story-read-big-message.html#ixzz36Rn4TbZz.

4. Matt Redman, "'You Never Let Go'—Devotional," PraiseCharts, http://www.praisecharts.com/you-never-let-go/.

Jeremiah 40:1–43:7

1. Some scholars, however, connect the assassination of Gedaliah with the return of the Babylonian commander Nebuzaradan to Judah in 582 BC, when he carries away another group of Judahites into captivity (Jer. 52:30) (Lundbom, *Jeremiah 37–52*, 115).

2. Lawrence T. Garaty, "Baalis," in *Anchor Bible Dictionary*, ed. David Noel Freedman, 6 vols. (New York: Doubleday, 1995), 1:556–57.

Jeremiah 43:8–45:5

1. Lundbom, *Jeremiah 37–52*, 163.

2. There probably is an allusion to this verse in Luke 9:51: "[Jesus] set his face to go to Jerusalem" (ESV).

3. Lundbom, *Jeremiah 37–52*, 164.

4. See Kevin and Sherry Harney, *Organic Outreach for Families: Turning Your Home into a Lighthouse* (Grand Rapids: Zondervan, 2012); and Kevin Harney, *Organic Outreach for Churches* (Grand Rapids: Zondervan, 2011).

5. "Under the Influence: Consumer Trust in Advertising," *Nielsen*, September 17, 2013, http://www.nielsen.com/us/en/insights/news/2013/under-the-influence-consumer-trust-in-advertising.html.

Jeremiah 46:1–28

1. See the discussion in Lundbom, *Jeremiah 37–52*, 208.

2. Ibid., 201.

3. Fretheim, *Jeremiah*, 583.

4. Shaw and Nicholson, *Dictionary of Ancient Egypt*, 31–32.

5. Kay Arthur, *Beloved: From God's Heart to Yours* (Eugene, OR: Harvest House, 1994), 19.

6. Quoted in Michael Milton, "A Hero's Story at Christmastime: Colonel Roger Ingvalson, USAF-Retired (June 20, 1928–December 24, 2011)," http://michaelmilton.org/2011/12/26/a-heros-story-at-christmastime-colonel-roger-ingvalson-usaf-retired-june-20-1928-december-24-2011/.

7. Roger Ingvalson's interview can be found on the Library of Congress website at http://lcweb2.loc.gov/diglib/vhp-stories/loc.natlib.afc2001001.09773/#vhp:clip.

Jeremiah 47:1–49:39

1. A few scholars argue that "Bethel" refers to the name of a god. See Lundbom, *Jeremiah 37–52*, 268.

2. Fretheim, *Jeremiah*, 579.

3. C. S. Lewis, *Mere Christianity* (New York: Macmillan, 1960), 109.

Jeremiah 50:1–51:64

1. Pate and Hays, *Iraq*, 35–38.

2. Lundbom, *Jeremiah 37–52*, 370; ZIBBCOT 4:350–51.

Jeremiah 52:1–34

1. ANET 308.

2. Lundbom, *Jeremiah 37–52*, 535.

3. Ibid., 522–23.

4. Eugene Peterson, *A Long Obedience in the Same Direction: Discipleship in an Instant Society*, 2nd ed. (Downers Grove, IL: InterVarsity, 2000), 132.

Introduction to Lamentations

1. ZIBBCOT 4:375–76; Longman, *Jeremiah, Lamentations*, 332–33.

2. House, *Lamentations*, 305.

3. Translation, with minor modifications to spellings, from Pietersma and Wright, *New English Translation of the Septuagint*, 935.

4. See the extensive discussion of this issue in House, *Lamentations*, 283–303.

5. Ibid., 300.

6. For a good discussion of the theology of Lamentations, see House, "Outrageous Demonstrations of Grace."

7. Other alphabetic acrostics in the Hebrew text of the Bible include Psalm 119 and Proverbs 31:10–22.

Lamentations 1:1-22

1. Translation, with minor modifications to spellings, from Pietersma and Wright, *New English Translation of the Septuagint*, 935.

2. Longman, *Jeremiah, Lamentations*, 344.

3. Frederick Buechner, *Peculiar Treasures: A Biblical Who's Who* (San Francisco: HarperSanFrancisco, 2003), 47.

Lamentations 2:1-22

1. *NIDOTTE* 1:275.

2. Walton, Matthews, and Chavalas, *IVP Bible Background Commentary*, 687.

3. *ZIBBCOT* 4:385–86.

4. *NIDOTTE* 3:828–29.

5. For a good discussion, see Ames, "Warfare and Divine Warfare."

6. C. S. Lewis, *Mere Christianity* (New York: Macmillan, 1960), 37.

7. Ibid., 39.

8. Ibid., 38.

Lamentations 3:1-66

1. Longman, *Jeremiah, Lamentations*, 363; Berlin, *Lamentations*, 84–85; Parry, *Lamentations*, 94–95.

2. This basic outline is developed from Parry, *Lamentations*, 92–93.

3. Berlin, *Lamentations*, 86.

4. *NIDOTTE* 3:317.

5. Both the MT and the LXX read first-person plural, "we will not come to an end." Arguing from the parallelism, syntax, and Targums, several commentators propose to emend the reading to "they [i.e., Yahweh's *heseds*] never come to an end" (e.g., Berlin, *Lamentations*, 83). Thus the NRSV reads, "The steadfast love of the LORD never ceases," the gist of which is reflected in the NLT, NASB, and ESV.

6. Anderson, *Out of the Depths*, 56–57.

7. Matt Roper, "Loyal Dog Ran Away from Home to Find His Master's Grave," *Daily Mail*, September 13, 2012, http://www.dailymail.co.uk /news/article-2202509/Loyal-dog-ran-away-home -dead-masters-grave--stayed-years.html.

Lamentations 4:1-22

1. Longman, *Jeremiah, Lamentations*, 386.

2. Parry, *Lamentations*, 136; Berlin, *Lamentations*, 107.

3. Berlin, *Lamentations*, 103–4.

4. Other possibilities for the meaning of "the blood of the righteous" are viable. Berlin (*Lamentations*, 110–11) argues for idolatry; Parry (*Lamentations*, 139) proposes the attempts to kill Jeremiah and the execution of Uriah (Jer. 29).

5. Centers for Disease Control and Prevention, "Child Passenger Safety: Get the Facts," http://www .cdc.gov/Motorvehiclesafety/child_passenger_safety /cps-factsheet.html.

Lamentations 5:1-22

1. House, *Lamentations*, 460.

2. For a good discussion of the various options, see House, *Lamentations*, 470–72.

3. Ibid., 471–72.

4. The term "cheap grace" was brought into the theological vocabulary of the church through Dietrich Bonhoeffer's classic work *The Cost of Discipleship*, originally titled *Nachfolge* and published in 1937.

5. Philip Yancey, *What's So Amazing about Grace?* (Grand Rapids: Zondervan, 1997), 49–51.

6. Ibid., 51.

Bibliography

Recommended Resources

Berlin, Adele. *Lamentations*. Old Testament Library. Louisville: Westminster John Knox, 2002.

Boda, Mark J., and J. Gordon McConville, eds. *Dictionary of the Old Testament: Prophets*. Downers Grove, IL: IVP Academic, 2012.

Fretheim, Terence E. *Jeremiah*. Smith & Helwys Bible Commentary. Macon, GA: Smyth & Helwys, 2002.

Hays, J. Daniel, J. Scott Duvall, and C. Marvin Pate. *An A-to-Z Guide to Biblical Prophecy and the End Times*. Grand Rapids: Zondervan, 2007.

House, Paul R. *Lamentations*. Word Biblical Commentary 23B. Nashville: Thomas Nelson, 2004.

———. "Outrageous Demonstrations of Grace: The Theology of Lamentations." In *Great Is Thy Faithfulness? Reading Lamentations as Sacred Scripture*, edited by Robin A. Parry and Heath A. Thomas, 26–51. Eugene, OR: Pickwick, 2011.

Longman, Tremper III. *Jeremiah, Lamentations*. New International Biblical Commentary. Peabody, MA: Hendrickson, 2008.

Longman, Tremper, III, Peter Enns, and Mark Strauss, eds. *The Baker Illustrated Bible Dictionary*. Grand Rapids: Baker Books, 2013.

Lundbom, Jack R. *Jeremiah 1–20: A New Translation with Introduction and Commentary*. Anchor Bible 21A. New York: Doubleday, 1999.

———. *Jeremiah 21–36: A New Translation with Introduction and Commentary*. Anchor Bible 21B. New York: Doubleday, 2004.

———. *Jeremiah 37–52: A New Translation with Introduction and Commentary*. Anchor Bible 21C. New York: Doubleday, 2004.

Martens, Elmer A. *Jeremiah*. Believers Church Bible Commentary. Scottdale, PA: Herald Press, 1986.

Parry, Robin A. *Lamentations*. The Two Horizons Old Testament Commentary. Grand Rapids: Eerdmans, 2010.

Thompson, J. A. *The Book of Jeremiah*. New International Commentary on the Old Testament. Grand Rapids: Eerdmans, 1980.

Varughese, Alex. *Jeremiah 1–25: A Commentary in the Wesleyan Tradition*. New Beacon Bible Commentary. Kansas City: Beacon Hill Press, 2008.

Walton, John H., ed. *Zondervan Illustrated Bible Backgrounds Commentary: Old Testament*. 5 vols. Grand Rapids: Zondervan, 2009.

Other Works

Alexander, T. Desmond, and Brian S. Rosner. *New Dictionary of Biblical Theology*. Downers Grove, IL: InterVarsity, 2000.

Ames, F. R. "Warfare and Divine Warfare." In *Dictionary of the Old Testament: Prophets*, edited by Mark J. Boda and J. Gordon McConville, 827–35. Downers Grove, IL: InterVarsity, 2012.

Anderson, Bernhard W. *Out of the Depths: The Psalms Speak for Us Today*. Philadelphia: Westminster, 1974.

Aune, David E. *Prophecy in Early Christianity and the Mediterranean World*. Grand Rapids: Eerdmans, 1983.

Avigad, Nahman. "Jerahmeel and Baruch: King's Son and Scribe." *Biblical Archaeologist* 42, no. 2 (Spring 1979): 114–18.

Calvin, John. *Isaiah 59–Jeremiah 32:20*. Vol. 5 of *Calvin's Commentaries*. Wilmington, DL: Associated Publishers, n.d.

Chambers, Joseph. *A Palace for the Antichrist: Saddam Hussein's Drive to Rebuild Babylon and Its Place in Bible Prophecy*. Green Forest, AR: New Leaf Press, 1996.

Clements, Ronald E. *Jeremiah*. Interpretation. Atlanta: John Knox, 1988.

———. *Old Testament Prophecy: From Oracles to Canon*. Louisville: Westminster John Knox, 1996.

Dearman, J. Andrew. *Jeremiah, Lamentations*. NIV Application Commentary. Grand Rapids: Zondervan, 2002.

Dyer, Charles. *The Rise of Babylon: Sign of the End Times*. Wheaton: Tyndale, 1991.

Fretheim, Terence E. *The Suffering of God: An Old Testament Perspective*. Overtures to Biblical Theology. Philadelphia: Fortress, 1984.

Hays, J. Daniel. *From Every People and Nation: A Biblical Theology of Race*. New Studies in Biblical Theology 14. Downers Grove, IL: InterVarsity; Leicester: Apollos, 2003.

———. "From the Land of the Bow: Black Soldiers in the Ancient Near East." *Bible Review* 14 (August 1998): 28–33, 50–51.

———. "Jeremiah, the Septuagint, the Dead Sea Scrolls, and Inerrancy: Just What Exactly Do We Mean by the 'Original Autographs'?" In *Evangelicals and Scripture: Tradition, Authority and Hermeneutics*, edited by Vincent Bacote et al., 133–49. Downers Grove, IL: InterVarsity, 2004.

———. *The Message of the Prophets: A Survey of the Prophetic and Apocalyptic Books of the Old Testament*. Grand Rapids: Zondervan, 2010.

Hill, Andrew, and John Walton. *A Survey of the Old Testament*. Grand Rapids: Zondervan, 2009.

Knowles, Michael. *Jeremiah in Matthew's Gospel: The Rejected Prophet Motif in Matthaean Redaction*. Journal for the Study of the New Testament: Supplement Series 68. Sheffield: JSOT Press, 1993.

McKane, William. *Jeremiah*. 2 vols. International Critical Commentary. Edinburgh: T&T Clark, 1986–96.

Pate, C. Marvin, and J. Daniel Hays. *Iraq: Babylon of the End Times?* Grand Rapids: Baker Books, 2003.

Pietersma, Albert, and Benjamin G. Wright, eds. *A New English Translation of the Septuagint*. New York: Oxford University Press, 2007.

Rata, Tiberius. "Covenant." In *Dictionary of the Old Testament: Prophets*, edited by Mark J. Boda and J. Gordon McConville, 100–102. Downers Grove, IL: IVP Academic, 2012.

Richards, E. Randolph. "The General Epistles and Hebrews: In Exile but on the Brink of Restoration." In *The Story of Israel: A Biblical Theology*, edited by C. Marvin Pate, 232–54. Downers Grove, IL: InterVarsity; Leicester: Apollos, 2004.

Shaw, Ian, and Paul Nicholson. *British Museum Dictionary of Ancient Egypt*. London: British Museum Press, 1995.

Tiemeyer, L.-S. "Manasseh." In *Dictionary of the Old Testament: Historical Books*, edited by Bill T. Arnold and H. G. M. Williamson, 674–77. Downers Grove, IL: InterVarsity, 2005.

Van Groningen, Gerald. "אָצָנ." In *Theological Wordbook of the Old Testament*, edited by R. Laird Harris, Gleason L. Archer Jr., and Bruce K. Waltke, 2:879–80. Chicago: Moody, 1980.

Walton, John H. *Ancient Near Eastern Thought and the Old Testament: Introducing the Conceptual World of the Hebrew Bible*. Grand Rapids: Baker Academic, 2006.

Walton, John H., Victor H. Matthews, and Mark W. Chavalas. *The IVP Bible Background Commentary: Old Testament*. Downers Grove, IL: InterVarsity, 2000.

Wise, Michael O., Martin G. Abegg Jr., and Edward M. Cook. *The Dead Sea Scrolls: A New Translation*. San Francisco: HarperSanFrancisco, 1996.

Index

everlasting covenant, 238–39, 314. *See also* new covenant

evil, 128, 165, 170, 171, 194–95, 197, 319

evil heart, 124

exile, 3, 4, 7, 101, 176, 183, 214–15, 315, 326, 350

  in New Testament, 214–15

exiles, list of, 319, 321

exodus, 17, 101, 113–14, 164, 167, 237, 250

"exodus reversal," 150

eyes of God, 176, 177–78

Eyptians, 2

Ezekiel, 177

fair wages, 160

faith, 239

  inheritance of, 351

faithfulness, 257

false gods, 90

false prophets, 28, 29, 94, 95–96, 169–74, 195, 199–200, 351

  devastating results of, 205–10

  pride and arrogance of, 203

false teaching, 54–55, 91, 200, 208–9

false worship, 54

families of Israel, 224

famine, 95, 96, 100, 145, 202, 273, 289, 320, 330, 349–50

fatalism, 128

fatal sickness, 221, 223

fatherless, 47, 354

fear, 9, 262, 302, 304

fear of God, 64, 65

fertility cult practices, 16

fertility-gods, 22

field, purchase of, 236–40, 267

figs, 175–76, 178, 190, 288

final judgment, 132

fire, 120, 261, 267

flock, 164

foolish, 34, 37

footstool, 336

foreigners, 36, 149–52

forgetting, 171, 173

forgiveness, 232, 244, 314, 315–16, 322, 345

"formless and empty," 30

fortress, 114

four (number of completeness), 101

freedom, 250–51

fruitful, remnant as, 165

funerals, 111–12, 114, 356, 358

Gedaliah, 2, 287, 288, 321, 363

Gehenna, 132

gems, 348

gentiles, inclusion of, 166, 256–58, 275, 284, 310

Gilead, 53, 302

global south, 264, 284

God

  anger of, 118–19, 120, 190, 319, 335–36, 345

  compassion of, 226, 343, 345

  as Creator, 65, 243

  emotions of, 102–3

  as enemy of Jerusalem, 338–39

  faithfulness of, 110, 253, 343, 346

  as Father, 73, 354

  hatred of, 84

  as husband to Israel, 17, 24, 224, 230–31

  justice of, 31, 58, 60, 102, 136, 146, 303, 315

  lamenting of, 308

  love of, 31, 60, 227, 244–45, 304, 343, 345

  name of, 94

  patience of, 73, 74, 85, 339

  presence of, 49–50, 176–78, 238, 243, 320, 322

  promises of, 221, 322

  rejection of Judah and Jerusalem, 356

  relenting of, 126, 194, 196–97, 289

  righteousness of, 36, 60

  as shepherd, 167, 168

  sovereignty of, 64, 127, 183, 185, 191, 304

  as warrior, 140, 338

  weeping of, 99, 100, 102

  wrath of, 27, 30–31, 32, 41, 60, 73, 89, 96, 102, 145–47, 187, 190–91, 239, 283, 314, 338–39, 342, 345, 357

gold, 348

Gomer, 333

Gomorrah, 38, 308–9

gospel, rejection of, 298

grace, 220, 356–57

grapes, 189, 288

great assembly, 225

guilt of Israel, 314

Hamath, 320

Hammurabi, 250

Hananiah, 199, 205–8, 211, 212

hate, 83, 84

Hazor, 306

healing, 53, 219, 221, 223

hearing. *See* listening, to the word of God

heart, 77, 118–19, 127, 140, 158, 170, 171, 176, 213, 226, 239

  deceitfulness of, 119

  hardening of, 134

  renewal of, 177–78

heavenly council, 171, 172

heavens, as witness, 15–16

hebel, 64, 101

Heliopolis, 295

hell, 115

hesed, 113, 224, 244, 343

Hezekiah, 144, 196
high places, 131, 132
holiness, 252
Holy Spirit
  indwelling of, 23, 50, 109, 172, 173, 233
  and renewed hearts, 178
hope, 239–40, 245, 323–24, 327, 342–43, 344,
  346, 357, 358
horizontal relationship, 152–53, 160
Hosea, 22, 204, 333
house of the Lord, 194
human trafficking, 155
hyena, 83
hypocrites, 49–50

idols, idolatry, 37, 50, 54, 64–67, 72, 90, 101,
  117, 118–19, 121, 134, 149, 153, 177, 295,
  301
incense burning, 296
"in Christ," 173
individualism, 351
inheritance, 66, 81–84, 351, 354
  of faith, 351
injustice, 158
innocent blood, 47, 132, 134–35, 149, 151, 195,
  350
instant gratification, 214, 216
intercessory prayer, 71, 72, 95, 99, 101
iron, 106–7
Ishmael, 288
Ishtar, 295
Israel
  as a prostitute, 21–22
  as a tree, 36, 233
  as a wayward wife, 22

jackals, 348–49
Jacob
  name of, 119
  peace of, 303
  represents Israel as unified entity, 219
  as servant, 302–3
Jehoahaz, 2, 150, 152, 156–57
Jehoiachin, 2, 90, 150, 156–57, 176, 206, 211,
  361
  restoration of, 319, 321–22
Jehoiakim, 2–3, 150, 152, 156–57, 175–76, 182,
  194, 196, 206, 260, 301
Jenkins, Philip, 284
Jereboam I, 307
Jeremiah
  arrest of, 268
  call of, 9–10
  discouragement of, 108, 140–41
  intercessory prayer of, 101, 103
  lament of, 137, 140

murder plot against, 76–77, 79, 127, 128
not to intercede, 72, 95, 99, 267
not to marry, 111–14
opposition to, 78, 137, 138–39, 208
as persecuted prophet, 1, 140, 198, 269–70,
  278
in prison, 236, 245, 268
protected by God, 197
rebuked by God, 106, 107
suffering of, 79
summary of ministry of, 125
Jericho, 281, 320
Jerusalem, 28–29
burning of, 249–50, 267
crying out, 94
as daughter, 100
destruction of, 3, 7, 71, 78, 133, 195, 215, 266,
  269–70, 279, 287, 309, 319, 348
destruction of (in AD 70), 78, 140, 147,
  269–70, 284
as grieving widow, 329–31
judgment on, 60
as personification of nation, 72
pride of, 89
rebellion of, 330–31
renown of, 244, 245
siege of, 40, 248–50, 266, 273
unfaithfulness of, 52, 54
as unfaithful wife, 330, 333
voice of survivors, 341–42
walls of, 337
Jesus Christ
  establishes *shalom* in kingdom, 215
  as fulfillment of new covenant, 246
  intercession of, 103
  as king, 246
  persecution of, 269
  as priest, 246
  rejection of, 332
  sacrifice of, 72
Job, 108
Johanan, 290
Jonah, 196
Josiah, 2, 8, 100, 131, 150, 152, 157, 158, 301
joy, 113, 226, 227, 244, 355
Judah
  broken the covenant, 3
  destruction of, 296
  mourning of, 94
  national interests of, 202–3
  rebellion of, 30, 118
  as unfaithful bride, 16–17
Judahites, in Egypt, 294–97
judgment, 3–4, 10, 11, 20, 25, 30–31, 36, 51, 54,
  102, 103, 128, 134, 175
  averted by true repentance, 196–97

Contributors

General Editors
Mark. L. Strauss
John H. Walton

Associate Editors, Illustrating the Text
Kevin and Sherry Harney

Contributing Author, Illustrating the Text
Dann Stouten

Series Development
Jack Kuhatschek
Brian Vos

Project Editor
James Korsmo

Interior Design
Brian Brunsting

Visual Content
Kim Walton

Cover Direction
Paula Gibson
Michael Cook

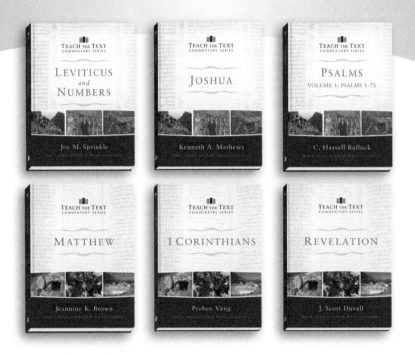

Printed and bound by CPI Group (UK) Ltd, Croydon, CR0 4YY

13/04/2025

14656456-0005